WINDOWS OF OPPORTUNITY

WINDOWS OF OPPORTUNITY
From Cold War to Peaceful Competition in U.S.–Soviet Relations

Edited by

GRAHAM T. ALLISON and WILLIAM L. URY

with

BRUCE J. ALLYN

BALLINGER PUBLISHING COMPANY
Cambridge, Massachusetts
A Subsidiary of Harper & Row, Publishers, Inc.

International Standard Book Number: 0-88730-349-8
0-88730-379-X (pbk.)

Library of Congress Catalog Card Number: 88-34416

Printed in the United States of America

Library of Congress Cataloging-in-Publication Data

Windows of opportunity : from cold war to peaceful competition in
  US-Soviet relations / edited by Graham T. Allison and William L. Ury
  with Bruce J. Allyn.
      p.   cm.
   Bibliography: p.
   Includes index.
   ISBN 0-88730-349-8. ISBN 0-88730-379-X (pbk.)
   1. United States—Military policy. 2. Soviet Union—Military
policy. 3. Nuclear warfare. 4. World politics—1945-   .
5. United States—Foreign relations—Soviet Union. 6. Soviet
Union—Foreign relations—United States. 7. United States—
Foreign relations—1981-   . 8. Soviet Union—Foreign
relations—1975-   . I. Allison, Graham T. II. Ury, William L.
III. Allyn, Bruce J.
UA23.W48   1989
355'.0217—dc19   88-34416
                                                       CIP

CONTENTS

FOREWORD

David Hamburg

When this project began a decade ago, I could not have imagined that it would turn out as it has. Events of truly historical import have underscored the significance of the enterprise and made it possible to move beyond the constraints of an earlier era.

In 1978, it was my privilege to convene in Geneva, under Pugwash auspices, a workshop on crisis management and crisis prevention involving scientists and scholars from a variety of countries but principally the United States and the Soviet Union. Over several intensive days and nights, we explored critical subjects bearing on the human future. We began with research on crises of the twentieth century, both nuclear and nonnuclear. Examining the record of analytical studies of particular crises, most significantly the Cuban missile crisis, we asked: how is it possible to emerge from a crisis in our time without a disastrous war, let alone a nuclear war?

It seemed to me that it would be valuable for scholars to reach a consensus on principles of crisis management and then to convey this consensus to policymakers in Washington, Moscow, and other world capitals. In any future crisis, it might be of the utmost practical significance for leaders of the superpowers to grasp these principles. As the Geneva group considered formulations that might be of practical use, we were deeply impressed with the difficulty of adhering to such guidelines in time of crisis. The immense strains of international crisis, and particularly of nuclear crisis, test the limit of human capacity to adapt and to behave in ways that could avert catastrophe. Therefore, we shifted to a consideration of crisis *prevention.* Whatever the level of armaments and whatever the animosity between the superpowers, it seemed simply a matter of prudent self-interest to stay away from the brink of nuclear crisis, since the tasks of crisis management are so exceedingly difficult, perhaps impossible to carry out.

Prior to the meeting, the American participants had been somewhat apprehensive about the Soviet response to these ideas. There had been only limited contacts between U.S. and Soviet scholars pertinent to these issues. During the meeting, while the Soviet participants listened attentively and raised reasonable questions, they often seemed tense and apprehensive. In private sessions with one senior Soviet participant, I found a good deal of suspicion and even some hostility. I left the meeting feeling that the outcome was highly uncertain.

Within a few weeks, however, I was pleasantly surprised to receive an invitation to visit Moscow. Over the next few years, Graham Allison and Alexander George, my principal collaborators, had useful and stimulating contacts with Georgy Arbatov, director of the Institute of the U.S.A. and Canada, Vitaly Zhurkin, now director of the Institute for Western Europe, and others. Gradually, understanding grew. Alex George pursued these ideas by putting together a landmark book, *Managing U.S.-Soviet Rivalry* (Boulder, CO.: Westview Press, 1983), which explored how a crisis prevention approach could diminish the nuclear danger.

In 1982, when I accepted the presidency of Carnegie Corporation of New York, U.S.-Soviet relations were under severe strain. The brutal Soviet invasion of Afghanistan and the reaction to it in the United States exacerbated the cold war. To those who had been working in this field, the possibility of nuclear crisis did not seem remote. Accordingly, one of my first acts at the foundation was to encourage a remarkable group of scholars at Harvard University to undertake a broad-gauged, interdisciplinary project on avoiding nuclear war. In connection with that project, I asked Graham Allison to explore the possibility of a joint U.S.-Soviet study group on crisis prevention. Soon such a group had been organized, with Allison chairing the U.S. team and Georgy Arbatov the Soviet side.

Since then, we have met about twice a year, with substantial preparation between meetings, including exchange visits of younger scholars to pave the way. These meetings have been characterized by civil discourse and mutual respect. The American participants recognized immediately that they were interacting with highly intelligent, well-informed, and seriously concerned individuals. Naturally, there were major differences in perspective on many issues. But we were all keenly aware of the dangers of accident, miscalculation, and misjudgment, and deeply concerned about the nuclear danger.

The American participants were sufficiently stimulated by the meetings, and the increasingly candid discussions between meetings, to crystallize some of their reflections and in due course to write papers. After some discussion of these papers among ourselves, we invited comment from our Soviet counterparts. We were glad to have reasonably candid, informal appraisals from them but did not think it would be feasible for them to write papers with us as a joint effort.

But it soon became clear that the Gorbachev era was different, and we began to explore the "new thinking." We felt our way beyond crisis prevention to the possibility of basic improvement of U.S.-Soviet relations. How could such possibilities be usefully explored, perhaps even facilitated, by U.S. and Soviet scholars? At the same time we realized that *glasnost* would offer the Soviet participants a chance to write with greater candor. Although conditions are still not optimal from our perspective, they are far better than they were a few years ago. Not only could the Soviet scholars go beyond official positions, but the official positions themselves have changed for the better. We decided the time was right for a joint volume on central problems of international security.

This book is unusual in that its chapters reflect joint work by U.S. and Soviet scholars in considerable depth over an extended period of time. Differences could be explored rationally, and consensus points specified. Moreover, there is something novel, refreshing, and hopeful about the relative freedom of expression of the Soviet participants. They and their American counterparts have both become much more significant advisers to government leadership than they were when the project began. This volume exemplifies the increasingly useful and dynamic interplay between scholars and policymakers in leading countries throughout the world.

PREFACE

Graham T. Allison
Georgy Arbatov

Our conversation about U.S.–Soviet relations began fifteen years ago. Almost a decade has passed since, at the urging of David Hamburg, scholars from the Soviet Union and the United States began talking about crises and the risks of inadvertent war. Over the past five years, the two of us have cochaired an outstanding group of American and Soviet academics exploring how crises can be prevented in U.S.–Soviet relations.

When our joint study began in 1983, U.S.–Soviet relations were at a low point. Having campaigned against détente and the SALT II arms control agreement, President Reagan came to office denouncing the Soviet Union as an "evil empire." The explicit rejection of arms control in favor of rebuilding U.S. military might, new defense guidance that called on the United States to "prevail" in a nuclear war, and the virtual cessation of candid direct consultations between the two governments signaled a revived cold war. On the Soviet side, difficulties included a series of successions (four leaders in as many years), errors made when making the decision to send troops to Afghanistan, a series of mistakes made during and especially after the Korean Airlines flight 007 incident, and a not very gracious walkout of Soviet negotiators from the intermediate-range nuclear forces (INF) talks in Geneva in November 1983.

Around the globe the superpowers encountered each other in settings where various third parties posed risks to both. In Lebanon and Syria, U.S. and Soviet military personnel stood but fifty miles apart. The two nations were supporting opposing forces in wars in Afghanistan, Nicaragua, the Persian Gulf, and elsewhere. The threat loomed large that misperceptions and miscalculations would combine with actions of third parties, accidents, or inadvertence to produce confrontations between the superpowers that neither would have chosen.

Most previous conferences of Soviet and American academics and policymakers had been confounded by combinations of propaganda, concepts that defied translation, and practices that made communication difficult if not impossible. At the dinner before the first session of our joint study, we announced that "accusations and mutual recriminations will begin at 6:30 tomorrow morning; those uninterested in an exercise of this sort need not arrive until 9:00."

We all came to the meeting at 9:00 prepared for serious, candid discussion. As the chapters and commentaries in this book demonstrate, when unnecessary rhetoric and propaganda are set aside, Soviet and American scholars can understand and learn from each other. We met alternately in the United States and the Soviet Union for discussions around the table and in informal settings— at one point fishing for sturgeon in the Amur River in Eastern Siberia, at another riding dolphins in the Florida Keys.

In our conversations, Americans not infrequently disagreed with other Americans about American views, and the Soviets disagreed among themselves about Soviet views. We two cochairmen have disagreed as often as we have agreed—learning more from our disagreements than from our agreements. Neither of us agrees with all of the statements in this book written by his countrymen. But we jointly commend with enthusiasm such candid conversations between American and Soviet scholars for the purpose of clarifying issues of relevance to both governments. Moreover, we commend the product of this conversation, in the chapters and commentaries that follow, to policy analysts and policymakers in the United States and the Soviet Union.

U.S.-Soviet relations have substantially improved over the past five years and are now evolving toward a relationship that may be sustainable. We are pleased to think that some precursors of the new thinking in the Soviet Union and the United States, and some of the proposals for ways to deal more effectively with one another, were already visible in discussions that produced this joint volume. As we began, we looked forward to a period of improving relations between the superpowers, in which a better understanding of the past and a common framework for understanding the present could motivate actions that would lead to a more stable relationship in the future. We both believe that window of opportunity is open now.

The elements of a stable relationship between the United States and the Soviet Union have evolved. The basic guidelines for a relationship of "peaceful competition" are now relatively clear. Such a relationship does not mean peace and harmony on all fronts, nor does it require the transformation of either nation. Indeed, it begins with realism about the fundamental differences of philosophy, values, and interests that divide our two countries. But it is equally realistic about the overriding common interest we share: to avoid a general war of which the two superpowers would be the primary victims. Refining the elements of a relationship well beyond cold war but short of perpetual peace, so that war and the threat of war recede while profound differences remain, is the fundamental challenge for the leaders of our two countries. This book provides solid evidence about the extent to which serious, candid conversation can lead to mutual understanding. The guidelines for a stable, peaceful competition proposed in these chapters give us hope that this challenge can be met.

ACKNOWLEDGMENTS

Our first thanks must go to our colleagues in the joint study, who not only contributed their papers but also offered continual counsel on the shaping of this volume. In particular, we would like to express our gratitude to our Soviet colleagues. Georgy Arbatov and his able deputies, Vitaly Zhurkin (now head of the new Institute on Western Europe), and Henry Trofimenko made it possible for this book to reflect candidly both American and Soviet perspectives.

We would also like to thank those scholars and policymakers who participated in some of our meetings and gave us their ideas and feedback: Yevgeny Primakov, Valentin Falin, Alexander Bovin, Vladimir Gantman, and Vladimir Baranovsky on the Soviet side and General David Jones on the American. We are also grateful to the members of the Avoiding Nuclear War working group for their feedback, as well as to Richard Haass and Mark Kramer, both of whom read the manuscript in its entirety and gave us their counsel. For able editing, we thank Stephen Bates and Nancy Jackson. For an excellent translation of the Soviet contributions from Russian to English, we thank our colleague Bruce Allyn.

Our joint study has benefited from superb staff work. We thank the staff of the Institute of the U.S.A. and Canada, especially Vladislav Chernov and Alexander Dvoretsky, who patiently guided and assisted us on trips to Moscow and Khabarovsk. At all our meetings, we were especially fortunate to have the aid of Ellen Meyer; she not only worked organizational wizardry, but also made the conference sessions much easier for all by recording the talks on large sheets of paper in front of the group. Her warm and enthusiastic spirit animated our meetings. Lucia Miller organized our conferences with remarkable efficiency, attention to detail, and courtesy.

The principal burden of the book was tackled by Linda Lane, who brought to bear her effective administrative and clerical skills, patience with endless drafts, and unfailing cheer. We would also like to thank Brad Woodworth and Astrid Tuminez for research assistance with endnotes.

We cannot fail to mention our collective debt to the International Research and Exchanges Board (IREX), which administered our exchange, took care of visas, travel, and financial reimbursements, and helped us learn from the experience of past exchanges. In particular, we would like to thank Alan Kassof, Wesley Fisher, and Arlen Hastings.

Without the generosity of the Carnegie Corporation, there would have been no joint study and hence no book. Fritz Mosher and Deanna Arsenian were unfailingly helpful.

Finally, we would like to thank our editor at Ballinger Publishing Company, Carolyn Casagrande, who in wisely pressing us to edit and re-edit has made the reader's task much easier.

INTRODUCTION
Competition Without War

Graham T. Allison
Georgy Arbatov

We begin by recognizing the most extraordinary achievement of the nuclear age. More than four decades have passed without a nuclear war or indeed any general war—more than twice as long as the period of peace following World War I. Coming after four centuries in which war was more the rule than the exception in European international relations, the limitation of warfare over the past forty years is especially remarkable. The antagonisms and instabilities World War II left in place were at least as likely to lead to conflict as conditions after the hostilities Woodrow Wilson described as "the war to end all wars." A number of tense U.S.-Soviet confrontations might have led to war: over Berlin, over missiles in Cuba, and more than once over the Middle East. Other crises have involved wars between nations allied to one or both of the superpowers. But an even larger number of dogs have not barked: potential crises have been avoided or prevented. For example, both the United States and the Soviet Union refrained from direct military involvement in the war between Iraq and Iran.

The recent experience of the superpowers in the Persian Gulf offers an instructive example of crises avoided. During the early 1980s, when bad political relations precluded candid direct negotiations, each government nonetheless felt its way to a tacit understanding of the other's vital interests and the limits of the actions it could

1

accept. Any U.S. military action in Iran that brought U.S. troops to the Soviet border in Azerbaijan would almost certainly have been unacceptable to the Soviet Union, just as the United States could not have tolerated Soviet military action against Iranian or other Persian Gulf oil fields. Similarly, from 1981 through 1983, U.S. troops in Lebanon and Soviet personnel in Syria stood fifty miles apart in a theater that included many independent, unguided actors. Americans were killed by terrorists, and Soviets also died. Yet no crisis erupted, in large part because of the caution exercised by both superpowers.

American and Soviet scholars are in substantial agreement in interpreting the experience of these four decades. Our most important finding concerns the dawning recognition of what could be called the facts of life in the nuclear age. These "objective conditions" crowd the visions and values of both superpowers. Leaders of each government have repeatedly sought to deny the most troublesome truths, but hard facts prove difficult to ignore. Over time, both governments have acknowledged that these realities define the challenge they face. The most important of these facts of life can be summarized under four headings: competition, unintended interdependence, a vital common bond, and uncontrollability.

1. Competition between Real Interests and Values.   The rivalry between the United States and the USSR has deep roots: in geopolitics, history, values, interests, and ideology. While misperceptions and misunderstandings contribute to the rivalry, a realistic approach to peaceful competition must begin with an appreciation of the real differences in philosophy, values, and interests that divide the two countries.

2. Unintended Interdependence.   Technology has established an unintended interdependence between the United States and the USSR that will persist for the foreseeable future: citizens of each nation live as hostages to the adversary's government. Each government has the capability, which it can exercise unilaterally at its own discretion, to execute a nuclear attack that will kill most of the citizens of its rival. Each chooses to hold the other at risk. Each would escape this situation were it able. Perhaps in time, technology may make possible some perfect defense of one's own society or some capacity to disarm the opponent. But for the next several decades at least, each nation's survival depends on the forbearance of its adversary.

3. A Vital Common Bond. These conditions create a historically unprecedented condition in which two primary adversaries are united by a vital common bond. Each government starts by seeking to defend its values and interests. But any attempt to defend those values and interests that leads to a nuclear war would constitute catastrophic failure. Technological conditions have thus created a solidarity of interest between the United States and the USSR: avoiding nuclear war is clearly neither nation's sole objective, but it is one that must be achieved if any other goal is to be reached.

4. Uncontrollability. The first three facts alone are telling arguments for caution. But the problem is even worse. Confrontations between the United States and USSR can arise not only from deliberate choices and real conflicts of interest, but also from uncontrollable events. Things happen that are not expected or intended. Third parties act independently. Misperceptions, misunderstandings, and miscalculations combine with accidents and irrationality to produce confrontations and even wars that no sane leader would have chosen. These uncontrollable ingredients are becoming increasingly important in relations between the United States and the Soviet Union. However either nation chooses to play the competitive game with its rival, the presence of elements of chance counsels additional constraints.

Rudimentary recognition of these objective conditions implies three necessities for policy. Policymakers must:

constrain the competition,
negotiate about each nation's security and its adversary's, and
balance competing and cooperative interests.

The Need to Constrain the Competition. The inescapable risk of destruction motivates a search for constraints that permit the defense of one's values and interests: competition without war. The most celebrated bumper sticker of the nuclear age captures the heart of the matter. As President Reagan and General Secretary Gorbachev affirmed in their Geneva summit communiqué, "The leaders of both nations agree that a nuclear war cannot be won and must therefore never be fought." Then the task becomes finding ways to avoid situations in which either government might believe that its best (or least bad) choice was an action that could trigger a chain of events leading to war. Over the past four decades, the superpowers have discovered a number of rules of prudence, some of which have been extended in written agreements and put into operation in institutions and procedures. Thus there has emerged a relationship that remains deeply competitive, but within constraints that preclude war.

The Need to Negotiate. Technology has denied either government the ability to provide *unilaterally* for its own survival. Each must therefore negotiate about its security, whether explicitly or tacitly. If U.S. actions in pursuit of American security make the USSR insecure, it can unilaterally choose to act in ways the United States finds threatening—and vice versa. The two nations face a mutual security problem in which the threat each one confronts is a result of actions taken by the rival, which are affected by the actions of the first. Thus each nation's security is shaped by a process of (at least implicit) negotiation.

The Need to Balance Competing and Cooperative Interests. Where one party's self-preservation requires cooperation with another to avoid actions whose consequences would destroy them both, interest in cooperation is solidly grounded. Just this solid is the common interest of the United States and the Soviet Union in avoiding major war in which they would be the first victims. Indeed, what competitive objective would justify overriding such a common interest?

At the same time, as President Kennedy noted a quarter-century ago, American policy "seeks not peace at the expense of freedom, but both peace and freedom." No American president would sacrifice freedom before risking peace, nor would a Soviet leader choose surrender rather than war. Thus a challenge for leaders of both governments is to assure that neither is forced to make such a fateful choice. (Asked whether they would "rather be red than dead," Americans should reply "neither"; so too for Soviets faced with an equivalent choice.)

When the question about competitive and competing interests is considered over decades rather than days, additional threats to both superpowers should accent cooperation. The proliferation of nuclear weapons; the spread of other technologies of mass destruction like biochemicals; terrorism; conventional wars between third parties that pose risks of escalation; environmental degradation—the list grows ever longer and the risks rise. Moreover, on the positive side of the ledger, there are attractive opportunities for joint gains, not only from trade but from expanded exchanges of scientists, artists, athletes, and citizens, plus opportunities to promote solutions to global problems.

Such common interests coexist with equally powerful competitive demands in each nation to solve its own problems and promote its values and interests. Finding an appropriate balance between competition and cooperation in preserving and advancing each nation's enlightened self-interest will remain policymakers' enduring challenge.

These elemental facts and implications form a substructure of a relationship that has permitted competition without war. As the chapters that follow demonstrate, American and Soviet scholars have found considerable common ground identifying the key elements of that relationship. Three such elements are rules of prudence, agreements, and institutions and procedures, discussed in chapters 1, 2, and 3, respectively.

Chapter 1 identifies various rules of prudence that constrain the U.S.-Soviet competition. The central factor motivating these rules of prudence is identified by Henry Trofimenko as a strategic nuclear parity that imposes an "objective nonaggression pact." Frequently unwritten and unarticulated (in the sense that there is no agreed statement of them), these rules derive their standing and force not from declarations by governments but from recognition of facts and calculations of self-interest.

Chapter 2 examines written agreements and norms that make it possible not only to avoid unintended crises (for example, by agreeing on rules of the road) but to clarify common interests and expectations about appropriate constraints. While some written agreements between the United States and the USSR have been essentially declaratory and rhetorical, other specific agreements prescribe communication in times of crisis, limit numbers and types of nuclear weapons, and guarantee the status of Berlin.

Chapter 3 explores a third element of this system: the institutions and procedures that make unwritten and written agreements operational. Although both governments recognized the costs of an incident like the downing of the Korean Airlines flight 007 and acknowledged an obligation to communicate about suspicious events or accidents, that tragedy still occurred. To be operationalized, such understandings must be embodied in institutions such as the newly established nuclear risk reduction centers and in procedures like those established by the North Pacific Air Safety Agreement.

Part II provides perspective on the evolution of this system for crisis prevention. Chapter 4 discusses the cardinal historical event that spurred the development of the system: the Cuban missile crisis. It offers for the first time a candid Soviet assessment of what happened, what was misperceived and misunderstood, and what lessons this event holds for avoiding future confrontations. Chapter 5 interprets the evolution of rules, agreements, and procedures as a process of learning and as the building of "partial security regimes." It places this evolution in the broader context of the changing U.S.-Soviet relationship over the last four decades. Chapter 6 takes a different cut: it explains the development of reciprocal rules (from the Soviet point of view) as the result not of the subjective process of learning but of changes in objective conditions—namely, the gradual development of strategic parity between the United States and the Soviet Union. Chapter 7 traces the evolution of a common language between Americans and Soviets, in which scholars and policymakers can understand crises and crisis prevention. A key element in this system for crisis prevention is the nuclear weapons themselves, and how they would be deployed and controlled in a time of crisis. Chapter 8 considers the question of strategic stability.

Part III builds on this understanding of the past to ask where we should go from here. Insights gained in an era of poor relations provide an impetus to proposals for action in the current window of opportunity. Finally, the concluding chapter draws from the body of the book to outline a set of guidelines for peaceful competition.

FOUNDATIONS OF PEACEFUL COMPETITION

1 PRIMITIVE RULES OF PRUDENCE
Foundations of Peaceful Competition

Graham T. Allison

During the Cuban missile crisis, John F. Kennedy spoke of "the precarious rules of the status quo." He believed that the USSR had violated these rules by secretly placing strategic nuclear weapons in Cuba, in direct contradiction of Khrushchev's private assurances to him. In Kennedy's judgment, it was not just the particular stakes in Cuba but rather Khrushchev's violation of these rules that demanded the firmest response—even if that response entailed a one-in-three chance of war. As he stated in his announcement of the United States' discovery of the missiles and initial response:

> This secret, swift, and extraordinary build-up of Communist missiles—in an area well known to have a special and historical relationship to the United States and the nations of the Western Hemisphere, in violation of Soviet assurances, and in defiance of American and hemispheric policy—this sudden, clandestine decision to station strategic weapons for the first time outside of Soviet soil—is a deliberately *provocative and unjustified change in the status quo* which cannot be accepted by this country if our courage and our commitments are ever to be trusted again by either friend or foe.[1] [emphasis added]

If Khrushchev could so misread the rules of the game, or miscalculate the consequences of their violation, or reinterpret them unilater-

In the preparation of this chapter, Doug Strand served not only as research assistant, but as a colleague and virtual co-author.

ally, then, Kennedy reasoned, war was likely. The president's "shocked incredulity" at the discovery of the missiles raised dark doubts about the Soviet leader: if Khrushchev was willing to attempt this after all his promises and denials, how could he ever be trusted on anything? As Theodore Sorensen recalls his own and Kennedy's reasoning: "The fact that Khrushchev had already made one major miscalculation—in thinking he could get away with missiles in Cuba—increased the danger that he would make more."[2]

Many of Kennedy's advisers feared that Berlin would be next. The Red Army had the physical capability to seize this enclave inside East Germany. The United States was committed to go to war to prevent that outcome. What preserved the peace, therefore, was a *web of mutual understandings* of what each superpower could and could not do—precarious rules of the status quo that Khrushchev could not be allowed to violate with impunity. To reassert these rules, Kennedy chose a course of action that he judged would raise the risks of war in the short run, in order to limit such risks in the longer run.

This chapter explores the concept of rules of prudence; articulates some critical unwritten rules of prudence that constrain the U.S.-Soviet competition; and assesses the extent to which these rules are understood by American and Soviet observers. After considering the broader context of factors that have produced four decades of peace between the superpowers since World War II, I examine the concept of "rules of prudence" and analyze those rules as perceived by Americans. In what form can these unarticulated rules be stated? What are key examples of behavior that observe the rule (where alternative behavior was plausible)? What are telling exceptions to the rule? How wide is the band of gray that separates black from white in defining the rule? Are there substantial disagreements about instances when a rule was observed, or infringed, or about where the gray areas begin? How acceptable is the formulation of the unstated rules advanced here? Finally I attempt to draw conclusions about the role of rules of prudence in peaceful competition.

FOUR DECADES WITHOUT WAR

More than forty years have passed without global war. What accounts for this prolonged peace—or at least the absence of global war?

Many factors are relevant, the most important of which can be grouped under three headings. The first is the *substructure of power.* For the first three decades after World War II, the Soviet Union, Japan, and Europe were recovering from devastating losses. Not until the 1970s were there two genuine superpowers. Even in that decade the Soviet Union's claim to superpower status rested on only one dimension of power: military capacity. Special domestic circumstances, both economic and political, have tempered ambitions in Japan and Germany. Only slowly has the Soviet Union become able to project power at a distance. As this substructure of power evolves, so too will the associated rules of prudence.

A second set of factors is the *distribution of aspirations and demands:* what is judged desirable, necessary, possible, or intolerable. In the aftermath of World War II, Soviet armies rarely retreated, but instead claimed for the Soviet Union a security buffer of Eastern European states. While the United States objected, it was not prepared to fight to change that situation on the ground. The enforced division of Germany has met the minimum requirements of both superpowers and other Europeans. While the question of West Berlin's survival as a Western enclave led to hard bargaining and some real risk-taking, that issue now seems settled. The status of the American claims to prevent foreign interference in the Western hemisphere was tested in Cuba—a success for the Soviet Union that defined a limited exception to the rule. Soviet and Cuban supply of local revolutionaries in Central America extends that test, but at low cost and risk. Other actors with revolutionary ambitions that might have incited global war have thus far lacked the power of their aspirations.

A third cluster of war-deterring factors has to do with the emergence of *a vital common interest between the U.S. and the Soviet Union*: an interest in avoiding the global war of which they would be the first victims. Churchill observed that "sublime irony" that made safety "the sturdy child of terror, and survival the twin brother of annihilation."[3] Nuclear weapons' capacity to destroy the adversary's society, combined with invulnerable delivery systems, has enabled the leaders of each country to see clearly that attack on the other would be suicidal. Technological forces beyond their control have, at least during this period, established a solidarity of interest between the superpowers, rooted in the basic instinct for self-preservation and the fundamental national interest in survival. This mutual necessity to avoid nuclear war has engendered a remarkable degree of caution and evolving practices of prudence in each nation's pursuit of its interests.

RULES OF PRUDENCE IN THE U.S.-SOVIET COMPETITION

American and Soviet participants in this study agreed broadly that "rules of prudence" have constrained both superpowers' competitive behavior. Indeed, there was also considerable agreement on the minimum content of these rules. Soviet scholars commented on the striking stability of these practices, even in periods of bad relations between the superpowers. Perhaps especially at such times, both governments have understood the need to observe these fundamental unwritten rules of prudence.

These practices have emerged over the course of the postwar period. The restraints reflect what our Soviet colleagues call "objective factors" and are grounded in realistic calculations of self-interest and short- and long-term risks, rather than sympathy for or concessions to the adversary. Such unwritten rules are ambiguous, fuzzy at the edges, and evolving; but where they have become embedded in interpretations of self-interest, they have constrained behavior much more powerfully than would mere declarations of principle.

A telling example is provided by recent experience in the Persian Gulf. In a period during which bad political relations precluded candid direct negotiations, both governments seemed to recognize that Soviet military action against the oil fields would be unacceptable to the United States; similarly any U.S. military action in Iran that brought American troops to the Soviet border in Azerbaijan would be unacceptable to the Soviet Union. From 1981 through 1983, when U.S. troops in Lebanon and Soviet personnel in Syria were only fifty miles apart, the caution exercised by both superpowers suggests an appreciation of an unwritten rule restraining direct confrontations of their military forces.[4]

There is no agreed statement of these rules of prudence. They are not formalized in treaties or other agreements (and some could never be).[5] But they go beyond mere calculations of short- and long-term self-interest and risk. They affect each government's understanding of its interests and its definitions of the problem it faces. They shape the prevailing conventions and simplifications that shrink the unlimited number of possibilities to manageable proportions. They become part of the actors' expectations of their adversary's behavior.[6] Nonetheless, the rules do not achieve the status of law, for they do not meet the standard criteria of unambiguous statement, authoritative interpretation, and formal sanction upon violation.

It has been suggested that the phenomena analyzed here should be described as "practices," rather than rules, of prudence. But more than a customary mode of behavior is involved here. These practices, at least in part, reflect *rules*. Webster's first definition of rules states: "a prescribed, suggested, or self-imposed guide for conduct or action." This concept applies in the literal sense to superpower interaction in the patterns we are examining. Repeated practices by intelligent governments are not due to mere habit or case-by-case calculation of interest but reflect at least a self-imposed guide for conduct. Each superpower seems to have adopted the practices described below as the preferrred procedures in the relevant situations. The motivation begins with the desire to minimize the risk of nuclear war, but also includes concern about public opinion, aversion to uncertainty, and a desire to limit complexity. In sum, these rules are analogous to precepts like "don't drive after heavy drinking" or "drive slowly when the roads are icy": well-known, prudent ways to avoid unnecessary risks, which can nonetheless be violated, and sometimes are.

Given the many possible paths to nuclear war, prudence should motivate the development of rules to limit risks in various arenas: nuclear weapons, accidents, crisis confrontation, "vital interests," areas of dominant security concern, limited war, unconventional warfare, and terrorism, to offer a partial list. We will focus here on five primary, salient, unwritten rules of prudence restraining the superpower competition.

RULES FOR SUPERPOWERS: AMERICAN PERCEPTIONS

From the American perspective, five key unwritten rules of prudence have governed the behavior of the superpowers:

1. Avoid any use (explosion) of nuclear weapons, except as a final resort.[7]

2. Avoid direct military action against the other superpower's vital interests.
3. Respect the other's area of dominant security concern.[8]
4. Avoid any direct use of force against the other's troops.[9]
5. Restrain allies and clients from inflicting a strategic defeat on the other superpower's allies or clients.[10]

Here we consider these rules in turn, giving examples of their application and of exceptions and gray areas.

1. Avoid Any Use of Nuclear Weapons

In 1945, a prediction that no nuclear weapons would be exploded in anger for the next four decades would have been dismissed as utopian. We should recognize that our record of abstention is remarkable, and should not presume it to be sustainable.

American thought and practice with regard to nuclear weapons have been schizophrenic. On the one hand, since the period of American monopoly, the United States has relied on nuclear weapons for defense on the cheap. Defense strategy, guidance, and plans call for deploying nuclear weapons to deter threats against U.S. vital interests and to defend these interests. For example, NATO acquires and positions nuclear weapons in Europe and trains for their use to deter Soviet aggression. NATO's plans for the defense of Europe call for the first use of nuclear weapons in the early weeks of war.

On the other hand, recognizing the risks of escalation and concerned about proliferation, the United States has played a major role in establishing the taboo against the use of nuclear weapons. The United States refrained from using nuclear weapons when it could have done so without fear of retaliation (e.g., in Korea and in the defense of Dien Bien Phu).

Soviet views and practices seem even more complex. When Soviet forces were most vulnerable to American pre-emption, the USSR adopted a declaratory policy of repeated nuclear threats (e.g., during crises over the Suez and Berlin and with regard to the defense of Cuba). The posture of its nuclear forces and its practices suggested no operational intent to use these weapons, however. After Soviet nuclear forces reached parity with those of the United States, the USSR adopted a declaratory no-first-use policy—but Soviet posture and practices appeared to anticipate pre-emption on warning.

Examples. Four key examples will illuminate this rule's consequences. Its influence on behavior has become more clearly recognized over time. In no instance has either superpower made advanced
preparations for nuclear war. Paul Bracken sums up the surprise here:

> Some people consider it remarkable that no nuclear weapons have been fired
> since 1945. Far more remarkable is the absence of a full Soviet-American
> alert. No American bombers have been launched in anticipation of enemy
> attack, at no time have nuclear weapons in Europe been dispersed from their
> peacetime storage sites, nor have all of the Soviet nuclear submarines been
> dispatched from their ports at one time.[11]

When Korean armistice talks bogged down, President Eisenhower
raised the nuclear option. In a message passed to the North Koreans
shortly after he took office, he threatened nuclear use if negotiations
didn't progress.[12] It appears, however, that he was conscious of an
emerging rule against such use. Recently declassified National Security Council (NSC) minutes indicate that on March 27, 1953, Eisenhower and Dulles agreed "that somehow or other the taboo which
surrounds the use of nuclear weapons would have to be destroyed."[13]
The president was impressed by the fact that nuclear weapons would
be more cost-effective than conventional attack.[14] Atomic weapons
were stationed in the vicinity, and although target opportunities in
North Korea looked poor, "the military were most anxious to make
use of nuclear weapons . . . outside Korea."[15] By the beginning of
1954 the Joint Chiefs and the State Department had settled on a
compromise plan: if hostilities recommenced, military targets in
North Korea and their supporting facilities in Manchuria and China
were to be bombed.[16]

Eisenhower recognized the taboo against nuclear use in at least
one other instance. When the French faced a great defeat at Dien
Bien Phu in 1954, an NSC paper presented to Eisenhower explored
uses of nuclear weapons. The president retorted: "You boys must be
crazy. We can't use those awful things against Asians for the second
time in less than ten years. My God."[17]

A third example concerns Vietnam. In a recent interview Nixon
said that he considered the nuclear option in one of his early assessments of the situation there but immediately ruled it out, dissuaded
by the fact that it would kill millions of North Vietnamese.[18] Kissinger has said he is not aware that the use of nuclear weapons was ever
seriously considered during his tenure (thus allowing the possibility
of Nixon's private deliberations). Kissinger finds it a "curious phe-

nomenon" that nuclear use was present only in the vague background of crises. Even when the administration thought China might come to the aid of Pakistan in its 1971 war with India, and the Soviets might then have threatened to fight the Chinese, the nuclear option was not considered.[19]

Finally, we have little evidence of Soviet deliberations on nuclear use. Vague Soviet threats were issued in the 1956 Suez crisis and during the Berlin crisis in the late 1950s. Khrushchev alluded to a nuclear defense of Cuba on July 9, 1960. After the U-2 affair, Khrushchev said that he had predelegated authority to the head of the Soviet rocket forces to launch missiles against any bases used for further illegal overflight.[20] Yet the evidence suggests the contrary, for example, in 1962 an American U-2 strayed over the Kola Peninsula and no retaliation followed.

Exceptions and Gray Areas. In 1969 the Soviet Union threatened a nuclear attack on China during their extended border war.[21] Kissinger reports that a Soviet diplomat sounded out the United States as to its likely reaction to a Soviet attack on Chinese nuclear facilities. Kissinger and Nixon were alarmed and seriously explored the contingency.[22] H. R. Haldeman gives a more explicit account based on first- and second-hand experience. The administration's diplomatic response—publicly approaching the Chinese to propose renewal of the Warsaw talks, with the aim of reopening relations between the two countries—"stave[d] off an incredible disaster: a Soviet nuclear 'surgical' strike at China's atom plants."[23]

Would the Soviet leadership today so seriously consider using nuclear weapons against a state that could not significantly retaliate in kind? Should a vigorous, aggressive nonproliferation regime threaten joint U.S.-Soviet action to destroy emerging nuclear capabilities of other powers?

According to Steve Meyer, Soviet military writings now show a preference for pre-emptive nuclear attack upon strategic warning of nuclear attack by the other side; such a warning might include full alert or dispersal of theater nuclear weapons. Generally, Soviet doctrine has evolved from an expectation that any superpower war would necessarily become a strategic nuclear war to acceptance of the possibility that a superpower conflict would remain conventional. With modernizations of conventional forces in Europe in the 1970s, the Soviet Union took a number of specific steps to develop a conventional option.[24]

As noted above, NATO strategy is based on nuclear deterrence—that is, the credible threat to use nuclear weapons to defeat a major conventional attack. If NATO were to initiate a limited nuclear attack to force the Soviet Union to one final pause before general war, would this be a "final resort" or a "penultimate resort"? Could smaller-yield, accurate nuclear weapons be used by both parties in a controlled manner that observed some deeper rule, such as an injunction to avoid the use of nuclear weapons against the adversary's homeland, or against cities?

2. Avoid Military Action Against the Other's Vital Interests

The issue of vital interests is an old nut that we will not try to crack here. At a minimum, we will assume, vital interests include a nation's territory and that of nations it is evidently willing to defend; here "evidence" would include a combination of stakes, explicit treaties, and military deployments. While neither a necessary nor a sufficient condition, a formal military alliance or security commitment clearly indicates the likelihood of a vital interest. Since 1945 the United States has taken direct military action (invasion or use of firepower) against ten nations. None of these nations had formal military alliances with the Soviet Union. Similarly, the Soviet Union has taken military action against five nations, all of which shared borders with the Soviet Union, and none of which was formally allied with the United States.[25]

Superpower attacks on vital interests of the other side have occasionally been plausible. The Soviet Union certainly considered using military force to assert control over West Berlin. More recently, it appears to have considered military action against Pakistan and Iran (especially after the severance of Iran's ties with the United States). The United States considered attacks on China in the Korean War and on Syria in recent years. In all cases, restraint prevailed.

Examples. According to two Czech émigré historians, in 1951 Stalin discussed plans to invade Western Europe before it recovered economically and began providing bases for American nuclear weaponry. The invasion was to happen within three or four years.[26] Soviet military spending rose sharply in 1951, but if such plans existed, they were never carried out.

Khrushchev's failure to win Western concessions on Berlin was used against him by his opponents within the USSR.[27] At the 1961 Vienna summit, he seemed to make a confrontation inevitable, asserting that "the decision to sign a peace treaty [with East Germany] was firm and irrevocable." The Soviet hesitation to use military force against Berlin is explained by an exchange between Khrushchev and Averell Harriman in 1959. If no concessions were made, Khrushchev swore, the USSR would close off the access routes to West Berlin. Harriman laughed and replied, "You're a very intelligent man, and that would mean nuclear war and you don't want that." After a moment's thought, Khrushchev replied, "You're right."[28]

Pakistan has provided sanctuary and support for Afghan rebels. In 1981, the Soviet Union reportedly warned Islamabad that continued aid to the rebels would eventually result in war with Afghanistan, which the Soviet Union would support.[29] The U.S. capacity to assist Pakistan, if attacked, is limited. Nonetheless, the Soviet Union has not made deep incursions into Pakistan or used airpower or artillery beyond limited attacks on rebel camps on the border, with consequently little impact on the rebels' war effort.

Since its withdrawal in 1946, the Soviet Union has refrained from military action against Iran, despite provocations. Afghan rebels operate out of Iran, Iranians have fired on Soviet helicopters in hot pursuit, and the Communist (and Soviet-established) Tudeh party and leftist Mujahadeen have been banned or persecuted. Given the current state of U.S.-Iranian relations, limited Soviet attacks on Iran would not violate the rule of prudence against attacking the other's vital interests, though a major military action would threaten U.S. vital interests in the oil fields.

Why has the United States made military air strikes on Libya but not Syria? The answer helps clarify this rule of prudence. Both states sponsor terrorism against the United States. Each has taken actions against U.S. interests: Syria in Lebanon, Libya in Egypt and the Sudan. But Syria has a military alliance with the Soviet Union, while Libya does not.

Exceptions and Gray Areas. The U.S. attacks on Libya in 1986 could appear to be an exception to this rule. However, there is little evidence that the USSR considers Libya a vital interest. The Soviet Union has spurned Qaddafi in his appeals for a friendship and cooperation treaty.[30] Furthermore, Soviet support before and during the attacks was exceedingly restrained. If the Soviet Union does not consider Libya a vital interest, the U.S. attack does not constitute an exception.

What about North Vietnam? Neither the United States nor the Soviet Union seems to have regarded North Vietnam as a vital interest of the USSR before or during the war. At the beginning of the war, Soviet support of Vietnam was very limited, and the latter's aid request in early 1963 was denied.[31] Indeed, the Soviet Union did not sign a formal alliance with Vietnam until 1978—well after the U.S. withdrawal.

Similarly, the USSR had no formal alliance with North Korea at the time of the war, and the U.S. attack was in response to an invasion of its ally. Moreover, the U.S. response was UN sanctioned and multilateral. The invasion spared one clear Soviet vital interest from attack on its territory: China.

A somewhat stronger case can be made regarding the U.S.-Syrian air battle over Lebanon in December 1983. However, the engagement was very limited and had been provoked by Syrian attacks on U.S. reconnaissance planes; moreover, the Soviet Union took actions to distance itself from Syrian activity in Lebanon and exempt itself from any obligations under the 1980 Friendship Treaty. Therefore this case is at most a partial exception—but it does help identify a fuzzy boundary. If an ally is intervening in another country, as Syria was in Lebanon, are attacks on these out-of-country forces an acceptable exception to the rule?

3. Respect the Other's Dominant Security Concerns

Both the United States and the Soviet Union vigorously deny the existence of this rule—each for its own reasons. Neither one is prepared to cede to the other by law, right, or legitimacy the claim to exercise a special authority over other independent states. Moreover, each is publicly committed to values, international agreements, and images of itself that conflict with making any such claim upon the rights and freedom of action of nations that might fall within its own area of dominant security concern. Thus one must look at actions rather than words.

A superpower's area of dominant security concern is one in which it exercises (what it considers to be) certain rights, restraining the freedom of action of governments of nations in the area, and one in which it expects its adversary to exercise restraint. Such areas need not represent "vital interests."

The contrast between Eastern Europe and Afghanistan is instructive. While the United States is not prepared to accept the legitimacy of Soviet domination of Eastern Europe, Soviet military interventions in Hungary, Czechoslovakia, and East Germany have triggered no military response. Indeed, the United States has not been prepared to provide military aid or advisers to support freedom-fighters in these countries. Soviet intervention in Afghanistan, however, has been met with verbal protest, and covert and overt military assistance.

Soviet involvement in the Western Hemisphere is a more complicated story. The issue of Cuba is discussed below as an exception to the rule. In the case of Nicaragua today, the United States has communicated clearly to the Soviet Union that military assistance to the Sandinista regime would be unacceptable if it included significant offensive capabilities such as MiGs, and the Soviet Union appears to have accepted that restriction.

What does it mean to "respect" areas of dominant security concern? This unwritten rule appears to impose stricter restraints on the United States than on the Soviet Union. It may be useful to attempt to spell out in somewhat more precise detail each power's understanding of the restraints it has been observing.

U.S. behavior and government statements suggest that the limits to Soviet involvement in the U.S. area of dominant security concern include:

1. No use or threat of force.
2. No substantial numbers of Soviet military advisers.
3. No establishment of facilities for Soviet power projection.
4. No arms transfers permitting the recipient to acquire a locally dominant offensive capability (e.g., for Nicaragua) or large-scale offensive capability.
5. No military response to U.S. military action in its area.
6. No alliance or friendship treaties.

The U.S. area here is taken to include the Caribbean (with the partial exception of Cuba, as discussed below), Central America (regarding Nicaragua, see below), and, to a lesser extent, South America.

Limits to U.S. involvement in the Soviet area seem to be stricter, including proscriptions corresponding to all those listed above, with two further additions:

1. No arms transfers of any kind.
2. No subversive aid of any kind beyond propaganda (may there be covert exceptions?).

The Soviet area is clearly understood to include Eastern Europe and Mongolia. Yugoslavia and Albania are in gray areas, as discussed below. Finland is not included, although Finnish foreign policy takes account of Soviet interests.

Examples. The Soviet reaction to the U.S. invasion of the Dominican Republic in 1965 provides a clear example of this rule. After the successful establishment of the Castro regime, the United States announced a "no second Cuba" policy. The first test came in the Dominican Republic, where the United States sent 25,000 American troops to keep the revolution from falling into the hands of Communist conspirators. As it had done following the CIA-assisted overthrow of the Arbenz government in Guatemala in 1954, the Soviet Union condemned the action before the international community, arguing that it violated the UN charter. Otherwise no punitive actions were taken; indeed, no warnings were issued to discourage such action in the future.[32]

The regime in Grenada sought to shape the state according to Marxism-Leninism. Its leaders courted Soviet support and assiduously backed up the Soviet position in international organizations.[33] The Soviet Union sent the Grenadians weapons and covert advisers.[34] Grenada would have been a significant strategic gain for the USSR, given its location near South America.[35] Yet despite pressure from the Cubans, the Soviet Union proceeded cautiously.[36] When the United States took military action against Grenada, the Soviet response was limited to rather low-level diplomatic protest and other verbal denunciation.[37]

U.S. restraint in Hungary in 1956 and in Czechoslovakia in 1968 are telling counterpoints. Early in the Eisenhower administration, American officials talked about "rolling back" the Iron Curtain in Eastern Europe. Options for covert and overt aid were explored. When the Soviet Union sent troops to suppress the Hungarian revolutionaries, there was a public outcry in the United States. Radio Free Europe broadcasts had encouraged the Hungarian revolt and suggested that the United States would rescue Hungary if the Soviet Union were to intervene. The CIA had specific plans to airdrop arms to the rebels.[38] Yet the U.S. government's reaction essentially stopped at words of condemnation. After the first Soviet intervention, on October 23, Eisenhower stated that Eastern Europe should be free, but not freed through force.[39] After the second intervention on November 4, the United States issued no warnings against Soviet intervention in the future.[40] Instead, Dulles remarked that the United States did not want to ally with states on the Soviet border hostile to the USSR.[41] Moreover, the United States reportedly felt that it could not even recognize a Hungarian government unfriendly to Moscow.[42]

Shortly before the 1968 Soviet invasion of Czechoslovakia, UN Ambassador George Ball (formerly undersecretary of state) gave a speech on the subject of containment. He argued that the concept "suggested in less clear outlines, the implicit acceptance by both sides of broad spheres of influence."[43] As Soviet troops marched into Czechoslovakia, the United States condemned the action. But during the crisis, NATO limited its force movements: reconnaissance flights over Czechoslovakia were halted, despite the intelligence loss.[44] The United States, as Valenta puts it, "sent unmistakable signals" to the Soviet Union that it would not interfere in Czechoslovakia (although for geographical reasons, the logistics for such interference would have been more favorable than in the Hungarian case). Phillip Windsor claims that the minister of state at the British Foreign Office told him that the USSR had sent a message to London: "If you interfere, we will blow you off the map."[45] (Windsor also asserts that some similar, though vaguer, warning was probably conveyed to the United States.) Casting doubt on this account, however, is the fact that Soviet troops were ordered to hold their positions without firing if they encountered Western troops in Czechoslovakia. Ultimately, American sanctions amounted to little more than a delay in ratification of the Nonproliferation Treaty, the cancellation of plans for President Johnson's trip to Moscow, and the postponement of the SALT talks. Within three months the United States sought resumption of the talks.[46] The United States seems to have given no warnings for the future.[47]

Exceptions and Gray Areas. U.S. ambivalence and uncertainty allowed Cuba to become a partial exception to the rule of respecting the adversary's area of dominant security concern. The Bay of Pigs was a clumsy, ill-planned, and ill-executed attempt to provide plausibly deniable support to Cuban rebels attempting to overthrow Castro. In resolving the Cuban missile crisis, the United States drew a line precluding the establishment of Cuba as a base for significant offensive action in the region, but accepting a Soviet outpost in the Western Hemisphere. (In Chapter 4 Sergo Mikoyan challenges the notion of unlimited duration, inquiring to what extent a rule against "Soviet arms transfers permitting Cuba a substantial offensive capability" holds today.)

In spite of Sandinista pleas, the Soviet Union has steadfastly refused Nicaragua any defense pledge and has shown qualitative restraint in its arms transfers.[48] In 1982, after preparation for Soviet shipments of advanced MiGs to Nicaragua, a warning from Shultz to Gromyko seems to have led the Soviet Union to exclude that level of armaments.[49]

The Soviet invasion of Afghanistan in 1979 alarmed the United States because it was the first major use of Soviet troops outside the Soviet area of dominant security concern. Though the Soviet Union had played a role in the coup of 1978 that brought Taraki to power, it never claimed and the United States never accepted any special Soviet right to exercise control in Afghanistan. Had the invasion been a success, Afghanistan might have been incorporated into the Soviet area of dominant security concern. Its status should become clearer in future agreements on Soviet withdrawal.

Rumania pursues an independent foreign policy. Moreover, President Johnson vaguely warned the USSR against allowing its invasion of Czechoslovakia to spill over into Rumania. ("Let no one unleash the dogs of war.") But U.S. interest seemed to be focused primarily on the security of Yugoslavia, which like Albania remains a state of uncertain status.[50]

4. Avoid Any Use of Force against the Other's Troops

In 1945, would anyone have forecast that the next forty years of geopolitical competition would see few American soldiers, sailors, or airmen killed by Soviets, and vice versa? Yet this is the record.

Historically, states have engaged in limited clashes outside the context of war and without provoking war (e.g., Britain and France in the nineteenth century). Military force can be used for limited purposes without causing war. Yet the United States and the Soviet Union have avoided the former as well as the latter. The superpowers have exercised extreme caution in situations where military forces might confront each other. In Berlin, the four-power agreement and processes for regular consultation have kept violence to a minimum. Moreover, each superpower has sought to keep its forces out of the other's way. Their Incidents at Sea Agreement is a limited codification of this practice for the two navies.[51] U.S. forces have avoided places where the Soviet forces were using firepower in conflict.[52] The Soviet Union has also steered clear of American military action. In cases where Soviet soldiers were in danger of American attack, intentional or unintentional, the USSR (sometimes with the cooperation of the United States) has downplayed their presence.

Examples. Berlin provides several good examples of this rule. During the 1948 blockade, Stalin did not challenge the airlift that destroyed his plans, and Truman rejected General Clay's advice to challenge the land blockade with an armed convoy.[53] Later, in the 1958–59 Berlin crisis, Eisenhower felt "that the Soviet challenge was not merely to the precarious Western position in Berlin, but extended to the entire strategic relationship between the USSR and the U.S. . . ."[54] But despite this perception, he avoided using force. In January 1959, incensed by the situation, he ordered: "Should there be any substitution of East German officials for Soviets, a small convoy with armed protection would attempt to go through, and if this convoy was stopped, the effort would be discontinued and the probe would fire only if fired upon. . . ."[55] The contingency did not arise.

During President Kennedy's Berlin crisis, the United States did send a probe—a 1,500-man battle group—down the autobahn to West Berlin, a move that gave Kennedy "some of his tensest moments."[56] But the Soviet Union did not challenge this retort. East Germany proposed a 150-meter no man's land on either side of the sector boundary. Kennedy countered by placing 1,000 troops with tanks along the boundary. No violence ensued. Later, when tanks from both sides confronted each other head on, Soviet forces withdrew without firing. Although obsessed with Berlin, Khrushchev repeatedly backed down from challenges without firing a shot.

This pattern was repeated in the Cuban missile crisis. Both sides avoided confrontation on the high seas. The Soviet Union recalled ships carrying missiles, testing the blockade cautiously with civilian cargos. The United States postponed boarding, inventing other options, including inspection by airplane. Under tremendous pressure to eliminate the intermediate-range ballistic missiles (IRBMs) before they became operational, Kennedy nonetheless sought alternatives to decisive military action. On the final Saturday he even overrode his previous order to retaliate against any surface-to-air missile (SAM) battery that fired on U.S. U-2s. Khrushchev also reacted cautiously, allowing the illegal (and unintended) overflight of another U-2 over the Kola Peninsula, even though he had threatened previously that retaliation would be automatic.[57]

Superpower restraint in adhering to this rule is particularly impressive in situations where another rule has already been broken. When the Soviet Union intervened in Czechoslovakia in 1968, Red Army commanders were briefed to hold positions without firing if they encountered troops in Czechoslovakia.[58] This restraint was observed in spite of a violation of rule 3. Before its air strikes on Libya in 1986, the United States had strongly hinted that Libyan SAM-5 batteries would be attacked from the fleet.[59] The Soviet Union then reportedly moved its subs out of the area, to avoid being mistaken for Libyan subs.[60] During that first attack, 300 Soviet advisers reportedly refused to leave a bunker when the Libyans begged them for help in installing new launch pads on a SAM site.[61] Apparently no Russians were killed.[62] According to Egyptian reports, the United States told the Soviet Union of the imminent attack one hour beforehand. This alert carried a high cost: the Libyans got the warning and were able to move their planes to safety in Sudan, and Qaddafi moved his headquarters, probably saving his life.[63] The 3,000 Soviets in Libya "mostly retreated" during the attack, even though the Libyans needed their help to avert defeat in battle, in the event suffering humiliation and exposing Soviet weaponry and aid to renewed criticism.[64]

During the fighting in Lebanon in 1983, the USSR never formally announced its manning of SAMs.[66] This approach—downplaying military presence when vulnerable to attack by the other superpower—has been a repeated Soviet practice. In Vietnam, the Soviet Union maintained a tacit agreement with the United States that neither side would note the presence of Soviets in combat roles, such as around SAM sites.[66]

Exceptions and Gray Areas. Various isolated, limited violent encounters have occurred. The United States apologized after the 1960 U-2 downing, since it was an illegal overflight of the type against which the USSR had long protested. The Soviet forces fired on U.S. reconnaissance planes twice during the 1959 Berlin crisis; American planes withheld fire. Apparently there were U.S.-Soviet air battles over northeast China, though the extent is unclear. The United States did not comment on one case in which a MiG-5 was shot down.[67] More blatant was an incident in October 1950, during which U.S. F-80s strafed Soviet territory, hitting an airfield sixty miles inside the USSR, near Vladivostok. The United States later admitted that "navigation error and poor judgment" were to blame and informed the UN that the Air Force had begun disciplinary proceedings. Official U.S. policy prohibited such behavior.[68] In the Vietnam War U.S. forces bombed and mined Haiphong Harbor, killing some Soviet sailors. Moscow took no punitive action in response, and indeed proceeded with the upcoming summit, at which the Basic Principles Agreement and the SALT I Interim Agreement were signed. However, there was significant disagreement in the Kremlin over the Soviet response to the American escalation.[69]

These cases suggest a range of potential exceptions. Violence against the adversary's soldiers or civilians may be tolerated if they get in the way when they are not the targeted party. When home territory or airspace is violated, action against the offending party may be acceptable. And perhaps some limited violence against the adversary's forces is tolerable if the presence of these forces has not been acknowledged, or has been denied.

5. Restrain Allies and Clients

Although this last rule has been seen as a corollary of the fourth, it does not necessarily follow. If each superpower refrains from engaging the other's forces, an ally of one could nonetheless defeat the other's ally. One author has argued that the history of the superpower interaction reveals a "bias in favor of the status quo." Consequently, when the status quo changes substantially against the interests of one superpower's client, then that superpower's intervention threshold is broken and "only that patron 'receives an invitation' to intervene whose client is on the defensive strategically."[70] Or as Kissinger represented the American attitude in a 1973 threat to the Egyptians, "Do not deceive yourselves, the U.S. would not either today or tomorrow allow Soviet arms to win a big victory, even if it was not decisive, against U.S. arms."[71]

Yet except for the War of Attrition discussed below, neither superpower has intervened directly to preserve an ally from an adversary supported by the other superpower. Each superpower has sought to prevent the other from intervening unilaterally in a war between allies. Attempting to restrain an ally from actions that invite intervention is the safest way to pursue this goal.

Examples. In the 1967 Arab-Israeli War, Moscow's most serious warning came when Israel threatened Damascus, on June 9, after the cease-fire agreement had been accepted. President Johnson put pressure on the Israelis to halt their offensive. Some American officials even privately expressed the view that if Israel did not hold back, Soviet intervention would be "legitimate."[72]

In the 1973 Arab-Israeli War, after failing to secure American agreement to joint intervention to enforce the cease-fire, Brezhnev issued one of the strongest Soviet threats since 1945: "I will say it straight, that if you find it impossible to act together with us in this matter, we should be faced with the necessity urgently to consider the question of taking appropriate steps unilaterally. Israel cannot be allowed to get away with the violations."[73] At this point Israel was actively considering attacking Damascus and was in a position to do so.[74] Israel had also surrounded Egypt's critical Third Army and threatened its liquidation. The road to Cairo was clear, and the Israeli forces certainly had the option of taking it.[75] The USSR backed up its intervention threat with the requisite military preparations.[76] The United States responded in turn with a worldwide alert of its forces (DEFCON 3), including its strategic nuclear forces. The Soviet threat, the American response, and further pressure on Israel finally led America's ally to retreat.[77]

In May 1969, Soviet officials "begged Nasser to use every effort to halt the 'War of Attrition' across the Suez canal." The Soviet government was said to fear that Egyptians would miscalculate or the situation would get out of hand.[78] The Soviet Union again urged restraint on Nasser when it decided to come to Egypt's aid, signaling its client that Soviet aid was not to be used to attack across the canal.[79] Egyptian requests for weaponry that would have allowed extensive forays into Israeli-held territory were denied.[80]

Exceptions and Gray Areas.   In the War of Attrition, Israel dominated Egyptian forces and sought to overthrow Nasser.[81] Only the Soviet intervention—manning SAMs in Egypt—blocked achievement of that objective and turned back the Israeli assault. Soviet hopes that the United States would restrain Israel were disappointed. Kissinger apparently thought that Israeli escalation was a legitimate response to Nasser's initiation of the war, though several lesser administration officials disagreed.[82] Besides domestic political obstacles, the basic reason for American acquiescence to Israel's unlimited goals may have been the failure of U.S. intelligence to realize how desperate Nasser's situation was.[83] Nixon later faulted Israel for the extent of the crisis, and the administration postponed arms sales to Israel.[84]

Did the Soviet Union restrain North Vietnam from participating in the rout of the South Vietnamese regime? The U.S. domestic situation, including congressional attitudes, suggested a weakening U.S. commitment to Vietnam. Congress voted on July 31, 1973, to bar any future military operations in Indochina, and this became a law binding the Nixon and Ford administrations. Soviet analysts noted the U.S. domestic constraints.[85] Under such conditions, perhaps exceptions to the rule should be expected, as in Afghanistan today.

CONCLUSIONS AND IMPLICATIONS

Several conclusions and implications can be drawn from this exploration of the foundations of peaceful competition between the United States and the Soviet Union.

First, the most powerful constraint on the competition between the two superpowers over the past four decades has been these primitive rules of prudence emerging from a sober assessment of self-interest. This basic point was clearly recognized by both Americans and Russians in our joint study. The motive for most of these unwritten rules of prudence is the superpowers' common interest in avoiding a major nuclear war.

As chapters contributed to this volume by Soviet participants in the joint study show, they have found the concept of "unwritten rules of prudence" understandable and useful. It is consistent with the "new thinking" that reflects General Secretary Gorbachev's more pragmatic approach to international affairs. From the Soviet perspective, the fact of forty years without war has been due to the increasing strength of the socialist camp—an "objective" fact that "forces" restraint on the United States (and provided a rationale for Khrushchev's 1956 declaration that world war was no longer inevitable). Some Soviet specialists have argued that the unwritten rules of prudence are more fundamental than written agreements because they are grounded in "objective" reality. In this regard, Henry Trofimenko notes that the fact of strategic parity can be seen as "an objective nonaggression pact," which is much stronger as an impediment to aggression than the solemn pledges of "classical" nonaggression treaties.[86] Another Soviet participant argued that SALT II and the Anti-Ballistic Missile Treaty "actually achieve the same as a treaty to renounce first strike."

The rules of prudence are thus rules of self-preservation, more fundamental than any written agreement because they are grounded in objective reality. As such they provide a solid foundation for competition without war, for what the Soviets think of as "normal relations."

Second, just as the "objective reality" supporting these rules is not static, neither are the rules themselves. As the correlation of forces evolves, so too will the rules. Our first rule—avoiding the use of nuclear weapons—is a prime example of this evolution. Once the Soviet Union achieved real parity in second-strike capability, both superpowers backed away from using the nuclear threat to advance their security interests. We should not, however, assume that all future changes will be gradual, or even that a new rule will necessarily re-enforce the stability of this regime.

Third, in many areas these primitive rules of prudence can be written down, agreed in public, and operationalized in institutions and procedures. Where this can be done, so much the better. But the articulation of these rules, and their mutual agreement, does not always enhance their understanding. In fact, once officially stated in agreements, they may seem to be merely propaganda or truisms; paradoxically, the real footing on which they stand is thus obscured by open recognition. Thus the challenges for both superpowers is to articulate and institutionalize these rules without losing sight of the realities underlying them.

Fourth, there are genuine reasons to hesitate to write down some primitive rules, such as those relating to each power's dominant area of security concern. Governments are often unwilling to acknowledge facts publicly, whether for reasons of domestic or international politics, or simply because of a reluctance to give public recognition to certain facts. The validity of these primitive rules should not be discounted simply because they are not fully acknowledged.

Though the official Soviet conceptual framework resists the concept of "vital interests," emphasizing common security instead, Soviet specialists understand the term and use it for analytical purposes. One Soviet participant in our discussions developed a typology of conflict based on the relative interests of each side in particular regions. Another urged a "principle of equality in definitions of vital interests." "When a great nation defines its vital interests," this participant argued, "it should be ready to accept the right of the opponent to have exactly the same vital interests and be ready to comply with these and avoid direct assaults. If a nation is not ready to recognize the vital interests of the other, it should limit its own."

Fifth, each government has a stake in the basic framework of constraints on competition provided by these primitive unwritten rules as well as in the specific instances in which the rules apply. Thus each has special reasons for caution when approaching a rule-defined boundary—and for reacting firmly when a boundary is violated. Both superpowers have substantial stakes in the "precarious rules of the status quo" and should maintain them vigilantly.

Sixth, serious, sustained conversations between American and Soviet specialists can elaborate further primitive rules of prudence. The rules discussed in this chapter could be the beginning of a much longer list. Our joint discussions have identified a number of other candidates for a more complete catalog of rules of prudence observed in practice.[87] Soviet participants suggested additional possibilities.[88]

Even more important than discussions to formulate further rules of prudence would be joint explorations of regional instances in which they can be applied. Meetings of experts from both nations focused on specific regional conflicts or specific functional problems would do well to examine the recent record of emerging constraints and cooperation for clues to further rules of prudence, written norms, and procedures.

Finally, because primitive rules of prudence are sometimes unwritten, and in any case subtle, the issue of institutionalizing their understanding and interpretation becomes especially difficult when new individuals come to government. Through research like this joint study, scholars in both nations can assist in clarifying the fact and importance of such rules. Especially at a time of transition between national regimes, each government should take steps to assure an adequate understanding of the fundamental framework that constrains the competition between the two nations.

NOTES

1. *New York Times*, October 23, 1962.
2. Theodore Sorensen, *Kennedy* (New York: Harper & Row, 1965), p. 681.
3. Quoted in Bernard Brodie, *War and Politics* (New York: Macmillan Publishing Co., 1973), p. 377, n. 1.
4. Alexander George notes that the Soviets explicitly informed the United States which Israeli attacks on Syrians would elicit a Soviet response (attacking Soviet surface-to-air missiles [SAMs] in Syria) and which would not (attacking Syrian forces in Lebanon).
5. The superpowers have written into treaties and other agreements approximations of some of the rules highlighted here. For example, the 1973 Agreement on the Prevention of Nuclear War includes in Article IV a provision that if relations between the United States and the USSR or between one of them and another state "appear to involve the risk of nuclear conflict . . . [the superpowers] , acting in accordance with the provisions of this Agreement, shall immediately enter into urgent consultations with each other and make every effort to avert this risk."

   But the unwritten versions preceded the written statements and persisted after the statements had been forgotten or had become inoperative. The unwritten rule on nuclear use, furthermore, later motivated another written approximation in the communiqué from the 1985 Geneva Summit between President Reagan and Secretary Gorbachev: "The sides . . . have agreed that a nuclear war cannot be won and must not be fought. Recognizing that any conflict between the USSR and the U.S. could have catastrophic consequences, they emphasized the importance of preventing any war between them, whether nuclear or conventional."

6. "Perhaps the most fundamental factor underlying the content of the rules governing conflict behavior and the institutionalization of the rules are the recurrent practices preceding explicit rules. Repeated practices come to be expected and after a while derivations become not only violations of expectations but illegitimate. . . . The way things are done is the way they should be done because that is the way they have been done." (Louis Kriesberg, *Social Conflicts*, 2nd ed., [Englewood Cliffs, N.J.: Prentice-Hall, Inc., 1982], p. 122.) On bounded rationality and rules of thumb, see Robert Keohane, *After Hegemony* (Princeton, N.J.: Princeton University Press, 1984), chap. 7.

7. Alternate statements include those of John Lewis Gaddis and Stanley Hoffmann. Gaddis: "Use nuclear weapons only as an ultimate resort . . . reserving military use . . . only for the extremity of total war" ("The Long Peace," *International Security* 10, Spring 1986, p. 136). Hoffmann, writing of the rules Kissinger inherited, lists the "nonresort to atomic weapons by one against the other, or the other's allies" (*Primacy or World Order* [New York: McGraw-Hill Book Company, 1978], p. 11).

8. "Respect Spheres of Influence. . . . Defections from one sphere would be exploited by the other only when it was clear that the first either could not or would not reassert control" (John Lewis Gaddis, "The Long Peace," *International Security* 10, Spring 1986, pp. 133–34). Alternative statements come from Paul Keal and Isaak Dore. Keal: "What is understood is: (i) that the U.S. will not intervene militarily in Soviet actions in eastern Europe . . . ; (ii) that the Soviet Union will not intervene militarily in the Americas . . ." (Paul Keal, *Unspoken Rules and Superpower Dominance* [New York: St. Martin's, 1983], p. 2). Dore: "Whenever bloc intervention takes place for the preservation of intrabloc solidarity, there is to be no active resistance from the rival bloc" (Isaak Dore, *International Law and the Superpowers* [New Brunswick, N.J.: Rutgers University Press, 1984], p. 74).

9. Alternative statements include those of Gaddis and Phil Williams. Gaddis: "Avoid Direct Military Confrontation" (Gaddis, p. 135). Williams: "Not content with avoiding nuclear warfare against each other, the United States and the Soviet Union have been scrupulous to avoid *any* type of open and violent conflict: the *threat* of violence has been permissible, its actual *use* against each other's forces virtually outlawed. In fact, it is little exaggeration to suggest that the coercion-violence threshold has been almost religiously observed" (Phil Williams, *Crisis Management: Confrontation and Diplomacy in the Nuclear Age* [New York: John Wiley and Sons, 1976], p. 102).

    The Basic Principles Agreement, objective two, includes a statement that the United States and the USSR agree to "do their utmost to avoid military confrontations," which may be considered a written reflection, to some degree, of this unwritten rule.

10. Carsten Holbraad provides an alternative statement: "Encourage your allies or clients only up to the point where the danger of major war becomes real; then check them—if you can." (Carsten Holbraad, *Superpowers and International Conflict* (New York: Macmillan, 1979), p. 110.

11. Paul Bracken, *The Command and Control of Nuclear Forces* (New Haven: Yale University Press, 1983), p. 2.

12. Dwight D. Eisenhower, *Mandate for Change 1953–1956* (New York: Doubleday, 1963), p. 181. Cited in Honoré Catudal, *Nuclear Deterrence—Does It Deter?* (Berlin: Berlin Verlag, 1985), p. 455.

13. Quoted in Catudal, p. 458.

14. Ibid.

15. NSC Notes, May 13, 1953, quoted in Walter Pincus, *Washington Post*, July 22, 1985, p. A8.

16. Catudal, p. 459.

17. Stephen Ambrose, *Eisenhower: The President* (New York: Simon & Schuster, 1984), p. 184.

18. *Time*, July 29, 1985, pp. 52–53. Nixon says he considered the use of nuclear weapons in several other instances, but the seriousness of the consideration and the reasons for rejecting nuclear use are unclear.

19. Interview in the *Washington Post*, August 11, 1985, p. L8.

20. Deputy Secretary of Defense Roswell Gilpatric, letter to Hubert Humphrey, quoted in Bracken, p. 42.

21. Thomas Robinson, "The Sino-Soviet Border Conflict," in Steven Kaplan, ed., *Diplomacy of Power: Soviet Armed Forces as a Political Instrument* (Washington, D.C.: Brookings, 1981), pp. 280–81.

22. Henry Kissinger, *The White House Years* (Boston: Little, Brown and Co., 1979), pp. 183–86.

23. Arkady Shevchenko, *Breaking with Moscow* (New York: Knopf, 1985), pp. 165–66. H. R. Haldeman, *The Ends of Power* (New York: Dell, 1978), pp. 129–30. One primary analyst of the Sino-Soviet border war, Thomas Robinson, finds doubtful any Soviet intention of carrying out the threat (Robinson, pp. 281, 291–92). Shevchenko claims that he indirectly learned "that the Soviet leadership had come close to using nuclear arms on China." In this account, Defense Minister Grechko "actively advocated a plan to 'once and for all get rid of the Chinese threat.'" Ogarkov opposed it, however, on the grounds that world war would follow. The Politburo remained stalemated for several months over nuclear options until signals from the United States that such action would seriously risk a Soviet-American confrontation ended its consideration (Shevchenko, pp. 165–66).

24. Steve Meyer, "Soviet Perspectives on the Paths to Nuclear War," in Graham Allison, Albert Carnesale, and Joseph Nye, eds., *Hawks, Doves and Owls: An Agenda for Avoiding Nuclear War* (New York: W.W. Norton, 1985), pp. 179–80, 183, 203.

25. The United States took action against North Korea, North Vietnam, Cambodia, Laos, the Dominican Republic, Cuba (1961 and 1962), Grenada, Lebanon (1958 and 1983), Nicaragua (mining harbor), and Libya; the USSR against East Germany, Hungary, Czechoslovakia, China, and Afghanistan.

26. Account of Karel Kaplan as summarized by N. Tolstoy, *Stalin's Secret War* (London: Pan Books, 1981), pp. 361–62. Michael Rejman is the confirming Czech historian cited in M. Heller and A. Nekrich, *Geschichte der Sowjetunion, Vol. II, 1940–80* (Koenigstein: Athenaeum, 1982), p. 427. Cited in Alex Schmid, *Soviet Military Interventions Since 1945* (New Brunswick, N.J.: Transaction Books, 1985), p. 41.

27. Robert Slusser, "The Berlin Crises of 1958–59 and 1961," in B. Blechman and S. Kaplan, eds., *Force Without War* (Washington, D.C.: Brookings, 1978), pp. 343–439.

28. McGeorge Bundy, "Risk and Opportunity: Can We Tell Them Apart?" in Catherine Kelleher, Frank Kerr, and George Quester, eds., *Nuclear Deterrence: New Risks, New Opportunities* (New York: Pergamon-Brassey's, 1986), p. 34.

29. J. Bruce Amstutz, *Afghanistan: The First Five Years of Soviet Occupation* (Washington, D.C.: National Defense University, 1986), p. 356.

30. *New York Times*, April 13, 1986, p. 18.

31. Schmid, p. 49.

32. Paul Keal, *Unspoken Rules and Superpower Dominance* (New York: St. Martin's, 1983), p. 154.

33. Peter Shearman, "The Soviet Union and Grenada under the New Jewel Movement," *International Affairs*, Autumn 1985, pp. 664, 666. For Grenada's approach to the Soviet Union, see numerous analysts and documents in J. Valenta and H. Ellison, eds., *Grenada and Soviet/Cuban Policy: Internal Crisis and U.S./O.E.C.S. Intervention* (Boulder, Colo.: Westview Press, 1986).

34. Evidence indicates that a small number of Soviet military advisers have been present in Nicaragua and Peru. Currently the numbers are reportedly 50 and 160, respectively (International Institute of Strategic Studies, *The Military Balance, 1986–87* [London: IISS, 1986], p. 46).

35. Dov Zakheim, "The Grenada Operation and Superpower Relations: A Perspective from the Pentagon," in Valenta and Ellison, p. 178.

36. Jorge Dominguez, "Report to the Political Bureau, Central Committee, Communist Party of Cuba, from the Special Task Force on the US Imperialist Aggression Against Grenada," in Valenta and Ellison, p. 83.

37. *New York Times*, November 2, 1983, pp. 17–18 and October 26, 1983, p. A19. Cited in Raymond Duncan, "Soviet Interests in Latin America: New Opportunities and Old Constraints," *Journal of International Studies and World Affairs* 26, May 1984, p. 172.

38. Ambrose, p. 355.

39. *New York Times*, October 26, 1956, p. 1. Cited in Keal, p. 120.
40. Keal, p. 154.
41. *Department of State Bulletin*, January 7, 1957, pp. 3-4. Cited in Keal, p. 122.
42. *New York Times*, October 27, 1956. Cited in Keal, p. 121.
43. *Department of State Bulletin*, August 26, 1968, p. 221. Cited in Keal, p. 128.
44. Bracken, p. 72.
45. Philip Windsor, "Yugoslavia, 1951, and Czechoslovakia, 1968," in Blechman and Kaplan, p. 478.
46. John Newhouse, *Cold Dawn, The Story of SALT* (New York: Holt, Rinehart & Winston, 1973), pp. 130-36, 162. Cited in Keal, p. 129.
47. Keal, p. 154.
48. *Boston Globe*, May 13, 1985.
49. Raymond Garthoff, *Détente and Confrontation: American-Soviet Relations from Nixon to Reagan* (Washington, D.C.: Brookings Institution, 1985), p. 1066.
50. Windsor, pp. 486-98.
51. For more on this agreement and its background, see Sean Lynn-Jones, "A Quiet Success for Arms Control: Preventing Incidents at Sea," *International Security* 9, Spring 1985, pp. 154-84.
52. Kaplan, p. 675.
53. Lucius Clay, *Decision in Germany* (London: Heinemann, 1950), p. 374. Also Harry S. Truman, *Memoirs, Vol. II: Years of Trial and Hope 1946-52* (New York: Signet, 1965), p. 151. Cited in Phil Williams, *Crisis Management*, p. 103.
54. Slusser, p. 367.
55. Dwight Eisenhower, *The White House Years: Waging Peace, 1956-1961* (Garden City, N.Y.: Doubleday, 1965), p. 341. Quoted in Slusser, p. 368.
56. Sorensen, p. 594. Cited in Slusser, pp. 425-26.
57. Gilpatric, op. cit.
58. Victor Suvorov, *The Liberators* (London: Hamish Hamilton, 1981), pp. 158-59. Cited in Meyer, p. 193.
59. David Shipler, *New York Times*, March 26, 1986, p. A9.
60. Michael Gordon, *New York Times*, March 28, 1986, p. A12.
61. *New York Times*, April 14, 1986.
62. Edmund Schumacher, *New York Times*, March 29, 1986.
63. UPI in *Boston Globe*, April 27, 1986.
64. Edward Schumacher, *New York Times*, April 27, 1986, p. 17.
65. Robert O. Freedman, "Moscow, Damascus, and the Lebanese Crisis of 1982-84," in Paul Marantz and Blema Steinberg, eds., *Superpower Involvement in the Middle East: Dynamics of Foreign Policy* (Boulder, CO.: Westview, 1985), p. 98.
66. William Zimmerman, "The Korean and Vietnam Wars," in Kaplan, p. 347.

67. Robert Futrell, *The United States Air Force in Korea, 1950-1953* (Duell, Sloan and Pearce, 1961), pp. 477, 567. Cited in Zimmerman, p. 331.

68. Catudal, p. 460, footnote 60.

69. Garthoff, pp. 99-100. One Politburo member was demoted following his direct opposition to the summit; other Politburo members may have supported him on this issue.

70. James McConnell, "The 'Rules of the Game': A Theory on the Practice of Superpower Naval Diplomacy," in B. Dismukes and J. McConnell, eds., *Soviet Naval Diplomacy* (New York: Pergamon Press, 1979), p. 249.

71. *New York Times*, December 5, 1973, p. 18. Cited in Amos Jordan and William Taylor, Jr., *American National Security: Policy and Process* (Baltimore: Johns Hopkins Press, 1981), p. 264.

72. Jonathan Trumbull Howe, *Multi-crisis: Sea Power and Global Politics* (Cambridge: MIT Press, 1971), pp. 117, 122. Cited in McConnell, p. 268.

73. Marvin Kalb and Bernard Kalb, *Kissinger* (Boston: Little, Brown, 1974), p. 490.

74. Chaim Herzog, *The War of Atonement* (Boston: Little, Brown, 1975), pp. 128-29. Cited in McConnell, pp. 272-73.

75. Lawrence Whetten, *The Canal War: Four-Power Conflict in the Middle East* (Cambridge: MIT Press, 1974), p. 291. Cited in McConnell, p. 274.

76. Interview with James Schlesinger in Walter Pincus, *Washington Post*, July 25, 1985, p. A14.

77. Insight Team of the London *Sunday Times, The Yom Kippur War* (Garden City, N.Y.: Doubleday, 1974), pp. 432-33; Edward Sheehan, *The Arabs, Israelis, and Kissinger* (New York: Readers Digest Press, 1976), pp. 36-37; Whetten, *The Arab-Israeli Dispute* (Adelphi Papers 125, London: International Institute for Strategic Studies, 1977), p. 32. Cited in McConnell, p. 276.

78. George Breslauer, "Soviet Policy in the Middle East, 1967-1972: Unalterable Antagonism or Collaborative Competition?" in Alexander George, ed., *Managing US-Soviet Rivalry: Problems of Crisis Prevention* (Boulder, CO.: Westview, 1983), p. 77.

79. McConnell, p. 270.

80. Breslauer, p. 78.

81. Whetten, pp. 83, 89-90. Cited in McConnell, p. 270.

82. Yaacov Bar-Siman-Tov, *The Israeli-Egyptian War of Attrition, 1969-1970* (New York: Columbia University Press, 1980), pp. 157, 236. Cited in Breslauer, p. 80.

83. Alexander George, "Missed Opportunities for Crisis Prevention: The War of Attrition and Angola," in *Managing US-Soviet Rivalry*, p. 197.

84. Ibid., p. 194.

85. Daniel S. Papp, *Vietnam: The View from Moscow, Peking, Washington* (Jefferson, N.C.: McFarland and Co., Inc., 1981), p. 194.

86. Henry Trofimenko, "The Third World and the U.S.-Soviet Competition," *Foreign Affairs* 59 (Summer 1981): 1037.

87. These rules might include the following:

1. Avoid sudden, secret military deployments that importantly affect the strategic or regional military balance.
2. "Do not seek to undermine the other side's leadership" (Gaddis, p. 138).
3. Refrain from unconventional warfare in the territory or against assets of the other.
4. Avoid "those confrontations which bring an adversary to the choice of either a humiliating defeat or a nuclear war" (Robert F. Kennedy, *Thirteen Days: A Memoir of the Cuban Missile Crisis* [New York: Norton, 1971], p. 104).
5. Establish and maintain close contact in a crisis.
6. Refrain from lying in private discussions with one's diplomatic counterpart.
7. Exercise strict control over forces in the field at the highest political level when a clash with the other superpower threatens.
8. Keep military intervention localized.
9. Seek arms control agreements that reconfigure forces to reduce the risks of war.
10. Keep talking: don't break diplomatic relations.

88. Among these were:

1. "No false accusations against each other." One Soviet participant argued that "most propaganda is counterproductive."
2. "Carry out gentleman's agreements" (e.g., regarding emigration and most favored nation status).
3. "Codify whenever possible unwritten rules." In contrast, other Soviet participants argued that it is better to leave certain rules unwritten tacit: it avoids the inference that whatever is not prohibited is permissible; the superpowers will behave more cautiously if the rules are somewhat murky; interpretations of written rules would differ, and tension would be exacerbated.
4. "Make more use of diplomacy, less of signaling."
5. "Practice restraint internationally." To try to keep a free hand is too risky.
6. "Behave in predictable patterns during crises."
7. "Include unwritten rules of *cooperation*, such as gentlemen's agreements."

SOVIET VIEW

Viktor Kremeniuk

I would like to discuss Graham Allison's rules of prudence in turn, examining how each one functioned in different crisis situations. The first rule is to avoid any use of nuclear weapons. In most crises, it is true, the use of nuclear weapons was never regarded as a genuine option. Nuclear threats have been made, however. American leaders have used nuclear threats in 33 cases, including Dien Bien Phu (1954), Cuba (1962), and the Middle East (1973).[1] American specialists recall Suez (1956) and Cuba (1962), among other occasions, as times when the Soviets made nuclear threats. The fact is that when a nation has nuclear weapons in its arsenals, there is always a possibility that it would use them in a major crisis. This observation underlines the importance of making transparent one's intentions to avoid nuclear use, as the Soviet Union did in 1982 when it pledged no-first-use of nuclear weapons. The elimination of offensive, destabilizing weapons systems in the arms control process can contribute greatly to the same purpose.

It is important to understand the motivation that lies behind this rule. Is it merely a reaction to the fact of mutual assured destruction (MAD)? Or does it reflect a deeper understanding of the need to avoid the use of nuclear weapons, regardless of whether the other side would retaliate? Former Secretary of State Alexander Haig once remarked that there are things more important than peace. His statement was widely criticized in both East and West because it touched on one of the most important questions of today's world: is there any more important value than the survival of humanity? This question was answered in part in the 1985 Geneva summit declaration, which announced that a nuclear war cannot be won and therefore should not be fought. In their adherence to this rule of prudence, both nations were apparently guided not only by their fear of retaliation, but also by the understanding that the necessity of avoiding nuclear war takes precedence over the pursuit of other national interests.

While the establishment of the unwritten rule of avoiding nuclear use is a positive achievement, it does not go far enough. It is, in Allison's terms, too precarious and needs to be reinforced by declaratory pledges and by the reduction of nuclear arms in a balanced and verifiable manner.

The second rule of prudence is to avoid direct military action against the other side's vital interests. The problem is that these interests have never been clearly defined and agreed upon. Most crises have been triggered by a failure to make others accept one's own definition of one's vital interests. Self-proclaimed vital interests had to be supported by military threat or force, which in turn provoked a reaction. The impasse could be resolved only through a crisis. As Allison points out, it is significant that even in such perilous times, when the two great powers could not agree on their respective vital interests, they adhered to the rule of not using their own forces against a unilaterally proclaimed vital interest.

With all due respect to American concerns about the threat posed by Soviet missiles in Cuba, I cannot agree that the Soviet decision was a case of "breaking the rules." The U.S. decision to install Thor missiles in Turkey had signaled its view that the rules of the game allowed putting missiles close to the territory of the other side. Any action that threatens the other side's national security will almost certainly be pursued by the other side once it acquires similar capabilities. That is why we attach such importance to the fact that the resolution of the Cuban missile crisis reflected an understanding of reciprocity in dealing with each other's national security interests (the agreement to exchange the withdrawal of Soviet missiles from Cuba for American missiles from Turkey).

The third rule is to respect the other's areas of dominant security concern. Here we should note that the definition of security has changed significantly since the end of World War II. Then security seemed simpler: national territory to be defended against aggression, allies to be defended, and areas of vital economic interest to be safeguarded. Now the whole world system is changing. The value of military power has diminished. The interdependence of nations has become an objective reality in the 1980s. No nation can achieve security unilaterally at the expense of others' security. The only possible solution is common security, which can be attained only through a comprehensive and logical system of international negotiation. Moreover, interdependence extends to the economy and the environment; we can survive and thrive only by working together.

Society today is increasingly vulnerable to disruptions such as terrorism, sabotage, and subversion. There has been a misguided tendency to understand these new sources of threat in cold war terms—old thinking. Because of turbulent change and conflicts in the Third World, for example, regional conflicts have assumed an increasingly important role in U.S.-Soviet relations. This process, which began during the Kennedy administration and has continued into the mid-1980s, encouraged an overreaction to Third World conflicts and a dangerous exaggeration of their importance as areas of dominant security concern.

The fourth rule is to avoid any direct use of force against troops of the other great power. The troops of each nation have participated in regional conflicts. Indeed, the United States has done so more frequently than the USSR; Blechman and Kaplan (1978) count almost 150 instances of U.S. intervention. If force had ever been used against the troops of the other great power, a global crisis would have begun. The leaders of both nations have always understood this boundary and made certain it was never crossed. This rule was clearly followed during the Cuban missile crisis and the Middle East crises of 1967 and 1973.

It is important to recognize that troops can be drawn into a clash without the leaders' intentions or knowledge. The Incidents at Sea Agreement (1971) was a natural step forward to embody this understanding in the standard operating procedures of each navy. Thus far, the agreement has worked throughout the ups and downs of U.S.-Soviet relations.

The final rule of prudence is to restrain allies and clients from inflicting a catastrophic defeat on an ally or client of the other. A striking conclusion emerges from the history of regional conflicts since World War II: almost never did one side achieve a definite military victory, even when a great power intervened. Wars in Korea, the Middle East, Southern Africa, and elsewhere have all ended in a political stalemate. There have been exceptions, notably in Vietnam, but even this outcome can be understood in the light of the withdrawal of U.S. troops in 1973. Even where a decisive military victory occurred, as in the 1967 Middle East War, no final settlement ensued, and the military and political struggle continued. Certain American leaders recognized at the time of Vietnam that a great power in conflict with a regional power can never expect a victory if the other great power supports its opponent. This principle deserves more attention than it has received from military and political leaders. It explains the limits of possible gain through the use of military force in any occasion and in any region.

It is important that each of the great powers has exercised self-restraint and restrained its allies and clients from inflicting a defeat on the allies and clients of the other. But the situation is changing. Increasingly, regional conflicts take place without significant involvement of the great powers. The Iran-Iraq war is an example. The time has passed when one could rely on the great powers to intervene in a moment of crisis to prevent a regional conflict from spreading and escalating. The rule of seeking to restrain allies may soon lose its efficacy. Although President Reagan once called South Africa a "natural ally" of the United States, there seems to have been little the United States could do to stop South African forays into Angola. Similarly, the administration chided Israel strongly for its brutal suppression of riots in the West Bank and Gaza in early 1988, but could not persuade the Israeli government to accept the idea of an international conference. In effect, the great powers' influence over regional actors is declining. The more importance the great powers place on these regional conflicts, the more powerful the regional actors will feel, believing they can play one power against the other.

These rules of prudence may be fragile, but they have played a powerful role. Those who doubt their validity (or even existence) may be forgetting that none of the dozens of crises since World War II have escalated into a major clash between the two great powers.

There remains the question of what to do next. The acceptance of these rules will not guarantee a sense of security if a crisis should occur. Such confidence can come only from believing that the world situation is crisis-proof (at present an unrealistic condition) or from an unbreakable and verifiable agreement on standard operating procedures to be pursued during a crisis. Such an agreement in turn is likely to exist only in an atmosphere of mutual confidence based not on mutual assured destruction, but on shared assumptions and goals. The recognition of unwritten rules, at least by experts, may thus become a starting point for going "beyond the hot line" (in William Ury's words), not only to a network of nuclear risk reduction centers, but also to a shared understanding of what each side will not do if a crisis erupts.

NOTE

1. Barry M. Blechman, Stephen S. Kaplan, and David K. Hall, *Force Without War: U.S. Armed Forces as a Political Instrument* (Washington, D.C.: Brookings Institution, 1978).

2 THE SEARCH FOR AGREED NORMS

Alexander L. George

Chapter 1 examined some tacit understandings that have constrained important dimensions of U.S.-Soviet competition. I will discuss proposals for a more formal, explicit code of conduct or standards of behavior by which the two superpowers might moderate and regulate their rivalry.

After considering the importance of articulating a basic political framework of relations between the two nations, I will review the efforts of U.S. and Soviet leaders to build this kind of framework during the 1970s, and the aftermath of the 1980s. The significance and utility of four types of formally agreed-upon norms can then be assessed. Finally, I will try to sum up the discussions on these questions that took place during our joint study, to illuminate Soviet and American perspectives on the desirability and feasibility of seeking agreement on formal, explicit norms of behavior.

THE IMPORTANCE OF A BASIC POLITICAL FRAMEWORK OF RELATIONS: SOVIET AND AMERICAN PERSPECTIVES

More than their American counterparts, Soviet leaders attribute considerable importance to developing a formal, written document that articulates the fundamental bases of the political relationship be-

45

tween the two nations. The difference in views on this point, which continues to the present day, was first noted as the two sides prepared for the historic Nixon and Brezhnev summit in 1972. Five months before the two leaders were to meet in Geneva, Henry Kissinger notes in his memoirs, the Soviet ambassador to Washington, Anatoly Dobrynin, raised the possibility of including on the summit agenda an agreement on a declaration of principles. Dobrynin's request was not unexpected; U.S. policymakers knew of the Soviet leaders' predilection for formalizing the basis of their relations with other states and had noted Moscow's success in engineering such joint declarations with French and Turkish leaders.[1]

The language of the Basic Principles Agreement (BPA) signed by Nixon and Brezhnev in 1972 was marked by troublesome imperfections and ambiguities. However, we should not dismiss out of hand the possibility that agreement on a basic political framework of relations could help the United States and the Soviet Union structure an appropriate relationship. Such an agreement would facilitate efforts to move toward a more constructive, stable relationship. After the sobering experience with the BPA and with détente generally, however, the two sides—and particularly U.S. leaders—have approached this task with greater caution and more modest expectations.

The more fundamental question is whether the two superpowers are close enough in their conceptions of the desired relationship to permit an agreement. Both sides would have to share a realistic conception of the competitive nature of their relationship, and of ways to mute and control the dangerous implications of their rivalry. In addition, they would have to focus on those aspects of their relationship in which cooperation would be mutually beneficial. To the extent that the two sides share a conception of an acceptable mixed competitive-collaborative relationship, then an agreement on a basic political framework for the relationship is possible and can be useful. Within such a framework, progress could be made in developing cooperation on various specific issues. An important lesson derived from the disappointing experience with détente in the 1970s is that agreement on a framework of relations is at best only a start toward, and not a substitute for, the hard work of developing more specific norms of competition and cooperation.

A basic framework of relations—indicating how the two sides view each other, how they identify common or parallel interests in various issue areas—would provide an element of political stability that could help the nations weather occasional downturns and setbacks in their relations. Security for both sides in the "anarchic" international system is affected by the quality of their overall relationship, its political as well as its military dimensions. Arms control is indeed important, but cannot in itself compensate for fundamental problems in the relationship. Political stability is just as important as strategic stability, and the two are not unrelated. Besides, the full potential of arms control probably cannot be realized in the absence of a viable basic framework of U.S.-Soviet relations.

Agreement on a basic framework can help define the longer-range objectives the two sides believe to be worth pursuing. A basic framework can strengthen the "shadow of the future," increasing U.S. and Soviet incentives to find cooperative, mutually acceptable solutions to at least some of their problems.[2] Without a basic political framework that holds out a credible promise of important mutual benefits in the long run, a superpower is more likely to take advantage of opportunities for unilateral short-term gains at the expense of its adversary.

THE EXPERIENCE OF THE BASIC PRINCIPLES AGREEMENT OF 1972

In practice, as the Nixon-Brezhnev détente demonstrated, it can be difficult to formulate a workable basic framework. The two leaders attempted to provide just such a framework at their first summit meeting in Moscow in May 1972. The Basic Principles Agreement constituted a sort of charter defining the basis for the further development of détente. In this document the two leaders agreed that in the nuclear age "there is no alternative to conducting their relations on the basis of peaceful coexistence." Moreover, "differences in ideology and in the social systems of the U.S.A. and the U.S.S.R. are not obstacles to the bilateral development of normal relations based on the principles of sovereignty, equality, noninterference in internal affairs and mutual advantage." Continuing, they agreed that "the prerequisites for maintaining and strengthening peaceful relations between the U.S.A. and the U.S.S.R. are the recognition of the security interests of the parties based on the principles of equality and the renunciation of the use or threat of force." More specifically, the two leaders agreed to "attach major importance to preventing the development of situations capable of causing a dangerous exacerbation of their relations." Accordingly, they pledged to "do their utmost to avoid military confrontations and to prevent the outbreak of nuclear war," to "exercise restraint in their mutual relations," and to "be prepared to negotiate and settle differences by peaceful means." U.S.-Soviet discussions and negotiations in the future were to be conducted "in a spirit of reciprocity, mutual accommodation and mutual benefit." And, in this connection, Nixon and Brezhnev agreed that "efforts to obtain unilateral advantages at the expense of the other, directly or indirectly, are inconsistent with these objectives."

The two leaders placed this statement of goals and desiderata within the larger framework of strengthening the international system. They recognized their special responsibility as permanent members of the United Nations Security Council to reduce international tensions and "to promote conditions in which all countries will live in peace and security and will not be subject to outside interference in their internal affairs."

In the BPA, Nixon and Brezhnev also identified the specific issue areas in which they would seek to promote their mutual interests—that is, they reached what we will call an "agenda-setting" agreement (discussed below). They resolved to continue efforts to limit armaments and to develop long-term economic, scientific, and cultural ties between their two countries in order to strengthen their relationship.

The basic framework established by the BPA was at best a contractual agreement of a very loose and general character; the specifics remained to be clarified and filled in over time. In the parlance of nineteenth-century European diplomacy, the BPA was in the nature of a rapprochement: an agreement to go beyond a mere relaxation of tensions in relations to search for specific agreements on various issues. In fact, the BPA also pointed to the possibility of going beyond rapprochement to an entente, a term that in classical diplomacy refers to the recognition of a general similarity of views and interests on certain (though not all) issues.

In effect the BPA registered a mutual desire to develop a relationship of what might be called collaborative competition (as opposed to the confrontational competion of the cold war). Such a relationship would require the development of clear, mutually understood, and accepted norms of cooperation and competition. However, as many observers have noted, important ambiguities and divergent interpretations of key concepts imbedded in the BPA—with respect to "equality," "equal security," "restraint," "reciprocity," "no unilateral advantage"—and the persistence of conflicting interests left the basic framework highly vulnerable. It was not long before mutually inconsistent hopes and expectations from détente surfaced in Moscow and Washington that were bound to result in disappointment and recriminations. Although important progress was achieved in arms control, in scientific and cultural exchanges, and in movement toward political stabilization in Europe, Nixon was unable to overcome congressional resistance to improving trading arrangements with the Soviets. Soviet military programs and assertive Soviet policies in Africa raised doubts in the United States regarding the value of détente. And, in general, a variety of domestic constraints made it difficult for Nixon, Ford, and Carter to formulate and pursue a consistent, coherent policy of détente toward the Soviet Union.[3]

The result was a gradual erosion of the framework and political stability that the BPA was supposed to provide for the further development of the relationship. For all practical purposes détente was dead after Afghanistan, to be replaced by a revival of cold war rhetoric, greater reliance on unilateral efforts to strengthen security, and confrontational posturing.

Although Carter and Brezhnev formally reaffirmed the Basic Principles Agreement when they signed the SALT II agreement in 1979, the next U.S. president made it clear that he considered the BPA as no longer operative. Moreover, the Reagan administration displayed little interest in formulating a new basic framework of relations. Instead, policy was strongly influenced by the desire to develop a "position of strength" from which to deal more effectively with the Soviet Union.

American participants in the dialogue reported in this volume have expressed serious reservations about the utility of the "general principles" approach favored by the Soviets. In conversation with our Soviet colleagues and in publications, we noted that the unsatisfactory experience with the Basic Principles Agreement of 1972 and similar efforts had led American leaders to be extremely wary of subscribing to such general statements. If Reagan participated in a new summit, we cautioned, he would *not* reaffirm, as Carter had done in his 1979 summit with Brezhnev, adherence to the BPA; some other basis would have to be found for a joint statement acceptable to the

Reagan administration. Our Soviet colleagues insisted that American adherence to declaratory principles, such as Chernenko's March 1984 proposal for "norms of relations among the nuclear powers," was essential to convey the government's "political will" to achieve improved relations. As one Soviet academician argued, "general declarations create the spirit to move ahead on specifics."[4]

The question of a basic political framework re-emerged in connection with the summit meeting of Gorbachev and Reagan in November 1985. Statements by the two leaders and their joint communiqué never alluded to the Basic Principles Agreement of 1972. Neither side accepted the other's draft proposal for a joint declaration (the contents of the drafts have not been disclosed). During the summit there was even considerable doubt as to whether any joint statement would be issued at the conclusion of their meeting. Finally, as a result of a last-minute compromise, a joint statement was issued. Notably absent were any references to "peaceful coexistence," "equality," and other symbols associated with the BPA. However, the Gorbachev-Reagan statement did contain a few points of agreement that might be regarded as constituting a minimal basic agreement on interests and objectives. The paragraph on "security" contained three important declarations:

1. The two leaders "have agreed that a nuclear war cannot be won and must never be fought."
2. "Recognizing that any conflict between the U.S.S.R. and the U.S. could have catastrophic consequences, they emphasized the importance of preventing any war between them, whether nuclear or conventional."
3. "They will not seek to achieve military superiority."

A fourth declaration elsewhere in the joint statement reaffirmed "the tasks set down in the joint U.S.-Soviet agreement of January 8, 1985, namely to prevent an arms race in space and to terminate it on earth, to limit and reduce nuclear arms and enhance strategic stability." The leaders also agreed to continue "exchanges of views on regional issues on the expert level," which were said to have been useful, thus reaffirming a procedure the two nations had been following during the year preceding the summit. (In fact, these discussions had quite limited objectives, and their usefulness to the Reagan administration, at least initially, was primarily to provide a forum for restating and pressing its objections to Soviet foreign policy in various parts of the world.)

Much remained unclear as to what kind of long-range relationship the Reagan administration wished to develop with the Soviet Union. Indeed, fundamental disagreements persisted within the administration regarding the correct "image" of the Soviets, whether and to what extent the United States should "squeeze" the Soviet Union, and whether and in what ways to "deal" with it. Within the administration there was strong agreement on the need to develop a "position of strength," but substantial disagreement and uncertainty as to the objectives to be served by that strength. Also unclear was the desired mix of cooperation and competition in the relationship with the Soviets. The only certainty was that the administration preferred for the time being to rely on unilateral efforts to pursue its most important security and foreign policy objectives rather than to enter into risky arms control agreements.

Despite the absence of a broader political framework of relations during the Reagan years, the superpowers held talks on a variety of subjects. In 1986 arms control discussions addressed a variety of issues: nuclear and space arms, confidence-building measures, mutual and balanced force reductions, chemical weapons, nuclear testing, nuclear risk reduction centers, and incidents at sea. Other subjects under discussion included nuclear energy, regional problems, cultural and scientific exchanges, trade, human rights, and people-to-people exchanges.

Finally, in 1987 intensified negotiations on intermediate-range nuclear forces (INF) and strategic arms reduction (START) resulted in agreement on an INF Treaty, ratified by the U.S. Senate just before the fourth summit in Moscow in May 1988. In this improved atmosphere Gorbachev unsuccessfully sought Reagan's approval of a joint statement that echoed some of the language of the BPA of 1972. Gorbachev's draft statement would have had the United States and the Soviet Union agree that "peaceful coexistence is something that we resolve as a universal principle of international relations, and that the equality of all states, non-interference in domestic affairs, and freedom of socio-political choice should be recognized as inalienable and mandatory for all."[5] In a news conference Gorbachev complained that Reagan had initially conveyed a favorable view of the proposed statement but that by the end of the summit his advisers had persuaded him to reject it. Secretary of State George Shultz and other advisers were said to have reacted negatively to Gorbachev's proposed joint declaration. One unnamed U.S. official called it "ambiguous, freighted with the baggage of the past," too similar to some of the language of the BPA; he specifically objected to the phrase "peaceful coexistence" as a propagandistic Soviet term, and rejected "noninterference in internal affairs" as possibly undercutting U.S. appeals for improvements in the Soviet human rights record.[6] Instead, the joint statement finally agreed to by the two leaders, said to have been written by the American side, reiterated the minimal basic framework established at their first summit and stated that despite "the real differences of history, tradition and ideology" the "political dialogue" they had established "represents an increasingly effective means of resolving issues of mutual interest and concern."[7]

A TYPOLOGY OF AGREED NORMS

Agreement on a basic political framework of relations is, of course, only one type of formal, explicit agreement that can help stabilize and improve U.S.-Soviet relations. As Soviet academicians Henry Trofimenko and I. Sheidina have reminded us, many "mutual commitments" can be found in written U.S.-Soviet agreements and documents of the 1970s.[8] According to their summary, the two superpowers agreed they would:

Develop contacts and cooperation on a firm and lasting basis.

Make efforts to eliminate completely and as soon as possible existing international conflicts and to prevent the emergence of new ones.

Avoid military confrontations and show restraint in mutual relations.

Prevent situations that could lead to a dangerous deterioration of bilateral relations.

Make no attempts to gain unilateral advantages at the expense of the other side.

Not seek military superiority, since it could only lead to dangerous instability, raise the level of armaments, and do nothing for the security of either side.

Do everything possible to avert nuclear war.

Consult each other in situations involving a risk of nuclear conflict.

Take measures to prevent accidental or unsanctioned use of nuclear weapons.

Notify each other of incidents involving nuclear weapons.

Notify each other in advance of planned launchings of missiles if they are to cross borders of one side in the direction of the other.

Implement bilateral measures to limit and reduce strategic armaments on the basis of strict observance of the principle of equality and equal security.

Undertake further efforts aimed at disarmament, including limiting and reducing strategic armaments and all types of mass-destruction weapons in general.

Exchange information on a voluntary basis in order to strengthen confidence in fulfillment of the obligations taken.

Consult each other when changes occur in the strategic situation affecting the Soviet-American agreements on strategic arms limitations.

Not make available to other countries weapons that only the two sides possess, a principle stemming from Article 9 of the anti-ballistic missile (ABM) treaty.

Try to increase the effectiveness of the United Nations.

This list is a useful reminder of the variety of important subjects that can be encompassed in such formal declarations. Although in some sense they all represent "commitments," they vary widely in significance and utility. A more refined analytical framework will therefore be useful in assessing the value of formal, written statements of this kind in structuring and regulating U.S.-Soviet relations.

In the first place, it is necessary to distinguish among the various possible *functions* of written declarations and agreements. What purpose does an agreement or declaration serve? What aspect of relations between the two superpowers does it attempt to define or regulate? Five types of functions can be identified, ranging from the most general affirmations to efforts to regulate quite specific dimensions of the evolving relationship:

Type I Agreement. Statements of principles or desiderata—as in the Basic Principles Agreement of 1972[9]—intended to characterize an agreed-upon framework for the overall U.S.-Soviet relationship (e.g., the relationship should be based on principles such as "equality and equal security," or "normalization" of relations).

Type II Agreement.   Statements that identify *priority objectives* on which Soviet and American leaders agree to cooperate (e.g., avoidance of nuclear war, avoidance of nuclear proliferation, reduction of strategic nuclear weapons) without specifying the means for achieving these objectives. The minimal basic agreement contained in the joint statement issued at the end of the first Reagan-Gorbachev summit is an example of this type of agreement.

Type III Agreement.   Statements that serve an *agenda-setting* function by identifying the issue areas in which the two governments agree to try to develop improved, mutually beneficial relations. This was done in the BPA of 1972, which Nixon characterized as a kind of charter or road map for cooperative efforts to improve relations.

Type IV Agreement.   Statements of general norms and principles that suggest or indicate possible *ground rules for regulating global or regional competition.* For example, in the first few articles of the BPA, the two sides agreed that in the nuclear era their relations would be based on "peaceful coexistence" and they would exercise "restraint" and forego efforts to obtain "unilateral advantages" in their foreign politics.

Type V Agreement.   Specific agreements designed to enhance mutual Soviet-American security (e.g., ABM and SALT treaties, Nuclear Nonproliferation Treaty, the Incidents at Sea Agreement).

   Each type of agreement can play a useful role in structuring Soviet-American relations. While all of them involve the acceptance of "mutual commitments," the commitments in question are of a quite different character. Moreover, it is both analytically and politically important that the two sides share the same understanding of a particular commitment and of the type of agreements.
   Serious political misconceptions can arise from lack of clarity or disagreement as to the nature of an agreement. In the first place, Soviet and American leaders may differ in the significance they attach to a particular type of agreement. Thus, for example, Soviet

leaders appear to attach greater importance to a Type I agreement than do American leaders. Indeed, one of the lessons of the Nixon-Brezhnev détente is that the Soviets saw much greater significance in the Basic Principles Agreement—a Type I agreement—than did Nixon and Kissinger, and interpreted it as bestowing advantages and benefits on the Soviet Union that the U.S. leaders were not fully aware of and had not really agreed to.[10]

Another serious misconception occurs when the public and opinion leaders within the United States or the Soviet Union diverge from their political leaders in their understanding of the commitment the two superpowers have agreed to. For example, important elements of the American public and influential political leaders regarded Soviet support of Egypt's attack on Israel in October 1973 as inconsistent with the commitments implied by the Basic Principles Agreement; they also criticized the Soviet failure to inform the United States of the forthcoming attack as a violation of the Agreement on Prevention of Nuclear War signed by Brezhnev and Nixon at their second summit in June 1973. While this type of misconception is more likely to assume importance in a democratic political system, it can occur also in the Soviet Union. Thus Brezhnev felt obliged to give repeated assurances to influential people in the Soviet Union that his agreements with Nixon did not mean that the Soviet Union would curtail support to national liberation movements or to "progressive forces" in the Third World.

Political damage may also result from a misunderstanding of the precise nature of the commitments entered into and/or overly optimistic expectations on the part of one signatory to the agreement. For example, while a Type II agreement is, strictly speaking, no more than a commitment to try to cooperate to achieve a priority objective, such as a 50 percent reduction in strategic nuclear weapons, one or both sides may come to believe (or to assert) that the other side was not sincere in entering into such a commitment or is now deliberately obstructing achievement of the goal. Elements of the public, eager for achievement of the announced goal and perhaps unaware of the technical complexities of the issue, may mistake a declaration of intentions for a virtual guarantee that the goal can be achieved in a way consistent with security requirements.

This brief discussion reminds us of some of the risks of trying to use written agreements to improve superpower relations. Nevertheless, if carefully crafted and clearly explained, formal declarations and written agreements can play an indispensable role in structuring U.S.-Soviet relations. To heighten sensitivity to the strengths and limitations of written declarations and agreements, it seems useful to call attention to several key variables associated with the *content, status*, and *implementation provisions* of such agreements.

First, the *content* of U.S.-Soviet agreements that state or imply a mutual commitment may be very general or quite specific, very precise and clear or ambiguous. Further, agreement may be reached on the *substance of an issue* or on the need to create *procedural mechanisms* for dealing with substantive issues. U.S.-Soviet declarations of a very general character may be appropriate in certain types of agreements. But ambiguity or lack of precision in articulating "mutual commitments" in joint declarations may lead to mutual recriminations that damage U.S.-Soviet relations.

Second, the *status* of the presumed norms, principles, and/or commitments imbedded in written U.S.-Soviet documents can vary greatly, in ways that affect their force and utility. Diplomatic practice assigns a quite different stature to various kinds of agreements. One needs to distinguish between recognized principles of international law to which states usually adhere and those to which lip service is given; the aspirations and injunctions of the United Nations Charter, to which both superpowers subscribe but which they often interpret differently; bilateral and multilateral treaties in which the two superpowers participate; U.S.-Soviet agreements that do not have treaty status; joint statements by American and Soviet leaders; and coordinated unilateral statements by U.S. and Soviet leaders, such as announcements of adherence to a nuclear test moratorium.

Finally, the force and utility of some written agreements may depend critically upon *viable arrangements for implementation.*[11] Procedural mechanisms or new institutional structures may be created for this purpose (for example, the creation of the Standing Consultative Commission for the ABM and SALT I treaties; the use of the Nuclear Risk Reduction Centers for implementation of the INF agreement; the implementation procedures for the Berlin Quadripartite Agreement of 1971; procedures to monitor, clarify, and implement the Incidents at Sea Agreement of 1972). The implementation of other written agreements may depend on the good will and independent actions of the two sides; adherence may be determined by calculations of utility and risk entailed in violating the terms or spirit of the agreement.[12]

AMERICAN AND SOVIET PERSPECTIVES
ON NORMS OF GLOBAL COMPETITION

One of the objectives of Type IV agreements, which state ground rules for global competition and for regulating superpower involvement in regional developments, is to avoid crises involving the United States and the Soviet Union, whether or not such confrontations pose the danger of war.

Crisis avoidance is indeed an important objective in U.S.-Soviet relations—one that is pursued in a variety of ways, not merely through efforts to develop norms of competition. Each superpower employs deterrence policy to dissuade the other from encroaching on the most important of its worldwide interests. The likelihood of crises is also reduced by the efforts Moscow and Washington make to increase the internal stability and security of their allies and neutral countries. On occasion the superpowers ask third parties to mediate regional conflicts that might otherwise lead to their own involvement and a confrontation. On a few occasions the two superpowers have acted together or in concert with other nations to create neutralized or buffer states. Finally, of course, each superpower's recognition of the other's sphere of dominant interests and influence helps prevent dangerous crises.

Even taken together, these traditional modalities do not guarantee success in avoiding U.S.-Soviet crises in the Third World. Thus the superpowers have good reason to consider still other ways in which they might cooperate to reduce the possibility of dangerous clashes. With this in mind, both sides have given thought to the possibility of an agreement on general principles, "rules of the game," or a "code of conduct" that might help regulate and moderate their global rivalry.

This issue was addressed by participants in the Soviet-American dialogue. Members of the American group expressed serious doubts as to the possibility of developing *general* principles or norms of competition that could contribute significantly to crisis avoidance. They pointed to the disappointing results of Brezhnev's and Nixon's efforts to establish this approach. In the first few articles of their Basic Principles Agreement, the two leaders referred to the need to base U.S.-Soviet relations on the principle of "peaceful co-existence," to deal with each other on the basis of "equality," to operate with "restraint" in their foreign policies, and to avoid seeking "unilateral advantages" at each other's expense. Given the ambiguity of these principles and norms, these articles of the BPA might best be considered a pseudo-agreement. The document did not clarify how the Soviet conception of "peaceful coexistence" could be reconciled with the agreement to observe mutual "restraint" and to forego seeking "unilateral advantages." And it soon became obvious that the two sides, in pursuing their foreign policy interests, had quite different, self-serving conceptions of what "restraint" and "no unilateral advantage" meant in practice.

At their second summit, in June 1973, Nixon and Brezhnev signed a more specific agreement on consultation to deal with situations posing the danger of nuclear war. This Agreement on Prevention of Nuclear War (APNW) was severely tested by the Egyptian attack on Israel in October 1973, which raised questions in the United States as to whether the Soviet Union had complied with the provisions of the agreement.[13] Although both U.S. and Soviet leaders expressed the view that their détente relationship facilitated cooperative efforts to end the October War, many Americans felt that the war demonstrated the shallowness of détente and the ineffectiveness of the agreed-upon crisis avoidance principles.

Members of the American group also tried to persuade their Soviet colleagues that cooperation in crisis avoidance cannot be limited, as Soviet leaders in the 1970s seemed to believe, to situations in which one or both sides perceived a risk of nuclear war. While conceding that avoidance of nuclear war certainly has the highest priority, American participants emphasized the importance of averting lesser regional crises, such as those brought about by Soviet and Cuban activities in Africa in the 1970s, which severely damaged the overall U.S.-Soviet relationship even though they did not raise the danger of war. One of the most important lessons that needs to be learned from the collapse of détente is that competition for influence in the Third World, if carried too far, will jeopardize the overall political relationship between the superpowers, which deserves greater priority.

For their part, Soviet participants in the dialogue strongly echoed the complaints made by Soviet leaders regarding the failure of the United States to live up to important norms contained in the Basic Principles Agreement. To charges that the Soviet Union did not operate with "restraint" in pursuing assertive policies in Africa in the

1970s, but rather sought unilateral advantages contrary to the norms of the BPA, Soviet participants responded by noting that Kissinger systematically excluded the Soviet Union from the Middle East, particularly after the October 1973 War.

Perhaps the most important norm in the BPA, from the Soviet perspective, was the acknowledgement of superpower "equality." In the Soviet view, this norm gave Moscow a legitimate role in deciding questions of regional security throughout the world. At our first meeting a Soviet participant argued that the major reason for the failure of détente was that the United States was not prepared to treat the Soviet Union as an equal. At our second meeting a Soviet academician said the United States treated the Soviet Union as an "outsider"; continuing, he argued:

> During World War II there was cooperation; the Soviet Union was co-founder of the UN. Then the United States was trying to exclude the Soviet Union, trying to conduct business without account of the lawful interests of the Soviet Union. In the détente era, the United States reversed its policy: it began to treat the USSR as a member of the international system. The United States officially recognized the principle of peaceful coexistence. Under Reagan, there is an effort to push out the Soviet Union as not contributing to the development of norms. . . ."

During our discussions, however, there was some convergence of views regarding the U.S. efforts to link the central relationship between the superpowers and their competition in peripheral areas. Traditionally, the Soviets view processes of change in the Third World as internally generated, clearly implying that regional changes and conflicts should be considered as distinct and separable from the basic détente relationship. In the late 1970s Soviet leaders explained Western efforts to link Third World issues to the central U.S.-Soviet relationship as motivated by right-wing elements in the United States who wanted to sabotage détente and to substitute for it a U.S. military superiority that would enable Washington to dictate to Moscow from a "position of strength." More recently some Soviets began to realize that such linkage is inevitable in a populist democracy such as the United States. A prominent Soviet participant stressed this point at several of our meetings ("There were good intentions to insulate arms control negotiations, but we saw it just did not work.") A recent Soviet book on international conflict, and its spokesman in our discussions, referred to the "interconnection," and "feedback" between regional conflicts and the central relationship. At the same time, however, Soviet participants in our discussions continued to stress the importance of recognizing a "hierarchy of interests" and of giving priority to the central U.S.-Soviet relationship.

The possibility of formulating general principles, or "rules," for moderating U.S.-Soviet competition in Third World areas has also been discussed by Soviet and American academicians in several meetings of the Dartmouth Conference Task Force on Regional Conflicts.[14] Like our own group, the Dartmouth Conference made some progress toward clarifying the difficulties encountered by the general principles approach. At an early meeting of the task force several years ago, the Soviet and American delegations each formulated a new set of principles, but the two drafts had so little in common that the participants agreed to try a different approach. Subsequent meetings were devoted to examining actual crises and potential flashpoints to see how proposed general principles or norms might apply in concrete cases. In discussions of specific crisis scenarios the two sides attempted to identify the respective interests of the United States and the Soviet Union. The two delegations also tried to assess how threatening each superpower would find certain actions taken by the other in a given country under hypothetical but not unlikely conditions, and how it might respond to different threatening actions. Both Soviet and American participants felt that a shift in focus from general norms to analysis of specific situations was worthwhile from an analytical standpoint, even though it did not prove easy to agree on how their two governments might deal with the specific situations examined.

Participants in our own dialogue have reached conclusions similar to those of the Dartmouth Task Force. While some members of these two discussion groups (particularly in the Soviet delegations) continue to urge a U.S.-Soviet agreement on general principles, such as those set forth in the BPA and the APNW, they recognize the need to refine such general norms. Other members (particularly in the American delegations) believe that general norms and principles do not take into account that the relative interests of the superpowers vary considerably from one geographical area and country to another. There are many different forms of direct and indirect intervention; it will not be easy to agree on which types of intervention are permissible. The types of restraints and understandings needed for crisis avoidance depend on whether the area in question is one in which (a) both sides have high interests; (b) one side has dominant interests; (c) neither side has major interests; or (d) the superpowers disagree or are uncertain as to the balance of interests.[15]

From the outset American participants in these dialogues suggested that a more promising cooperative approach to avoiding crisis would be to strengthen a traditional but underutilized diplomatic practice. We argued that the two superpowers should seek to develop, through timely, intensive discussions, a series of individual ad hoc understandings on how they would limit their competition and involvement in a particular country or region. The agreed-upon restraints would reflect the specific configuration of each case: what was at stake for each side; what was the danger of unwanted escalation; whether other external actors were or might become involved, and what might be done to limit their involvement; what developments and outcomes of the local situation would and would not be acceptable to each of the superpowers; whether diplomatic solutions could be found.

The proposed approach would bring the two superpowers together in the most serious kind of diplomatic conversations at an early stage in the development of a local situation that threatened to get out of hand. Even if their effort to devise an ad hoc agreement covering a specific situation proved abortive or only partially successful, timely diplomatic exchanges could clarify interests engaged by that situation, correct possible misperceptions of each other's intentions and activities, and encourage efforts by third parties or the United Nations to arrive at solutions before the superpowers were drawn in more actively.

Soviet participants in our dialogues have also recognized for many years that the two superpowers need to establish some kind of procedural mechanism for dealing with differences that could lead to a clash in the Third World. It was gratifying, then, when the United States and the Soviet Union agreed to hold periodic discussion of regional issues at the expert diplomatic level. The first step was taken by President Reagan in an address to the United Nations on September 24, 1984, in which he proposed a series of Soviet-American regional discussions to alleviate tensions. The first of these meetings was held in Vienna on February 19 and 20, 1985, to discuss Middle East issues. Other meetings were held later to discuss issues involving southern Africa, Afghanistan, and the Far East.[16] Although the first few talks were limited to a rather sterile exchange of already familiar views, their very existence had symbolic importance.

In the joint statement issued at the conclusion of their Geneva summit, Gorbachev and Reagan agreed to continue meetings on regional issues "on a regular basis." In recent years, reportedly, the two sides have begun to use these sessions for serious diplomatic explorations of possible agreements or adjustment of policies, rather than merely repeat and argue on behalf of their positions.

On the other hand, Moscow and Washington have made no progress in developing better written norms, a code of conduct, or general principles that might help them avoid confrontations. Ideological differences between the two superpowers make it difficult for either side to accept written norms that seem to legitimize the ideological thrust of the other's foreign policy. Soviet leaders are highly unlikely to accept any proposed code of conduct that implies modification of the ideological position that the Soviet Union is bound to lend assistance to "progressive forces" in the rest of the world. Similarly, after the disillusioning experience with the Basic Principles Agreement and the souring of the Nixon-Brezhnev version of détente, American leaders will balk at accepting the Soviet concept of peaceful coexistence in a statement of general norms.

The so-called Reagan Doctrine represents a strong counter to the idea of peaceful coexistence.[17] The administration openly committed itself to provide meaningful support to "freedom-fighters" resisting Soviet-supported communist regimes in Afghanistan, Southeast Asia, southern Africa, and Central America. It challenged the legitimacy of these regimes as it also challenged Moscow's long-standing insistence that Soviet gains are irreversible. Thus, insofar as communist regimes in Angola, Afghanistan, Cambodia, and Nicaragua were concerned, the Reagan Doctrine went somewhat beyond the traditional U.S. policy of containment. Its message was that Moscow should reconcile itself to giving up recently acquired positions of influence in these countries.

Therefore, despite the introduction of a procedural mechanism for U.S.-Soviet discussion of regional issues, superpower competition in certain regions was intensified. Yet the Reagan administration's policy of going beyond containment was restricted to areas (with the possible exception of Afghanistan) that could not be regarded as of vital interest to the Soviet Union. Moreover, although the administration set itself ambitious objectives in these countries, it sought to limit the risks of escalation by restricting the means it employed for these purposes. Underlying the Reagan Doctrine and lending a certain optimism to its objectives was the belief that U.S. military and economic strength had been re-established and that Moscow, having overreached itself globally and suffering severe domestic economic problems, would eventually have to come around. "For the United States," Reagan stated in the March 1986 message to Congress, "these regional conflicts cannot be regarded as peripheral to other issues on the global agenda. They raise fundamental issues and are a fundamental part of the overall U.S.-Soviet relationship." Not surprisingly, therefore, the Reagan administration tried to use the periodic discussions of regional issues with the Soviets to press for diplomatic solutions of the type it favored.

Although formidable difficulties still stand in the way of U.S. and Soviet efforts to moderate their global rivalry, it is possible that the two superpowers may eventually redefine their global aspirations and their broad, pervasive conceptions of the geopolitical requirements for their security. In recent years both nations have been drawing sober lessons from costly and frustrating experiences in the Third World. Both have ample cause to reconsider the limits of military power and of their economic resources for maintaining or extending their global positions. Both countries are coming to recognize that growing instability in the Third World will reduce their influence in many parts of the globe.

Thus the analyst of U.S.-Soviet relations might well predict that both superpowers will need to redefine their conceptions of a viable global role. This task will be difficult and at times painful; it could also accentuate the competitiveness and instability of superpower global rivalry, especially if one superpower attempts to exploit for its own advantage the difficulties the other is experiencing in some part of the Third World. One can hope, however, that pressures to reduce their involvements abroad might lead instead to mutual restraint and tacit cooperation in facilitating this process for each other.

CONCLUSION

Discussions among Soviet and American participants helped to clarify our perspectives on the utility of formally stated, explicit norms as against tacit understandings of the kind discussed by Graham Allison in chapter 1. Our dialogue helped to narrow some of our initial differences with regard to Type I and Type IV agreements. Views expressed by Soviet participants helped Americans to appreciate the value of a basic political framework for U.S.-Soviet relations (i.e., a Type I agreement), if it is well defined.

Similarly, the Soviet participants listened carefully to the reservations American participants expressed as to the utility of written agreements setting forth uniform ground rules to distinguish between impermissible and permissible superpower behavior in the Third World (i.e., Type IV agreements). Noteworthy in this respect was the explicit recognition by Yevgeny M. Primakov that efforts to codify impermissible superpower behavior may have the serious disadvantage of legitimizing all other behaviors not explicitly prohibited.[18]

More generally, tacit understandings have several advantages over formal norms of an explicit character. Tacit norms are more flexible and adaptable. Moreover, real or apparent violations of formal, explicit norms are more likely to lead to public charges and countercharges of violations, bad faith, and so on. Tacit norms may more easily survive occasional behavior that seems to deviate from the implicit standards. Imperfect adherence will not destroy their utility.

At the same time, some issues in U.S.-Soviet relations might be better handled through formal, explicit agreements. A written agreement may lend authority to agreed-upon norms and procedures and make it more difficult and costly to violate them. Also, the task of formalizing norms may force the two sides to clarify the ambiguity that often marks tacit understandings. And commitments undertaken in a formal, written mode may be less vulnerable to a deterioration of overall U.S.-Soviet relations. But we should remember that on certain issues, only tacit agreements will be possible; these accords may nevertheless be just as important as those that can be expressed in formal documents and declarations.

NOTES

1.   Henry Kissinger, *White House Years* (Boston: Little, Brown & Co., 1979), p. 1132.

2.   The term "shadow of the future" was introduced by Robert Axelrod in his important game-theoretic contribution to cooperation theory. [See *The Evolution of Cooperation* (New York: Basic Books, 1984), particularly

pp. 126–32.] He points out that concern about future interactions with an adversary can promote cooperation on more immediate issues. The more the outcomes of future interactions are valued relative to the payoff of current interactions, the less the incentive to behave in an uncooperative manner in the present.

3. For a more detailed discussion see especially chapters 2, 5, 6, 7, 13, and 15 in A. L. George, *Managing U.S.-Soviet Rivalry* (Boulder: Westview Press, 1983). See also Raymond Garthoff, *Détente and Confrontation* (Washington, D.C.: Brookings Institution, 1985).

4. Chernenko's proposal would have all nuclear powers agree "(1) to consider the prevention of nuclear war to be the principal goal of any power's foreign policy, and to prevent situations fraught with the danger of nuclear conflict and to hold urgent consultations if such situations arise; (2) to renounce the propaganda of nuclear war (either global or limited); (3) to make a commitment not to be the first to use nuclear weapons; (4) not to use nuclear weapons against nonnuclear powers; (5) to prevent nuclear proliferation; (6) to eliminate nuclear weapons step-by-step." (*Pravda* March 3, 1984).

5. Gorbachev disclosed at least part of the text of his abortive proposal in a news conference held immediately after the Moscow summit. (*New York Times*, June 2, 1988, p. 18.)

6. *San Francisco Chronicle*, June 2, 1988.

7. *New York Times*, June 2, 1988.

8. H. Trofimenko and I. Sheidina, "USSR-US: Half Century of Peaceful Coexistence" (Moscow: Novosti Press, 1983), pp. 71–72.

9. The BPA also includes articles that I regard as examples of Type III and Type IV agreements.

10. For a detailed discussion, see George, *Managing U.S.-Soviet Rivalry: Problems of Crisis Prevention*, especially chap. 5.

11. For a general discussion, see Philip J. Farley, "Managing the Risks of Cooperation," in Alexander L. George, Philip J. Farley, and Alexander Dallin, eds., *U.S.-Soviet Security Cooperation: Achievements, Failures, Lessons* (New York: Oxford University Press, 1988).

12. In one of our discussions, a Soviet participant pointedly remarked that the problem with the "rules" in the UN Charter, the Basic Principles Agreement, the Helsinki Accord and other declarations is that "there is no enforcement mechanism, no central authority. Thus, it comes down to the problem of consensus or demonstrating to the other side that it is against its interests not to observe it."

13. For a detailed discussion of the experience with these two crisis avoidance agreements see George, chaps. 5 and 7.

14. The experience of the Dartmouth Conference Task Force on Regional Conflicts is summarized in A. L. George, "Mechanisms for Moderating Superpower Competition," in Harold H. Saunders, ed., *The Superpowers*

in the Middle East, special issue of the *AEI Foreign Policy and Defense Review* 6 (1), 1986.

15. This typology of interests and its implications for norms of crisis avoidance were discussed in George, *Managing U.S.-Soviet Rivalry*, pp. 381–89.

16. *New York Times*, February 13, 20, and 21; June 19; September 7, 1985. Since then additional talks have been held but with a minimum of publicity.

17. The most comprehensive statement of these policies was provided in President Reagan's message to Congress on March 14, 1986, which was entitled "Freedom, Regional Security, and Global Peace." See also the commentary by Leslie Gelb in the *New York Times*, April 5, 1986, and the op. ed. by Robert W. Tucker, "The New Reagan Doctrine Rests on Misplaced Optimism," *New York Times*, April 9, 1986.

18. This point, rarely acknowledged in Soviet writings, was sharply stated in a recent article by Yevgeny M. Primakov, director of the Moscow Institute of World Economy and International Relations and a member of the USSR Academy of Sciences. Commentary on the limited utility of "rules of conduct, however, thoroughly thought over, agreed upon in detail, and linked to specific situations," he noted that "the formulation of such rules is fraught with some danger, because they may be taken for the 'limits of the permissible.' Thus interpreted, which is inevitable, they may even stimulate activity, which in itself would lead to a dangerous aggravation of the situation." (Y. Primakov, "The Soviet Union's Interests: Myths and Reality," in *The Superpowers in the Middle East*, p. 30.)

SOVIET VIEW

Viktor Kremeniuk

The rules of prudence discussed by Graham Allison in chapter 1 have helped to prevent war thus far, but there is no guarantee they can continue to do so. Bilateral and multilateral efforts are needed to create new norms for avoiding nuclear war. Some of these agreed norms will encapsulate existing experience; others will suggest new guidelines for thinking and acting.

The very first agreed norm, to have stable and reliable communication in time of crisis, was first embodied in the 1963 agreement to establish the Washington-Moscow hot line. If, before the Cuban missile crisis, it was sometimes considered advantageous to conceal one's intentions from the other side, attitudes are quite different today. Communication before, during, and after a crisis is considered not only expedient but an integral part of the relationship between the superpowers. The second norm was to prevent any unauthorized or accidental event that might aggravate a crisis. This norm was embodied in the Accidents Agreement and the Incidents at Sea Agreement, both signed in 1971. The Basic Principles Agreement of 1972 represented an attempt to create a norm to avoid any actions that would jeopardize world peace, which was extended in the Prevention of Nuclear War Agreement of 1973. Unfortunately, further work to codify these norms was stopped in the 1970s, after fierce attacks by Americans who argued that such efforts were against the national interest.

Although the Basic Principles Agreement was widely criticized in the United States, we should not be discouraged from building on this attempt to develop some broad norms for preventing or constraining U.S.-Soviet conflict in the Third World. The BPA was a first effort to bring some order into the delicate area of crisis management. In a sense, it prepared both sides for the type of crisis illustrated by the Iran-Iraq war. The agreement suggested that both sides abstain from actions that could add fuel to the fire and endanger world peace. It also opened the way to discussions of certain regional conflicts, as in the Geneva Conference on the Middle East in 1975. Unfortunately, Henry Kissinger's shuttle diplomacy, aimed at gaining unilateral advantage, created doubt as to the sincerity of the U.S. administration in those areas considered most critical by both sides. The quest for unilateral short-term gain led to long-term losses for both sides.

Written agreements can be elaborated in two ways. One is to perfect the substance of the norms and to ensure that they address the potential sources of crisis as these sources evolve. An attempt should be made to discuss each side's underlying assumptions about the likely sources and forms of crisis. We should try to evolve a common language that, without requiring a convergence of theoretical views, will permit us to turn hitherto unwritten rules into mutually acceptable agreements.

The second approach focuses on the implementation of written norms. It is useless and even dangerous to sign an agreement and leave the two sides to implement it in any way they please. Cross-cultural differences, differences in national political structures, and the legacy of distrust would inevitably turn implementation into another source of conflict, as happened with the Basic Principles Agreement. Both sides need to agree on procedures to implement the norms and to establish standing consultative committees to exchange views and information. Without such machinery, the written agreements can easily become worthless sheets of paper.

In sum, written norms represent a first glimpse at the new thinking in the area of crisis avoidance. They reflect the two sides' understanding of their security interdependence and the mutual obligation to avoid steps that might seem to offer unilateral advantage but would inevitably bring both nations, and the rest of the world, to the brink of war.

3 DEVELOPING RISK REDUCTION INSTITUTIONS AND PROCEDURES

William L. Ury

On June 8, 1967, Israeli planes and gunboats attacked a U.S. communications ship, the *Liberty*, off the coast of the Sinai Peninsula. Washington soon learned of the attack, but as President Johnson recalled, "For seventy tense minutes we had no idea who was responsible."[1] Both the United States and the USSR had sizable and vulnerable navies in the eastern Mediterranean. The Soviets' intentions were unclear. U.S. Secretary of Defense Robert McNamara "thought the *Liberty* had been attacked by Soviet forces."[2]

Johnson ordered carrier-based aircraft to investigate and sent Moscow a message on the Direct Communications Link (otherwise known as the hot line) explaining this action and giving assurances that the United States was not about to intervene in the war. An hour later, when the Israelis discovered they had made a tragic mistake, their apology to Washington was also passed along on the hot line. McNamara later remarked, "Thank goodness our carrier commanders did not launch immediately against the Soviet ships who were operating in the Mediterranean."[3]

I would like to acknowledge, in particular, my colleague Richard Smoke. Many of the ideas in this article derive originally from a report we co-authored for the U.S. Arms Control and Disarmament Agency in March 1984, entitled *Beyond the Hotline:–Controlling a Nuclear Crisis* (Cambridge, Harvard Law School Nuclear Negotiation Project). For useful suggestions, I would like to thank my colleagues in the joint study as well as Richard Haass and Elizabeth Sherwood.

The *Liberty* incident illustrates the dangers of unintended run-away escalation that may arise in a superpower crisis. It also demonstrates the wisdom of establishing in advance joint institutional mechanisms, such as the hot line, for use in heading off a dangerous superpower confrontation.

This chapter will begin by sketching out the kinds of events and decision-making pressures that could lead to unintended escalation. I will then discuss how joint risk reduction procedures and institutions can assist in preventing unintended escalation, complementing other approaches such as arms control. After surveying existing arrangements and their possible insufficiencies, I suggest five measures—or classes of measures—that could make the U.S. and Soviet governments better able to deal with dangerous triggering events.

Chapters 1 and 2 have discussed rules of prudence and agreed norms for preventing crises. This chapter will focus on concrete procedures and institutions for applying these rules and norms in specific conflict situations and for coping with perceived violations. (These procedures and institutions would constitute what George calls Type V agreements.) I will limit myself to measures that might be adopted jointly by both governments, while acknowledging that unilaterally undertaken measures, such as permissive action links safeguarding against unauthorized use of nuclear weapons, are just as important in reducing the risk of inadvertent war.

POSSIBLE TRIGGERS OF UNINTENDED NUCLEAR WAR

Most experts agree that the most likely path to a nuclear war lies in a nuclear crisis rather than a calculated launching of a general war. Despite a desire on both sides to avoid war, an intense Soviet-American confrontation could escalate into war through a series of miscalculations, miscommunications, and accidents.

The Cuban missile crisis of 1962 was one occasion when the superpowers appeared to come perilously close to nuclear war. During several other crises, including the Middle East wars of 1967 and 1973 and the Berlin crises of 1948 and 1961, the perceived possibility of a nuclear war rose noticeably.

Three main kinds of events might trigger unintended escalation: regional conflicts, inadvertent encounters between deployed American and Soviet forces, and nuclear incidents.

Regional Conflicts

On any given day, a number of wars are being fought around the world, and others may be on the verge of erupting. In many of these conflicts, the United States and the USSR support opposite sides. As in the Middle East War of 1973, there exists a serious possibility that both nations will be drawn into such a confrontation against their original intentions.

The potential danger grows as nuclear weapons—and long-range missiles and bombers to carry them—proliferate. India, Pakistan, Israel, and South Africa now have, or are close to having, nuclear weapons. Additional countries are likely to join the list in the future.[4] The possibility of a serious nuclear threat, or even of a nuclear detonation, in a regional conflict will make the superpowers more cautious, but will correspondingly make a confrontation significantly more risky.

Inadvertent Military Encounters

American and Soviet forces operate in close proximity over much of the globe. Both navies patrol the same seas, and their planes constantly pass in the skies. Dangerous encounters occasionally occur. In normal times, such incidents can damage relations; during crises, they could lead to inadvertent escalation. The *Liberty* incident was dangerous because it came at a time of crisis, and the proximity of Soviet ships led to the initial misinterpretation. At the height of the Cuban missile crisis, a U.S. reconnaissance plane on a routine mission over the North Pole strayed over Soviet airspace, triggering Soviet fears that an American attack was imminent.[5]

A related kind of risk stems from the proximity, and routine interaction, of American and Soviet strategic nuclear systems. When Soviet submarines, for instance, approach the shores of the United States, the American warning and command systems automatically cause precautionary actions to be taken. The equally automatic warning systems on the Soviet side observe these actions and may in turn prompt similarly precautionary military actions, which of course are noticed and may be responded to immediately by the American system. In a time of crisis, when forces are on alert, this back-and-forth process might ratchet dangerously upward. Safeguards exist, of course, but some danger remains and tends to increase over time as U.S. and Soviet warning and command systems become more tightly coupled and the flight times of missiles become shorter.[6]

Nuclear Incidents

There is always a tiny but appreciable danger that one or more nuclear weapons could be set off by technical accident or by false alarm. Accidents have occurred, as when a twenty-four-megaton nuclear bomb was jettisoned over Goldsboro, North Carolina, in 1961.[7] Missiles have strayed off course; in December 1984, a Soviet cruise missile accidentally overflew a NATO nation, Norway, and crashed in Finland.[8] False alerts have been triggered by flights of geese, the rising of the moon, a faulty computer chip, and the accidental insertion of a war game tape.[9] Both superpowers have instituted substantial fail-safe systems and procedures to protect against such incidents and misinterpretations. Still, the possibility of catastrophic failure cannot be ignored altogether, particularly as American and Soviet nuclear and control systems become more complex. The safeguards are designed primarily to protect against isolated failures; with compound accidents, the number of possible reactions is so large that no safeguard can be entirely foolproof.[10]

An unauthorized launch is not impossible either. The possible consequences of mental strain were vividly imagined in the movie *Dr. Strangelove*, which depicted a commander of a remote bomber base suddenly breaking under pressure and dispatching his bombers. Probably more serious are the dangers of misunderstood instructions and misguided judgment. Though absolutely small, because of careful safeguards, this risk is greatest on submarines, where the officers have more discretion, and during conditions of tension and nuclear alert, when some of the safeguards may be removed.

Nuclear terrorism is another source of danger. One possibility is blackmail—for example, a threat to blow up a major city unless demands are met for some immediate political outcome and/or large sum of money. Terrorists might also threaten nuclear use to demonstrate the importance of their cause, or to wreak vengeance on a nation they perceive as the enemy. In some cases, especially if the group were perceived by one side as receiving even indirect support from the other, such an event could trigger a superpower confrontation; coming in the middle of a crisis, a terrorist incident could raise the risk of war.

Deliberately triggering such a confrontation would be the object of *agent provocateur* attacks, also called "disguised third-party attacks." Imagine the dangers if the West German Cessna that penetrated Soviet airspace and landed in Red Square in May 1987 had dropped a bomb on the Kremlin.[11] Imagine further that it was an atomic bomb. It is conceivable, if improbable, that a terrorist group, or even a nation, might try to trigger a Soviet-American war, perhaps by the use of a nuclear weapon, in the belief that it would be in a better position in a post-World III world.

A Deadly Combination

Within these categories—the escalation of regional conflicts, inadvertent military encounters, and unusual nuclear events—countless scenarios might lead to an intense Soviet-American confrontation, and perhaps to a nuclear war. Any particular path to unintended nuclear war may be extremely unlikely, but the sum of all potential paths poses a cumulative risk that cannot be ignored.

Perhaps the most worrisome danger is the possibility of several events occurring at about the same time and interacting to produce effects none of them could cause by itself. A coincidence of unexpected events and accidents occurring at a time of high Soviet-American tension could produce consequences almost impossible to foresee, and perhaps a fast-moving train of U.S. and Soviet escalations.[12]

Paul Bracken describes one such instance that took place in 1956, while the Hungarians were revolting, the British and French were trying to take the Suez Canal back from Egypt, and the Soviets were making veiled nuclear threats against London and Paris:

The headquarters of the U.S. military command in Europe received a flash message that unidentified jet aircraft were flying over Turkey and that the Turkish air force had gone on alert in response. There were additional reports of 100 Soviet MiG-15s over Syria and further reports that a British Canberra bomber had been shot down also over Syria. (In the mid-1950s only the Soviet MiGs had the ability to shoot down the high-flying Canberras.) Finally, there were reports that a Russian fleet was moving through the Dardanelles.

... The White House reaction to these events is not fully known, but reportedly General Andrew Goodpaster was afraid that the events "might trigger off all the NATO operations plan." At this time, the NATO operations plan called for all-out nuclear strikes on the Soviet Union.

As it turned out, the "jets" over Turkey were actually a flock of swans picked up on radar and incorrectly identified, and the 100 Soviet MiGs over Syria were really a much smaller routine escort returning the president of Syria from a state visit to Moscow. The British Canberra bomber was downed by mechanical difficulty, and the Soviet fleet was engaging in a long-scheduled exercise.[13]

If this coincidence of events and miscalculations had been suggested as a "scenario," it would have been dismissed as too improbable to take seriously. Yet it actually occurred. This is not to suggest that such perilous interactions are probable, but simply that we do not know how likely they are.

DECISION MAKING IN CRISES

Decision making in times of crisis appears to be qualitatively different from the normal flow of governmental decision making. The "warp," or diminished rationality, that prevails during crisis decision making has been conceptualized in various ways.[14] One somewhat simplified scheme emphasizes four main factors: there is little time for making crucial decisions; the stakes are high; critical information is often lacking, leading to dangerous uncertainty; and few usable options are available.

Little Time

However grave the issues at stake, an event is usually not considered a crisis if plenty of time is available to resolve the conflict. The 1973 Middle East war became an acute superpower crisis when the Israelis encircled the Egyptian Third Army and were on the verge of capturing it, which would have been a grave humiliation for Egypt and its Soviet patrons.[15] Little available time is a defining characteristic of crises.

High Stakes

In the Berlin crises of 1958 and 1961, the credibility of the NATO alliance was perceived to be at stake.[16] If the stakes are not high, decision makers may see themselves as "putting out fires" rather than dealing with a genuine crisis. An international, and especially a nuclear, crisis is distinguished from the normal flow of decision making (which often includes short deadlines and a feeling of urgency) by expectations of severe losses—in other words, high stakes.

High stakes result from an increase in either the magnitude of a potential loss or the probability of that loss (or both). After tens of thousands of U.S. troops had been committed to Vietnam, for example, Washington's stakes became much higher. In the Berlin crises of 1958 and 1961, there was little change in what was at stake for the West—the credibility of NATO—but as the crisis intensified, the perceived probability of the threat to those stakes rose.

High Uncertainty

Decision makers often report a sense of great uncertainty at moments of crisis. Not enough clear information is available, and they feel that they are groping in a fog.

Three kinds of uncertainty in a crisis can be distinguished. The simplest is a lack of critical information about what is going on. To what degree are the other side's forces mobilized? Where are they deployed? What exactly is occurring? Factual data generally are incomplete.

Almost always there is great uncertainty about the other side's intentions. During the 1973 Middle East war, American intelligence discovered that the Soviets were shipping nuclear material through the Bosporus. What did this suggest about Soviet intentions? Did it portend an escalatory move, a nuclear threat? (There was a lack of simple factual information too: were these weapons nuclear waste, reactor fuel rods, or what?)[17]

The final kind of uncertainty has to do with the likely escalation sequences that might result from the current situation. In the Cuban missile crisis the Executive Committee of the National Security Council (ExComm) worried that Khrushchev might suddenly move against Berlin or take other drastic action.[18] The Western responses to such moves were uncertain as were, of course, the Soviet counter-responses, and the Western counter-counterresponses.

Few Usable Options

In a crisis, decision makers perceive there to be fewer realistic policy options than in normal times, and the ones available are likely to be more extreme. Generally, the more intense the sense of crisis, the more this will be so. In the first two days of the Cuban missile crisis, the only two options seriously examined by the United States were to do nothing but issue a diplomatic response, or to carry out an air strike on Cuba, which risked escalation toward war.[19] In a crisis, the options often come, as it were, "sliced thick," whereas more "fine-tuned" options can be developed in normal times.

In many crises, considerably more options are available than decision makers perceive to be usable. Many things could be done, but very few of them would simultaneously defend national interests and limit the risk of severe escalation to follow.

The Intensification of Crises

The combination of little time, high stakes, high uncertainty, and few usable options creates among decision makers a strongly felt need to act. As a crisis intensifies, decision makers typically sense that all four factors are becoming more serious. The press of time becomes more noticeable. The stakes may be rising. As actions of ambiguous import are taken, the uncertainties may also rise. As a crisis mounts, decision makers often feel they are rapidly approaching the point where they will have only a few and extreme options left. This sense of constricting possibilities is a psychologically distinctive feature of the crisis experience. In the various Berlin crises, Western decision makers sometimes found themselves only a couple of steps away from ordering major military action, which might have provoked a European war. At points in the 1973 Middle East crisis,

U.S. officials felt they were only a few steps from an intense East-West confrontation.[20]

APPROACHES TO PREVENTING
INADVERTENT WAR

Besides nuclear weapons themselves and the doctrine for their use, four other factors contribute to the risk of inadvertent war. All were present in the *Liberty* incident. First, the political relationship that constituted the background for interpreting the incident was one of profound mistrust and fear. Second, American and Soviet military forces were in proximity on opposite sides of a shooting war. Third, an unexpected incident occurred "out of the blue," a possible trigger of U.S.-Soviet combat. Fourth, the incident was initially misread. These four factors—a tense relationship, a point of conflict, a trigger for combat, and a misinterpretation—together could create a situation that would spiral out of control despite the best intentions of leaders in Washington and Moscow.

The risk of inadvertent war springs from a deadly mix of inadvertent and "advertent" factors. The tense relationship and the point of conflict are basically advertent, reflecting the underlying conflict between the United States and the Soviet Union. The unexpected triggers and the misinterpretation, in contrast, are inadvertent, unwanted by either superpower.

Soviet scholars and policymakers have tended to focus on the first factor, stressing that the way to prevent inadvertent war is to create a "normal relationship."[21] With greater mutual confidence, unexpected triggers are less likely to be interpreted as indicative of hostile intent.

Chapters 1 and 2 focus chiefly on the second factor, discussing rules that constrain escalation as both powers carry on their conflict around the world. Such constraints, for instance, may have helped keep American and Soviet forces from engaging in actual hostilities, even against third parties, during the 1967 Mideast war.

Here we consider the other two factors: the unexpected triggers and the tendency toward misinterpretation of events. Joint institutions such as the hot line can be helpful in dealing with unexpected triggers like the attack on the *Liberty* and can correct hazardous misinterpretations like the initial suspicion of Soviet attack. The adequacy of communications, negotiations, and prior consultation with the other side may make a considerable difference should a crisis occur.

Joint Measures Already Taken to Prevent Inadvertent War

Recognizing the dangers of runaway escalation and the difficulties of decision making in crises, Washington and Moscow have taken steps to strengthen communication and negotiations, so as to head off unintended escalation. The hot line was created in 1963 in the wake of the Cuban missile crisis, during which President Kennedy and Premier Khrushchev had had to improvise awkward and roundabout ways to communicate, such as passing notes through a news reporter.[22] The hot line was established to allow direct, prompt, and confidential communication at the highest level.

Since then, additional steps have been taken:

In 1971 the hot line was made more reliable. Two satellite links were added; the sea and land link was kept as a back-up.

In 1971 the United States and the USSR signed the Accidents Agreement, which commits each side to notify the other at once in the event of an accidental unauthorized occurrence that could lead to a threatening detonation; to give notice of any missile test firings in the direction of the other's homeland; "to act in such a way as to reduce the possibility" of actions being misinterpreted should a nuclear incident occur; and to maintain and improve internal arrangements intended to prevent unauthorized or accidental nuclear war.

In 1972 the Incidents at Sea Agreement (INCSEA) created navigation rules for naval vessels and procedures for coping with accidental collisions and near-misses.

In 1973 the Prevention of Nuclear War Agreement was signed, requiring consultation between Washington and Moscow in any situation carrying a higher than normal risk of nuclear war.

In 1975 "Basket One" of the Helsinki Final Act included two confidence-building measures: a requirement of prior notification of major military maneuvers in Europe, and provisions for the exchange of observers at these maneuvers.[23]

In 1984 the hot line was improved again, gaining the capability to transmit whole pages of text, photographs, and graphics.[24] In 1987 the U.S. and Soviet governments signed an agreement to establish nuclear risk reduction centers in Washington and Moscow, to be linked by high-speed communications and to be used for arms control notifications as well as for any risk reduction functions both governments decide to assign them.[25] Designated at the principal channel for communications about inspections to verify the INF Treaty, the centers began operating in March 1988.

The Inadequacy of Existing Arrangements

Existing diplomatic procedures have served Washington and Moscow well over these last forty years of tension. But certain gaps need to be filled by supplementary procedures and institutions.

To deal with the risk of inadvertent war, it is valuable to have in place mechanisms for U.S.-Soviet consultation that can:

1. Interpret and exchange specialized military-technical knowledge of the kind involved in military incidents or nuclear detonations.
2. Anticipate unexpected incidents, head them off where possible, and design contingency procedures for defusing them.
3. Respond quickly to a threatening situation.

Existing diplomatic arrangements—at least until the nuclear risk reduction centers are fully functioning—do not always meet these criteria. Diplomats rarely have the specialized knowledge needed; very little anticipatory discussion about possible inadvertent incidents takes place; and time-urgent communication procedures are sometimes inadequate. At one point in the early 1980s, for example, American diplomats sought to notify Soviet authorities that a malfunctioning American satellite might crash on Soviet territory, but were unable to contact anyone in the Soviet Ministry because it was a weekend.[26] Such a danger had not been discussed, contingency procedures for consultation were nonexistent, and routine channels were inadequate.

It is also valuable to insulate institutions from the vagaries of U.S.-Soviet relations so that they can continue their functions if superpower relations turn cold. During phases of tension in the overall relationship, discussions that are directly in the interest of both nations, such as those on nonproliferation, are often suspended because of the hostile atmosphere. Unwanted incidents pick their own timing, however. Institutionalizing consultations on preventing inadvertent war would help ensure their continuation during tense times, when they might be most needed.

Risks of Risk Reduction Mechanisms

Risk reduction mechanisms, unfortunately, must be established in a context of deep-seated conflict between the superpowers. It is not easy to promote their shared interest in preventing inadvertent war while protecting vital national interests against perceived threats from the other side.

The very information, for instance, that one may wish both sides to know *during* a crisis, in order to defuse it, might, if known *before* the crisis, encourage one or both sides to believe that launching a crisis would be relatively safe. There is no escape from this basic paradox. However promising risk reduction mechanisms may become, a very large realm of uncertainty and risk will always remain.

Many possible measures are vulnerable to misuse. New channels such as risk reduction centers, for instance, could be used for gethering intelligence or for sending false information at a critical time. Safeguards can and should be carefully designed. Moreover, since U.S.-Soviet risk reduction measures could be misinterpreted as evidence of superpower condominium, it is important to consult carefully with friends and allies before negotiating any agreements.

IMPROVING AND ADDING RISK REDUCTION MEASURES

Five classes of measures could help reduce nuclear risks. The sketches offered here are intended to stimulate discussion and to elicit criticism and improvements, not to be used as blueprints. Although each has its own merits (and risks), what matters most is the establishment of a systematic approach for preventing and defusing dangerous incidents.

Nuclear Risk Reduction Centers in Washington and Moscow

The agreement signed in September 1987 mandates the creation of two nuclear risk reduction centers, in Washington and Moscow, to be staffed around the clock and linked by telecommunications. This is a significant first step toward realizing the proposal advanced by many political leaders and acacemics, including Senators Sam Nunn and John Warner.[27]

Initially the functions of the centers will be limited to transmitting notifications of launches, military exercises, and inspection visits specified in bilateral arms control treaties. As the use of the centers for verifying the implementation of the INF treaty demonstrates, the mandate is flexible. The centers can be used for whatever confidence-building communication functions both governments assign them.[28] The agreement provides for annual meetings between governmental experts of each side to consider subjects of mutual concern.

Over time, as the centers are integrated into the existing infrastructures of both governments, they could serve as a place where working groups drawn from agencies of each government could meet to discuss their concerns about the various inadvertent triggers, jointly analyze past incidents or future hypothetical ones, and share their thinking. For example, participants might focus on events that could lead to the acquisition of nuclear weapons, materials, or equipment by unauthorized parties. Or the centers might facilitate exchange of information about the problem of detonations of unknown origin. American and Soviet officers might consider, for instance, the hypothetical scenario of a nuclear weapon suddenly exploding on national soil. In such a case, the nation "attacked" would naturally suspect the other. The center staff might discuss observable actions (and the absence of actions) that could make a denial of responsibility credible.

Working groups might also design contingency procedures for consultation and/or action in the event of particular incidents. Occasionally these contingency procedures might become embodied in a common understanding such as the one reached in June 1985 concerning the use of the hot line during a nuclear terrorist incident.[29] More often, these procedures would simply remain informal "scripts" that could, if appropriate, be followed or adopted on a case-by-case basis before, during, or in the wake of dangerous incidents.

One of the greatest benefits of such discussions would be to stimulate the development of better internal procedures within each government. Indeed, it would be valuable, if not essential, for each government to assess and improve internal procedures before they meet jointly.

Government agencies could use the centers as a place to raise concerns about inadvertent incidents with their counterparts in the other country, and to work out helpful procedures that would then be implemented not by the centers but by the agencies themselves. Further, the centers could be used as a channel for the exchange of technical information that would help Washington and Moscow prevent inadvertent escalation of an incident—for example, an errant satellite, an accidental launch toward a third country, or a nuclear terrorist threat.

In time, the centers might also become a channel for technical coordination of actions needed to implement a political formula agreed upon by both governments (e.g., after the political settlement of a crisis). For example, if a subnational group threatened to detonate a nuclear bomb, the centers might be used to work out the details of coordinated operations agreed upon by both leaderships. A less dramatic example could have been technical discussion of the two countries' readings on South Africa's nuclear capabilities and readiness to test in 1977. In this case, when the Soviets reported that South Africa was digging a hole as if in preparation for a test, several weeks were available for diplomatic discussions before the suspected test. Suppose, however, that the South Africans had been observed connecting up electrical wires, and only a day or two remained before the test. Under these circumstances, the White House and the Kremlin might have worked through the risk reduction centers, had they existed.

I have stressed that the centers would be concerned with the exchange of technical rather than political information. Admittedly, the distinction between "technical" and "political" will be blurred; in a particular incident it will be a matter of judgment whether to use the hot line, the centers, or both. In general, however, it would probably detract from the centers' long-term usefulness if they were used as a channel for political discussions *during* an acute U.S.-Soviet confrontation, when either or both sides were jockeying for political or military advantage. For example, it would seem inappropriate to use the centers for the kinds of political and diplomatic conversations that took place during the Middle East crisis of 1973.

Unless handled with considerable care, these functions for the nuclear risk reduction centers pose certain risks, including disinformation at critical moments, intelligence leaks, added bureaucracy, and foreign perceptions of U.S.-Soviet condominium. It would be best therefore to take an incremental approach, starting with items on which U.S.-Soviet mutual interest is greatest (e.g., dealing with an errant satellite). Then gradually, as confidence develops, officials from both governments could work toward more complex cases.

It would also be wise to keep the arrangements flexible. It should be understood that other functions will be added only if in a particular situation both sides want them. There should, for instance, be no obligation to share information about missing nuclear weapons unless either government wish to do so.

Incidents Agreements

The Incidents at Sea Agreement sprang from a series of incidents between American and Soviet naval vessels that both sides viewed as dangerous. The incidents took many forms, such as "blocking," "shouldering," and "playing chicken" for the purposes of testing the other side's vessels, disrupting their mission, and perhaps embarrassing their officers. As time went on, the incidents took on a life of their own, leading to reprisals and escalation. There were several near collisions, and the intimidating behavior came to include the aiming of guns and missiles.[30]

American and Soviet officials negotiated an agreement in 1972 to control the competitive behavior and forestall a potentially explosive incident. The Incidents at Sea Agreement created a joint naval working group, which developed agreed-upon "rules of the road" and a common code book that could assist commanders on the spot in communicating to avoid or cope with a naval incident. A joint review group, drawn from naval officers on both sides, meets annually to review any incidents that occur and to improve procedures for coping with them. In addition, a special communication procedure was established to deal immediately with serious problems that cannot wait. In the fifteen years since the agreement was reached, these procedures have reduced considerably the number of risky naval incidents.[31]

This is an excellent example of how joint Soviet-American operating procedures can reduce the likelihood of a crisis. Such procedures operate preventively: routine mechanisms operate at working levels, defusing any incident well before it even is defined as a crisis or requires attention from top political leaders.

The annual review conducted under the Incidents at Sea Agreement has functioned in a relatively nonpolitical way, with few exceptions.[32] Because both sides find the routinized procedures helpful in preventing unwanted incidents, they continue in operation, comparatively free of linkage to political issues.

The principles of the Incidents at Sea Agreement can readily be extended to other kinds of incidents, in the air, on the ground, or in space.

Incidents in the Air Agreement. From time to time, one side's aircraft have accidentally strayed into the other's airpsace. Because an accidental air intrusion during an intense crisis would be very dangerous, it would be valuable to develop agreed-upon procedures for coping with such an incident. After a U.S. reconnaissance plane strayed into Soviet airspace at the height of the Cuban missile crisis, Khrushchev wrote to Kennedy: "Is it not a fact that an intruding American plane could easily be taken for a nuclear bomber, which might push us to a fateful step?"[33] Even during normal times, such emergency safety procedures could be valuable, as the tragic downing of Korean Airlines flight 007 in 1983 reminds us. A useful first step was the North Pacific Air Safety Agreement signed in July 1985, which established links among Soviet, American, and Japanese air traffic control centers.[34] It could usefully be extended to other regions of the world and to military aircraft.

Incidents on the Ground Agreement. Occasionally patrols lose their way and blunder across the border between the alliance zones in Europe. Such incidents have never yet caused a crisis, and by themselves are unlikely to. But in a time of high tension, and especially in the midst of a serious European crisis, such an incident could be serious. At all times such mistakes lead to confusion, tension, and unnecessary irritation. An Incidents on the Ground Agreement, again patterned loosely after the Incidents at Sea Agreement, may be negotiable and beneficial. Such an agreement might include procedures under which designated ranking officers from NATO and the Warsaw Pact nations could communicate directly with each other to clarify and defuse any incident without its immediately escalating to an issue between Washington and Moscow. Such contacts would help implement the unwritten rule to avoid any direct use of force against troops of the other superpower, as discussed in Chapter 1.

The superpowers might extend this understanding, perhaps informally, to other points around the world where forces come into close proximity. In 1983 and early 1984, for instance, American Marines stationed in Beirut found themselves only about fifty miles from Soviet military personnel in Syria, at a time when rival factions in Lebanon were fighting almost continuously. U.S. Navy aircraft bombed positions between the Marines and the Soviets, and at times the battleship *New Jersey* fired into the Lebanese melee. In that situation, American military commanders wisely took great care to keep their fire away from Soviet positions. But accidents can always occur. In some future tangle, American and Soviet forces might be even closer, the regional fighting even more intense, and the danger—and hence the need for understandings—even greater.

Incidents in Space Agreement. The superpowers could agree to restrict their satellites and spaceships from making close high-speed passes or passes in geosynchronous orbit near the other's satellites and spaceships. Since a surprise attack might be preceded by an attack on monitoring satellites, near-collisions and collisions in outer space can create a dangerous reaction. As space technology evolves, such dangers may increase, suggesting the importance of an incidents agreement as well as arms control initiatives in this area.[35]

Regular Military-to-Military Exchanges

In addition to incidents agreements and the attendant military-to-military exchanges, a strong case can be made for regular meetings with a broad scope between the military leaders of each side. Each side spends a lot of time studying the capabilities of the other, but each has much to learn about the other's intentions. In a crisis situation, a correct assessment of the intentions that lie behind the other side's force deployments or military actions may well be the determining factor in avoiding inadvertent escalation. Moreover, an established working relationship between U.S. and Soviet military officers could be exceedingly important in defusing a tense confrontation.

There have been sporadic contacts over the years, most notably a few between the U.S. and Soviet commanders-in-chief in Europe, and mostly during the era of détente. There was little contact at the highest levels until recently. During the December 1987 summit in Washington, the chief of the Soviet general staff, Marshal Akhromeyev, came to the Pentagon to meet with his American counterpart, Admiral Crowe. In March 1988, Secretary of Defense Carlucci met with Soviet Defense Minister Yazov for three days in Bern, Switzerland.[36] In August Carlucci paid an official visit to the Soviet Union.[37] Both sides agreed to expand military contacts and to exchange information on each other's forces. They also discussed the establishment of a new channel for dealing with military incidents and actions involving both sides.

Such exchanges would be useful at both higher and lower levels and for both civilian and military defense officials. The scope of conversation should be broad enough to encompass such issues as force posture, deployments, military uses of space, and weapons programs. Exchanges might usefully entail visits to active units. Discussions could focus on ambiguities in each side's military stance. Currently, both the United States and the USSR are uncertain about the real meaning of various deployments and military actions of the other. Each could make inquiries and receive at least limited explanations at an authoritative level. Simply hearing the other's concerns about nuclear and conventional posture may be valuable.

Useful discussion would probably revolve around basic assumptions and the intentions of each side, so as to reduce the chance of miscalculation and misunderstanding. Should a crisis occur, officials already would have established a working relationship with their opposite numbers, a wish frequently expressed by American participants in past crises.

Such talks carry, of course, certain risks of misunderstandings and false confidence, as well as intelligence leaks and disinformation. While considerable caution is advisable, many American military experts, in and out of the armed forces, believe that the concept of regular exchanges is practical and that the potential benefits outweigh the inevitable risk.[38]

Expanded Regional Consultations

A joint review of the Cuban missile crisis by American and Soviet participants has revealed the tantalizing possibility that, if the U.S. and Soviet governments had held serious talks about Cuba earlier in 1962, the crisis might have been averted altogether. Khrushchev had known that Kennedy had no intentions of invading Cuba with an American force, and certainly if he had known how strongly Kennedy was likely to respond to the introduction of Soviet missiles, he very well might not have taken the perilous step of placing missiles in Cuba.[39]

Perhaps the most likely source of superpower confrontation is a regional crisis in the Third World. Since 1985 American and Soviet diplomats have been meeting regularly to discuss specific regional hot spots such as Afghanistan, the Middle East, and Central America. While such talks have reportedly often descended into unproductive posturing, mutual accusations, and recitations of well-known positions, they at least have the potential to reduce misperceptions about intentions and likely responses to actions taken by the other side. As one Reagan administration official, interviewed in March 1987, commented, "The Soviets think we have a secret game plan to put military forces close to their southern border. . . . They look at our Rapid Deployment Force, the marines in Beirut, now the patrol in the Persian Gulf. It is useful to tell them that that is not our purpose, that our concern is with freedom of navigation. They may not believe us, but it helps."[40]

These consultations could be extended to clarify the global ground rules that the United States and the Soviet Union have gradually built up to limit their worldwide competition, as discussed in Chapters 1 and 2. Such rules are open to conflicting interpretations. A case in point is Cuba.

During the Cuban missile crisis, Kennedy and Khrushchev reached a loose understanding that the Soviets would never place combat forces in Cuba that were capable of offensive operations. Still, much ambiguity remained about the exact meaning of "offensive." In 1979 a brief, and quite unnecessary, crisis occurred when the Carter administration suddenly "discovered" a Soviet combat brigade in Cuba and publicly demanded its withdrawal. Moscow pointed out, correctly, that thousands of Soviet troops had been in Cuba for many years to train Cuban forces. When U.S. intelligence searched for evidence that the brigade had the capability to fight outside Cuba and found none, Carter had no choice but to back off from public confrontation. The "crisis" blew over—but not before damaging the ratification prospects for the SALT II agreements.[41] A recognized confidential forum for clarifying—and where appropriate extending—specific understandings could avert such crises, which, even if they pose no danger of war, damage the relationship and retard progress on arms control.

Intensified consultations may lead to agreements, formal or informal, to restrict arms sales or the introduction of military advisers in specific regions. They may also lead to joint or parallel action to bring about a ceasefire or progress toward the resolution or the containment of a particular conflict. Although the outcome is uncertain at the time of this writing, conversations between American and Soviet officials on the subject of Afghanistan in 1985–86 clearly helped clarify each side's political interests and even included tentative commitments that provided a basis for General Secretary Gorbachev's decision to withdraw Soviet troops.

Such consultations also help develop useful working relationships between American and Soviet officials. As one American diplomat said of the current regional consultations, "It does develop personal contacts, contacts which can be used if a crisis develops."[42]

Consultations, like all the crisis prevention measures discussed, are not without certain risks. Discussions of ground rules, especially about hot spots, could generate misunderstandings, especially false confidence between the superpowers. Officials would need to take great care in what they said and conveyed.

CONCLUSION

The greatest danger of nuclear war lies in a process of miscalculation, miscommunication, and inadvertent incidents in time of crisis. Against such a threat, rules of prudence and agreed general norms of behavior are not sufficient. Operational institutions and procedures are needed to implement the rules and norms. Some, such as the hot line, already exist. The nuclear risk reduction centers, incidents agreements, military-to-military talks, and regional consultations would combine with existing crisis prevention and management measures to constitute a risk reduction system of procedures and institutions that could play a substantial role in the prevention of nuclear war.

NOTES

1. Lyndon Baines Johndon, *The Vantage Point: Perspectives of the Presidency* (New York: Holt, Rinehart, and Winston, 1971), p. 300.
2. "Sect. Rusk and Sect. of Defense McNamara Discuss Vietnam and Korea on 'Meet the Press,'" *Department of State Bulletin* 83 (1496), February 26, 1968, p. 271.
3. Ibid.
4. Steve Weissman, *The Islamic Bomb* (New York: Times Books, 1981), p. 64.
5. Graham T. Allison, *Essence of Decision: Explaining the Cuban Missile Crisis* (Boston: Little, Brown, 1971), p. 141.
6. Paul Bracken, *The Command and Control of Nuclear Forces* (New Haven and London: Yale University Press, 1983), pp. 59–65.
7. Stockholm International Peace Research Institute, *Yearbook of World Armaments and Disarmaments* 2 (London: Duckworth, 1969), p. 261.
8. *New York Times*, January 4, 1985, p. A9.
9. The incident involving a faulty computer chip is discussed in *Recent False Alerts from the Nation's Missile Attack Warning System*, a report to the Committee on Armed Services of the U.S. Senate, October 9, 1980.
10. Bracken, *Command and Control*, p. 53.
11. *New York Times*, May 30, 1987.
12. Ibid.
13. Ibid., p. 66.
14. Thomas Schelling, *A Strategy of Conflict* (Cambridge: Harvard University Press, 1960), p. 21.
15. Scott Sagan, "Lessons of the Yom Kippur Alert," *Foreign Policy* 36 (Fall 1979), p. 168.
16. Alexander George and Richard Smoke, *Deterrence in American Foreign Policy: Theory and Practice* (New York: Columbia University Press, 1974), p. 400.
17. Barry M. Blechman, "The Political Utility of Nuclear Weapons," *International Security* 7 (1), Summer 1982, p. 137.
18. Graham Allison, *Essence*, p. 60.
19. Ibid.
20. Blechman, "Political Utility," p. 137.
21. This point was made again and again by Soviet participants in our joint study conversations.

22.   Robert F. Kennedy, *Thirteen Days: A Memoir of the Cuban Missile Crisis* (New York: W. W. Norton, 1971), p. 71.

23.   This and previous agreements are described in U.S. Arms Control and Disarmament Agency, *Arms Control and Disarmament Agreements: Texts and Histories of Negotiations* (Washington, D.C.: Government Printing Office, 1980), p. 112.

24.   *New York Times*, July 17, 1984.

25.   Formally entitled "Agreement Between the United States of America and the Union of Soviet Socialist Republics on the Establishment of Nuclear Risk Reduction Centers," the agreement was signed by Secretary of State George Shultz and Foreign Minister Edward Shevardnadze on September 15, 1987, at the White House.

26.   Personal interview with Thomas Simon, American diplomat, June 25, 1986.

27.   Sam Nunn, "Washington, Moscow need improved emergency communications," *Atlanta Constitution*, November 17, 1981. Senators Nunn and Warner cosponsored Senate Resolution 329, "Relating to Nuclear Risk Reduction Centers," *Congressional Record of the 98th Congress* 130, no. 8 (February 1, 1984). For further discussion of the centers concept, see John W. Lewis and Coit D. Blacker, *Next Steps to the Creation of an Accidental Nuclear War Prevention Center* (Stanford: Center for International Security and Arms Control, 1983); William L. Ury and Richard Smoke, *Beyond the Hotline: Controlling a Nuclear Crisis (A Report to the United States Arms Control and Disarmament Agency)* (Cambridge: Harvard Law School Nuclear Negotiation Project, 1984); and Barry Blechman, ed., *Preventing Nuclear War* (Bloomington: Indiana University Press, 1985).

28.   Article 3 of Protocol I reads: "Each Party also may, at its own discretion as a display of good will and with a view to building confidence, transmit through the Nuclear Risk Reduction Centers communications other than those provided for under Article 1 of this Protocol."

29.   *New York Times*, July 6, 1985.

30.   See Sean Lynn-Jones, "Avoiding Incidents at Sea," in John Borawski, ed., *Avoiding War in the Nuclear Age* (Boulder, Colo.: Westview Press, 1986), pp. 73–78.

31.   Ibid., pp. 81–82.

32.   In June 1984, for the first time in the history of the Incidents at Sea Agreement, a meeting that was to be held in Washington was postponed. In response to the Soviet shooting on March 24, 1984, of U.S. military liaison officer Major Arthur D. Nicholson, Jr., Secretary of Defense Caspar Weinberger decided to cut short the scheduled exchange. In response, the Soviets canceled their trip. Leslie Gelb, "U.S.-Soviet Session on '72 Naval Accord Canceled," *New York Times*, June 19, 1985, pp. A1, A9.

33.   David L. Larson, ed., *The "Cuban Crisis" of 1962: Selected Documents and Chronology* (Boston: Houghton Mifflin, 1963), p. 164.

34. See "Monitoring Pact Aims to Keep Jets from Straying," *Boston Globe*, July 31, 1985, p. 7.
35. For this brief discussion of an incidents in space agreement, I am indebted to Sean Lynn-Jones. See his article on "Avoiding Incidents at Sea," in John Borawski, ed., *Avoiding War in the Nuclear Age* (Boulder, Colo.: Westview Press, 1986), pp. 85–86. Also see Paul Stares, *Space and National Security* (Washington, D.C.: Brookings Institution, 1987), p. 169.
36. *New York Times*, March 18, 1988, p. A3.
37. *New York Times*, August 2, 1988, P. A3.
38. Colonel Wade Williams interviewed twenty individuals, including former commanders-in-chief of U.S. Army Europe, chiefs of military intelligence agencies, and a former chairman of the Joint Chiefs of Staff. With one exception, they felt that an expanded program of exchanges was beneficial. See Williams, "Expanding the US-USSR Military Dialogue," in Blechman, op. cit..
39. This impression is derived from a private conference between American and Soviet participants in the crisis, held at the John F. Kennedy School of Government under the auspices of its Avoiding Nuclear War Project on October 12–13, 1987. See chapter 4.
40. *New York Times*, March 29, 1987, p. E3.
41. See Gloria Duffy, "Crisis Prevention in Cuba," in George, *Managing U.S.-Soviet Rivalry*, pp. 298–314.
42. *New York Times*, March 29, 1987, p. E3.

SOVIET VIEW

Mikhail Mil'shtein

The prevention of accidental nuclear war remains one of the most urgent and complex problems of our time. A series of technical accidents have forcibly drawn the attention of scholars, the public, and political leaders in both the West and the East to the danger of accidental or unauthorized use of nuclear weapons, which in today's world could have incalculable consequences.

The danger of accidental or unauthorized use has grown continuously, as a consequence of the increase in the number of nuclear weapons, their constant qualitative modernization, and the development of new means of delivery, most notably intercontinental ballistic missiles (ICBMs) and submarine-launched ballistic missiles (SLBMs) with speeds as high as 24,000 kilometers an hour. Such speed has irrevocably shrunk the time available for collecting and analyzing information on which to base rational decisions. Human capabilities have become too slow and are giving way to complex automated technology. Thus gradually man is becoming a prisoner of technology of his own making. This paradox must be kept in mind when evaluating the effectiveness of mechanisms to make accidental nuclear war less likely. While some technological improvements can reduce the risks of accidents (for example, in the early warning system or in the system of command and control), more mistakes may occur in the perception and evaluation of information, even in the new nuclear risk reduction centers.

Ury correctly notes that the danger of inadvertent use of nuclear weapons sharply increases in crisis situations, in regional conflicts, and in times of increased tensions between East and West. In these conditions, mutual suspicion increases, and each side evaluates the other's actions with worst-case thinking. As the time available for decision is compressed, the chance of miscalculations that might provoke a chain reaction sharply increases. One must agree with Ury that the most likely path to nuclear destruction lies not in the calculated launching of a war but in the inadvertent escalation of a crisis through miscalculation, miscommunication, or accident.

The danger of accidental nuclear war will increase markedly if American pursuit of the Strategic Defense Initiative (SDI) undermines the Anti-Ballistic Missile Treaty, and offensive systems are introduced in space. This move would destabilize the strategic balance and accentuate the distrust between our nations, thus increasing the risk of accidental war.

Ury correctly describes the factors creating the risk of inadvertent war. His point that nuclear proliferation can increase the risk of U.S.-Soviet nuclear war in a crisis suggests the necessity of strengthening the Non-Proliferation Treaty, of accelerating the ratification of the Threshold Test Ban Treaty and the Peaceful Nuclear Explosions Treaty, and ultimately of stopping testing altogether. He also highlights the potentially dangerous interaction of the two sides' automatic warning and command systems. If an American strategic bomber, for instance, flying close to the Soviet Union in a time of crisis, were to misfire a cruise missile, the consequences could be incalculable. The danger lies not only in accidental and unauthorized launches but also in the misinterpretation of situations independent of an incident. Dozens of circumstances—ranging from a flock of geese to the rising moon—might be misperceived as evidence of an attack.

The main focus of Ury's work is the creation of a general mechanism to prevent accidental war. He begins with an overview of the joint measures already taken toward this end. Indeed progress has been made recently in this area, with the creation in 1988 of national centers in Moscow and Washington to reduce the risk of nuclear war.

The establishment of such centers had been discussed at both the political and scientific levels in the United States since 1982. At the 1985 Geneva summit meeting General Secretary Gorbachev and President Reagan agreed to a preliminary study of the centers proposal at the expert level. When the study was completed, negotiations began, and an agreement to establish the centers was signed on September 15, 1987, in Washington, D.C. The creation of the centers represents a breakthrough in the effort to build an effective and continually active mechanism to reduce the risk of accidental nuclear war. The centers can be considered the main link of such a mechanism. Undoubtedly, with the accumulation of experience and the improvement of the means of communication, the work of the centers will play an important and perhaps indispensable role in reducing that danger. Significantly, the INF Treaty (Article 13) calls for the systematic use of the nuclear risk reduction centers to provide constant communication of the data necessary to carry out the spirit and letter of this agreement.

It is important, however, not to overestimate what the risk reduction centers can do. They cannot substitute for political and military confidence-building measures that reduce the risk of misperception. (By misperception, I mean misjudgment, misinterpretation, exaggerated suspicions, and the evaluation of each accident from a worst-case point of view.) Nor can the centers substitute for the hot line or for meetings between military and political leaders.

Ury discusses possible future functions for the centers, such as establishing joint working groups to analyze dangerous incidents that have occurred in the past and to discuss hypothetical ones that might occur in the future. While these functions are important, they are better dealt with through channels other than the centers.

Ury goes on to discuss other links in a general mechanism for reducing the risk of inadvertent nuclear war. Soviet scholars and political figures, he observes, have focused on improving political relations as the main approach to preventing inadvertent nuclear war. In conditions of tension, of constant confrontation and exacerbation of the political atmosphere, the danger of accidental nuclear war sharply increases. Accidental or unauthorized use of nuclear weapons could well trigger a general nuclear catastrophe. As Ury has written elsewhere, "a single spark conceivably could start a fire that, if allowed to burn out of control, might ultimately become an inferno that destroys our societies."[1] This recognition has convinced many Soviet leaders and thinkers that confidence in each other's intentions is one of the most, if not the most, important factors in avoiding nuclear war. The adequacy of communications, negotiations, and prior consultation with the other side can, as Ury indicates, make a considerable difference should a crisis occur.

Ury also suggests that joint meetings on a high military level would play a positive role. It is hard to disagree. When the defense ministers of the two nations met in Bern, Switzerland, in March 1988, and in Moscow in the summer of 1988, both sides expressed their satisfaction with the progress made. In May 1987 the Warsaw Pact proposed to hold meetings with NATO to compare the military doctrines of the two alliances and to examine jointly their further evolution. The aim of such meetings would be to remove mutual suspicion and mistrust accumulated over the years, to better understand each other's intentions, and to develop military concepts and doctrines for both alliances based entirely on a defensive posture. The NATO leadership has not yet responded to this proposal.

The proposals discussed by Ury for agreements on the prevention of incidents in air and in space, modeled after the existing Incidents at Sea Agreement, are worthy of discussion. An agreement on incidents on the ground might be included in an understanding on reducing conventional forces in Europe. As a whole, Ury's work is a definite contribution to our understanding of the problem of how to reduce the risk of accidental nuclear war.

NOTE

1.   William L. Ury, *Beyond the Hotline* (Boston: Houghton Mifflin, 1985), p. 4.

SOVIET VIEW

Viktor Kremeniuk

William Ury is correct in considering regional crises as a major potential source of nuclear war. In a condition of great power rivalry, such crises contain elements of escalation that inevitably aggravate tensions even if there is no direct cause for confrontation. Those few times when both nations have come close to war have occurred during regional crises, notably the 1962 Cuban crisis and the 1973 Middle East crisis.

Clearly no U.S. or Soviet interest in any regional conflict would warrant a nuclear showdown. Nevertheless regional crises could trigger a sequence of events that might lead to such an outcome. Characterizing one side or the other as "aggressive" or "subversive" does little to explain the potential for such escalation. Even the most peace-loving nation can make decisions in crisis that could aggravate the situation. Conversely, an "aggressive" nation can show a degree of prudence and restraint that will stop the escalation. Sometimes aggressive behavior produces a sobering effect on the conduct of other nations; other times it adds fuel to the fire. While such categorizations may be useful in analyzing long-term trends in a nation's policy, a different set of concepts, such as the one Ury discusses, is more useful in understanding crisis behavior.

Nations in crisis are intensely interdependent. As Ury describes, each move by one side is matched with a move by the other, time for thinking about a response is short, and communications sometimes become confusing or impossible. Policymakers take certain actions hoping that the other side will properly infer their intentions. With the obvious exception of those who are deliberately seeking to go to war, national actors usually hope to achieve an accommodation that will prevent open hostilities with a minimal loss to their interests, including their prestige, domestic position, and international reputation.

The system of procedures and institutions of which William Ury writes can become an efficient instrument to prevent an inadvertent nuclear war. Both the United States and the Soviet Union have come to understand the need for such a system and have gradually developed the concept. There is a problem, however, in relating these procedures and institutions to existing decision-making practices in both countries, given the difference in domestic political structures. It might easily happen that one side was better able to deal expeditiously with a crisis because its internal communications were not blocked by bureaucratic procedures, or because its personnel were better trained, or because its leader was more fit. Simply because the other side was slower, it might be accused of "cheating" or "double dealing." The asymmetry of internal standard operating procedures (as Graham Allison pointed out in *Essence of Decision*) could thus aggravate tensions. A critical task of the system suggested by Ury will be to coordinate both sides' crisis decision-making procedures so as to reduce dangerous misperceptions.

AMERICAN VIEW

David Hamburg

Most experts now agree that the greatest risk of nuclear war would arise through escalation out of crisis, probably involving miscalculation of consequences. Thus it is in both superpowers' national interests to stay well back from the brink, since mechanical and human errors and misjudgments are all too likely to occur under the incredibly complex stress of nuclear crisis.[1]

History is replete with mistakes leading to war and mistakes exacerbating destruction once war has broken out. Even the most respected, disciplined, science-based professions such as medicine provide many vivid examples of error and misjudgment in life-and-death circumstances. There is a growing research literature on iatrogenic (medically induced) illness. In fact, serious errors of judgment under great stress are observed in every field. In relations between the superpowers, unfortunately, the characteristics of the interacting nuclear alert systems substantially increase both the risks of human and mechanical error and the interaction between the two.

Effective crisis management would be made much more difficult by the temptation to subject the opponent to coercive diplomacy for bargaining purposes, particularly if the opponent feels urgent pressure to comply with the demands and if the demands are backed up by credible threats to inflict damage. But if either side resorts to strong coercive pressure of this kind, as they have in past crises, then the confrontation readily takes on a dangerous character analogous to the game of "chicken."

The task of crisis management becomes more complicated when the United States and the Soviet Union are drawn into a regional conflict involving their allies or client states. In the Middle East wars of 1967, 1970, and 1973, for example, each superpower confronted a difficult policy dilemma: how far to go in assisting its local ally without risking a dangerous confrontation with the other superpower. In such situations the superpowers must control not only their own forces, but also those of their regional ally. Some of the important requirements for managing crises become much more difficult to fulfill in regional conflicts of this kind.

An international crisis is a highly stressful experience for leaders and their advisers. Such stress jeopardizes the quality of decision making.

For all those reasons it is vital to develop a regime for crisis prevention rather than settle for crisis management. Some of the main points in the crisis prevention approach have been discussed in this book by William Ury. Additional crisis prevention activities might emerge from regular meetings of foreign and defense ministers, as well as regular summits. Measures aimed at crisis prevention could, with arms control agreements, contribute to a tangible and durable improvement in working relations between the two countries. This approach is not a substitute for arms control or for improvement in the general U.S.-Soviet relationship. But it is at least an antidote to complacency and a prudent, practical response to visible risks.[2]

The crisis prevention approach would be strengthened by the adoption of the following guidelines for improving U.S.-Soviet relations, applicable to the leaders of both nations.

1. No dehumanization or harsh deprecation of the other. Criticize in civil discourse. Make carefully differentiated assessments rather than sweeping pronouncements.
2. Try to relate principles of decent human relations to specific actions of the two countries.
3. Hold regular consultations at various levels (e.g., summits, mini-summits, regional meetings).
4. Make agreements explicit. Build a cumulative series of crisis prevention agreements in this mode.
5. Do not put the other in a humiliating position, either directly or in relation to its allies.
6. Resist the temptation to exploit local situations drastically.
7. Safeguard systematically and incessantly against inadvertent or accidental war.
8. Do not sponsor terrorism against the other, directly or by client. View terrorism as a long-term danger to the relationship between the two countries.
9. Conduct ongoing serious negotiations of the central strategic balance. Build a cumulative record of arms control agreements

that enhance stability, are verifiable, are enforced, and greatly reduce the level of the stockpiles.

10. Avoid grandiose interpretations of national interest. Learn to live in a multicentric world that respectfully accommodates many vigorous nations.

11. Expand contacts widely in different spheres of activity and sectors of society; leading edges might include scientific and scholarly exchanges, cultural exchanges, and business transactions.

If the United States and the Soviet Union alter their behavior along these lines, as they have begun to do in the late 1980s, the risk of inadvertent war will surely diminish.

NOTES

1. David A. Hamburg and Alexander L. George. "Nuclear Crisis Management," *Bulletin of Atomic Scientists*, June/July 1984, pp. 24–28.
2. Graham T. Allison, Albert Carnesale, and Joseph S. Nye, Jr., eds., *Hawks, Doves, and Owls* (New York: W. W. Norton and Company, 1985), p. 282. Barry M. Blechman, ed., *Preventing Nuclear War* (Bloomington: Indiana University Press, 1985), p. 197.

LOOKING BACK
How Did We Arrive Here?

4 NEW THINKING ABOUT AN OLD CRISIS
Soviet Reflections on the Cuban Missile Crisis

Fyodor M. Burlatsky
Sergo A. Mikoyan
Georgy Shakhnazarov

The following comments were prepared for this book by the Soviet participants in an October 1987 conference on the 25th anniversary of the Cuban missile crisis, organized by the Center for Science and International Affairs at Harvard University's John F. Kennedy School of Government. The participants discuss Soviet motives behind the missile installation, the course of events during the crisis itself, and lessons of the crisis.

SOVIET MOTIVES BEHIND THE MISSILE INSTALLATION

Fyodor Burlatsky

In assessing the motives that guided the Soviet Union to station its missiles in Cuba, we must differentiate between direct and deeper causes. The direct reason was, of course, our desire to help the Cuban leaders defend the island against intervention originating in the United States. The well-known adventure at the Bay of Pigs showed that the U.S. administration was ready to render all assistance—weapons, money, and military training—and to bring Cuba's neighboring Central American states into the conflict, in order to overthrow the Cuban leadership.

But the incident also reflected more profound causes associated with the balance of forces between the United States and the USSR. Khrushchev asked at that time, "Why do the Americans have the right to surround us with missile bases on all sides, and we have no such right?" Standing on the shore of the Black Sea, another Soviet leader observed, "There, on the other side of the sea, in Turkey, is an American missile base that in a short period could destroy the major centers of the Ukraine, as well as Moscow and Leningrad." If I am not mistaken, that is when the idea first arose that we might deploy missiles in Cuba, close to the U.S. border.

Not long before, in 1961, our successful tests of a powerful nuclear device had inspired Khrushchev with the sense of growing Soviet might. Although the United States then had some 5,000 warheads and we had only 300, an important goal of stationing the missiles in Cuba was to take the first step toward strategic nuclear parity. In my view, since our bases could be destroyed by a U.S. first strike, the deployment of missiles had less military than political significance—as a new factor in the correlation of forces between the two great powers.

In distinguishing direct and deeper causes for deploying our missiles in Cuba, it is essential to understand the psychological factor. Scholars tend to search for exclusively rational explanations of political events, but this approach is misguided. Political decisions are not taken by machines but by people, typically under the influence of various circumstances—accurate or erroneous information, intelligent or not so intelligent advice, personal relationships between leaders, and so forth. Such considerations are especially important in analyzing Khrushchev's actions; he had an astute political mind and was extraordinarily emotional and impulsive. To this day, I am not convinced that he had a precise, concrete concept of what might happen as a result of stationing our missiles in Cuba, or how President Kennedy might respond, and how we might respond to those U.S. actions. In short, I do not think he had well-thought-out, considered alternatives and options for all eventualities. It was, of course, a test of strength in a new situation after the Soviet Union had at last acquired the potential for a retaliatory nuclear strike that could inflict irreparable damage on the other side.

Here we may ask: why was the camouflage during the missile deployment so poorly prepared that the Americans could so easily, so quickly discover our missiles in Cuba? It is not credible to argue that our leadership wanted the Americans to discover them immediately and to enter into negotiations. I think the explanation again is psychological. Having made a decision, Khrushchev was prone to act unusually quickly, and often successfully. Witness how little time passed between the taking of the decision and the beginning of its execution. Contrary to what may be thought in the West, I think that in general we Russians do not plan our action very well. It is a great paradox: our nation made the first attempt to plan the economy and social life as a whole, yet a Russian usually has difficulty in planning even one day of his life or his family's!

Were any nuclear warheads deployed on the island? The answer, I am convinced, is no. Knowing Khrushchev's psychology, I think it improbable that he would immediately throw all his cards on the table. More likely, he wanted to deploy the missiles, see what impression that made on the American administration, consider the reaction, and then make a decision regarding warheads. This was particularly so because this action was especially dangerous. Moreover, had nuclear warheads been deployed on the island, the American side certainly would have known about it, for they had at their disposal sufficient means of intelligence, including agents in Cuba. They would have used this fact in their public announcements and secret negotiations with us.

Sergo Mikoyan

Why did the Soviet Union decide to install nuclear missiles in Cuba? Kennedy was absolutely correct when he spoke of mutual misunderstanding. The thinking of Khrushchev and other Soviet leaders proceeded as follows. First, the American landing at the Bay of Pigs had ended in a humiliating defeat, because President Kennedy relied too trustingly on the mistaken assessments of the Central Intelligence Agency (CIA). We saw him as susceptible to being under the thumb of agencies like the CIA or the Pentagon—apparently because of lack of assurance, youth, and inexperience. Second, the Soviet leadership reasoned that the CIA and Pentagon would conclude from the Bay of Pigs that an invasion must be carried out by American armed forces. Kennedy would give in to their plans in order to regain the prestige he lost in April 1961. The whole operation would last only a few days—not long enough for the USSR to react, except in some other region. But to act after the fait accompli would be too late. Third, if Soviet missiles with nuclear warheads were installed on Cuba, along with many thousands of Soviet troops, an attack on Cuba would either be equivalent to an attack on the USSR, with all the resulting consequences, or it would provoke a nuclear response from the territory of Cuba (again with all the resulting consequences). Under those conditions, the United States would refrain from invading and would reconcile itself both to the new face of Cuba and to the presence of Soviet missiles there. Finally, the presence of Soviet missiles would improve the position of the USSR in a military-strategic confrontation with the United States; it would restrain American aggressiveness and reduce the U.S. capacity to conduct any negotiations from "a position of strength."

Study of all accessible materials, and especially discussions with Robert McNamara, McGeorge Bundy, and Ted Sorensen, suggests that the logic of Kennedy and those around him, proceeded as follows. First, the Soviet Union was installing the missiles secretly, making it impossible to predict what would occur after all or most of them were operational. Second, an ultimatum might follow regarding West Berlin, where several serious crises had already emerged, including one during the Kennedy administration. Third, to have Soviet missiles next door was an extremely tense situation under any conditions; but when they were installed contrary to official assurances, it challenged the prestige of the entire administration and its leader. Fourth, the president had already learned through bitter experience that you should not thoughtlessly follow the prescriptions of the CIA; therefore an invasion of Cuba was removed from the agenda. But, in this case, the responsibility for a moral-political and military-strategic U.S. defeat in a confrontation with the USSR would rest with the president. Therefore an invasion of Cuba was again on the agenda.

All this, of course, is only a fundamental outline. The more people, then the more shades of opinion, new views, and different logic. On the Soviet side, the leadership sent Marshal Biriuzov, head of Strategic Rocket Forces, to Cuba in May 1962. He convinced a majority of the leadership of the possibility of secretly installing the missiles (although Politburo member Anastas Mikoyan considered it to be impossible). He also convinced Fidel Castro, and explained that such an action would more or less equalize the position of socialism, which was threatened by the aggressive actions of the United States.

Biriuzov's fervent desire to believe his own arguments and to convince the others may have arisen primarily from his calculation of the correlation of warheads at that time—17 to 1 (5,000 U.S. and 300 USSR). Perhaps the minister of defense, Malinovsky, was unable to forget these figures, as well as the presence of American missiles close to Soviet territory—even when the political leadership was thinking about the defense of Cuba.

Or let us take the American side. On October 28, General LeMay regretfully said that a peaceful resolution of the crisis deprived the United States of the opportunity to strike Cuba under the pretext of the threat of Soviet missiles. And, according to Robert Kennedy, somebody proposed—despite the agreement reached—to strike Cuba and conduct an invasion on Monday the 29th. Unlike John Kennedy, these people were thinking about the first step of escalation, and not the fourth, fifth, or especially the sixth (when "there is no one around to do so").[1] A "strike on Cuba" and an invasion would have inevitably meant military action against the Soviet armed contingent and against the military installations, several of which were ready for battle—and nobody was going to surrender them without a battle.

Many researchers consider it possible that the missiles had no warheads. The whole story then would have been a "bluff by Khrushchev." Robert McNamara is, of course, correct that the Executive Committee of the National Security Council (ExComm) had to proceed as if warheads were located close to the missiles. And the point of being able to bring them quickly to working order, was certainly not merely to act on the nerves of those in the White House. The primary concern was the capability to bring the missiles to battle readiness in order to force the United States to refrain from invasion. To do this, warheads were needed next to the missiles, not 10,000 kilometers away. Even here, however, a misunderstanding occurs: from the point of view of John Kennedy, this action turned into a *casus belli*; by the same token, it was the agreement to dismantle the missiles that yielded the guarantee not to invade Cuba. Some American works on the crisis speculate that the missile installations were deliberately not camouflaged in order to bring Kennedy to negotiations. In fact, the absence of camouflage was only one of the many manifestations during the crisis of McNamara's Law, which says: "It is impossible to predict with a high level of certainty the effects of the use of military force because of the risks of accident, misperceptions, miscalculation, and inadvertence."

Georgy Shakhnazarov

Americans inevitably regard the deployment of Soviet missiles on Cuba as the starting point of the Caribbean crisis. But each cause has its own cause. If we want to probe the sources of a crisis seriously, not superficially, then we must begin with the evolution of the pre-crisis situation.

Since the proclamation of the Truman Doctrine, the policy of all American administrations has been guided by the idea of "containment" or "rollback" of communism. In effect, the Soviet Union and other socialist states have been held continually in the nuclear gunsights. I am not contending that U.S. presidents have wanted to drop their nuclear arsenal on the Soviet Union as quickly as possible. But plans were developed and updated that envisaged the destruction of hundreds of Soviet cities ("Dropshot," "Off-tackle"). Since such plans had been formulated, there might always be people who, given the opportunity, would put them into effect. All this was no secret to the Soviet leadership. The U.S. nuclear threat hung over our country like a sword of Damocles, forcing it into continual efforts to strengthen national security.

More than the security of the Soviet Union was at stake. Shortly before the Caribbean crisis, Cuban counterrevolutionaries landed at the Bay of Pigs, directly supported by the U.S. government. Although this adventure ended in failure, Cuba received a stream of threats. Any responsible historian would acknowledge that these threats might have been followed by new acts of aggression, this time involving the direct participation of American troops. In short, Cuba would almost certainly have suffered the fate that befell Grenada some two decades later.

Robert McNamara says that the Kennedy administration had no such intentions. Let us suppose not. But what of subsequent U.S. administrations? Periodic philippics against the recalcitrant island, White House threats to punish it, calls to invasion from the hawks on Capitol Hill—these became permanent features of American political life. The constant threat hanging over Cuba compelled its leadership to seek ways to ensure its national security.

In other words, the primary cause of the Caribbean crisis was the hostile American policy toward the Soviet Union, Cuba, and other socialist states, a policy calculated sooner or later to destroy them and, until then to keep them in constant fear of nuclear attack.

Still another serious cause of the crisis was the United States' historically colossal advantage in nuclear arms. Among the political and military leadership this advantage engendered a psychology that could be called the arrogance of power. The conviction developed that the United States had the right to encircle the Soviet Union with naval and air bases equipped with nuclear weapons, whereas the Soviet Union could not deploy its nuclear forces anywhere near U.S. territory. These attitudes clearly reflected an unwritten rule that has for millennia dominated relations among states: "Between two equal rights, only force decides."

One can understand the U.S. unwillingness to live with nuclear missiles next door aimed at its territory. But the same reasoning applies to the Soviet Union. Had American politicians been ruled by a single standard, consonant with the spirit and principles of contemporary international law, they would have had to accept Soviet missiles in Cuba as an inevitable if unpleasant fact, or to negotiate with the USSR to rid both nations of the sword of Damocles on a reciprocal basis.

Thus one of the most important causes of the crisis was the American leadership's firm confidence in its military superiority. The unfolding of the crisis in October 1962 forced a genuine rethinking of this conviction; there was a gradual recognition that the correlation of forces had changed and that the United States should meet security guarantees from the other side with equivalent assurances and guarantees.

DURING THE CRISIS: CAUSES
OF ESCALATION

Fyodor Burlatsky

A question worthy of serious analysis is the cause of the escalation of the Cuban crisis during those famous thirteen days. Discovery of the secret deployment of our missiles in Cuba in itself did not force a steady increase in the tension of the conflict. Having discovered our missiles, John Kennedy had various options for response. He chose an open announcement, made on October 22 in the toughest language. He issued what appeared to be an ultimatum and announced the blockade of Cuba.

Of course, this statement seems mild in comparison with the recommendations of several American military and political leaders: an air strike against Soviet military installations. But Kennedy did have another alternative: to try diplomatic means first. He might have deferred public actions until he had informed the Soviet leadership that their preparations to create a missile base in Cuba had been detected and waited for their response. Had Kennedy sent a notification directly to Khrushchev, I am almost 100 percent certain that further escalation of the conflict would have been prevented. Of course, Khrushchev would have tried to set certain conditions regarding the return of our missiles from Cuba. But there would have been an opportunity to resolve the problem by diplomatic means, without the public confrontation that caused such shock waves in world public opinion.

In this regard, I think psychological factors played a large role. Kennedy was shocked by the secret shipping of missiles to Cuba, reflecting differences between American and traditional Russian political cultures. But, in any case, the two political leaders had the right to expect the truth, and only the truth, from each other in the negotiations. This is a most important prerequisite for mutual understanding. Kennedy was probably stunned and personally wounded that Khrushchev would take such a step after their meeting in Vienna.

In my view this was one of the least successful summit meetings of Soviet and American leaders. I have studied the transcripts of their talks and was surprised to see how much attention they devoted to ideological and even philosophical questions concerning the relationship between the two systems—socialist and capitalist—and how little time they spent discussing specific political problems. Perhaps this is why the two leaders came away with less than a fully accurate view of each other.

As a result of the meeting, Khrushchev concluded that Kennedy was still a very young politician, perhaps "too intellectual" to take firm decisions in a crisis. Kennedy, in turn, attached too much significance to Khrushchev's ideological statement, believing that he continued to nurture ideas of "world revolution" and was guided by this philosophy in his practical policy. Kennedy's idea was entirely erroneous; at the Twentieth Party Congress in 1956 it was Khrushchev who announced an abrupt turn in the direction of peaceful coexistence between the two social systems of East and West, who declared the possibility of preventing a world war, and who came out in defense of other countries' peaceful transition to socialism. This is a graphic example of mutual misunderstanding of the motives, objectives, and actions of the other side.

The crisis culminated in the destruction of an American U-2 plane over Cuba and the death of the pilot. Conservatives in the Kennedy administration used this event to whip up psychological tension, and urged the president to take extreme measures, including the bombing of Cuba. There is much speculation about who shot down the American plane. Soviet officers had received strict orders to avoid any action that might provoke the American side in the difficult situation. It was said that the downing of the plane stunned Khrushchev, who feared the situation was escalating out of control. It was crucial to find a way to resolve the problem quickly.

In sum, one can cite a whole series of concrete causes of the escalation of the Caribbean crisis: the secret stationing of missiles on the island, President Kennedy's blockade announcement, the destruction of the U-2 plane, the public exchange of confrontational messages. But there were deeper reasons as well, notably deep-seated mutual distrust. Each side regarded the other as, so to speak, a pirate who was only waiting for the right moment to spring an ambush. Throughout the postwar period, many Western political leaders and representatives of public opinion expected a Russian tank attack against Western Europe, and built their entire strategy on this assumption. The West's proclamation of the right to use nuclear weapons first is connected with this scenario. Similarly, Soviet leaders and representatives of public opinion feared a surprise nuclear strike from the United States, especially before we had nuclear weapons. Nothing of the kind happened. Each side was mistaken about the other's intentions. But in the period of the Caribbean crisis the cold war mentality was still active. The meeting between Khrushchev and Kennedy did not dissipate the former prejudices, but even strengthened mutual suspicion. Fear of a nuclear first strike was the most important factor prompting the escalation.

The ambition of great powers also played a role. The public exchange of messages between Kennedy and Khrushchev unfortunately activated the mechanisms of pressure from the political elite and public opinion of both sides. Both leaders were, of course, concerned with their own roles, personal authority, and prestige. Each was expected to exhibit character and to stand up to the other side. This pressure was especially significant for Kennedy, who had to consider the criticism of hawks within his administration, and the vigorous efforts of Republicans in Congress to portray the president as weak, incapable of opposing communism and actively countering its spread. Pressure from the conservative press added to the confusion, producing an edginess that worked against the taking of considered decisions.

It is unlikely that Khrushchev was subject to serious pressures from inside the Soviet leadership, although he undoubtedly had to deal with alternative proposals regarding practical steps. He also had to consider the position of the Cuban leadership, and especially the fact that Chinese leaders were trying to use the conflict to damage Soviet-American relations and to undermine the personal prestige of the Soviet leader.

During the final stage of the Caribbean crisis, John Kennedy and Nikita Khrushchev acted as genuine world leaders, with profoundly global thinking. Each proceeded from a conviction of the absolute inadmissibility of nuclear war. Khrushchev faced a much more difficult dilemma than Kennedy: to remove the missiles from Cuba under active monitoring by the United States and the world community. He was able to set aside such traditional concerns as national prestige and personal authority and to take the single correct decision that would save the world from catastrophe. We should also give him credit for his diplomatic skill, by which he artfully achieved two extremely important concessions: a U.S. guarantee against a direct or indirect invasion of Cuba, and the removal of the Turkish nuclear base.

President Kennedy deserves credit for understanding in a most difficult situation that the crisis could only be resolved through compromise and mutual concessions. He took a large risk relative to his own authority (which was especially important given the coming elections) when he conveyed through Robert Kennedy the secret promise to liquidate within six months the American base in Turkey. This move, made behind the backs of many ExComm members, the Congress, and the NATO allies, was the best confirmation of something Kennedy had written in his younger years: "The true political figure is the one who is capable, when necessary, of going against the current."[2] Kennedy's decision to guarantee the security of Cuba was made even more difficult by the fact that anti-Cuban sentiment had reached a high point in the United States at that time.

Sergo Mikoyan

Why was the American U-2 surveillance plane shot down over Cuba on October 27, 1962? One might equally well ask why another American U-2 accidentally strayed over Soviet territory on that same day. How could it have violated Soviet airspace at such a tense time? John Kennedy is said to have remarked, "There is always some SOB who doesn't get the word."[3]

Kennedy's explanation applies to many puzzles about Khrushchev's behavior during those critical days. The shooting down of the U-2 seemed to contradict what he had said in his letters to Kennedy; it was tantamount to announcing an intention to reject the proposed agreement. In theory, it could be construed to reflect a political decision by the Soviet Union to take military actions if the United States insisted on its ultimatum that Soviet missiles be removed.

In fact, the downing of the American U-2 was a spontaneous, automatic decision of a commander in a tense circumstance when the plane passed through the zone of fire for two minutes, leaving no time to obtain approval. The officer was trained to think within the limits of military regulations.

McNamara spoke personally with the admiral assigned to organize the blockade of Cuba, emphasizing that the quarantine was a political signal rather than a textbook military operation and ordering him not to shoot without his express permission. What would have happened had McNamara not made this effort, had the president himself not focused attention on preventing error and loss of control? Might the admiral, fully conversant with the military regulations, have sunk a Soviet ship that did not obey commands to stop or let its cargo be examined? And how would Soviet submarines located in the Atlantic have reacted? In prewar conditions, and more so in war, experience shows that the command and control of the actions of those who carry out orders become highly unreliable. The lower in the military hierarchy, the less the reliability. Therefore it is senseless to repeat that an attack on Cuba should not become a reason for a global nuclear conflict. In practice, the smallest careless step of the highest political leaders could lead to catastrophe, or have the effect of an avalanche in the mountains. To push any of the participants into a corner might provoke an action that could not remain unanswered. The geographic range of the crisis, the level and speed of action, would snowball. At some point the two leaders would no longer be able to stop the headlong rush to catastrophe.

And so, having begun as a kind of adventuristic reaction of one superpower to the adventuristic and aggressive behavior of another, the installation of Soviet missiles on Cuba led to a confrontation. Any further adventurism at this point would, in my view, have inevitably led to a catastrophe.

Georgy Shakhnazarov

The impact of the strategic nuclear balance during the Caribbean crisis has been much discussed. At the time, the Soviet Union lagged significantly behind the United States in many parameters of military power—in the number of missiles, warheads, submarines, and bombers. Robert McNamara argues below that the "band" of parity is very wide, and that, in effect, strategic parity existed in 1962. He means that either side could deal a devastating retaliatory strike.

But this condition, it seems to me, is not equivalent to parity. The palpable U.S. strategic advantage led many American specialists to believe that the USSR could inflict a serious but not mortal strike on the United States. They estimated that the number killed might not exceed one-quarter of the U.S. population. Deplorable as such losses would be, the country would survive and be able to inflict a second strike completely destroying the USSR. Ever since the Caribbean crisis, the Pentagon has continued to develop and refine plans for a preemptive strike against the USSR. The United States has resisted the obligation not to use nuclear weapons first.

It is generally recognized that full military-strategic parity was reached sometime in the late 1970s or early 1980s. Today parity is measured not only and not simply by the criterion of devastating second-strike capability, but by approximate equality of the two nations' military-strategic forces (given the obvious differences in their structures). The American recognition of parity provided a starting point for a reappraisal of the military-strategic situation as a whole, and then for joint efforts to lower the level of parity.

During the Caribbean crisis, the American leadership began to realize that no political objectives can be achieved by unleashing nuclear war. This process has continued, with its ups and downs, to this day. At the 1985 Geneva meeting between Mikhail Gorbachev and Ronald Reagan, this truth was officially acknowledged for the first time and recorded in the joint statement.

LESSONS OF THE CRISIS

Fyodor Burlatsky

One lesson of the crisis relates to the role of uncontrollable actions and bureaucratic distortion of government decisions. John Kennedy reportedly gave the order to dismantle the American base in Turkey several months before the Caribbean crisis, but it was never carried out. Khrushchev, of course, knew nothing about Kennedy's order. We can only regret that the American administration did not inform the Soviet leadership of its firm decision to liquidate the base. Perhaps this information would have prevented many of the subsequent events. To a large degree the Cuban crisis was provoked by the people who failed to carry out Kennedy's order to liquidate the base— illustrating the real threat posed by actions outside the control of governmental decision makers, and the possibility that unintended conflicts and crises could result from decisions taken by middle-level executives.

What have we learned from the Caribbean crisis? First, the most important lesson is to avoid by all means a direct military confrontation between the United States and USSR. In other words, do not allow a nuclear crisis to emerge. Second, there follows the imperative for truthfulness and full sharing of information concerning any possible situation that might provoke a crisis. Adventurism, unexpected actions, efforts to drive the other into a corner, and provocation should be absolutely excluded. Under no circumstances should American and Soviet soldiers fire at each other. Third, the modernization of the hot line between the leadership of the USSR and the United States, and the establishment of risk reduction centers have particular significance, for these steps provide modern means of information exchange and a direct communication link between the military and foreign departments of the two sides. Fourth, the direct contacts between Kennedy and Khrushchev, and the more recent Gorbachev-Reagan summits have shown the great advantages of this form of political diplomacy. Such meetings are vitally necessary, no matter what the political weather, even in precrisis and crisis periods. It is especially important to use direct diplomatic channels before public appearances, which make the settlement of political conflicts more difficult. Finally, conflict in our time can only be regulated through compromise and mutual concessions, understanding each other's interests, as well as the global interests of humanity. The threat of apocalypse has made senseless many traditional values, methods, and views in international relations.

The Caribbean crisis demonstrated the need to discard the old way of thinking and embark on a new one adequate to the threats of the nuclear age, to the interests of survival and general security. A question arises, however: why, after the severe jolt of the Caribbean crisis, did the arms race gain new strength? Undoubtedly, the death of Kennedy and the dismissal of Khrushchev from the Soviet leadershp played a major role in this regard. It sometimes seems that Providence, according to its own laws or purposes, takes from the political arena those figures who are capable of preventing the destruction of humanity.

The way out is simple and yet extremely complex. It lies in the transition from traditional thinking to the new thinking proclaimed with such force by Mikhail Gorbachev. This means new thinking about military strategy and about universal security. It means new thinking by Americans about Soviet people and by Soviet people about Americans. It means a firm orientation toward the implementation of long-term plans for the reduction and elimination of nuclear weapons, as well as other instruments of human destruction. It means a return to the humanism of the best thinkers of the past, the development of a new humanism based on tolerance, reason, and amity among the various civilizations that coexist on our small planet.

Sergo Mikoyan

The Cuban missile crisis was one of the most important events in the history of international relations. To date, the United States has fulfilled its obligations as part of the agreement achieved on October 28, 1962, not to attack Cuba. But occasionally Western scholars argue that the condition of inspection was not fulfilled.[4] There are serious and weighty objections against such a thesis, as a brief summary of the postcrisis history shows.

First of all, the White House failed to recognize the threat to Cuba as the cause of the emplacement of the missiles, nor did it see the necessity of conducting negotiations with Cuba once the crisis began. To expedite matters, Moscow agreed to conduct such negotiations without the direct participation of Cuba. Ambassador Alekseev, however, kept Fidel Castro constantly informed about the negotiations and transmitted to Moscow the opinion of the Cuban government on various questions. One of the arguments against negotiations with Cuba, even after the direct danger of war had been eliminated, was that there had been no official agreement between the USSR and Cuba—the missiles were installed secretly.

But what would have happened if the USSR and Cuba had openly signed an agreement to install the missiles? There might have been such a stir in the United States that the White House would have reached exactly the same decision about a quarantine, though perhaps with less support in the United Nations. Besides, there was a Soviet agreement with Cuba, and the sites proposed for inspection were located on Cuban territory. In a memo sent to Anastas Mikoyan after the agreement on the missiles had been reached, Adlai Stevenson added the IL-28 bombers supplied to Cuban armed forces to the list of offensive arms subject to removal from Cuba. The memo also mentioned torpedo boats, which in general had no relation to offensive arms. Exasperated, Mikoyan immediately gave the letter back to V. V. Kuznetsov and said, "Return this to Stevenson and tell him that I not only am not planning to consider these additions, but in general I consider that I never received this letter." All the same, the content of the letter was transmitted to Moscow by diplomatic channels, and Khrushchev gave in. In the interests of peace, the USSR did not object. And Cuba, albeit with difficulty, agreed to the terms added by the American side after the initial agreement.

Fidel Castro announced to U Thant and publicly that Cuba would not allow any inspections on its territory. Similarly the USSR could not agree to on-board inspections of Soviet ships, whether conducted by Americans or UN representatives. On November 1–2, 1962, Anastas Mikoyan, first deputy chairman of the Council of Ministers, was in New York en route to Cuba. To prepare for the difficult negotiations that awaited him, he held a preliminary discussion of the details of the Kennedy-Khrushchev agreement with Adlai Stevenson and John McCloy, the individuals authorized by the U.S. president. It was John McCloy, aware of the Cuban and Soviet positions, who proposed an inspection of Cuban territory from the air, and of Soviet ships from the decks of American ships at a sufficiently close range to see the missiles, which would be located in plain view on the decks. It was completely clear that McCloy had agreed in advance with President Kennedy on this proposal. Those were precisely the details of the agreement—proposed by the American side.

At the end of November 1962, Mikoyan arrived in Washington from Cuba and had a long discussion with Kennedy, who did not say then that the agreement had not been fulfilled. The discussion was occasionally sharp, however, despite their personally amicable relationship. Raymond Garthoff asserts that in the course of those negotiations, the president said that the agreement about inspections remained unfulfilled relative to the nonintroduction of missiles to Cuba in the future.[2] This is absolutely incorrect. Garthoff refers to his own information about these negotiations, the text of which remains unpublished at the time of this writing.

According to Mikoyan, whose account of the negotiations was recorded immediately afterward, the U.S. president stated that the condition of inspection would not be fulfilled *if the American side was unable to conduct aerial surveillance of the territory of Cuba*, which required unhindered flights of U-2 aircraft over its territory. Mikoyan protested that such surveillance would be a violation of international law and an infringement of the sovereignty of Cuban airspace and its national dignity. Kennedy said that although he had no wish to assault the national dignity of Cuba, he saw no alternative. Mikoyan suggested a way out: aerial photos could be taken from planes flying over the open sea along the shores of Cuba. According to Soviet information, the United States possessed sufficient reconnaissance aircraft to carry out this plan. Kennedy asserted that it was not technically possible, however. He granted that low-altitude flights would affront the national dignity of Cuba, but emphasized that he was talking about flights at a very high altitude, which would be difficult to notice.

Thus President Kennedy considered that the conditions of inspection would be fulfilled by aerial surveillance. In any case the United

States has acquired the capability, through satellites and modern photo reconnaissance technology, to photograph practically any region of the earth and even to determine, for example, the make of an automobile. So to continue speaking about the nonfulfillment of the conditions for inspection, and citing President Kennedy in this regard, is absolutely without legal basis.

In November 1963, Anastas Mikoyan again arrived in the United States, to attend the funeral of John Kennedy. The new president, Lyndon Johnson, twice affirmed in a meeting with Mikoyan that the United States remained and would remain true to the obligation it took upon itself as a result of the agreement reached in October-November 1962.

Yet if one can believe the journalist Tad Szulc, at the end of 1964–1965 the Central Intelligence Agency, with the approval of the same President Johnson, developed a plan to kill Fidel Castro and then to conduct a rapid invasion by hired mercenaries, apparently to be given much greater support than at the Bay of Pigs.[5] The plan was set aside only in connection with the intervention in the Dominican Republic in April 1965; then the war in Vietnam clearly finished the matter. More than once, however, even in the 1970s, the question arose, under various pretexts, of whether the Soviet-American agreement was binding—for example, in connection with the short visits, for technical reasons, of Soviet submarines to Cuban ports (not identified by the United States as a violation of the agreement).

Then suddenly, on September 14, 1983, President Reagan tossed out the remark that the agreement was "annulled." Soon his friend William Clements, a former governor of Texas and a member of the Kissinger Commission on Central America, included in the commission's findings his "personal" addition that in general there had never been an agreement or understanding. In February 1984, he developed this idea in an appearance at a luncheon in Dallas. Wayne Smith, who was present at the luncheon, writes about it in his book *The Closest of Enemies*. Contradicting himself, Clements added that the agreement had not been fulfilled by Cuba.

Both international law and political considerations based purely on common sense argue against any attempt to deactivate the agreement. One should not take every sentence from the letters of Kennedy and Khrushchev as articles of an international treaty. The United States, for example, would not agree with everything in Khrushchev's letters. In the same way, the Soviet Union cannot endorse every sentence of Kennedy's letter. For example, in connection with the inspection, he wrote that the United States should have a guarantee that missiles would not be acquired by Cuba in the future. Does the United States then have a right for all time to inspect the holds of all Soviet ships going to Cuba? Or, if it does not make such inspections, to describe the agreement as unfulfilled?

The very statement of the question shows its absurdity. At the same time, if we treat the letters as we do political documents, you will find they contain few if any specific words about inspections. It is stated that an inspection should be "appropriate," and a guarantee for the future should be "suitable." These words open the way for detailed, concrete agreements—as were developed in practice in the framework of the U.S.-USSR-Cuba triangle. So we speak about the lessons of the crisis—but it turns out that we forget them very quickly.

Today, as never before, it is important to assimilate the positive lessons from our shared history. Some have to do with how we should extricate ourselves from an acute, dangerous crisis. They speak of the kind of patience, caution, cool-headedness, and wisdom that was manifested then by many important government officials. We must learn these lessons, lest a crisis bring us to catastrophe. But, of course, the most important lesson of all is not to allow situations to reach a similar level of acuteness. It was not without reason that the hot line (sometimes called the "red telephones") was installed in the Kremlin and in the White House in precisely those years. All these lessons can be summed up by saying that the Cuban missile crisis forced us to agree that the fate of humanity is more important than winning on some chessboard, which is how the political map of our planet (and now even the space that surrounds it) is sometimes regarded. This outcome of the crisis should be kept in mind as a promising direction in the psychology of any foreign policy action.

The agreement reached in 1962 turned out to be one of the first elements of a new approach to regional and global conflicts—the approach that, beginning in 1985, began to be formulated in Gorbachev's concept of new political thinking.

Georgy Shakhnazarov

There is good reason to believe that the Caribbean crisis, which brought the world to the edge of nuclear conflict, has been a decisive factor in averting a nuclear conflagration over the subsequent twenty-five years. Like the fever induced by inoculation with an immunizing vaccine, the moment of fear and illumination experienced in October 1962 has mobilized the body's defenses.

The first and main lesson of the Caribbean crisis should also be seen in a broader context. October 1962, like a flash of lightning, revealed the most essential feature of international relations in the nuclear age—*the impossibility of providing national security at the expense of the security of others.* But it took a quarter-century for this idea to be developed into a theoretical concept and made government policy. In the documents of the Twenty-seventh Party Congress, in the speeches by Mikhail Gorbachev, and in documents submitted by the Soviet Union to the United Nations, the quintessence of the new political thinking found expression: the growing interdependence of states makes it necessary to create a comprehensive system of international security, which would allow humanity to bypass the minefield of our days and enter a nonnuclear, nonviolent twenty-first century.

Besides analyzing the causes and the actual course of the Caribbean crisis, it is also important to assess the actions of political leaders who played a key role in the crisis. Had Shakespeare based a dramatic production on these events, he would have portrayed them as a clash of characters and shown how the dramatis personae were able to rise above their polar differences in world views, mindsets, life experiences, and many other qualities, cross the barrier of ideological intolerance, and understand the necessity of a compromise.

The political wisdom exhibited by the main characters of the Caribbean drama—Khrushchev, Kennedy, Castro—can be seen as an example of new thinking in the nuclear era, though at the time nobody gave particular thought to such lofty theoretical concepts or even to the fact that, perhaps for the first time, the fate of all humanity hinged on the decisions of the leaders of the two most powerful states with different sociopolitical systems.

One final lesson of the Caribbean crisis has to do with the time factor. The paradox is that in the late 1980s it would be extraordinarily dangerous to take as a model the methods that were successful in settling a conflict in October 1962. In other words, it is a lesson by negative example.

The Caribbean crisis unfolded over the course of two weeks, or, in a wider interpretation, an even longer period. During this time there were fits of anger on both sides, and confusion gave way to desperate resolve. Had decisions been taken in those moments, history might have ended with a tragic finale. The reserve of time helped the leaders to cool off, to think through again all the possible consequences of their actions, to consult not only with their inner circle, but with a wide circle of experts, and to exchange views with allies.

Today we have no such reserve of time. At best the time left for decisions will be counted by hours, or even minutes, provided those decisions are to be made by people and not computers. In other words, reliance on nuclear deterrence becomes illusory. This is one of the strongest arguments in favor of eliminating nuclear weapons.

But even if the method of settling the Caribbean crisis is not directly applicable to an emergency that plays itself out in hours, it is highly instructive with regard to the political-diplomatic procedures used then. An analysis of the details of the crisis brings us to a general conclusion: *the more stable and broader the constant communication between the parties, the greater the chances of controlling any unexpected crisis situation that flares up.*

In recent years much has been done to give a regular character to contacts between the governments of the USSR and the United States. Besides meetings at the summit and high political levels, experts consult on questions of arms control; citizens interact through telebridges, peace marches, and other means; and scholars of international relations hold symposia and conferences.

During the celebration of the seventieth anniversary of the October Revolution, I had occasion to describe to Fidel Castro the October 1987 U.S.-Soviet conference on the Caribbean crisis. The Cuban leader stressed the importance of a profound analysis of the dramatic events of October 1962, and of its lessons, which have not lost their significance today.

NOTES

1. Robert F. Kennedy, *Thirteen Days: A Memoir of the Cuban Missile Crisis* (New York: Norton, 1971), p. 76.
2. Dean Rusk has told us that John Kennedy had made preparations to promise publicly to eliminate a U.S. nuclear base in Turkey. The need for a public statement was obviated when the Soviet leadership, satisfied by the president's secret promise to eliminate the Turkish base and the public guar-

antee of nonaggression against Cuba, made public its decision to withdraw the missiles on October 28. It was a courageous decision. Both Khrushchev and Kennedy proved to be up to the demands of the extraordinary situation of a nuclear crisis. They saved the world from disaster.

3. Ibid.

4. Raymond Garthoff, "Karibskii krizis (Kubinskii raketnyi krizis) 1962 g.: razmyshleniia amerikanskogo uchastnika" [The Caribbean Crisis (Cuban Missile Crisis) of 1962: Reflections of an American Participant), *Latinskaia amerika* (Latin America) no. 1, 1988] pp. 40–58.

5. Tad Szulc, *Fidel, A Critical Portrait* (New York: William Morrow and Co., 1986).

AMERICAN VIEW

Robert McNamara

In 1962 the members of President Kennedy's ExComm wondered: What in God's name did Khrushchev think he was doing putting those missiles in Cuba? We did not have much of an answer then, and we doubted we ever would. For the next twenty-five years we kept wondering.

At the conference marking the twenty-fifth anniversary of the event, American members of the ExComm met with Soviets to discuss the crisis candidly for the first time. As our Soviet colleagues Fyodor Burlatsky, Sergo Mikoyan, and Georgy Shakhnazarov have already pointed out, at the time of the crisis both countries held profound misperceptions. Mikoyan accurately contrasts U.S. and Soviet assumptions leading up to the crisis. We were ignorant as to each other's vital interests, intentions, and probable responses to military action.

From the Cuban missile crisis, we can draw several lessons. The most important is that we must do all we can to avoid such crises. Crisis management is too uncertain and difficult to rely on; we must keep crises from arising in the first place. How? Two principles will help. First, each side must be clear as to its interests and state them succinctly. Our failure to do this well in 1962 contributed to the Soviets' miscalculation. Second, over time we must address a basic source of friction between our two countries: deep-seated mistrust. With Gorbachev we have already made progress in reducing tension in East-West relations, but more can be done, particularly with respect to superpower involvement in regional conflicts.

The second main lesson of the crisis is that we must avoid even small risk of a nuclear confrontation. Thus we must improve the conventional force balance, either by negotiation—Gorbachev has indicated a willingness to engage in such negotiations—or by building NATO's conventional forces.

The third main lesson is that the band of nuclear parity is very, very wide. Several years ago Dr. Sagdeev, then director of the Soviet

Institute for Space Research, asked me when our countries had achieved parity. I said, "I don't know when we reached parity, but in one sense it existed in October 1962 despite an imbalance in strategic warheads of 5,000 to 300." He was astonished, but I believe I was correct. In 1962, neither side could have used its nuclear forces to achieve military or political ends. Had we launched our 5,000 warheads against the Soviet Union, a sufficient number of their 300 would have survived to inflict unacceptable damage on the United States. For that reason alone, we were deterred from using or threatening to use such force. Recognizing that parity extends across a broad range of force levels, not just at a point of numerical equivalence, will affect our decisions with respect to arms control agreements, verification procedures, and military strategy.

In addition to these general lessons, the events of the Cuban missile crisis point to several ways of improving our crisis management capabilities. First, we must remember that human beings are fallible—prone to misjudgment, misinformation, miscalculation, and emotion. On the basis of that fact, I have formulated McNamara's Law: "In the nuclear age, it is impossible to predict with a high degree of certainty the effects of the use of military force by the superpowers, because of the risks of accident, misperception, miscalculation, and inadvertence."

Second, we must ensure that crisis managers are adequately prepared. They need to think in advance about how to deal with crises, especially ones that involve even a remote possibility of a nuclear response. One problem is that we have no institutional memory. Each new administration starts all over again. I came to the Pentagon straight from Ford Motor Company, knowing next to nothing about the application of military force—particularly nuclear force—and the risks associated with it. This is very dangerous, as the Bay of Pigs illustrates. In that case, we had no experience, and we did not know what we were doing. Some of us learned very quickly; still, it is dangerous to give authority to individuals who are totally illiterate about handling superpower relations and managing international crises. The situation has not changed. Georgy Shakhnazarov asked me this fall if the Reagan administration had been adequately briefed by the prior administration on superpower relations and crisis management. I am confident the answer is no.

The third lesson in crisis management is more specific: take time to plan. Thank God we did so in the Cuban missile crisis. I agree with my colleague George Ball that had we been forced to decide within the first forty-eight hours, we might have chosen an air strike. The consequences would have been incalculable.

The fourth lesson is to provide the president with knowledgeable associates. He and his advisers must draw on the experience of informed people. I came to the Pentagon on the condition that I be able to choose associates to tutor me (the other part of my schooling was learning from just plain being wrong umpteen times). During the Cuban missile crisis our advisers included Chip Bohlen, Tommy Thompson (who was there twenty-four hours a day), and George Kennan, people who were real students of the Soviet Union. They were the unsung heroes of the crisis.

The fifth lesson is to maintain communication. Anatoly Dobrynin played a crucial role, not only in the Cuban missile crisis, but during the whole time he was in Washington. He was an extraordinarily sophisticated diplomat.

The sixth lesson is always to look at a problem or action from the adversary's point of view. For instance, our decision in the 1970s to MIRV our missiles quadrupled the number of warheads in the inventories of the two superpowers. We failed to put ourselves in the Soviets' shoes and anticipate the obvious consequence: that the Soviets would follow suit. In the middle of the Cuban missile crisis, in contrast, we did try to recognize the Soviet perspective. Both the U.S. and the Soviet leaders rapidly became more sensitive to each other's positions, which significantly contributed to the successful outcome.

The final lesson is not to force the adversary into a corner. Do not force them into taking some desperate action. Always leave them a way out.

Where does that leave us today? When we add the potential for human error to the availability of nuclear weapons, the consequences of mistakes become unthinkable. Nuclear weapons cannot be used as such; they serve only to deter a potential opponent from their use. This fact argues strongly for a new understanding between superpowers. Burlatsky speaks of the need for a new way of thinking that matches the threats of the nuclear age. Mikoyan says we must never again let tensions rise to the boiling point. Shakhnazarov advocates more frequent and comprehensive communication between our two powers to limit misperceptions. They are all saying what I have come to believe: that the best hope for survival in a world of nuclear weapons lies in avoiding crisis—crisis avoidance deserves much more attention than it has received.

In the last twenty-five years we have made little progress in applying that lesson. Grave misperceptions and deep-seated mistrust still exist between our countries. We must seek to reduce them. From the American side, as Graham Allison develops in the conclusion to this book, we ought to probe Gorbachev's sincerity when he says he wants to reduce East-West political tensions. In particular, we should seek to reduce the numerical imbalance in the conventional forces in Europe. Though for twenty years we have overestimated the military capabilities of Soviet conventional forces, the Warsaw Pact does have a two-to-one superiority to NATO in tanks, artillery, and attack helicopters. This imbalance supports the view of those in the West who believe the Soviets are maintaining an aggressive posture. I think Gorbachev has recognized the contradiction between his words and reality, and as a result the Soviets have been suggesting a move toward "reasonable sufficiency" of forces, as opposed to superiority, and the adoption of a defensive, not offensive, posture. In addition, the general secretary has said he will accept "asymmetrical" cuts in East-West military forces to achieve those objectives.

Today we have an unparalleled opportunity—the greatest since the end of World War II—to test Soviet intentions and move toward a better understanding. The stage is set for the new administration to probe the potential for a dramatic shift in East-West relations. General Secretary Gorbachev has indicated he is willing to move in that direction. For the world's sake, let's take him up on it.

5 NUCLEAR LEARNING AND THE EVOLUTION OF U.S.-SOVIET SECURITY COOPERATION

Joseph S. Nye, Jr.

Current political concerns have always strongly influenced theories of international relations. The early 1980s proved no exception. With worsening U.S.-Soviet relations and increased fears of nuclear war, military studies again became the central focus of attention. The study of interdependence continued, but tended to be applied only to the international political economy. Thus the field of international politics split into two literatures: one in military security, rooted in the realist tradition, and the other in international political economy, incorporating some insights from the liberal tradition. Each tended to ignore the concerns of the other. Only recently have there been efforts to reunite the two fields.[1]

SECURITY REGIMES

Most theory about international regimes has been developed in the area of international political economy, with little recognition of its

I am indebted to Alexander George for permission to use the papers of the Stanford Project on U.S.-Soviet Efforts to Cooperate on Security Matters; to attendees at the Harvard Avoiding Nuclear War Project Conference in July 1986; to Hayward Alker, James Blight, Robert Bowie, Peter Haas, Stephan Haggard, Stanley Hoffmann, Robert Jervis, Robert Keohane, William Ury, Ted Warner, and David Welch for detailed comment, and to William Jarosz for both comments and research assistance. An earlier version of this chapter was published in *International Organization* 41 (3), Summer 1987.

potential application to security studies. The concept of a regime—a range of principles, norms, rules, and procedures constraining states' behavior and focusing actors' expectations with respect to a given issue—became identified with liberal international relations theory, although it could also fit easily with realist theory.[2] Egoistic self-interest can lead states to create regimes in security as well as economic issues. It may be more difficult to ascertain intentions, and the stakes at risk in case of defection may be higher for most security issues than for most economic issues, but such differences are matters of degree.[3]

A few interesting attempts have applied the concept of international regimes to the U.S.-Soviet relationship.[4] But the concept has often been used loosely. Practices and policies were not always distinguished from norms and rules. We are told that the absence of nuclear war is explained in part by a regime of primitive rules ("no direct conflict between the superpowers," "no use of nuclear weapons," "respect for spheres of influence"). But the rules are more tacit than explicit. Their existence is inferred from the absence of war, which is, in turn, attributed to the existence of such rules. Thus this concept risks tautology by using the same evidence to establish both the cause and the effect of the regime.

Robert Jervis has attacked such efforts to categorize the U.S.-Soviet security relationship as a regime. If cooperation can be explained on the basis of short-run self-interest, such as avoiding the disproportionate costs of nuclear war, then regimes become a redundant explanation. In Jervis's view, "The links between states' restraint and their self-interest are too direct and unproblematic to invoke the concept [of a regime]."[5] Moreover, he argues, the participating nations' preference for the status quo is a necessary condition for a security regime, and the United States' and the Soviet Union's different ideological interpretations of events make the independent restraining force of rules highly improbable.

However, the skeptics' judgment may be premature. The critiques are justified when applied to the overall U.S.-Soviet relationship, but the existence of regimes is a matter of degree. There are variations in scope, adherence, duration, and degree of institutionalization. Even in the economic area, regimes are far from perfect. Tariffs, quotas, and protectionist sentiments persist, but the GATT (General Agreement on Tariffs and Trade) regime has still had a significant effect on international trading behavior.

Rather than debate whether the overall U.S.-Soviet relationship can be categorized as a security regime, we should view it as a patchwork quilt or a mosaic of subissues, some characterized by rules and institutions we would call a regime and others not. Differentiating by subissue facilitates comparative observations of the effect of regimes on state behavior. It also allows us to raise interesting questions about the dynamics of both learning and redefining interests, about how learning may lead to the creation of regimes and how regimes may promote further learning.

Skeptics may object that it makes no sense to use the regime concept when dealing with the relations between a status quo power and a revolutionary power. Skeptics say that the notion of a regime is a status quo concept, which attracts U.S. theorists because they are attracted to stability.[6] From a Marxist point of view, if regimes delay dynamic forces of history, there can be no agreement upon international regimes. Over the last decade the Soviets have made increasing use of the term.[7] However, the critical question is whether Soviet *behavior* can be consistent with the rules and institutions of a regime.

In this regard, one must consider the nature of Soviet goals and the role of ideology in the Soviet system. The best judgment must be mixed. To describe the Soviet Union as a rigidly ideological and totalitarian society does not fit current reality. Seweryn Bialer sees the society as not yet traditional authoritarian, but no longer totalitarian. As Richard Pipes describes, its leadership has become bureaucratized and its ideology has eroded.[8] The role of the party and state in mobilizing the society has greatly diminished since the Stalinist days, when the concept of totalitarianism was originally formulated.

At the same time, ideology still plays a role in legitimizing the Soviet political elite and in providing many categories through which they approach the world. Within the last decade, however, Western concepts have been incorporated into Soviet thinking about international relations. Marxist categories have not been discarded, but have been supplemented by more flexible concepts and categories. Joanne Gowa and Nils Wessell argue that "as the USSR acquired a stake in the stable operation of the international political system and particularly as it relied on treaties as an instrument of its foreign policy, its leadership came to value the role international agreements play in the defense of established interests."[9] The Soviet view of international politics is far more differentiated and complex today than it was in Stalin's day. For example, it is hard to imagine a Soviet leader in 1989 abolishing an entire institute of world economy as Stalin did simply because he was displeased by its accurate but optimistic description of the prospects of the capitalist economies.[10] Mikhail Gorbachev's "new thinking" in foreign policy is rooted in a longer evolution of Soviet thinking about nuclear and international affairs.

Nor is it helpful to see the Soviet Union as a purely revolutionary or purely status quo actor in international politics. There is often a revolutionary and expansive tone to Soviet foreign policy pronouncements, and sometimes to Soviet behavior. But the latter is far more cautious and risk averse than the former. Support for proletarian revolutions has always come second to the safety of the Soviet state. In Europe, which the Soviets still see as the heart of the global balance of power, the Soviets tend to be a status quo, rather than a revolutionary, actor in the short term of decades. In a sense, both the United States and the Soviet Union were the great winners of World War II. Neither is eager to reverse the partition that took the German problem off the front burner of international politics. Neither wants a nuclearized Germany. Neither has made strenuous efforts to reverse the de facto division of Europe into spheres of relative interest.

If Hitler's Germany is the polar example of a revolutionary world power for which the concept of security regime is totally meaningless, then clearly the Soviet Union is considerably closer to the center of the continuum between revolutionary and status quo powers. Caspar Weinberger did not see "any real change or any real possibility of modification of their basic policies," but this need not prevent limited cooperation on security regimes.[11] Such cooperation can be based on risk aversion without requiring agreement on the long-term course of history. In the words of Brent Scowcroft, "the Soviets, whatever their view of history and the 'inevitable outcome' which 'history' promises—are very cautious and very conservative."[12] On this basis, cooperation on security is possible, though it will remain limited by ideology and competition.

LEARNING

Perception of national interests may change in several ways. The most obvious occurs after domestic shifts in power. An election, or coup, or even generational change can bring to power leaders with quite different perceptions of national interest. In other words, some changes in "national interest" depend not upon new affective or cognitive views in the society at large, but merely on changes of political elites. Such political change may occur because of domestic issues largely unrelated to foreign policy. National interest may also be redefined through normative change. The practices or interests of one period become downgraded or even illegitimate in a later period. Changed views of slavery or colonialism are examples.

A third way in which national interests may change is through cognitive change or learning. In this sense, to learn is to develop knowledge by study or experience. New information alters prior beliefs about the world. Learning often involves a shift from overly simple generalizations to "complex, integrated understandings grounded in realistic attention to detail."[13] Learning occurs internationally when "new knowledge is used to redefine the content of the national interest. Awareness of newly understood causes of unwanted effects often results in the adoption of different, and more effective, means to attain one's ends."[14] In such instances, a simple power or pressure model of policy change may be highly misleading. To take a case from my personal experience, in the mid-1970s, the United States wanted France to cancel its sale of a plutonium reprocessing plant to Pakistan. France refused for some time on the grounds that the plant was for civil purposes. But France decided to cancel the sale in 1977 when the United States provided new information showing that the plant would be misused. Most press accounts attributed the change to U.S. arm-twisting, but they were wrong.

The alteration of beliefs by new information does not always increase effectiveness. Sometimes new information can be misleading or wrongly applied. Misread "lessons of history" and inappropriate analogies have often prevented leaders from attaining their goals.[15] Large macrohistorical analogies (as to "Munich" or "Vietnam"), which are laden with emotional and domestic political content, can be particularly misleading. Neither individuals nor societies are clean slates. New information affects prior beliefs, but its reception and interpretation are also affected by those prior beliefs. The extent and accuracy of learning depends upon the strength of the prior beliefs and the quantity and quality of the new information.[16] Some beliefs may be so strong that new information is ignored, and no learning, or only highly distorted learning, occurs. Psychological studies of perception and misperception help us to understand such barriers to learning, but so do political and institutional factors. Learning is often blocked or distorted by affective and power variables. Russell Leng has shown, for example, that in crisis bargaining, experiential learning from the last crisis is not a powerful predictor of behavior in the next crisis until it is combined with prior beliefs about the importance of demonstrating power and resolve.[17]

Learning can be a slippery concept, for two reasons. One problem is the tendency to build effectiveness into the definition. For simple situations, this connotation is intuitively obvious. It seems odd to say that one has "learned" that two plus two equals five. But the situation is different with complex social phenomena. The Keynesian revolution in economics meant that some "laws" learned in the 1920s were wrong in the 1930s. Some economists today believe that early Keynesian formulations about inflation were far too simple. The effectiveness of newly accepted cognitive beliefs is sometimes discovered only after great delay, and sometimes not at all. A second problem is that the notion of learning has positive connotations for many people: when the observer approves of the new conception of self-interest, it is called "learning"; disliked changes are not. But by my definition, negative, as well as positive learning, can occur. The question is whether the new information or skills have enabled the actors to achieve their purposes better, regardless of whether the observer likes those purposes or not. Of course, choices of definition are to some extent arbitrary, but the danger of building effectiveness and positive value into the definition of learning is that it inhibits one's ability to observe variation. The spare definition chosen here is designed to avoid these pitfalls, and provides a more useful research tool in an important but murky area.

There are also different degrees of learning along a continuum of ends-means relationships, from very simple to highly complex. Simple learning uses new information merely to adapt the means without altering any deeper goals in the ends-means chain. The actor simply uses a different instrument to attain the same goal. Complex learning, by contrast, involves recognition of conflicts among means and goals in causally complicated situations, and leads to new priorities and tradeoffs.[18] Simple learning is relatively easy for an observer to assess, but complex learning can be elusive when deeper goals may have changed. This distinction helps us to avoid needless semantic disputes over whether or not changes in behavior are examples of learning. For instance, most changes in nuclear behavior are adaptations to changed circumstances. Only a few involve the readjustment of goals and the development of new norms. Both types of learning are important, but complex learning may be more so. At the same time, complex learning is sometimes difficult to ascertain objectively because perceptions and ideology play a larger role in assessing consequences when human affairs have long and complex causal chains. Thus complex learning often involves evaluative ambiguity, and we must be explicit about the values involved.

The Bay of Pigs episode in 1961 helps illustrate the distinctions. Khrushchev seems to have learned (incorrectly) that Kennedy would respond weakly, and this interpretation may have led him to the risky actions that brought on the Berlin and Cuban missile crises. Kennedy seems to have learned very important but simple lessons about managing bureaucracy and crises. Whether he "failed" to learn more complex lessons, which would have effectively altered his goals in Cuba, is more controversial.[19] In any case there would be a higher ideological evaluative component in assessing whether complex learning led to greater or lesser effectiveness in the achievement of his higher-priority goals.

Some events seem to have a larger effect on leaders' learning than others. Robert Jervis argues that early firsthand experiences are particularly important. He also notes the power of analogies and overgeneralization when leaders do not have the experience of alternative explanations. They usually have sharper reactions to failure than to learning about the limits of success.[20] Sometimes nothing fails like success.

Finally, individual learning is a necessary, but insufficient, basis for organizational learning. Societies and governments are complex entities. Not everyone learns the same lessons or at the same rate. Shifts in social structure and political power determine whose learning matters. In organizations, there must be an institutional memory and procedures that affect old and new members throughout the organization. In James Rosenau's terms, they are pools of habits.[21] As John Steinbruner points out, organizations tend to divide complex problems and reduce uncertainty so that their cybernetic learning is slower and more constrained than analytic causal learning.[22] Finally, in societies, one needs to understand not only the social and generational divisions over the interpretation of common experiences, but also the transmission belts between mass public opinion, societal groups, and political elites.

Skeptics may argue that we know too little about internal Soviet processes to be able to apply such theories of learning. Certainly the secretive nature of Soviet society makes this task difficult, but it is not impossible. In terms of the simple learning criterion, one can observe Soviet responses to experience and new information. With regard to complex learning, one can see glimpses of more sophisticated thought, which goes deeper into the chain of ends-means relationships even if it does not challenge ultimate ideological goals. As Thane Gustafson argues, "there is evidence from many different fields that the scope and quality of specialists' advice to policy makers . . . have increased."[23] Alexander Dallin sees "a learning process that has led to growing sophistication and 'emancipation' from doctrinal stereotypes on the part of a relatively small number of members of the intellectual and political elite. . . ."[24] Rose Gottemoeller notes an increased complexity of Soviet decision making for arms control.[25]

Soviet writings about nuclear weapons in world politics have also become more detailed and sophisticated.[26] Arkady Shevchenko described the strategem by which Foreign Minister Andrei Gromyko involved the reluctant Soviet military in arms control negotiations. He lobbied to have rising young officers placed on the Soviet delegation and insisted on a unique procedure by which all seven delegates had to sign cables to Moscow. "'It's hard to discuss the subject with the military,' Gromyko told me, 'but the more contact they have with the Americans, the easier it will be to turn our soldiers into something more than just martinets.'"[27]

The Soviets tend to understate the degree to which their positions change and to stress continuity almost as much as Americans emphasize evolution and change. Organizational learning is likely to be slower in centralized systems with limited access to outside information and a concern for doctrinal continuity. But if the Soviets are slower to learn, Americans may be quicker to forget. Because of the frequent turnover of political officials, the American government has a weak institutional memory, and new leaders often have to relearn old lessons.

NUCLEAR LEARNING

One difficulty in evaluating nuclear learning is the uncertainties of deterrence. No one knows exactly what weapons are necessary for deterrence. Moreover, deterrence of conventional war or political aggrandizement demands capability and credibility greater than is needed to deter a strike against one's homeland. Thus, much of what passes for nuclear knowledge rests upon elaborate hypothetical argument, abstractions based on assumptions about rational actors or the other nation's unknown intentions, and simple intuitions. The ambiguous structure of nuclear knowledge makes it difficult for new information to alter prior beliefs. Obviously, this combination leaves much room for spurious knowledge, false learning, and occasional forgetting as coalitions shift in domestic politics. The uncertainties of deterrence also block transitions from simple to more complex learning. And because of differences in political and military cultures, divergent prior beliefs tend to lead each country to learn different lessons from new information. But sometimes common lessons are learned nevertheless.

Over the past four decades, new information about nuclear weapons and experiences with their handling have altered prior beliefs. In several areas, a core of consensual knowledge has developed that both countries share to a large extent. Both sides certainly share a greater knowledge about the destructive power of nuclear weapons. With the advent of the hydrogen bomb in the 1950s whole societies became vulnerable. More recently, public attention has focused on the unintended environmental damage that would be done by nuclear war. One result of this learning is that we recognize assured destruction as a present condition, even though we still have doctrinal differences about its desirability or the effectiveness of long-term efforts to escape it by building perfect defenses.

A second area of common knowledge is the command and control of nuclear weapons and the dangers of escalation. In the early days of few weapons, each side put nuclear control in the hands of a separate civilian agency (the Atomic Energy Commission in the United States and the KGB in the Soviet Union). As nuclear weapons systems became more numerous and complex, such simple solutions no longer worked. More elaborate technical and political procedures have been developed to cope with problems of control and to reduce risks of inadvertent nuclear war.

Common knowledge has also developed as to the spread of nuclear weapons to more countries. Both the United States and the Soviet Union acted somewhat naively during the 1950s and 1960s, when they believed that sharing nuclear technology with allies could be controlled, and that peaceful nuclear exports could be kept from military use. Better scientific knowledge and diplomatic experience have changed these attitudes and policies.

A fourth area involves forces and the volatility of the arms race. Some early illusions have been dispelled, such as the fallacy of the last move—that is, the belief that a technological innovation will not soon be acquired by the other side. The Soviets seem to have learned that they can tolerate some degree of "open sky surveillance," which they rejected in the 1950s. Both seem to have accepted the language of parity and recognized the link between offense and defense, though each appears at times to yearn for the superiority it has officially foresworn. Both seem to have learned the practice of formal arms control negotiations, but have disagreed about the value of arms control and have been reluctant to make major changes in force structures.

In a fifth area—what forces are needed for deterrence—the ambiguities and uncertainties of nuclear deterrence doctrine seem to have blocked further learning. Both sides recognize the value of having invulnerable forces for crisis stability, but both continue to wish for an ability to put the other sides' forces at risk as a means of deterring political aggrandizement.

Table 5–1 summarizes the four areas in which considerable nuclear learning has occurred, as well as the fifth area, in which learning has been more limited. In the first three areas, learning rests upon fairly concrete new information such as scientific, technical, and diplomatic experience; diplomatic experience has been most important in the fourth area; the fifth rests mostly upon theoretical studies and perceptions of strategic interactions—a type of new information that provides a less clear-cut basis for judging complex causal chains, and is less likely to alter prior beliefs than to be distorted by them. Nonetheless, changes in force structures have occurred, some of them convergent. The United States moved to flexible response in the 1960s, and the Soviets replied with a similar development of conventional capabilities in the 1970s. The Soviets developed significant counterforce options in the 1960s, and the United States replied with the countervailing strategy of 1970s. Whether these changes in doctrine and structure enhanced deterrence is more difficult to ascertain. In this area, though learning led to some concurrence in beliefs, it did not lead to explicit cooperation.

Moreover, much learning in the fifth area of force structure and deterrence seems to have been simple rather than complex. For ex-

Area of Common Knowledge	Resulting Beliefs	When Learned	How Known (Type of Information)	Were Regimes Created?
1. Destructive power	Assured destruction, inherent deterrence, and no-use	1950s H-bombs, 1980s environmental effects	Nuclear tests, theory, and some data	Yes, in part
2. Control problem	Crisis management practices, Accidents Agreement, PALs, and redundant sensors	Berlin, Cuba crisis, 1957–61 accidents and false alarms, 1970s alarms	Diplomatic experience, false alarms, accidents	Yes
3. Proliferation problems	Dangers of nuclear spread, problems of nuclear exports, co-operate to control	USSR/PRC 1959 US/Europe 1960s Both/India 1974	Diplomatic experience and scientific tests	Yes
4. Arms race stability	Interaction of force structure choices, acceptance of parity and offense-defense link; acceptance of surveillance	1960s buildup 1970s SALT I and SALT II	Diplomatic experience	Yes, but eroding
5. Deterrent force structure	Invulnerability for crisis stability; counterforce for credible threat; conventional for credibility	late 1950s and early 1960s 1960s USSR/ 1970s US 1960 US/ 1970s USSR	Theoretical studies; military doctrines; response to other side's posture	No, primarily unilateral actions

ample, the invulnerability of one's own forces was stressed more than the development of a norm of mutual invulnerability. Robert Mc-Namara welcomed the news that the Soviets were hardening their silos in the 1960s, and the Brooke Resolution tried to limit improvements in missile accuracy in 1969 and 1970, but these were isolated incidents.[28] Guided by complex notions of nuclear stability, both sides continue their attempts to threaten the other's nuclear forces, making it difficult to develop norms and explicit cooperation. Yet in the other four areas, learning and convergent knowledge did lead to explicit, albeit limited, cooperation. In the first three areas, as we shall see, regimes were established. In turn, these regimes helped to reinforce and develop the learning that had occurred. In the fourth area—arms control, where the nature of the information is less firm and strategic bargaining has a powerful impact—the regime has eroded and cooperation has become more problematic. A comparison of the five areas suggests that the extent to which cooperation is learned does indeed depend upon the strength of the prior beliefs (and who holds them) and the quantity and quality of the new information.

It is useful to consider these five areas in greater detail. First, regarding destructiveness and nonuse of nuclear weapons, both the American and Soviet governments have learned something during the nuclear era. Nuclear weapons were invented to be used. Yet today both sides frequently discuss them as though they are not usable or are useful for deterrence only. In the words of the Geneva communiqué of November 1985, "the sides have agreed that a nuclear war cannot be won and must never be fought. Recognizing that any conflict between the USSR and the U.S. could have catastrophic consequences, they emphasize the importance of preventing any war between them, whether nuclear or conventional. They will not seek to achieve military superiority."

Nonuse was not always the received nuclear wisdom. The United States actively considered using nuclear weapons at a high level several times in the 1950s (Korea, Dien Bien Phu, Taiwan). During one of the first National Security Council meetings in 1953, President Eisenhower and Secretary of State Dulles worried that public campaigns against nuclear weapons might hinder their usability as weapons of war. Since the early 1960s, however, there is hardly any evidence of high-level consideration of the deliberate use of nuclear weapons to achieve a political purpose (although the United States worried that nuclear weapons might be used in a crisis).[29] Overt incidents of coercive nuclear diplomacy have also declined.[30] Public opinion became more skeptical about the use of nuclear weapons during the 1950s.[31] While the United States has refused to declare it will never be the first to use nuclear weapons (because of the requirements of the doctrine of flexible response for extended deterrence in Europe), many observers believe that the de facto position is no-first-use. Early in the Reagan administration, officials discussed the possibility of protracted nuclear war, but public opinion forced them to revise the declaratory policy to the form eventually stated in the Geneva communiqué.

A similar evolution occurred in Soviet declaratory policy. Under Stalin, nuclear weapons were seen as military instruments of bombardment within an ideological context that declared the inevitability of war between the two great camps.[32] When Georgy Malenkov tried to alter this doctrine in 1954, Khrushchev used that move to help defeat Malenkov's bid for the succession. Nonetheless, by the twentieth party conference in 1956, Khrushchev had adopted Malenkov's position that war between the two camps was no longer inevitable in the nuclear age. Khrushchev bluffed openly with nuclear weapons after the major action had concluded during the Suez crisis of 1956 and the Taiwan Strait crisis of 1958, but the dangers of nuclear war in the latter case clearly enhanced Soviet caution.[33] This caution contributed to the Sino-Soviet split. In the early 1960s polemics between the Soviet and Chinese Communist Parties, the Soviets declared that nuclear weapons do not observe the class principle. These positions developed further in the various SALT-related agreements of the 1970s; in Brezhnev's Tula speech of January 1977, which cautioned against viewing nuclear weapons as usable; and in a series of statements by Andropov and Chernenko in the early 1980s.

In short, the two countries have changed their declared position about the usability of nuclear weapons. How significantly this change affects operational doctrine is an open question. For example, declaratory policy affects American strategic targeting plans (with certain lags), but they have always involved a more mixed set of targets than pure declaratory policy would suggest. On the Soviet side, most analysts distinguish between the political and the operational levels of strategic doctrine, the former enunciated by party leaders and the latter by military officers.[34] In general, the political doctrine has become more defensive; nuclear weapons will not be used unless the

Soviet Union is attacked. In 1982, Soviet leaders formally declared a doctrine of no-first-use. On the other hand, the military doctrine is pre-emptive. If an attack appears imminent, it is better to strike first than second.[35] These two positions are not necessarily contradictory, but it is important to note the limits of declaratory policy. Nonetheless, knowledgeable experts report that changes in declaratory policy have an influence. Soviet policy changes sometimes start because of tactical or propaganda advantage, and later take on a life of their own.

In contrast to the apparent learning and development of some common norms at the level of rhetoric, much less learning has occurred in the fourth and fifth areas (arms control and deterrent force structures). Both countries continue to develop new nuclear systems, including those designed for prompt attack against the other's hardened nuclear forces. Yet similar simple learning seems to have occurred on both sides, and some convergent views exist. Both sides have gone to considerable expense to develop forces that are relatively invulnerable to a first strike. This development may be explained simply as prudent adaptation; it may also have been affected by American efforts to persuade the Soviets of the value of a seaborne deterrent during arms talks in the 1970s. While the Soviets have placed far fewer of their warheads at sea, they have invested heavily in developing a submarine-based force that can be held in protected sanctuaries. Similarly, while some Americans worry about the vulnerability of fixed land-based missiles, it is worth remembering that the ICBMs constitute only a quarter of American strategic warheads. Despite their leaders' rhetoric, both sides have made heavy investments in redundant and invulnerable second-strike capabilities, which contribute to stability in a time of crisis.

Why, then, do both sides resist agreement on a common norm of second-strike forces only? Why do they continue to invest in forces that could be used in a first strike against missile silos? Some observers explain that the two sides have totally different concepts of nuclear stability. Certainly differences in force structure reflect conceptual and historical differences.[36] However, both countries are in much the same situation. The classic usability dilemma has blocked the development of a norm about nonuse and its incorporation into force structures on both sides.[37] If no one believes nuclear weapons can be used, they lose their deterrent value. Yet if used, they may destroy the values they are supposed to protect. This dilemma creates ambivalence in both countries and limits the development of the doctrine of nonuse. Instead, both sides have developed a complex notion of nuclear stability that trades off different values.

Crisis stability refers to the absence of incentives to pre-empt in time of crisis. Arms race stability refers to the absence of incentives to accelerate the development of new arms. Political stability refers to the absence of incentives to take political actions that might lead to crises or nuclear war. Asked why they have invested so much in the development of large, vulnerable, land-based missiles that threaten American ICBMs, the Soviets often reply that such missiles frighten the Americans and deter Washington from taking risky actions that might lead to war.

Americans make similar arguments. For example, Defense Department officials justify the placement of MX missiles in silos by arguing that they threaten the Soviets and keep them from risky political actions. As one U.S. Air Force officer put it, "Deterrence is more important than survivability."[38] In both countries certain groups stress one dimension of stability more than another. Both countries' force structures and doctrines have become more similar over time. In fact, the Soviet force structure strongly affected the development of the American countervailing strategy of the late 1970s.[39] While important differences remain (most notably in air defense), both countries are investing heavily in crisis stability—albeit as a unilateral goal for their own forces rather than for their adversary. The Soviets are developing mobile land-based missiles and increasing the capabilities of their submarine forces, while the Americans debate the prospect of mobility and enhance their submarine forces.[40]

The result, of course, is not always helpful for arms race stability. But some learning has occurred. Both sides seemed to have learned the importance of maintaining invulnerable second-strike retaliatory capabilities, but they differ somewhat internally and with each other over the allocation of investment between the three dimensions of strategic stability. As for the arms race, both sides have eschewed superiority, at least at the declaratory level, which is a change from earlier postures. Neither has developed as many nuclear weapons as it physically could. As Ernest May has shown in the American case, this outcome has been due in part to the larger number of groups now involved in nuclear decision making.[41] Similarly, Soviet participation in arms limitation talks during the period of détente presumably helped to broaden the range of actors involved in their weapons acquisition process. More recently, civilian involvement in military affairs has increased. A clause in the 1986 Party Program "breaks ground by reserving for party leaders the right to formulate Soviet military doctrine, which includes forecasting the probability of war." When a Soviet marshal wrote in 1985 of analogies to the 1930s, Gorbachev contradicted him at a Moscow rally, telling the crowd that "the present world is absolutely unlike that of the 1930s."[42]

There is clear evidence of nuclear learning about avoiding inadvertent and accidental nuclear war. If one divides the forty-year postwar period, the first half involved far more serious crises (such as those over Berlin and Cuba) than the second. Alexander George has argued that during such crises, as well as those in Korea, Hungary, Suez, and the Middle East, the two sides learned de facto rules of prudence.[43] In Zbigniew Brzezinski's words, they are "a code of reciprocal behavior guiding the competition, lessening the danger that it could become lethal."[44] These rules include avoiding direct fighting with each other (which hasn't occurred since Soviet pilots manned MiGs over Korea in 1950); no use of nuclear weapons even in limited wars; the importance of communication during crisis (as Eisenhower signaled to Khrushchev in 1956); not pressing each other's clients to the wall in regions such as the Middle East; and rough respect for areas of primary interest to the other side. During informal discussions with the Soviets, both sides have acknowledged common rules of prudence, although exact formulations and the length of the list are still ambiguous.

The prospect of accidental nuclear use can be seen as advancing deterrence. As one Soviet put it, "such measures [against nuclear accidents] are like having perfect seat belts in cars. They may encourage reckless driving. Since we believe your president has a tendency for reckless driving, the last thing we want to do is provide him with the belief that he has a perfect seat belt." At the same time, another Soviet explained the other side of the same dilemma: that "nuclear accidents are so frightening that nobody will believe in perfect safety belts. Safety measures are critical."[45] In general, given American proclivities for technical solutions and Soviet preferences for political solutions, Americans have often pressed accident-prevention measures more than the Soviets. In addition, the Soviets find some advantage in stimulating concerns about accidents as a way of draining confidence in the West while controlling the Soviet domestic audience.[46]

Despite these differences, both sides agree upon a number of measures. The most frequently cited is the hot line, or direct communication link, which has become so widely accepted that it is hard to remember that many Americans once opposed it, thinking it might sap deterrence.[47] Since the early 1970s, when the two sides signed an Accident Measures Agreement, they have worked out codes and procedures for communication during crises and developed an understanding on consultations to occur in the event of nuclear terrorism. The Incidents at Sea Agreement has reduced the number of dangerous incidents between the navies of the two countries. In the area of surveillance and inspection, which can help limit misperceptions, change has also been gradual. Although Soviet secrecy is still pervasive, they now accept satellite surveillance and on-site inspection.

Not all cooperation in this area has been formal. For example, after the Americans developed the electronic safety devices called permissive actions links (PALs), they deliberately leaked information to the Soviet Union, hoping that they would begin to develop similar devices. By the time the question of such devices was raised in formal negotiations in 1970 and 1971, the Soviets told the Americans that they did not need their assistance.[48] It seems reasonable to believe that, in this case, informal cooperation was successful. Nuclear learning has occurred as new information gradually altered prior beliefs and definitions of interest.

Finally, learning has been particularly impressive in efforts to slow the spread of nuclear weapons to new countries. Both sides took nearly a decade to appreciate this seemingly obvious common interest. Even after they recognized its significance in the early 1950s, both sides first tried unilateral efforts at restriction, then turned to sharing nuclear technology with allies. When Khrushchev found that this policy involved higher risks with Chinese nuclear weapons than he originally intended, he tried to control his Chinese ally by confronting the American opponent and proclaiming his leadership of the Sino-Soviet alliance. At the same time, the United States was trying to balance two concerns: (1) sharing operational control of nuclear deterrence with its allies and (2) developing broader norms for slowing the spread of nuclear weapons. Only after these unilateral efforts failed did the two sides turn to cooperative solutions in the mid-1960s, developing international institutions to slow the spread of nuclear weapons.[49] Once again, learning occurred: initial beliefs and definitions of interest altered as a result of new information and experience.

THE INCOMPLETE MOSAIC
OF SECURITY REGIMES

Although the overall U.S.-Soviet security relationship cannot be described as a security regime, the two countries largely agree upon broad and specific injunctions in a number of subissues, and one can argue that a jointly recognized regime exists in such areas.[50] Table 5-2 portrays this incomplete mosaic in terms of the five areas of nuclear learning, showing whether a regime exists, and how it affects state behavior. The columns represent the operational definitions for a regime's existence (the ability to identify agreed-upon broad and specific injunctions) and a regime's effects (whether it constrains short-run and reshapes long-run definitions of self-interest).

Structural factors and ideological differences lead the two countries to compete politically, but the awareness of nuclear destructiveness makes them avoid war with each other. Despite the acceptance of certain basic rules of prudence (no direct fighting, no nuclear use, communication during crisis, and so forth), there are no stable bilateral institutions, such as regular summitry or fully worked-out agreements for codifying the ambiguous rules and for managing the overall competition. (The multilateral United Nations has limited effects on the relationship.) There is no agreement on the legitimacy of the overall status quo. It is doubtful whether the rules constrain the short-run self-interest of the participants; prudence sufficiently explains the effect. Nor is it clear that these rules affect states' reshaping their long-run self-interest or provide a point around which expectations can converge, although some learning may occur from the formal and informal discussions of such principles.

In the most important area of the political competition, however, some broad and specific injunctions constrain behavior. At least a weak regime seems to exist in Europe, reflecting agreement on the division of Germany, the legitimate role of the United States and the Soviet Union in European security, and mutually recognized spheres of concern. The implications and implementation of these principles are spelled out in various ways, including the Berlin agreements and

Table 5-2. U.S.-Soviet Security Regimes.

Area of Common Knowledge[a]	Does a Regime Exist?		What Effects?	
	Broad Injunctions (Principles and Norms)	Specific Injunctions (Rules and Institutions)	Constrain Short-run Self-Interest	Reshape Long-run Self-Interest
1. Destructive power	Limit competition to avoid war	Yes in Europe, no in Third World		
A. Europe	Divide Germany and respect spheres of influence	Berlin agreements; Conference on Security and Cooperating in Europe	Yes	Yes
B. Third World	No consensus on status quo, but prudence in crises	Only vague or tacit	No	No
2. Control problems	Reduce risk of accidents; crisis management and prevention	Hot Line; Accidents Measures Agreement; Incidents at Sea meetings	Yes	Yes
3. Proliferation	Slow the spread; priority to nonproliferation	Nonproliferation Treaty; International Atomic Energy Agency; Suppliers' Group	Yes	Yes
4. Arms race stability	Accept parity; limit offense and defense	ABM Treaty SALT II	Yes	Uncertain
5. Deterrent forces	Ambivalence prevents significant limits on counterforce and conventional threats	No	—	—

a. See Table 5-1.

the Final Act of the Conference on Security and Cooperation in Europe.

The early efforts at establishing a postwar peace treaty or settlement for Europe failed. The original intention was not to divide Germany or to leave an anomalous Berlin in the midst of East Germany, but it proved impossible to agree upon a set of rules and institutions for a united Germany and a European peace treaty.[51] However, both the United States and the Soviet Union gradually redefined their interests, and their expectations gradually converged around the existing principles. The 1958–61 Berlin crisis raised nuclear fears that reinforced the importance of adhering to these principles. Subsequently, specific agreements laid out the rules and the institutional framework for meeting to discuss the issues, in a manner that fits the description of a partial security regime.

The rules and institutions help constrain the short-range self-interest of the United States and the Soviet Union in Europe. Both sides have closely adhered to cooperation on access to Berlin, the neutrality of Austria, and the de facto division of Germany. The 1985 slaying of an American major in East Germany was noteworthy because it occurred in the gray area of what is permissible in intelligence gathering, and because it did not severely disrupt or change either state's behavior in this issue. Similarly, the brief efforts of East German authorities to restrict diplomats' freedom of access in Berlin in 1986 were not sustained.

It is more difficult to ascertain whether this partial regime has provided a point around which expectations converge, and thus reshaped both sides' definitions of their long-range self-interest. While high American officials have occasionally given speeches about reversing the Yalta agreement and Soviets have occasionally complained about revanchism in West Germany, the main lines of expectations have apparently converged around the rough status quo, at least since the agreements of the early 1970s. At the same time, the European regime has limitations. Formal cooperation on disarmament has been elusive, although tacit cooperation may have occurred. When it seemed Congress might compel a unilateral withdrawal of U.S. troops, Brezhnev made a speech suggesting talks on conventional forces; his speech helped the Nixon administration successfully oppose Congress.[52] Eastern Europe remains an area of potential instability that could disrupt a neutralization regime. The Helsinki Agreement of 1975 is at best a de facto rather than de jure peace treaty for the region.

No regime limits the political competition in the rest of the world. As for broad injunctions, the Basic Principles of Agreement signed in 1972 are ambiguous and vague. They did not agree about the legitimacy of the status quo, the legitimacy of each other's actions in support of particular groups, or for wars of national liberation. They had little effect on Soviet or American behavior in the Third World. As for specific rules and institutions, prudent practices have aided the management of crises, particularly in the Middle East. But as Alexander George has noted, simple rules of crisis management are easier to learn than the complex changes involved in crisis prevention. Meetings to discuss regional issues have had little effect. In general, there is little evidence of rules or institutions that constrain both sides' short-range self-interest or that help to reshape their definition of their long-range self-interest.

The area of managing the arms race has also seen mixed results. For at least a decade, the SALT agreements formed a partial security regime based on the acceptance of parity, recognition of mutual vulnerability, and agreement to limit both offense and defense.[53] These principles and norms were supplemented by specific rules in treaty form and in an institutional framework called the Standing Consultative Commission (SCC) for discussing issues of compliance. Both sides redefined their short-run interest by adhering to rules (such as not interfering with the national technical means of verification) and by dismantling nuclear systems that exceeded treaty restraints. Given Soviet proclivities for keeping redundant systems and given the American debate over dismantlement of Poseidon submarines, these actions constitute evidence that the rules and institutions indeed affect the definition of short-range self-interest. Moreover, bureaucratic definitions of self-interest have evolved. A former chairman of the Joint Chiefs of Staff observed, "As we got deeper into arms control came recognition of its increasing importance—that neither side could gain through a nuclear war." During debates about whether or not to abide by SALT II early in the Reagan administration, "the arguments not to undermine SALT II were by these military officers."[54] On the Soviet side, William Jackson argues that the SALT regime tipped the Politburo balance between contending long-run expectations about the United States in the moderate direction.

Shevchenko confirms that the arms control process broadened the thinking of the Soviet military.[55]

On the other hand, the SALT regime's definition of long-range self-interest and the convergence of expectations gradually eroded—at least among part of the American political elite. It proved impossible to insulate the SALT regime from political competition in the Third World, which helps to explain why SALT II was not ratified. Brzezinski's comment that SALT II died in the sands of the Ogaden may have been premature, but Afghanistan doomed its ratification.

A second cause of erosion was the worsening U.S.-Soviet relationship and the confrontational manner used to discuss issues of verification and compliance. Soviet compliance frequently rested on narrow interpretations of the letter of the agreements and seemed to violate their spirit. Their behavior came closer to the specific than to the diffuse end of the spectrum of reciprocal behavior, which suggests a weak regime.[56] Nonetheless, in the 1970s the Soviets changed their behavior after contentious issues were raised in the SCC. In a quieter period the SCC might have dealt with the main charges of Soviet noncompliance in the 1980s—the Krasnoyarsk radar, the second new land-based missile, and the encryption of telemetry—but the deterioration in the overall political relationship allowed groups opposed to the arms control regime to turn these peripheral questions into central issues, which were used as a litmus test of Soviet reputation and intentions. This development suggests that a third cause of erosion was the political power shift in the United States. The 1980 election brought to power elites who had learned different lessons about arms control. Unlike the Joint Chiefs of Staff, they assimilated information about Soviet arms control behavior in a way that led to negative assessments. For example, Eugene Rostow, then director of the Arms Control and Disarmament Agency, argued that the Soviets used arms control to seek superiority in the 1970s. Assistant Secretary of Defense Richard Perle argued that "far from *learning* from the experience of 1972, we will simply repeat it."[57]

Finally, the regime eroded because changes in technology and politics called in question the basic principles of parity, mutual vulnerability, and the offense/defense relationship, which reflected the conditions of the early 1970s. The prospects of space-based defense pose special challenges to the ABM Treaty. If the erosion continues, and no new agreements are reached, the strategic arms control regime may turn out to be not only limited but also short-lived. Nonetheless, the return of the Reagan administration to arms control negotiations, as signified by the INF Treaty and efforts to conclude a strategic agreement, suggests that the regime has influenced public and administration expectations.

The problem of control has been more successfully dealt with: there is a regime for avoiding accidental nuclear war. The broad injunction of the regime is to reduce risks of accidental nuclear war; the specific rules and institutions are the Accidents Measures Agreement, the hot line, and the obligation to consult and communicate. These rules and institutions have constrained the short-range self-interest of states in a limited way. As argued earlier, cooperation to avoid accidental nuclear war is not as clear or easy as it might at first appear: short-range self-interest could have encouraged the Soviets to play the danger of accidents for short-run political advantage in the West. These rules and institutions probably also helped to reshape the long-run self-interest of the two states. The continued discussions and gradual development of additional agreements in this area suggest that both countries take the issue seriously.

Within the regime to prevent accidental nuclear war is a subsidiary regime to regulate and prevent incidents at sea. It reduces both risks and costs to the two navies. The two bureaucracies have elaborated quite specific rules and a series of regular meetings to implement the agreement. When one looks at the change in naval behavior on both sides since the 1972 agreement, one can argue that interests were redefined and that the rules and institutions have constrained the short-range self-interest of the two states.[58]

Another successful area is the regime for nonproliferation of nuclear weapons. The key injunctions are to slow the spread of nuclear weapons and weapons-usable technologies to third parties and to place nonproliferation concerns before political advantage with allies or third parties. A number of specific rules and institutions have been developed to implement these norms—for example, the Non-Proliferation Treaty (NPT), the International Atomic Energy Agency, and the Nuclear Suppliers' Group. While these are multilateral institutional devices, they are supplemented by regular bilateral nonproliferation talks between the United States and the Soviet Union. Moreover, these rules and institutions have constrained short-range self-interest. In a number of instances, the Soviet Union could have gained impressive short-range political advantages with third countries, but decided to forego them (for example, over South Africa in the United Nations in 1978, or over the issue of a test ban at the 1985 NPT Review Conference). Even when overall political relations between the Soviet Union and the United States worsened in the early 1980s and Soviets cut off other forms of arms negotiations after the deployment of the new NATO missiles in 1983, the non-proliferation talks continued. A high-level participant observed, "Our early discussions were somewhat rigid regarding the hard cases, but after seven or eight meetings, they have become more frank. They now give us detailed information, and when they bring up our hard cases, it is not in the old rhetorical way. The talks definitely improved with time."[59]

The rules and institutions not only constrained short-range self-interest, but they helped to reshape long-range self-interest, so that nonproliferation has become a major interest for both states. This is quite a contrast to President Reagan's declaration (as a candidate in 1980) that nonproliferation was none of our business. It also indicates that regular meetings in an institutional framework help detach an issue from vicissitudes of the overall political relationship. The hostility of the 1980s generally overwhelmed the cooperation that had been established earlier, but in some cases, such as nonproliferation, the superstructure of regime made the area of cooperation less vulnerable to the rising tide of hostility.

Finally, limited regimes, such as agreements on neutralization, are not related to nuclear learning, but they have some effect on the security relationship. The basic principles and norms of these regimes isolate certain areas from the overall U.S.-Soviet competition. The specific rules and institutions vary. For example, an effective multilateral agreement in Antarctica prohibits the implanting of nuclear devices on the seabed. Other specific regimes neutralize particular countries, such as Austria. There is evidence that such rules and institutions have constrained the short-range self-interests of states. For example, Deborah Shapley shows how the Antarctica regime helped reshape the long-range self-interest of states from relatively incoherent positions to longer-term cooperation.[60]

In short, while no overall United States-Soviet security regime constrains or reshapes the two countries' definition of self-interest, partial security regimes exist in Europe, for strategic arms control, for preventing accidental nuclear war, for encouraging nonproliferation, and for neutralizing certain issues. Moreover, some evidence (independent of that used to identify the regimes) suggests that the regimes have shaped both countries' security behavior. Further, their behavior in areas where regimes have been identified differs from their behavior in the overall security relationship. While additional evidence of internal processes within the Soviet Union would help determine how significant a role regimes play in Soviet learning and redefinition of interest, this information will be hard to get. But observable behavior and hypothetical arguments suggest that agreed rules and institutions have helped to make the security relationship in some issues different from areas without regimes.

REGIMES AND LEARNING

One should not assume that regimes make a difference, however. The most parsimonious explanation of governmental learning is that leaders notice changes in the structure of the situation that modify their effectiveness, and they adapt their behavior as a result of anticipation or experience. Starting with the simplifying assumption that states are unitary actors, we can ask whether experience in playing a game leads to learning. The experience of playing iterated games of prisoner's dilemma in situations with a long shadow of the future may teach players the value of cooperation to maximize their payoffs over time.[61] Or learning may occur simply through perceptions of change in the structure of the situation. For example, the weakening of alliances and the perceived erosion of bipolarity in the mid-1960s may have helped the United States and the Soviet Union learn that they had a common interest in cooperation as a means of slowing proliferation of nuclear weapons. One need not think of regimes or even overt negotiation to imagine conditions in which cooperation between countries can be learned. Changes in the structure of power can produce learning without the intervening variable of regimes. Cooperation can evolve as a choice of unitary rational actors who are redefining their self-interest in response to changes in the structure of the game—and that is itself an optimistic conclusion.[62]

In some instances, however, the existence of a regime may affect learning. Its principles, rules, and institutions may have two types of effects. First, they may restrain state behavior. In this sense, one can seek evidence of restrained behavior either in external changes or arguments used in domestic processes. Do the specific injunctions cause states to act differently than if they merely followed their short-run self-interest? Second, the injunctions of a regime may create a focal point around which expectations converge. One can look at the behavior of states to see to what extent interests and expectations are redefined around such principles, norms, and rules. Has the expectation of rule-governed behavior become so firm that self-interest is defined in a way that takes the existence of the regime as given?

Regimes exercise their influence in several ways. First, their principles and norms may be internalized by states or by important groups within states. This process raises the costs of defecting from cooperative solutions and makes it more important to establish a reputation for reciprocity. Second, regimes may provide information that changes key participants' understanding of their interests, or lets them see cause-and-effect relationships that were not previously understood. Included in this information may be procedures for transparency and timely warning through inspection or verification, which then tend to discourage worst-case assumptions.[63] More specifically, the institutionalization of regimes can: (1) change standard operating procedures for national bureaucracies; (2) present new coalition opportunities for subnational actors and improved access for third parties; (3) change participants' attitudes through contacts within the framework of institutions; and (4) provide means to dissociate a particular issue from changes in the overall political relationship by regular formal meetings. If regimes make a difference, we should see different behavior between those areas of security cooperation where regimes exist and those where they do not. To a large extent, we have found this to be the case.

PROSPECTS AND PROBLEMS

Prospects are mixed for the partial regimes in the complex mosaic of U.S.-Soviet security relations. For some, the future is unclear. It is uncertain whether the ABM Treaty will collapse completely, or whether the treaty will be surpassed by a stable strategic accord. While the regime established in Europe in the early 1970s seems relatively stable, it has not yet led to significant reduction in nuclear or conventional armaments. Moreover, it may weaken if changes threaten Eastern Europe and tempt the United States to cross the historical dividing line by, for example, assisting those nations' human rights. The agreements less central to U.S.-Soviet competition may be more durable and better insulated from the vagaries of the overall relationship. These include the regimes for nonproliferation, for avoiding accidental nuclear war, and for neutralizing certain areas and countries.

Looking at subissues of the U.S.-Soviet security relationship in terms of learning and regimes does not solve problems—it raises questions. How have the two countries learned in the nuclear area? What causes definitions of interest to change? Why has learning been faster in some areas than others? When has learning led to the development of institutions and regimes, and when has it not? What difference does it make when such institutions and regimes have been developed? What are the impediments to learning? How can learning be accelerated? Can societies plan to take advantage of crises and discontinuous learning to create new regimes and lock in the learning?[64] At this stage, we have more questions than answers, but one task of a good research program is to raise important questions as both sides explore new thinking about international affairs.

NOTES

1. See the special issue of *World Politics* 38 (October 1985) edited by Kenneth Oye.

2. Robert Keohane, *After Hegemony* (Princeton, N.J.: Princeton University Press, 1984).

3. Janet Gross Stein, "Detection and Defection: Security Regimes and the Management of International Conflict," *International Journal* 11 (Autumn 1985); Charles Lipson, "International Cooperation in Economic and Security Affairs," *World Politics* 37 (October 1984); Robert Jervis, "Security Regimes" in Stephen Krasner, ed., and "From Balance to Concept" in Oye, *World Politics* 38. *International Regimes* (Ithaca, N.Y.: Cornell University Press, 1983).

4. Dan Caldwell, *American-Soviet Relations: From 1947 to the Nixon-Kissinger Grand Design* (Westport, Conn.: Greenwood Press, 1981); Michael Mandelbaum, *The Nuclear Revolution* (Cambridge: Cambridge University Press, 1981), chap. 3; Joanne Gowa and Nils Wessell, *Ground Rules: Soviet and American Involvement in Regional Conflicts* (Philadelphia: Foreign Policy Research Institute, 1982); David Gompert, Michael Mandelbaum, Richard Garwin, and John Barton, *Nuclear Weapons and World Politics* (New York: McGraw-Hill, 1977).

5. Jervis, "Security Regimes," p. 359.

6. See Susan Strange, "Cave! Hic Dragones: A Critique of Regime Analysis," in Krasner, *International Regimes.*

7. Based on conversations with Soviet academicians in Moscow, June 1986. Note also M. Gorbachev's recent suggestion of "an international regime for the safe development of nuclear energy" (*New York Times,* June 4, 1986) or his 1985 tribute to the "international non-proliferation regime . . . as an effective instrument of peace" (*Soviet News.* No. 6289, August 28, 1985).

8. Seweryn Bialer, *The Soviet Paradox* (New York: Knopf, 1986), p. 40; Richard Pipes, *Survival Is Not Enough* (New York: Simon and Schuster, 1984).

9. Gowa and Wessell, *Ground Rules*; see also the forthcoming work by Robert Legvold, Columbia University.

10. William Zimmerman, *Soviet Perspectives on International Relations, 1956-1967* (Princeton: Princeton University Press, 1973), p. 32.

11. Weinberger interview in Michael Charlton, *The Star Wars History* (London: BBC, 1986), p. 97.

12. Scowcroft interview in Charlton, p. 106.

13. Lloyd Etheredge, *Can Governments Learn?* (New York: Pergamon Press, 1985), p. 143; also "Government Learning: An Overview," in Samuel L. Long, ed., *Handbook of Political Behavior,* vol. 2 (New York: Plenum Press, 1981), pp. 73-161.

14. Ernst Haas, "Why Collaborate? Issue-Linkage and International Regimes," *World Politics* 32 (April 1980), p. 390.

15. Richard Neustadt and Ernest May, *Thinking in Time* (New York: Free Press, 1986). Also, John D. Steinbruner, *The Cybernetic Theory of Decision* (Princeton: Princeton University Press, 1974); Robert Jervis, *Perception and Misperception in International Politics* (Princeton: Princeton University Press, 1976), chap. 6.

16. For a discussion of theories of the effects of prior beliefs and some interesting examples, see Deborah Larson, *Origins of Containment* (Princeton: Princeton University Press, 1985).

17. Russell Leng, "When Will They Ever Learn?" *Journal of Conflict Resolution* 27, September 1983.

18. Chris Argyris and Donald Schon, *Organizational Learning: A Theory of Action Perspective* (Reading, Mass.: Addison-Wesley, 1978). Their terminology is single loop and double loop learning.

19. See Etheredge, *Can Governments Learn?*, for this interpretation.

20. Jervis, *Perception and Misperception,* chap. 6.

21. James N. Rosenau, "Learning in East-West Relations: The Superpowers as Habit-Driven Actors" (Los Angeles: Institute for Transnational Studies, mimeo, 1986).

22. Steinbruner, *Cybernetic Theory,* pp. 78-79.

23. Thane Gustafson, *Reform in Soviet Politics* (Cambridge: Cambridge University Press, 1981), chap. 6.
24. Alexander Dallin, "The Democratic Sources of Soviet Foreign Policy," in Seweryn Bialer, ed., *The Domestic Context of Soviet Foreign Policy* (Boulder, Colo.: Westview Press, 1981), p. 359.
25. Rose E. Gottemoeller, "Decisionmaking for Arms Limitation in the Soviet Union," in Hans Guenther Brauch and Duncan Clark, eds., *Decisionmaking for Arms Limitation* (Cambridge: Ballinger, 1983), pp. 53ff.
26. Robert Legvold (note 9). Compare to Zimmerman, *Soviet Perspectives.*
27. Arkady Shevchencko, *Breaking with Moscow* (New York: Ballantine, 1985), p. 270.
28. See Congressional Information Service, "ABM, MIRV, SALT and the Nuclear Arms Race" 72-608111 (Washington, D.C.: U.S. Government Printing Office, 1970); "Senate Unit Asks MIRV Test Cutoff," *New York Times*, March 17, 1970, p. 7; John W. Finney, "Senate Unit Urges Nuclear Arms Freeze, *New York Times*, March 21, 1970, p. 6.
29. John Lewis Gaddis, "The Long Peace: Elements of Stability in the Postwar International System," *International Security* 10, Spring 1986. "The pattern of caution in the use of nuclear weapons did not develop solely, as one might have expected, from the prospect of retaliation." It "may owe more to the moral- and public relations-sensibilities of Washington officials than to any actual fear of escalation" (p. 137).
30. Barry Blechman and Stephen Kaplan, *Force Without War* (Washington, D.C.: Brookings Institution, 1978).
31. Thomas W. Graham, "Future Fission," unpublished ms, Harvard University, Center for Science and International Affairs, 1987.
32. See David Holloway, *The Soviet Union and the Arms Race* (New Haven, Conn.: Yale University Press, 1983).
33. Benjamin S. Lambeth, "Nuclear Proliferation and Soviet Arms Control Policy," *Orbis* 13, Summer 1970.
34. See Derek Leebaert, ed., *Soviet Military Thinking* (London: George Allen and Unwin, 1981), and Robbin Laird and Dale Herspring, *The Soviet Union and Strategic Arms* (Boulder, Colo.: Westview Press, 1984).
35. Stephen Meyer, "Soviet Perspectives on the Paths to Nuclear War," in G. T. Allison, A. Carnesale, and J. Nye, eds., *Hawks, Doves and Owls* (New York: Norton, 1985).
36. William E. Odom, "The Soviet Approach to Nuclear Weapons: A Historical Review," *The Annals* 469, Sept. 1983. See Colin Gray, *Nuclear Strategy and National Style* (Boston: Hamilton Press, 1986) on this point and for general skepticism about Soviet learning.
37. See the discussion in Joseph S. Nye, *Nuclear Ethics* (New York: Free Press, 1986), pp. 53 ff.

38. Conversations at Offut Air Force Base, February 1986. On the Soviet side, General Talensky concluded in 1965 that "in our days there is no more dangerous illusion than the idea that thermonuclear war can still serve as an instrument of politics," while Lt. Col. Rybkin warned that "any a priori rejection of the possibility of victory is harmful because it leads to moral disarmament, to a disbelief in victory and to fatalism and passivity." Quoted in Holloway, *Soviet Union*, p. 164.

39. See Walter Slocombe, "The Countervailing Strategy," *International Security* 5, Spring 1981.

40. In the area of mobility, the Americans learned from observing the Soviets. The U.S. Air Force finally decided that garrison basing for rail-mobile missiles might be safe enough after they observed the Soviets using that system for their new SS-24 missile. Interview, Pentagon official, 1987.

41. Ernest May, "Why Doesn't the United States Have *More* Nuclear Weapons?", unpublished ms., Harvard University, 1986.

42. Gottemoeller, "Decision making"; Sidney Ploss, "A New Soviet Era," *Foreign Policy* 62, Spring 1986, pp. 54–56.

43. Alexander George, *Managing the U.S.-Soviet Rivalry* (Boulder, Colo.: Westview Press, 1983).

44. Zbigniew Brzezinski, *Game Plan* (Boston: Atheneum, 1986), p. 244.

45. Conversations with academicians in Moscow, January 1984.

46. See Barry Blechman, "Efforts by the U.S. and Soviet Union to Reduce Risks of Accidental or Inadvertent War," prepared for the Stanford project on U.S.-Soviet Efforts to Cooperate in Security Matters, May 1986.

47. See Webster Stone, "The Hot Line," undergraduate history thesis, Harvard University, 1984; William Ury, *Beyond the Hotline* (Boston: Houghton Mifflin, 1985).

48. See "Report of a Conference on Permissive Action Links held at Harvard University," Center for Science and International Affairs, February 1986 (forthcoming).

49. See Joseph S. Nye, "Non-Proliferation," paper prepared for Stanford Project on U.S.-Soviet Efforts to Cooperate in Security Matters, May 1986.

50. I agree with Keohane that principles, norms, rules, and procedures shade into each other and are best distinguished as broad and specific injunctions (*After Hegemony*, p. 59).

51. See David Schoenbaum, "The World War II Allied Agreement on Occupation and Administration of Postwar Germany," paper for Stanford Project (note 49).

52. See John G. Keliher, *The Negotiations on Mutual and Balanced Force Reductions* (New York: Pergamon Press, 1981), pp. 25–27.

53. Condoleeza Rice, "SALT as a Limited Security Regime," paper for Stanford Project (note 49).

54. General David Jones quoted in Charlton, pp. 82–83.

55. William D. Jackson, "Soviet Images of the U.S. as a Nuclear Adversary, 1969–1979," *World Politics* 33, July 1981, 637. See also Raymond Garthoff, "The Soviet Military and SALT," in Jiri Valenta and William Potter, eds., *Soviet Decisionmaking and National Security* (London: Allyn and Unwin, 1984), pp. 16 ff.

56. See Robert O. Keohane, "Reciprocity in International Relations," *International Organization* 40, Winter 1986.

57. Eugene Rostow and Richard Perle quoted in Charlton, pp. 60, 114.

58. Sean Lynn-Jones, "A Quiet Success for Arms Control: Preventing Incidents at Sea," *International Security* 9, Spring 1985.

59. Interview, State Department, October 1986.

60. Deborah Shapley, "Antarctica: A Case History of Success," paper prepared for Stanford Project (note 49).

61. Robert Axelrod, *The Evolution of Cooperation* (New York: Basic Books, 1984). See also Hayward R. Alker and Roger Hurwitz, *Resolving Prisoner's Dilemmas* (MIT Center for International Studies, 1980).

62. Duncan Snidal, "Coordination versus Prisoner's Dilemma: Implications for International Cooperation and Regimes," *American Political Science Review* 79, December 1985.

63. See the articles in the special issue of *World Politics* 38 (October 1985), particularly those by Oye, Jervis, Axelrod, and Keohane.

64. See Robert Keohane and Joseph S. Nye, "Two Cheers for Multilateralism," *Foreign Policy* 60, Fall 1985.

SOVIET VIEW

Vladimir P. Lukin

Joseph Nye addresses the problem of learning, of progress, in the practice of world politics. He analyzes the formation of structures or regimes of collective security that have the capacity of self-development. In short, he poses the question of the theoretical and practical possibility of forming a rational world order in the nuclear epoch.

How we assess the possibility of a more rational world order depends on how we view the nature of the international system. Western scholars have long debated whether international relations are better described in terms of the doctrine of political realism or the so-called liberal tradition. The Soviet literature also includes some very heated discussions on this score, although a different terminology is used. For several decades the Soviet debate was dominated by advocates of a variant of political realism. Since the United States and the Soviet Union are the two most powerful states in the contemporary world, it was argued, there is a "natural antagonism" between them. Moreover, the reality of class struggle was directly transferred to inter-state, and in particular Soviet-American, relations. These simplified schemes gave rise to a bipolar antagonistic approach to Soviet-American relations. The problem was compounded by the fact that sensible, practical undertakings in relations between our countries were, on the Soviet side, tightly wrapped in the above-described conceptual package, sometimes completely hiding the real message contained therein.

This conception of international relations long dominated the Soviet literature, but it was not the only one. Another school noted that international politics develops with a significant degree of independence from geopolitical and historical factors. International politics corresponds to social-historical tendencies in the framework of a complex system.[1] The growing interdependence of the world has made human factors much more significant in the system and process of world politics. This realization is now becoming predominant in our literature.

In our country we prefer to speak not of a "balance of forces" but of a "balance of interests" as an instrument in the foreign policy process. Global interests in survival (nuclear, ecological, demographic) have become a most important component of national interests. These are now national, and both bilateral and global. This is where political realism meets the liberal tradition—the traditional vision of a civilized world order for our two countries and all of humanity.

Of course, a possibility and its realization are two different things, frequently separated by insurmountable barriers. These barriers are not only political but include the enormous difficulties of the process of learning. Rooted in the thicket of ages of history, in the impenetrable armor of human egoism, these difficulties are clothed in romantic, ideological garb.

Nevertheless the learning of civilized society proceeds, occurring in waves, accompanied by sharp zig-zags, serious backsliding, and the forgetting of lessons of the past. Qualities no less firm, no less organically inherent in human beings and humankind, underlie this advancing process. Perhaps most important is the colossal capacity of human beings to survive in extreme situations by overcoming their own dogmatic stereotypes. This capacity has been demonstrated repeatedly throughout history—in Soviet-American relations as in many other contexts. When the threat of Hitlerism hung over the world, for example, conceptual-dogmatic elements that militated against a sharp improvement in Soviet-American relations were quite rapidly thrust into the back seat.

One might object that such rapid learning under the influence of specific political circumstances is not true learning, and changed circumstances almost completely erase the psychological and intellectual experience accumulated during the period of military cooperation. In fact, however, this is far from the case. Although the political structure of cooperation was almost completely dismantled during the cold war, and the corresponding mass feelings subsided, the positive processes that arose in Soviet-American relations in the 1960s and 1970s did not by any means begin on an "empty page." In fact, as the great writer Bulgakov wrote in *Master and Margarita*, "manuscripts do not burn." In the manuscript of Soviet-American relations, the memory of cooperation remained alive, beneath the dogmatic stratifications that had formed in both our countries, awaiting comprehension and utilization. Some theories of Soviet-American relations, dominated by "single-measure" social and geopolitical factors, suggest that confrontation is absolutely inevitable. In fact, however, at least three types of relations between the USSR and the United States are possible: confrontation of the cold war type; peaceful coexistence in an essentially softer and more constructive détente form; and a military-political alliance. In other words, experience has turned out to be significantly broader than the various competitive dogmatic stratifications. And this experience is irreversible. Only incorrect or prejudiced interpretations can be undone.

Complications in the process of learning arise precisley here—at the level of interpretation. Here the real deadlocks and blockages begin, for dogmatic stereotypes seem to possess almost all the attributes of reality. Their charisma is at times so strong that they almost completely supplant the objective intellectual results of accumulated experience, raising doubts about the very possibility of learning.

In general the twentieth century has produced a more sober, realistic view of the possibilities of human advancement through learning the "truth" and realizing the fatally "false." But it is worth pointing out that this new view itself is a most important factor and result of learning. Those of us who are interested in the problem of learning in Soviet-American relations might usefully reflect on Karl Marx's simple and brilliant question: "Who teaches the teachers?" That is, in the system of bilateral inter-state relations, is there one side that teaches and one side that learns? Or should the discussion be about self-learning in the process of interrelating? Only as each side breaks from the first point of view and adopts the second, it seems to me, can learning occur in our relations. In moving toward "new political thinking," the Soviet side is now performing this most complex intellectual and psychological operation. I will say frankly that the situation seems significantly less defined on "the other shore." The future of security regimes, the tempo and continuity of work to develop them—the subject thoroughly investigated in the creative and substantial work of Joseph Nye—in large part depend upon a determined and positive stance by both sides.

NOTE

1.   See the author's book *Centers of Power: Concepts and Reality*, published at the beginning of 1983, though written much earlier: V. P. Lukin, *Tsentry sily: kontseptsii i real'nosti* (Moscow: Mezhdunarodnye otnoshenye, 1983), p. 15.

6 THE EMERGENCE OF MUTUAL SECURITY
Its Objective Basis

Henry Trofimenko

In Chapter 5 Joseph Nye describes the changes in perceptions of Americans and Soviets in the nuclear area. In my view, these changes in *perceptions* stem less from a process of learning than from changes in the *objective correlation of forces* between the two nations. For the first twenty-five years after World War II, while the United States maintained nuclear superiority, it used the threat of nuclear war to advance its security interests. When the Soviet Union achieved real parity in second-strike capability in the second half of the 1970s, the United States came to understand a new common interest in mutual security and thus to change the rules of the game. Under current objective conditions, the task of ensuring the security of our societies, and of human civilization, has become a mutual enterprise.

MUTUALITY AND THE COLD WAR

The problem of mutuality in the Soviet-American strategic relationship emerged immediately after World War II. With the other major world powers severely weakened economically, there were only two superpowers: the United States, a true superpower, and the Soviet Union, a fledgling one. The United States possessed tremendous economic wealth and the most powerful means of destruction and intimidation—an atomic bomb. The Soviet Union started with a severe handicap, since the wartime devastation of its European region had seriously damaged its economy. It had suffered tremendous human losses during the war, and it did not possess nuclear weapons. Its prime task during the first postwar decade was to hold fast and not allow the United States to overwhelm it. Though in one sense the two countries did not have much to quarrel about, they became locked in an adversarial relationship—a zero-sum game in which one side's gain was considered to be the absolute and equal loss of the other.

During the second half of the 1940s and the 1950s a real *balance* of fear was objectively still a distant matter. U.S. military planning documents of the period and the statements of American political and military leaders show complete confidence in victory over the Soviet Union in a nuclear war. U.S. strategic calculations were predicated on the use of nuclear weapons in a first strike against the USSR from numerous American air bases surrounding Soviet territory. After a U.S. bomber attack, documents stated, the Soviet Union would become a "smoking, radiating ruin at the end of two hours."[1]

By the beginning of the 1950s, the Soviet Union had a few nuclear weapons, but no means to deliver them across the ocean. In other words, the American-Soviet confrontation was asymmetrical: the United States possessed more powerful military forces. Exploiting its strategic superiority, the United States strove to impose upon the Soviet Union rules of international behavior that were one-sidedly pro-American. The Soviet Union naturally was not willing to accept such rules (though occasionally it had to yield).

Rejecting a dialogue with the Soviet Union as an equal and refusing to seek common rules of the game, the U.S. leadership made a qualitative leap in the arms build-up designed to sustain and enhance its superiority: it launched the hydrogen bomb project. As the famous NSC-68 memorandum stated: "Although the United States probably now possesses, principally in atomic weapons, a force adequate to deliver a powerful blow upon the Soviet Union and to open the road to victory in a long war, it is not sufficient by itself to advance the position of the United States in the cold war. The problem is to create such political and economic conditions in the free world, backed by force . . . that the Kremlin will accommodate itself to these conditions, gradually withdraw and eventually change its policies drastically."[2] But the Soviet Union tested thermonuclear weapons practically simultaneously with the United States, and it began to produce strategic bombers capable of reaching the continental United States from bases on Soviet territory.

THE BEGINNING OF JOINTLY
RECOGNIZED RULES

Realistic assessment of these new developments brought the U.S. leadership, for the first time, to a serious dialogue with the Soviet Union on a wide range of problems without any preconditions. Somewhere in the mid-1950s there occurred a transition from acute confrontation to constrained competition, to use Graham Allison's term. The 1955 Geneva Summit was the first international event after the Potsdam meeting of the Big Four at which the parallel and sometimes shared interests between the two groupings of nations were recognized. It was the beginning of a more or less clear understanding of some unwritten rules and development of more formal new rules of coexistence.

Were it not for the process of rapprochement begun in Geneva in 1955 and continued at Camp David in 1959, a number of East-West crises would probably have taken much more acute forms (the Hungarian events, the Suez crisis, the downing of the U-2 spy plane piloted by Gary Powers deep inside Soviet territory). During the Suez crisis of 1956, the United States and USSR actually took similar positions.

All of these developments in U.S.-Soviet relations were caused by the objective change in the correlation of forces improving the position of the USSR and the socialist states as a whole. The Soviet Union had broken the U.S. atomic monopoly in 1949, developed thermonuclear weapons and intercontinental ballistic missiles, and in 1957 launched Sputnik. Yet although both sides understood the need for mutual cooperation to ensure international security, and despite the existence of the objective prerequisites for the stabilization of the situation on the basis of "rough parity," U.S. pressure and Soviet counterpressure resulted in a confrontational trial of wills, which culminated in the Cuban missile crisis.

As Fyodor Burlatsky emphasizes in Chapter 4, Cuba represented the first Soviet "claim for parity." Though this claim was not presented in the best of forms, it made the U.S. leadership realize the need to approach a confrontation with the USSR more cautiously. The Soviet-American confrontation during the Caribbean crisis became a powerful impetus to observe some unwritten "rules of prudence" and to work out some written rules of the game to promote peaceful coexistence. The sense of danger that both sides experienced helped them realize the imperative to avoid similar or greater risks in their bipolar competition, to cooperate to ensure mutual security. As President Kennedy said later, "the experience led both not to see only a distorted and desperate view of the other side, not to see conflict as inevitable, accommodation as impossible and communication nothing more than an exchange of threats."[3] One of the first symbols of cooperative mutuality was the agreement in mid-1963 to establish a direct communication link (hot line) between the governments of the Soviet Union and the United States. Twenty-five years after the crisis in the Caribbean, the renowned American strategist Thomas Schelling remarked, "I firmly believe that the Cuban missile crisis was the best thing to happen to us since the Second World War. It helped to avoid further confrontation with the Soviets."[4]

During the cold war the USSR and United States managed, with very few exceptions, to avoid direct military confrontation. But there were some perilous episodes. In 1948 the Soviet Union blocked Western road access to Berlin, and the United States responded with an airlift. During the Cuban crisis, the United States instituted a naval blockade to prevent Soviet ships from reaching Cuba. Later, at the beginning of the détente era, mines planted by the United States in Haiphong Harbor hit some Soviet ships. More than once early warning systems have been tested with intrusive probes. Planes have been shot down and ships on spy missions shot at or captured. But these potential crises did not escalate because neither side was willing to risk nuclear war.

As the growth of Soviet strategic forces undermined the credibility of American nuclear policy, the Kennedy administration replaced the strategy of massive retaliation with one of flexible response. The new approach emphasized the "graduated" use of military force (in accordance with the scope of threat) and defined—in theory at least—nuclear weapons as the means of last resort in a military conflict.

In time this strategy was overtaken by the concept of mutual deterrence, as it was recognized that each side could inflict unacceptable damage in a second strike. This concept soon evolved into the somewhat sardonic formula of "mutual assured destruction" (MAD).

The MAD concept explicitly acknowledged the interconnectedness of the USSR and the United States in national security. In addition, it formally proceeded from the hypothetical equality of both sides to deter a nuclear attack.

The concept was enunciated by Robert McNamara as secretary of defense. Although McNamara, like all his successors, preferred to speak about assured destruction of the Soviet Union in the case of a nuclear war, the MAD concept was legitimized and appeared to be the publicly proclaimed U.S. strategy. In the mid-1960s, McNamara himself stated, "The fact is, then, that neither the Soviet Union nor the United States can attack each other without being destroyed in retaliation; nor can either of us attain a first-strike capability in the foreseeable future. . . . Further, both the Soviet Union and the United States possess an actual and credible second-strike capability against one another and it is precisely this mutual capability that provides us both with the strongest possible motive to avoid a nuclear war."[5]

When McNamara made this statement, the Soviet Union did not yet possess a second-strike capability equal to that of the United States. This was the reality perceived by U.S. defense strategists when they planned counterforce strikes against the Soviet military complex: its nuclear forces and command, control, and communication centers. But despite the optimistic scenarios designed by the military, American political leaders always had very strong doubts as to the feasibility of such war-winning strategies. As six former members of Kennedy's ExComm concluded in drawing lessons from the Cuban missile crisis,

> American nuclear superiority was not in our view a critical factor [in the resolution of the Cuban missile crisis], for the fundamental and controlling reason that nuclear war, already in 1962, would have been an unexampled catastrophe for both sides; the balance of terror so eloquently described by Winston Churchill seven years earlier was in full operation. No one of us ever reviewed the nuclear balance for comfort in those hard weeks. *The Cuban missile crisis illustrates not the significance but the insignificance of nuclear superiority in the face of survivable thermonuclear retaliatory forces. It also shows the crucial role of rapidly available conventional strength.*[6]

Even so, U.S. military and political leaders were convinced that U.S. nuclear advantages could be translated into bargaining leverage if a local conflict escalated. This confidence encouraged them to engage in nonmilitary coercion and small-scale local military operations in various regions of the world.

THE ATTAINMENT OF STRATEGIC PARITY

In the 1970s, the Soviet Union finally attained mutuality with the United States in its capability to survive a nuclear attack and inflict unacceptable damage in a retaliatory strike. At this point, the assured destruction concept became less attractive to American strategists. With both sides now truly equally vulnerable to retaliation, U.S. threats to use nuclear weapons became less credible. This actual parity was formalized by the SALT II Treaty. The United States had lost its former advantage, which it had used ostensibly to deter the USSR but in fact to ensure opportunities for pursuit of its own interests in the world arena—coercing "potential adversaries," neutrals, and even allies from a position of superior strength.

Henry Kissinger is one of the few American statesmen to acknowledge publicly that in the American view deterrence is essentially the intimidation of the opponent from positions of superior strength. At the Round Table conference of the Netherlands Atlantic Commission, he observed, "I have said it repeatedly and will say it again to the anguish of traditionalists, the notion of deterrence in its crude form presupposed American strategic superiority. It presupposed an American capacity for a plausible first-strike. To the degree that that capacity was diminished and to the degree that the diminution was accelerated by the pressures of our intellectual community, the classic notion of deterrence had to lose credibility."[7] This explains why U.S.-Soviet mutuality in retaliatory capabilities, a truly MAD situation, is absolutely unacceptable for many of those involved in the practical formulation of American strategy, and for like-minded politicians who have exercised significant influence on U.S. foreign policy in the 1980s. They were willing to flirt with the theory of MAD in public only as long as the Soviet Union lagged behind the United States in acquiring a capability for effective retaliation. During that fifteen-year lag, a "window of vulnerability" theoretically existed—not for the United States, but for the Soviet Union. Faced with unceasing military and political pressure from the United States, the USSR finally closed the window through a defense spending effort, just as it had earlier put an end to the American nuclear monopoly.

This change in objective circumstances, which created the threat of mutual annihilation in nuclear war, prompted the recognition of our shared interest in mutual survival. In their November 1985 joint statement that nuclear war cannot be won and must not be fought, General Secretary Gorbachev and President Reagan acknowledged this "nuclear learning." Nowadays all sober-minded politicians and strategists recognize that a nuclear conflict between the superpowers would have catastrophic consequences for global civilization, and could wipe the human species from the face of the earth.

This is a most important juncture in humanity's progress toward harnessing the powerful forces of nature. Our best minds and our most advanced production facilities have used the discovered laws of nature to perfect means of war, which now include weapons of mass annihilation. This result was not deliberately planned, but emerged through the logic of military competition. To legitimize and accept this situation on a permanent basis would mean committing the fate of the whole world to chance: to computer or human error.

Most politicians in the United States and in the Soviet Union would agree that deterrence on the basis of the "balance of fear" cannot be tolerated for long. The question is what to do about it. Different answers are given to this question in the two nations.

More than one answer is offered in the United States. Robert McNamara now believes that in order to avoid a catastrophe both sides will have to diminish drastically their reliance on nuclear weapons. He writes, "We can lay the foundation for entering the twenty-first century with a totally different nuclear strategy, one of mutual security, instead of war-fighting; with vastly smaller nuclear forces, no more than one thousand weapons in place of fifty thousand, and with a dramatically lower risk that our civilization will be destroyed."[8] McNamara's views appear to be supported by many responsible public figures in the United States and by the broad public as well. In the well-known pastoral letter on the issues of war and peace, American Catholics quote Pope John Paul II as stressing at Hiroshima that "from now on it is only through a conscious choice and through deliberate policy that humanity can survive."[9]

Under the Reagan administration, however, the United States pursued a dynamic program to build up offensive nuclear systems (Trident-2, B-1B, Stealth, MX, Midgetman). With state-of-the-art weapons design in both countries, Pentagon strategists have not been able to discover any way to outstrip the Soviet Union in the improvement of offensive weapons. So attention turned to defensive weapons. It was in these terms that President Reagan described his Strategic Defense Initiative (SDI) on March 23, 1983, challenging the USSR to a new round in the arms race. The Strategic Defense Initiative, he stressed, aims at "countering the awesome Soviet missile threat" with "the very strength in technology that spawned our great industrial base." [10]

By extending strategic arms to outer space, the intent was to replace a situation of mutual assured destruction with one of mutual assured survival (MAS). Thus, as Joseph Nye noted in Chapter 5, the regime for arms race stability is "uncertain." The SALT agreements had formed a partial security regime based on the acceptance of parity, recognition of mutual vulnerability, and agreement to limit both offense and defense. But the SDI calls into question all these principles.

Hoping to sell the SDI concept to American and world public opinion, the former president promised to share with the USSR the results of American defense research at some point in the future. It is hard for the Soviet side to believe this promise. As one of our American colleagues commented during our joint study, "If it doesn't work we will share it; if it works we'll keep it for ourselves." In his press conference following the 1985 Geneva summit Gorbachev stated:

> They say: believe us, if the Americans were the first to develop the SDI, they would share their experience with the Soviet Union. I then said; Mr. President, I call on you to believe us. We have already said that we would not be the first to use nuclear weapons and we would not attack the United States. Why, then, do you, while preserving the entire offensive potential on earth and under water, intend to start the arms race also in space? You don't believe us? This shows you don't. Why, then, should we believe you more than you believe us? [11]

Behind Washington's rhetoric of mutual assured survival lies a desire to return to the original rules of the game in the arms race—breaking through and leaving the other side behind, dealing with the rest of the world, including the Soviet Union, from a position of (at least relative) invulnerability. What was presented as "new thinking" was actually adherence to the traditional formula *si vis pacem, para bellum* (if you want peace, prepare for war).

Many compelling studies have proved that the SDI is not capable of hitting the myriad targets in space and that the projected "astrodome" will leak like a sieve. But, for the sake of argument, let us assume that a relatively impenetrable space "shield" could be created. What would happen if first the United States and then the USSR built such a shield? The first and most important effect would be the continuation of an unchecked arms race surpassing anything we have known so far—scientifically, technologically, and financially. Even now the arms race undermines the economies of all countries, particularly the nuclear powers, absorbing huge sums and resources that could otherwise be used to raise the living standards of their people and to assist developing nations. Such projects could also have unpredictable global ecological consequences (consider, for example, the problem of the ozone hole over the Antarctic).

If the United States were to build an impenetrable shield, discarding the mutual vulnerability formula, could it acquire a decisive advantage? The USSR obviously would not sit still and allow the United States to acquire significant strategic superiority. Forty years of the strategic arms race should have proved that neither side can attain absolute security by outstripping the other. It is conceivable that the United States could acquire a marginal superiority that could lead to bolder international behavior. But how much did the United States do against the USSR and its allies even when it had overwhelming superiority during the American nuclear monopoly and colossal predominance in strategic delivery vehicles? Is the acquisition of such provisional advantage worth all the effort and expenditures?

Let us imagine that the USSR then creates its own astrodome. A government that had invested hundreds of billions of dollars in demanding a unique, exceptional position for the United States could not stop there. Were the USSR to obtain equal capability in the sphere of defense, the United States would feel compelled to go farther, to ever new superexotic weapon systems. Henry Kissinger once observed that the road is endless: there is no final destination in the military competition between the superpowers. If a final station exists, it is beyond human civilization.

If a crisis developed and each side attempted to pierce the other's shield, what would happen to the thousands of nuclear warheads that, under the most optimistic assumptions, would be rendered impotent by ballistic missile defenses? They would simply fall to earth, as happened with the nuclear bombs that accidentally fell from an American B-52 bomber over Spain in the early 1960s. To this day, despite radical measures to sanitize the area through soil removal, and so on, there is reportedly an abnormally high level of radiation where those two or three bombs fell. In the case of a U.S.-Soviet nuclear exchange, the debris would consist of approximately 30,000 warheads. Has anyone calculated the consequences? Or does the "strategy" boil down to calculating how many weapons to deploy in space, and how many targets?

Finally, why should a potential adversary be willing to ensure a "smooth transition" to a new situation of American dominance? Is it not in this rival nation's interests to make the transition as rough as possible—for example, by increasing the number of deliverable offensive warheads so that the United States could not rely on its "shield" to protect it from the consequences of wanton international behavior? In other words, a strategic arms race in space will only deepen the sharp confrontation, producing a mutuality of negation in U.S.-Soviet relations. Forty years of the arms race, to say nothing of the whole human history of the sword versus shield approach, confirm the unsuitability of this attempt to achieve security.

The Soviet Union also believes that mutual assured destruction is unacceptable in the long run. Although the present nuclear balance provides security through equal danger, the level of the balance is too high. A continuation of the strategic arms race, as Mikhail Gorbachev has noted, could bring it to such a level that even parity would cease to be a factor of deterrence. With a continued arms race, he has observed "the situation in the world may assume such a character that it will no longer depend upon the intelligence or will of political leaders. It may become captive to technology, to military-technocratic logic. Consequently, not only nuclear war itself, but also the preparations for it, in other words, the arms race, the aspiration to win military superiority can, speaking in objective terms, bring no political gain to anybody."[12]

A NONMILITARY TRACK
TO MUTUAL SECURITY

We need an alternative, nonmilitary path to mutual security, with a basis in contractual agreement rather than unilateral actions. The Soviet Union has formulated its program for the creation of a comprehensive system of international security, which can be called a real system of mutually assured survival. It is based on the premise of mutual interdependence among all nations in security matters. The fundamental principles of such a system were elaborated by General Secretary Mikhail Gorbachev at the 27th Congress of the Communist Party of the Soviet Union.[13]

As the Soviet leadership has indicated, there are various ways to deal with the fundamental threat to mutual survival, and all should be pursued simultaneously. One approach is to adopt drastic measures of disarmament, especially nuclear disarmament. A second is to search for ways to ban the use of military force in the U.S.-Soviet competition. Most Soviet-American negotiations during the past twenty years have dealt with nuclear arms limitations. The Anti-Ballistic Missile (ABM) Treaty of 1972 was the most significant limiting measure, but its terms were challenged by the Reagan administration. Though no arms control agreements were reached during the first six years of the Reagan administration, the signing of the INF treaty, with its unprecedented verification measures, in December 1987 signifies a very important first step toward nuclear disarmament.

To achieve deep reductions in nuclear weapons, both sides will have to give up any lingering notions of achieving political or military advantage from superior types or numbers of nuclear weapons. All strategies of nuclear war-fighting must be jettisoned. The policy goal of the future should be just the opposite—to achieve the most stable framework of deterrence. Giving up the ABM treaty and moving to a major program of strategic defense would amount to rearmament. As noted earlier, if one side were to produce a successful defense against nuclear weapons, the other side would inevitably feel threatened because the balance of nuclear deterrence (understood as dissuasion) would be in jeopardy. Finally, all concepts of launch-on-warning or launch-under-attack must be abandoned. Deep cuts in nuclear arsenals, especially the elimination of first-strike weapons, would remove any justification for early launch procedures. The joint resolution of the Soviet and American governments to begin intensive discussion of the problem of strategic stability while pursuing strategic offensive weapon reductions is a positive step.

Other forms of disarmament are also very important, including a verifiable ban on the production of chemical weapons and the destruction of existing stockpiles of such weapons. A key problem is sharp reductions in conventional force levels in central Europe. Another important goal should be the phased mutual withdrawal of

U.S. and Soviet forces from overseas bases, including naval and air bases.

Most of the essential measures of disarmament will be very difficult to achieve until both sides have persuasively demonstrated that they no longer seek to advance their political objectives through military force. Political leaderships in both the Soviet Union and the United States will be unable to move very far toward disarmament as long as there is demonstrable evidence that the other side has offensive military intentions.

If we are to avoid nuclear war, we must demilitarize our competition. The United Nations Charter, the Basic Principles Agreement on U.S.-Soviet Relations of 1972, and the Helsinki Act of 1975 all provide that the signatories shall refrain from the threat or use of force against the territorial integrity or political independence of any state. The United States and Soviet Union have intervened, directly or indirectly, with combat forces on several occasions despite those agreements. The unilateral actions of the superpowers have weakened the international agreements. Furthermore, the example of the superpowers has provided a rationalization for smaller states to engage in military aggression without inhibition.

There are compelling reasons for the Soviet Union and the United States to reach an understanding that their relationship must be one of stable coexistence, in which the ideological competition is conducted without the use of military force. The first reason relates to mutual survival. The danger of unintentional nuclear war is growing, especially during periods of international crisis. Second, the continuing arms race jeopardizes the stability and growth of the economies of both nations. Third, the overwhelming majority opinion of other nations in the world favors an end to the cold war and the arms race.

The demilitarization of Soviet-American competition requires new political thinking. General Secretary Gorbachev and other Soviet leaders have already demonstrated new thinking about nuclear weapons and nuclear war. The Soviet Union has solemnly pledged never to be the first to use nuclear weapons. The Warsaw Pact countries have proposed to NATO countries that the ground forces and tactical aviation of both blocs be drastically cut—by 25 percent. The leaders of the Warsaw Pact countries have also affirmed that any regional problem can be settled in a just way by peaceful means, without outside interference. They oppose dividing the world into spheres of interest, or spheres of influence. The Soviet government's concept of universal security is based on the new thinking that stipulates concerted actions by the world community to reform the present system of international relations, with much more stress on political aspects of security, on basic human values and interests that should have priority over local or group interests. This system of universal security is viewed as a program to enhance the role of the United Nations and its charter as the main peace-keeping instruments.

Until the end of its eight-year tenure, the Reagan administration was more ideological and confrontational in its anti-Soviet rhetoric than any U.S. government since World War II. Some American political leaders, however, have questioned the assumptions and goals of U.S. national security policy during the first half of the 1980s. It is possible that strong elements of new thinking will emerge as the United States undergoes a change in leadership.

If the USSR and the United States seek to reach an understanding to demilitarize future competition, they should attempt to establish more clearly the ground rules for using military aid—only for defensive purposes and only in response to external aggression. The distinction between prevention and pre-emption may be difficult to make, but it should be less difficult in an atmosphere of reduced tensions. Soviet and American scholars have discussed together the possibility that the two superpowers might explore the feasibility of agreeing to cut military aid to countries engaged in fighting outside their borders, limiting the number of military advisers, and banning the use of so-called covert paramilitary or volunteer forces (usually such forces do not remain covert for long, because their source of support becomes exposed).

A demilitarization of competition could lead to greater Soviet-American cooperation in resolving tensions in the Middle East and the Persian Gulf—the two areas of greatest risk of crisis today. Clearly, the USSR and United States will have to work together toward a diplomatic solution if an explosive outcome is to be averted.

There is also a growing danger, if the arms race continues, that more nations will produce or acquire nuclear weapons. Such proliferation of nuclear capabilities will increase the risks of nuclear war, especially in the less stable areas of the world. Demilitarization of the U.S.-Soviet relationship could have significant influence in blocking further nuclear proliferation. Smaller powers bent on justifying their nuclear programs have often argued that, if the superpowers can continue such production, they should be able to do so too.

If the USSR and the United States stop the arms race, their joint influence could be substantial. If the two nations agree to compete through political, economic, and ideological means without recourse to military force, the nature of other world conflicts will be affected. The balance of power today throughout the world is substantially influenced by the Soviet Union and the United States, as it has been since mutuality in the Soviet-American relationship began at the end of World War II. The progressive militarization that came about during the cold war can be reversed through new thinking.

NOTES

1. Alan Rosenberg, "A Smoking, Radiating Ruin at the End of Two Hours," Documents on American Plans for Nuclear War with the Soviet Union, 1954–55, *International Security*, Winter 1981–82, pp. 3–38.
2. *Foreign Relations of the United States 1950*, vol. 1 (Washington, D.C.: Government Printing Office, 1977), p. 272.
3. Speech given at American University, Washington, D.C., June 10, 1963, quoted in John F. Kennedy, *The Burden and the Glory* (New York: Harper and Row, 1964), p. 56.
4. Quoted in J. Anthony Lucas, "Class Reunion: Kennedy's Men Relive the Cuban Missile Crisis," *New York Times Magazine*, August 30, 1987, p. 61.
5. Robert S. McNamara, *The Essence of Security: Reflections in Office* (New York: Harper and Row, 1968), pp. 55–56.
6. Dean Rusk et al., quoted in *Time*, September 27, 1982, p. 85.
7. H.A. Kissinger, "The Political Realities of the Transatlantic Relationship in the Future of European Deterrence," in *The Future of European Defence: Proceedings of the Second International Round Table Conference of the Netherlands Atlantic Commission on May 24 and 25, 1985*, edited by Frans Bletz and Rio Praaning (Dordrecht: Martin Nijhoff Publishers, 1986), p. 97.
8. Robert S. McNamara, *Blundering Into Disaster: Surviving the First Century of the Nuclear Age* (New York: Pantheon Books), p. 143.
9. *Origins* (Washington, D.C.: National Catholic News Service, May 19, 1983), p. 2.
10. *Weekly Compilation of Presidential Documents* (Washington, D.C.: Office of the Federal Register, National Archives and Records Service, General Services Administration: Supt. of Docs., U.S. G.P.O., distributor March 28, 1983, vol. 19, no. 12), p. 447.
11. *Pravda*, November 22, 1985.
12. M.S. Gorbachev, "Political Report of the CPSU Central Committee to the 27th Party Congress" (Moscow: Novosti Press Agency Publishing House, 1986), p. 83.
13. M.S. Gorbachev, *op. cit.*

AMERICAN VIEW

Joseph S. Nye, Jr.

Mutual security is now a popular slogan as well as an apt description of the U.S.-Soviet strategic relationship. In his thoughtful chapter Henry Trofimenko correctly points out that the problems of mutuality emerged at the end of World War II. Yet the understanding of the mutuality inherent in strategic interdependence has taken time to evolve. As Alexander George and his colleagues have written, "mutual adaptation and cooperation have been forced on leaders of the superpowers by their recognition of the limits of their ability to assure the security of their country by strictly unilateral policies. . . . The superpowers have been forced by their mutual dependence on each other for security to engage in a complex, continuing process of 'partisan mutual adjustment.'"[1]

I agree with Trofimenko that strategic mutuality developed after 1945, when the prewar multipolar balance gave way to bipolarity. Earlier there had been periods of both hostility and cooperation in U.S.-Soviet relations, but neither country was the primary security focus of the other. The prostration of the other powers at the end of the war left only the Soviets and the Americans. In one sense, Trofimenko is right that the two countries did not really have much to quarrel about. They were geographically distant; one is a maritime power and the other a land power. Both might have withdrawn from Europe, but as George Kennan pointed out, Europe was too critical to the global balance of power and the German problem too important to permit such a strategy. Instead the two countries found themselves cheek by jowl.

I also agree with Trofimenko that objectively the United States was in a stronger position and that the Soviet Union was only a fledgling superpower in 1945. The United States had suffered relatively little destruction and until 1949 was the only nation to possess nuclear weapons. But after the Americans demobilized their armies in 1945 and 1946, the Soviet Union had a conventional military preponderance on the European continent. Thus there was a balance of asymmetries.

Equally important are the psychological and perceptual dimensions of mutuality. Though objectively the Americans may have been stronger, they felt weak and threatened in Europe. The mutuality was one of fear, exacerbated by ideological differences that inhibited clear communication.

The Soviet development of nuclear weapons and progress toward nuclear parity reinforced such fears because they called into question the balance of asymmetries. At the same time, nuclear weapons added a new dimension to the mutuality of strategic interaction. While Trofimenko is correct that bipolar political competition tends to be zero-sum, in the sense that one side's gain is equal to the other side's loss, the possibility of mutual nuclear devastation added a non-zero-sum dimension to the relationship. The game now involved avoiding joint loss. The story of the last three decades has been one of slowly learning how to manage the non-zero-sum mutuality of the nuclear game while still locked in the zero-sum mutuality of the bi-polar political game. As I argue in Chapter 5, the learning process has been slow and imperfect. Nonetheless, it has occurred. As Trofimenko notes, staring into the abyss in 1962 may have quickened the learning on both sides.

Trofimenko's chapter raises two issues about which I am uneasy. One relates to the concept of "correlation of forces." Since this concept is very broad and covers a wide range of indicators, it is easily abused by political leaders. Is it true that the correlation of forces shifted from the 1970s to the 1980s, or was it more a shift in the psychology of leadership groups? And if subjective elements play a large role in the concept, can it not be politically manipulated by those on either side who wish to drive policy in risky directions? Perhaps in the development of new thinking about international affairs the two countries should try to clarify the concepts that express the two dimensions of their mutuality so as to minimize misperceptions.

I am also troubled by Trofimenko's conclusion that denuclearization will improve the U.S.-Soviet relationship. Arms control may help, but total denuclearization must await the development of a different political relationship. Otherwise it would remove the major current sources of non-zero-sum mutuality in the relationship and leave the zero-sum bipolar condition. Since nuclear weapons can always be reinvented (the knowledge cannot be destroyed), premature abolition might actually raise the risks of nuclear war. The dilemma was well expressed in the following dialogue between two thoughtful Soviet commentators.

Bovin: A 100% guarantee of survival can only be nuclear disarmament—the liquidation of nuclear arms.

Lukin: In that there is still a good deal to think over. You would agree the objective is not simply to reduce the quantity of arms. We want to reduce the danger of war. Let us assume that all nuclear weapons are eliminated. Will that mean as well the elimination of the danger of nuclear war? Not only M. Thatcher thinks that the elimination of the nuclear brakes of nuclear deterrence might increase the danger of non-nuclear wars, including major (world) wars. Doesn't it seem to you that an unambiguous answer to this question at this point is difficult to offer?[2]

NOTES

1. Alexander L. George, Philip J. Farley, and Alexander Dallin, eds., *U.S.-Soviet Security Cooperation: Achievement, Failures, Lessons* (Oxford University Press, 1988).
2. Vladimir Lukin and Alexander Bovin (Dialogue) "On the Threshold of the New Century," *MEMO (World Economy and International Politics)*, no. 12 (December 1987), p. 62.

7 TOWARD A COMMON FRAMEWORK
Avoiding Inadvertent War and Crisis

Bruce J. Allyn

Chapter 5 outlined five areas of nuclear learning in which the United States and Soviet Union have developed a core of consensual knowledge. The second of these areas—avoiding inadvertent war and crisis—has involved a long and (in historical perspective) dramatic evolution of views. After tracing the development of Soviet views on the subject, I shall compare Soviet and American understandings of key terms relating to crisis avoidance, focusing on the problem of finding a common language to deal with the problem.[1]

For decades, Soviet doctrine held that world war was inevitable and would be deliberately unleashed by the West. But since 1956 (when Khrushchev formally revised this doctrine), Soviet views have evolved toward greater recognition of the shared danger of inadvertent nuclear war. In the Gorbachev era, official Soviet pronouncements and specialist writings have stressed inadvertent paths to nuclear war as a major element of "new political thinking" in international affairs. A 1988 article in the authoritative party journal *Kommunist* all but ruled out the traditional Soviet scenario of deliberate attack by the West.[2] New emphasis has been placed on the danger of rapid escalation of a regional crisis (due to factors neither side can control), erroneous political decision making under severe time constraints in a crisis, and technical accident, the impact of which is magnified in times of tension and crisis. Gorbachev has raised the specter of a world "captive to chance."[3]

185

These changes in official doctrine reflect "nuclear learning" and a serious reassessment of the threat facing the Soviet state. At the same time, they have served Soviet domestic and foreign policy goals. The Gorbachev leadership appears to recognize that the power of a modern state is increasingly defined by the strength of its domestic economy. The official de-emphasis on the danger of deliberate war provides a rationale for shifting resources away from the military to the domestic *perestroika*. Soviet expressions of concern about inadvertent war have also played to public fears, as in the early 1980s during the Soviet "peace offensive" against deployment of American missiles in Europe. Yet Soviet statements and writings have shown growing awareness of the dangers of inadvertent war and crisis since the 1950s. Their thinking appears to have evolved as a result of learning from historical experience.

Beginning with the 1963 hot line agreement, the United States and the Soviet Union have made progress on various measures to avoid inadvertent war and crisis, during times when the countries sought to improve relations, and when competing interests did not override the cooperative interests in avoiding a war that neither side wanted. Measures to avoid inadvertent war, which are less central to the U.S.-Soviet competition and thus relatively easy to agree upon, can serve as an "entering wedge" to make progress on more difficult issues, such as arms control.[4]

THE KHRUSHCHEV PERIOD: CRISIS PREVENTION IN THEORY AND PRACTICE

The Possibility of Preventing War and Crisis

At the Twentieth Party Congress (1956), Khrushchev declared that world war was no longer "fatalistically inevitable," even though the capitalist threat had not been eliminated. Several factors influenced this abandonment of the earlier Soviet doctrine that war between the socialist and bourgeois states was inevitable. The Berlin Crisis of 1948 had not escalated to war; the Korean War had remained limited. According to the documents of the 1956 Party Congress and the Party Program of 1961, advances in Soviet military capability—the development of nuclear and thermonuclear weapons, and ICBMs—had made it possible to prevent a new world war. The socialist camp was now strong enough to deter the imperialist camp from a deliberate attack leading to global war.

Other factors lay behind the doctrinal shift. Khrushchev's program of "peaceful coexistence" included a new stress on the economic factors in the East-West competition; if war was not inevitable, then it was safe to proceed with Khrushchev's plan to channel more resources to domestic consumer goods and agriculture. Considerations of crisis stability also supported the new view. If an adversary took seriously the declared Soviet position that war was inevitable, it would have an incentive to pre-empt in an acute crisis.

The growing destructive power of nuclear stockpiles made modification of doctrine inevitable. Khrushchev's 1956 statement can be seen as the beginning of governmental learning regarding the destructive power of nuclear weapons. In fact, Soviet behavior during the 1950s suggests that the leadership believed a nuclear war would be catastrophic for both sides. Horrified by Mao Zedong's cavalier attitude toward use of nuclear weapons against the West, Soviet leaders decided in June 1959 to renege on the agreement to provide China with nuclear weapons.[5] Even more instructive is Andrei Gromyko's revelation that during the Taiwan Straits Crisis of 1958 the Soviet Union rejected a proposal by Mao to lure American troops into the interior of China, then attack them with nuclear weapons.[6]

But even after 1956, Soviet doctrine still held that a nuclear war would destroy only capitalism. The 1961 Soviet Party Program stated that "should imperialist aggressors unleash a new world war, the peoples . . . will sweep *imperialism* away and bury it" (emphasis added). This public Soviet position, however, was related primarily to Sino-Soviet polemics over leadership of the world communist movement. Ideological consistency demanded that the Kremlin espouse an official position of revolutionary, not preventive, diplomacy. The Soviet side generally refrained from publicly declaring that nuclear war would not further revolutionary purposes, although there were exceptions—like the 1963 *Pravda* article (directed toward the Chinese) that wryly noted, "The atomic bomb does not observe the class principle."[7] The statement regarding socialist victory in a new world war was not deleted until the new edition of the Party Program in 1986.

Gorbachev has argued that Khrushchev's 1956 doctrinal revision "implied that a future conflict could not just be postponed, and a 'peaceful respite' prolonged, but that any international crisis could be settled by peaceful means."[8] And if a *deliberate* world war could be prevented, it logically followed that attention should be directed to preventing a nuclear war through accident and inadvertence. Soviet military and civilian specialists began to consider these new scenarios in the late 1950s and 1960s.

Recognizing the Danger of Inadvertent Nuclear War

Given the historicist character of Marxist-Leninist ideology, the burden of Soviet argument has traditionally been to "reveal" the historically *determined* nature of war and conflict, and the *deliberate* premeditation to unleash war. In assessing the causes of World War I, for example, Soviet historians have traditionally emphasized the allegedly deterministic, deep causal elements in "the uneven development of capitalism."[9] According to recent Soviet historiography, the emergence of World War II was deliberate though not "fatalistically inevitable." The war resulted because Western nations failed to respond to the Soviet drive for collective security, which could have prevented fascist Germany from deliberately unleashing the war.[10]

After World War II, the scenario of deliberate surprise attack dominated Soviet thinking. The overriding lesson of the war was that surprise attack from Europe represented the primary threat to the Soviet Union, and that therefore a buffer of client states was needed for Soviet security. In this context, an international crisis was seen only as a prelude to deliberate war.

During the mid-1950s, the Soviet Union first expressed concern about preventing technical accidents and unauthorized launch of nuclear weapons. The official Soviet approach to the 1955 "Open Skies" proposal, as well as the 1958 Geneva Surprise Attack Conference, was to subordinate issues of data exchange and other specific technical proposals to calls for general and complete disarmament. Soviet commentators argued that the danger of technical accident is acute only if political relations are strained, particularly in conditions of an arms race. As one wrote, "Any technical device may fail, but a technical failure may lead to disaster only in *a climate of artificially heightened tensions.*"[11] By the early 1960s, Soviet military writings began to mention that accidents can be a *casus belli* in times of international tension.[12]

In the 1950s, Soviet specialists wrote little on the dangers of regional escalation. Anticipating continued growth in the socialist camp and the world communist movement, the Khrushchev leadership sought to win over Third World states. Even though a general world war was no longer considered inevitable, Soviet writings stressed that limited wars in the Third World were still likely, national-liberation wars were inevitable, and there might be wars among Western imperialist states, which would be plagued by economic and political crises.

Soviet and American perceptions of the danger of war during the 1961 Berlin crisis may have differed significantly. Though the stakes were high for the Soviets, Khrushchev may have felt he could turn the crisis on and off at will.[13] In the 1960s, for reasons assessed below, Soviet military and civilian specialists began to pay more attention to the risk that a regional crisis might escalate to the nuclear level.

Cuba 1962: The Role of Inadvertent Factors

Khrushchev and his colleagues may have learned from the Cuban missile crisis a profound lesson about the dangers of inadvertence (see Chapter 4). At the time, only the Soviet (and Cuban) leadership knew that certain critical events during the crisis were due to unintended and uncontrollable factors.

After conceiving the idea to install the missiles in April 1962, the Soviet leadership sent Marshal Biriuzov, commander of strategic rocket forces, to Cuba in early May. Biriuzov carried a letter proposing the missile installation if Castro agreed and if Biriuzov believed it could be done without American discovery.[14] Receiving affirmative answers, Khrushchev decided to try to install the missiles secretly. But construction crews followed standard operating procedures for installing nuclear missile sites (there had been no need to camouflage missile installations in the Soviet Union), and no one at the scene thought to camouflage the sites.[15] As a result, the missile sites were easily detected by American reconnaissance planes. A failure to coordinate with the Cubans may have been behind the blunder, perhaps because of the Soviets' insistence on strict self-reliance.[16]

More significantly, at the time of the crisis, only the Soviet (and Cuban) leadership knew that the shooting down of an American U-2 surveillance aircraft over Cuba on October 27 directly violated standing orders from Moscow. Though the ExComm took the shooting in stride, they could only assume it was a deliberate escalatory step in Khrushchev's coercive missile diplomacy.[17] In his memoirs, Khrushchev later blamed the Cubans for the shoot-down. Some American analysts have speculated that there was a Cuban-Soviet firefight for control of the SAM sites.[18] But Sergo Mikoyan reports a personal conversation with the Soviet commander who, most likely believing an American attack was soon to follow, gave the order to shoot down the plane. Evidence suggests that a Soviet commander, General Igor D. Statsenko, ordered the shoot-down and that Castro was willing to take the blame for the incident. Burlatsky reports (in Chapter 4) that Khrushchev was shocked to learn the plane had been shot down; the incident made it painfully clear that his control over developments in Cuba had evaporated. Members of the ExComm had their own reasons to be concerned about dangerous unintended events—especially after an American U-2 plane on a routine air-sampling mission accidentally strayed over Siberia at the height of the crisis.

Finally, during the crisis, only a few Soviet leaders knew that Khrushchev had no clear plan for action after the U.S. discovered the missile sites and publicly announced a blockade. Burlatsky highlights the importance of irrational, psychological factors. Because of his "emotional and impulsive" nature, Khrushchev acted without developing well-considered options for what to do if the Americans discovered the missiles and reacted in some way other than seeking direct negotiations. As Robert McNamara notes in Chapter 4, the U.S. side was convinced that Khrushchev had a contingency plan to take action in Berlin or Turkey if the United States acted to remove the missiles. Lacking direct knowledge to the contrary, the Americans interpreted the new data as part of a rational, planned strategy consistent with prior beliefs.

What did the Soviets learn about the dangers of inadvertence? In the Gorbachev era, the Cuban crisis has assumed symbolic importance as the beginning of "new thinking" in international affairs—particularly the recognition that the shared nuclear threat supersedes ideology and class interests. But to examine what Khrushchev and his immediate successors learned, we should briefly touch on changes in Soviet policy and behavior after 1962.

Following the crisis, both Khrushchev and Kennedy took steps to improve U.S.-Soviet relations. In 1963 the hot line agreement was signed, and the Limited Test Ban Treaty was successfully negotiated. As for the Soviets' management of nuclear operations, Western analysts had noted their strong concern about loss of control over events and forces well before the Cuban crisis.[19] Soviet leaders have always been extremely cautious with regard to control of nuclear warheads and relations with their allies. Until 1978, Soviet tactical nuclear delivery vehicles were housed in Eastern Europe, but their associated nuclear charges were kept on Soviet territory. And in the 1960s, the Soviet leadership spurned Eastern European efforts to gain access to nuclear warheads for tactical missiles.[20] Permissive Action Links (PALs) were introduced at some point after the crisis. But the reason may not have been further concern about loss of control, but a desire to have nuclear warheads remain on ICBMs which were on alert (with PALs to prevent unauthorized launch). In the latter part of the 1960s, Soviet ICBMs, IRBMs and SLBMs were armed with their nuclear charges and the KGB relinquished direct physical control over nuclear warheads (possibly for technical reasons).[21]

The Soviet military began to concern itself with the problem of escalation from conventional to nuclear warfare in the mid-1960s. But the independent effect of the Cuban crisis is difficult to assess, as the concern with escalation related directly to the evolution of the strategic balance and the military balance in Europe.[22]

The death of President Kennedy and the ouster of Chairman Khrushchev removed the two leaders who had absorbed most fully the central lessons of the event for crisis prevention and management. In the intense drama of the crisis, a personal relationship had been forged between the two men, not an insignificant factor for successful crisis management. In his memoirs, Khrushchev referred to Kennedy, after the crisis, as a man he could trust.[23]

It is often asserted that the Soviets also took from the Caribbean crisis a lesson about the importance of strategic nuclear parity. Vasily Kuznetsov, then first deputy foreign minister, is reported to have declared shortly after the crisis that the Soviet Union would "never again" tolerate the humiliation of having to back down under American pressure.[24] But it is not clear that the Cuban crisis was *primarily* responsible for the Soviet buildup to strategic parity; it may instead have been a *consequence* and a reinforcement of that buildup.[25] If

Khrushchev's plan to deploy missiles in Cuba was, as Burlatsky maintains, "the first step to strategic parity," the Soviets may have been bent on achieving parity anyway. In any case, the view that only strategic parity could restrain the United States ultimately prevailed and became the cornerstone of Brezhnev's foreign policy.

In retrospect, it appears that the lesson learned from Cuba may have been only to avoid those regional crises that threatened to escalate to nuclear war. In this sense, Cuba reinforced certain "rules of prudence," especially the practice of not threatening the other's vital interests or area of dominant security concern. Before 1962, the superpowers had not worked out norms of behavior governing Soviet activities in the Western Hemisphere. Apparently expecting the United States to acknowledge the Soviet Union's right to exercise the same prerogatives in the Caribbean that the United States had exercised around the Soviet periphery, Khrushchev misjudged the status of the Monroe Doctrine at that time. In Chapter 4, Burlatsky recalls Khrushchev's thinking as he vacationed on the Black Sea in April 1962, looking in the direction of the American missile base in Turkey: "Why do the Americans have the right to surround us with bases on all sides, and we have no such right?" Transcripts of the ExComm discussions held on October 27, 1962 (declassified 1987), show that President Kennedy expressed considerable concern about the "reasonableness" of the view that, if the United States had the right to place missiles in Turkey, then the Soviet Union should be able to do so in Cuba.[26] Once the Soviet Union attained strategic parity it would increasingly assert its "equal" right to pursue its interests globally.

Since 1962 both sides have redirected their competition to peripheral conflicts in the Third World. Zhurkin and Kremeniuk have argued that "After the shock of the Caribbean Crisis, . . . [the United States] began to transfer the policy of 'probe of force' onto the periphery, to the area of local conflicts."[27] The Cuban crisis marked the end of a period of acute U.S.-Soviet crises, as had occurred over Berlin. In the 1960s and 1970s, U.S. and Soviet involvement in peripheral Third World conflicts would move steadily to the center of the crisis prevention and management agenda.

THE AGREEMENTS OF THE 1970s: THE MIXED
LESSONS OF STRATEGIC PARITY

As Joseph Nye elaborates in Chapter 5, the two superpowers have learned to institutionalize shared interests through "partial security regimes" in Europe, for strategic arms control, avoiding accidental nuclear war, nonproliferation, and neutralizing certain areas. But no comprehensive regime has governed U.S.-Soviet competition in the Third World. For Cuba, the crisis prevention agreement has proven to be quite durable.[28] All the rules of prudence derive from the imperative to avoid nuclear war, which has the highest priority. But it remains an open question how to deal with peripheral conflicts (such as Angola in 1975) that do not risk an immediate superpower confrontation (what Alexander George refers to as U.S.-Soviet competition in the "gray areas" of low-interest symmetry).[29]

During the 1970s the United States and the Soviet Union began to recognize that it may not be enough to make the world safe for non-nuclear conflict: shared interests argue for preventing even those conflicts that do not threaten nuclear war.

Third Area Conflicts in the 1970s: Divergent
U.S.-Soviet Views and Interests

Western analysts usually trace heightened Soviet activism in Third World conflicts back to the achievement of strategic parity in the early 1970s. The Brezhnev leadership regarded the agreements of the early 1970s as formal U.S. acknowledgement of the Soviet Union's equal right to pursue its interests globally. Like Khrushchev pondering American missiles in Turkey, Soviet commentators of the 1970s wondered why it was permissible for the United States to supply advanced fighter aircraft to Pakistan, on the border of the Soviet Union, but impermissible for the Soviet Union to provide MiG-21s to Nicaragua?

Despite the Basic Principles Agreement (BPA) of 1972 and allusions to a "code of détente," there was no regime to regulate U.S.-Soviet competition in regional conflicts. Both U.S. and Soviet declaratory statements began to emphasize the prevention of crises, while passing over fundamental divergences in view that reflected major conflicts of interest.

The prevention of crises became a salient element of Soviet declaratory policy in the early 1970s, but it was based on Brezhnev's *offensive* view of crisis prevention. Soviet official policy and behavior in this area were heavily influenced by the psychological world view of the Brezhnev leadership, which had formed when the "correlation of forces" favored the United States. By the early 1970s, the Soviet Union was finally in position to reap the fruits of military-strategic parity, coupled with its growing force-projection capability: no longer could it be forced to back down.

How did Soviet officials and specialists explain the doctrine of crisis prevention to their internal audience? The same logic used by Khrushchev to declare that a world war could be avoided was now applied by Soviet theoreticians to the issue of international crises. A statement at the 1969 Conference of Communist and Workers' Parties signaled that the prevention of international *crises* could now be seen in the same way as the prevention of a new world *war:*

> Not just once in past years imperialism has provoked acute international crises, placing humanity on the brink of thermonuclear catastrophe. But U.S. imperialism is being forced to consider the correlation of forces which has formed on the international arena, the nuclear potential of the Soviet Union and the possible consequences of a nuclear war; it is becoming harder, more dangerous to gamble on unleashing a new world war.[30]

Military-strategic parity was to be the centerpiece of crisis prevention, which in the Brezhnev era meant forcing the West to desist from "provoking" crises. (Imperialist states were regarded as using crises to confront the USSR and advance U.S. foreign policy goals, a practice referred to in Soviet literature as Western "crisis diplomacy" or "crisis strategy".) No doubt the Cuban experience contributed to the highly charged Soviet view of U.S. crisis diplomacy.

Soviet specialists argued that as the USSR achieved strategic parity, the West's crisis diplomacy became too risky for its own security interests.[31] Specialists began to argue that after the USSR attained strategic parity, the United States engaged less often in coercive bargaining, especially the use of nuclear alerts to signal resolve in a crisis.[32]

Thus the Brezhnev leadership's approach to crisis prevention was based on the deterrent effect of strategic nuclear parity, not direct coordination or cooperation. Yet certain shared interests were reflected in the agreements of the early 1970s. The Soviet leadership wanted to improve relations with the West for a range of domestic and foreign policy reasons.[33] The Accidents Measures Agreement (1971) codified the long-term shared interest in preventing war through technical accident, and the broader concern to prevent inadvertent war was reflected in the Incidents at Sea Agreement (1972). The Soviets were also interested in direct cooperation with the United States with regard to certain third parties. Western analysts typically underestimate the Soviet leadership's concern in the early 1970s over how to manage a Chinese confrontation, which was a major element in the Soviet calculus underlying crisis prevention efforts with the United States.[34]

Parity and Soviet Risk-taking

Public Soviet documents throughout the 1970s made it clear that Brezhnev's offensive view of crisis prevention did not mean an end to Soviet assistance to "progressive" forces in the Third World. Soviet specialists emphasized that the "new possibility" for crisis prevention was the result of strategic parity and the Soviet capability "to apply wide, multilateral assistance to victims of local aggressive actions."[35] The Basic Principles Agreement of 1972 included both the preferred Soviet formulation "peaceful coexistence," which allowed "progressive" armed struggle, and the "no unilateral advantage" phraseology preferred by the United States. ("Peaceful coexistence" was then still defined in Soviet doctrine as a "specific form of class struggle"; this phrase was deleted at the Twenty-seventh Party Congress in 1986.) Given this divergence in view, the Basic Principles Agreement could not have been effective as a crisis prevention agreement (and neither side made any attempt to operationalize it).[36]

Western critics of the 1970s détente have focused on Soviet rhetoric regarding the changed "correlation of forces" and the allegedly consequent Soviet activism in Third World conflicts. Soviet assessment of the correlation of forces has traditionally been influenced by the general world view and analytical categories of Soviet ideology. From this perspective, there are three types of crisis: the "general crisis" of capitalism, cyclical crises of capitalist economies, and "international-political crises."

To what extent does Soviet risk-taking respond to perceived changes in the correlation of forces between the United States and the USSR—specifically to cyclical changes in American political and economic conditions, and to the policy of different administrations? Some observers believe that if the Soviets perceive the adversary is weak (in a state of deepening crisis and collapse), they will exploit opportunities to tilt the correlation of forces even further toward socialism. If the adversary is declared to be strong (no imminent collapse), then greater caution must be exercised.

Thus, the argument goes, with the United States in a political-moral crisis after Vietnam and Watergate, and a cyclical economic crisis (following the OPEC oil embargo), Soviet ideology proclaimed a sharpening of the crises of capitalism in the 1970s. Therefore the Soviet side was prepared to take more risks to exploit opportunities in the Third World, and the 1970s was a time of heightened Soviet (and Cuban) activism in Angola, Mozambique, Ethiopia, and South Yemen, culminating in the Soviet invasion of Afghanistan. Critics charge that Soviet behavior in third-area crises in the 1970s was inconsistent with the increasing declaratory stress on crisis prevention.

By the early 1980s, before the Gorbachev leadership came to power, some Soviet specialist writings began to suggest that the pursuit of marginal advantages in Third World conflicts might not serve Soviet interests, because of the damaging effects on the central U.S.-Soviet relationship, especially on arms control negotiations. This lesson implies a need to insulate the central relationship from regional conflicts and crises by developing specific agreements to delimit U.S.-Soviet competition in third areas, through mechanisms such as regional negotiations.

The standard Soviet view is that the linkage between Third World conflicts and the central U.S.-Soviet relationship during the 1970s was a Western ploy:

> . . . in the beginning of the 70s the policy of "linkage" developed as a whole as an attempt to achieve unilateral concessions from the USSR under the pretext of the necessity to consider U.S. interests and its allies in regional conflicts.[37]

Soviet commentators decried such linkage as a deliberate effort to sabotage détente. They observed that the Soviet leaders did not link the 1972 Nixon-Brezhnev summit to U.S. action against their North

Vietnamese ally, even though the United States mined the port of Haiphong on the eve of the summit. (This decision reportedly was contested at the Politburo level.[38]) Soviets also argue that they put détente above such losses as the swing of Egypt to the United States. Moreover, they argue, the Soviet Union did not make change in U.S. policy toward such countries as Chile a precondition for relations.

Yet Soviet specialists began to recognize that such de-linkage, however rational in some cases, is simply not possible in a populist democracy like the United States. Whether or not the United States actively pursues a policy of linkage, it is a political fact. A 1983 study of international conflict by the Soviet Institute of World Economy and International Relations (IMEMO) noted that, in the 1970s, local conflicts began to "interact" with the central U.S.-Soviet relationship and had "dangerous consequences for the development of détente itself."[39] A 1984 study by the Institute of USA and Canada (ISKAN) observed that "through a system of feedback, regional policy puts serious questions before global strategy and at times forces a correction of past policy. . . ."[40] In a rare official statement, General Secretary Andropov acknowledged that the invasion of Afghanistan poisoned the atmosphere for negotiations—as illustrated by the demise of SALT II.[41] As *glasnost* has come to international affairs, Soviet officials have expressed disagreement with the decision to invade Afghanistan, made by no more than four or five Soviet leaders. The Institute of Economics of the World Socialist System reportedly protested to the Politburo that the intervention would undermine the political atmosphere critical to arms control negotiations.[42]

The 1970s détente taught the Soviets not only that regional conflicts could hurt the central relationship and arms control, but that resolution of such conflicts could help. As Georgy Arbatov acknowledged in 1986, foreshadowing a new direction in Soviet policy:

> There were good intentions to insulate arms control negotiations; but we saw it just didn't work. Now we have even more complex arms control negotiations. Solutions of regional issues can have an important effect on improving the central relationship. Some understandings in the Middle East, or a solution in Central America based on the Contadora principles, may play a very positive role in the central relationship. You have to work wherever possible to save the central relationship and also if there is improvement, then it becomes easier to work on regional conflicts. . . ."[43]

Through the mid-1980s, however, no consensus emerged regarding involvement in specific regional conflicts. Soviet commentators argue that it was convenient for those opposing détente to charge that the Soviet Union had exploited it to spread influence in third areas. As Garthoff elaborates, there are wide divergences in U.S. and Soviet perspectives on involvement in the Third World in the 1970s.[44]

EFFORTS TO BUILD CONFIDENCE IN THE EARLY 1980s

Soviet risk-taking seems to have been responsive to the general state of U.S.-Soviet relations as well as to cyclical changes in U.S. political-economic conditions. In the early 1980s, U.S.-Soviet relations hit one of the lowest points in postwar history. Strained political relations led to Soviet polemics in which it was difficult to distinguish between the real and rhetorical components.

An enduring characteristic of the Soviet approach to security matters is an assessment of the "correlation of forces" in broad terms of political, economic, and military factors. In the early 1980s, the Soviet side analyzed measures to avoid inadvertent war and crisis within a larger political framework and evaluated U.S. proposals according to a hierarchy of Soviet political and economic objectives. In their view, the effectiveness of risk reduction measures depended largely on the state of the overall U.S.-Soviet relationship; therefore the priority should be on improving the general climate of relations. Second, Soviet expressions of concern about the danger of inadvertent war were often directed toward stopping U.S. weapons deployments during a time of rapid American military buildup; therefore Soviet commentators stressed the importance of arms control over risk-reduction measures. Finally, there were elements of substantive disagreement between—and among—Americans and Soviets over the risks and benefits of certain measures, such as the risk reduction centers.

Risk-Reduction Measures and the State of U.S.-Soviet Relations

Since the Khrushchev period, Soviet commentators have argued that an atmosphere of heightened tension greatly increases the danger of accidents and adversely affects perceptions; in tense conditions, U.S. and Soviet leaders are unlikely to believe each other, even with improved technical means of crisis communication. The reverse also applies. A high-placed Soviet adviser reported that because of the favorable U.S.-Soviet relations during détente, and the good communication between Kissinger and Dobrynin, the Soviet leadership accepted "with a smile" the U.S. DefCon 3 nuclear alert at the height of the 1973 Middle East War.[45] While the Soviet military may have taken a different view, Soviet civilian analysts have viewed the 1973 alert as designed to serve the domestic needs of a politically troubled Nixon administration. Similarly, tense U.S.-Soviet relations in the early 1980s may help explain Soviet restraint in potential crisis situations like Lebanon, Libya, and the Iran-Iraq war (though Soviet succession difficulties, domestic economic needs, and increased U.S. deterrent capability also played a part).

The Reagan administration questioned the entire framework of the U.S.-Soviet relationship, including the principles underlying the arms control process. The Brezhnev regime was by no means happy to abandon its central foreign policy achievement—détente with the United States. Soviet spokesmen argued that a crisis prevention mechanism was "completely unrealistic" without a return to the détente relationship. They emphasized the importance of "the political mood expressed in the treaties of the early 1970s" and the need to reaffirm the Basic Principles Agreement of 1972. Under Andropov, Soviet specialists began work on some revised "norms of relations among the nuclear powers," which were made public by Chernenko in March 1984.[46] (Because it was a multilateral, not bilateral proposal, the BPA was not mentioned.) Soviet commentators stressed the importance of joint affirmation of such norms—what Alexander George calls Types I, II, and III agreements (Chapter 2). Such declarations were not merely propaganda exercises—though they were certainly designed to influence world public opinion and gain prestige for Soviet initiatives—but represented useful starting points to improve relations.[47]

The Reagan administration, in contrast, focused on concrete proposals for nuclear confidence-building measures, while rejecting SALT II and proposing the "zero" option at the INF negotiations. In November 1982, the United States put forth proposals for nuclear confidence-building measures, including advance notification of major exercises involving nuclear forces, notification of missile launches, and expanded exchange of information on strategic and intermediate-range nuclear forces.

The Soviet side complained of a narrow U.S. interest in a bilateral crisis control mechanism consisting of upgraded technical facilities and exchange of information. The U.S. side dismissed Soviet declaratory statements as redundant atmospherics. The two approaches reflected a mixture of political posturing and differences in American and Soviet political culture: an American proclivity to begin by reaching agreement on specific technical measures versus a Soviet emphasis on context and principle.[48]

A similar deadlock occurred in negotiations at the Stockholm Conference on confidence-building measures. NATO proposals included information exchange about military command organization, advance notification of military maneuvers, provisions for observation and inspection, and the establishment of new bilateral hot lines. Soviet negotiators stressed the importance of joint "political-legal" declarations to re-establish basic intentions about the nonuse of nuclear and conventional force. "General declarations," a Soviet argued, "create the spirit to move ahead on specifics." Thus Soviet delegates argued that the no-first-use declaration was a "real way of averting every kind of war, including ones that might be touched off accidentally." To agree on military-technical measures outside a broader political approach would be "to erect a roof when the house still had no foundation."[49]

Soviet proposals also emphasized operational constraints on military forces. Arguing that they would give advantage to the Soviets, or restrict U.S. activities in unacceptable ways, the American side has rejected Soviet proposals at START and CDE for zones banning the use of antisubmarine warfare; buffer zones to keep aircraft carriers and planes away from the other side's territory; and advance notification for bomber takeoffs and cruise missile launches.[50]

Risk-Reduction Measures and Arms Control

The Soviet approach to risk-reduction measures in the early 1980s was also closely tied to efforts to stop U.S. weapons deployments. An official of the Soviet Ministry of Foreign Affairs criticized the American view that nuclear risk-reduction measures were "some kind of 'independent alternative' to disarmament, . . . an 'all-weather' instrument," able to function independent of the international climate.[51] Soviet commentators argued that the nuclear risk-reduction centers were designed to divert attention from the nuclear freeze movement and tranquilize the American public in a time of rapid military buildup. In response to President Reagan's June 1982 proposal to upgrade the hot line, a *Pravda* editorial rhetorically asked: "If 100 MX missiles are complemented by ten telephones—red or blue—directly linking Moscow and Washington, will that make those missiles any less dangerous?"[52]

The Soviet approach focused on the existence of the weapons systems themselves, rather than the danger of technical malfunctions. Without reference to their country's decision to deploy SS-20s, Soviet commentators criticized the American decision to deploy Pershing II and cruise missiles, which they argued increased the danger of inadvertent war. "If there is a technical error in the Pershing II," a Soviet asked, "should we blame it on the technology? No, we should blame the deployment." General Secretary Andropov, Defense Minister Ustinov, and Marshal Kulikov made dramatic statements about a major increased danger of inadvertent war.[53] It is not clear how much increase in risk the Soviets actually perceived, but such statements obviously served the purpose of conveying a sense of imminent danger to European and American public opinion, in hope of influencing the peace movement against deployment of American missiles in Europe.[54]

Soviet statements about the danger of inadvertent war were also directed against the decision to pursue the Strategic Defense Initiative (SDI). Soviet commentators stressed that SDI would increase the danger of accidental war by reducing decision time in crisis and increasing reliance on technical rather than human factors.[55] The primary goal was to stop deployment, not to consider measures that might reduce the danger once the weapons were deployed. A Soviet participant in joint discussions argued that the U.S. approach of proposing measures to reduce the risk of inadvertent war while deploying new weapons systems was like putting your feet simultaneously on the brake and the accelerator.

During the 1980s the two sides also disagreed about the risks and benefits of specific risk-reduction measures. Soviet commentators initially focused on the negative side of the paradox of crisis control: safety measures may encourage dangerous behavior precisely because they make such behavior less risky. If a complex risk-reduction mechanism would prevent them from stepping over the brink, Western leaders might take more risks in confronting the USSR. Thus Soviets initially argued that risk reduction centers would be a "safety valve," enabling the United States to apply force more flexibly on a global scale while lowering the nuclear risks involved. But these substantive disagreements were more apparent than real.

GORBACHEV AND A NEW POLITICAL FRAMEWORK

Both Khrushchev and Brezhnev sought to improve relations with the United States, opening the way to agreement on several important risk-reduction measures. After Gorbachev came to power, there was a similar opportunity to make progress. After the Geneva summit in November 1985 Soviet specialists began to give a more positive evaluation to risk-reduction measures, adding that they should not be a substitute for improving the state of U.S.-Soviet relations and achieving arms control agreements.[56] The public Soviet position began to change—suggesting that most of the risk-reduction measures were intrinsically beneficial but would not be accepted except as part of a political consensus to improve relations.

U.S.-Soviet joint discussions helped to establish the importance of pursuing measures to avoid inadvertent war and crisis *simultaneously* with efforts to improve the relationship and pursue arms control—rather than linking progress on the former to success on the latter. The two tracks can be seen as complementary. An influential Soviet participant in joint discussions initially emphasized the priority of an improved relationship and arms control, noting that a potential heart-attack victim should take long-term measures such as improved diet and jogging. But, another Soviet stressed, while the health of the patient improves, it is vital to have paramedics on hand. Thus, while pursuing arms control and long-term improvement of relations, the United States and the Soviet Union should take immediate steps to agree on risk-reduction measures, to avoid a catastrophic failure of deterrence.

When both sides desire to improve relations, agreement on risk-reduction measures can facilitate further negotiations on higher-priority matters such as arms control—as experience showed in 1963 (hot line), the early 1970s (the Accident Measures and Incidents at Sea Agreements), and again in the 1980s.

During the first half of the decade, the only U.S.-Soviet agreement on security issues was the hot line upgrade (1984). The agreement to study risk-reduction centers provided a specific achievement at the first Reagan-Gorbachev summit, where progress was made toward re-establishing the principles of the relationship: the cessation of hostile rhetoric, expressions of mutual respect, and the joint statement that nuclear war cannot be won. In September 1986, the Stockholm Conference agreed on measures to reduce the danger of surprise attack, miscalculation, and accident—especially in time of crisis. All these agreements preceded the signing of the INF treaty, in December 1987, and subsequent efforts to achieve a major cut in strategic arms. Measures to avoid inadvertent war are often the easiest to agree upon in times of tension, because they are less central to U.S.-Soviet competition and represent efforts to address a common threat.

SOVIET AND AMERICAN APPROACHES TO CRISIS: IN SEARCH OF A COMMON LANGUAGE

During joint discussions in the 1980s, the divergences in view of American and Soviet specialists were often complicated by underlying differences in definition of terms. Thus it may be helpful to contrast Soviet and American understandings of the vocabulary of crisis avoidance.

Since the early 1970s, when the first Soviet analyses of international crisis were published, Soviet writings have become increasingly sophisticated.[57] Initially no direct references were made to Soviet decision-making processes; the focus was almost exclusively on U.S. crisis decision making and behavior (based on Western sources). In the Gorbachev era, this is beginning to change, reflecting increased U.S.-Soviet contacts and Soviet exposure to Western writings. Meetings and conferences of academics and policymakers have helped establish a shared vocabulary and conceptual basis that has been important in reaching shared conclusions.

The Nature of Crisis

Much of the Western literature on international crisis is oriented toward crisis decision making and strategy. Thus American definitions of crisis often focus on attributes such as high threat or stakes, little decision time, high uncertainty, elements of surprise, and few available options.[58] Soviet definitions have traditionally given more emphasis to the historical context of a crisis. The major Soviet works define crisis as "the most acute phase" in the development of a conflict.[59] Soviet writings put specific conflicts in the broader context of *"konfliktnost'*," the propensity toward conflict, which is a function of history and the objective factors underlying the conflict.

Following Lenin's *Notebooks on Imperialism*, Soviet typologies of international conflict have been based on "objective" class interests, emphasizing the "just" historical struggle of "progressive" forces.[60] Studies of international conflict in the Brezhnev era defined three types of conflict and crisis: direct East-West confrontations; those between Western states and the forces of "national liberation" in developing countries; and those within the Western camp (there was no category for inter-socialist conflict, which is regarded an anomalous).[61]

Since 1985, the Soviet approach to international conflict and crisis has shown a new pragmatism. Gorbachev has used the category of "national" interest—as opposed to "progressive" (class) interests—and he has repeatedly referred to the need to achieve a "balance of interests."[62] Thinking has evolved significantly since Lenin's original typology, which argued that whether an "oppressed" state acted aggressively or defensively in the military sense, it was still a just war of "progressive" forces. This de-ideologization of Soviet foreign policy may relieve Soviet theoreticians of such awkward tasks as explaining the 1969 Sino-Soviet border clashes, or the Sino-Vietnamese border war, given that there is by definition no "objective class basis" for conflict among socialist states.[63]

In line with Gorbachev's new pragmatism, Fyodor Burlatsky suggested a typology of conflict and crisis based on relative interests (which closely resembles a typology of competitive games suggested by Alexander George).[64] Burlatsky's typology included:

1. Conflicts that create the threat of nuclear war or direct U.S.-Soviet confrontation (with the Middle East situation the most salient current example).
2. Conflicts involving the interests of both sides but without a nuclear threat (e.g., South Africa).
3. Conflicts where interests are ambiguous (e.g., Iran-Iraq).[65]

While there is a vast Western literature on the psychological factors in crisis decision making, dealing with the mental and physical condition of decision makers, their propensities toward risk taking and their general outlook, the subject remained practically untouched in Soviet writings until the 1980s.[66] With the Gorbachev leadership's new stress on the danger of inadvertence, Soviet official and specialist writings emphasize the danger of a mistake or miscalculation by political leaders forced to make decisions quickly in an unanticipated nuclear crisis.[67] To deal with this danger, Soviet specialist writings have begun to attend to the psychological elements in crisis decision making.

Soviet writings now emphasize the "relative independence" of an international crisis from the historical base. This position legitimizes the study of crisis processes outside the historical context of the conflict. Specialist writings state that an international crisis can get beyond the control of decision makers and develop "according to its own laws." Soviet specialists are thus able to focus on the "patterns of thinking" in crises, produced by the elements peculiar to a crisis situation. A study by Lukov and Sergeev identifies such elements as high uncertainty, little decision time, and few available options.[68] In a later work, the authors construct a computer model simulating Bismarck's thinking patterns, modeling the element of higher or lower stakes in a crisis by varying the effect a given input will have on different parties depending upon their particular foreign policy aims.[69] The 1983 IMEMO study of international conflicts devotes an entire chapter to social-psychological factors.[70]

Crisis Management and Coercive Diplomacy

Until the Gorbachev era, Soviet civilian specialists emphasized crisis prevention to the almost complete exclusion of crisis management, which was equated with the coercive diplomacy of Western states. The term crisis "management" (*upravlenie*) was understood to refer exclusively to coercive bargaining and thus had pejorative connotations in Soviet usage.[71] The Soviet experience in the Cuban missile crisis probably contributed to this negative view of "crisis management." In the early 1980s Soviet participants in the Dartmouth task group on regional conflicts called for a renunciation of the "use" of crises "in confrontation with each other." Yevgeny Primakov repeatedly criticized the United States for efforts to exclude the USSR from the Middle East peace process, using crises to confront the USSR and advance unilateral U.S. foreign policy aims.[72] Soviet commentators made this charge during the Israeli invasion of Lebanon in 1982. The term "crisis management" was, however, conditionally rehabilitated in a 1983 Soviet academic study.[73]

Crisis "settlement" (*uregulirovanie*) is the Soviet preferred term, envisaging direct negotiation and diplomacy to achieve a peaceful settlement. Soviet analyses of international crisis identify two "schools" of American specialists, favoring "crisis diplomacy" and crisis "settlement" respectively. As a key founder of the former school, Thomas Schelling is identified as highly influential on U.S. government crisis planning, assisting U.S. ruling circles during crises to "dictate their will to the opposing side."[74]

The political component of Soviet military strategy in crisis management has traditionally not included direct discussion of coercive bargaining—though actual Soviet behavior in crises has been highly sophisticated, involving manipulation of risk and threat.[75] The application of military force to achieve certain goals was treated only at the military operational level, as in Admiral Gorshkov's writings. Soviet civilian specialists limited themselves to noting the utility of "shows of force." Anatoly Gromyko observed that Soviet nuclear weapon tests during the 1961 Berlin crisis had "a sobering effect upon the hotheads in the United States"; Kulish discusses the utility of Soviet ships in the Mediterranean "to restrain the imperialists and local reactionaries."[76]

In general, Soviet civilian writings do not discuss the achievement of security goals through nuclear threat. Soviet analysts accept the fact of nuclear deterrence, but the theory of deterrence as understood in America (a theory of bargaining) is not publicly developed in the Soviet Union. Soviet specialists argue that the mere contemplation of coercive bargaining makes brinkmanship (and thus war) more likely. The same logic is applied to the issue of "limited" or "protracted" nuclear war. Detailed discussion of coercive bargaining implies a certain confidence in the controllability and manageability of a crisis situation. The first direct discussions of coercive bargaining in Soviet civilian writings began to appear in the late 1980s.[77]

Soviet analysts still emphasize the need to improve relations, so that crisis management measures are less necessary. With regard to signaling in crisis, an influential Soviet commented, "If you cannot say what you really want and need a nuclear alert to do it, then you are in a bad situation." Signals are always ambiguous and subject to different interpretations. An influential Soviet participant privately said that the Soviet evacuation of civilian personnel from Egypt was a signal, a warning of impending war. "If the U.S. did not detect it, it is not our responsibility." Moscow may have tried to restrain Syria and Egypt, and it may have been uncertain about the exact timing of the attack.[78]

Crisis Prevention

Brezhnev's offensive definition of crisis prevention was based on deterrence through military-strategic parity. The Gorbachev leadership has suggested that crisis prevention should no longer be treated as a problem of military strategy (a lesson facilitated by the Soviet deployment of SS-20s in Europe, which called forth the NATO deployment of Pershing II and cruise missiles). At the Twenty-seventh Party Congress, Gorbachev questioned the future reliability of strategic parity.[79] (This questioning was necessitated by the political decision to promote nuclear disarmament: if parity is a reliable guarantee of security, then there is no need to rid the world of nuclear weapons.) Soviet specialists still maintain, however, that parity serves as the basis for efforts to prevent a global conflict. Yet a Brezhnevian icon has been smashed; as one Soviet specialist candidly put it, "The cult of parity is ending . . . parity does not solve all problems." Gorbachev included the resolution of international crises as a basic element in the political (as opposed to military) sphere of the Soviet proposal for a "comprehensive security system."[80]

Soviet policy now puts greater stress on multilateral approaches to crisis prevention. Brezhnev and Gromyko emphasized bilateral superpower efforts to prevent certain third parties from provoking a crisis. Gorbachev has stressed a multilateral "mechanism," with much attention to the United Nations. The Soviet side has supported the creation of a multilateral risk-reduction center based at the UN, as well as reviving the UN Military Staff Committee.[81]

Under Gorbachev, declaratory policy toward the Third World has changed dramatically. His report to the Twenty-seventh Party Congress omitted the usual rhetoric regarding Moscow's military role in supporting "national liberation movements." The 1986 Party Program repeatedly refers to the stage of national liberation in the past tense. Significantly, "peaceful coexistence" is no longer defined as a form of class struggle.

Have Soviet goals in the Third World actually changed? Adam Ulam argued that the Brezhnev leadership sought to enhance its domestic legitimacy through Third World successes.[82] Under Gorbachev, the needs of the Soviet economy provide an objective basis for changing foreign policy priorities—redirecting resources from the military to the domestic *perestroika*. The new emphasis on "liberated" countries' becoming more self-reliant and independent has an objective underpinning in the cases of client states that impose a large economic burden, such as Vietnam and Cuba. Soviet writings now openly acknowledge that the economic burden for the Soviet Union in Third World conflicts is "much greater" than for the United States.[83] Soviet foreign policy has shown heightened interest in developing capitalist states like Mexico, Brazil, and India, some conservative Middle Eastern states, and Southeast Asian countries.[84]

In addition, the Soviets appear to be recognizing that the stakes in the Third World are not as high as both sides once thought. Political influence sought through military aid has often proven ephemeral, as in Egypt, Somalia, and Ghana. As Kremeniuk noted in 1983, given "economic problems, territorial quarrels, ideological differences, religious and ethnic conflicts" in Third World states, the "primary political interests and goals" of states can become "subordinated to the inertia of the conflictual interaction."[85] A Soviet participant in joint discussions candidly argued that, on balance, the overall geopolitical situations of the two superpowers have not changed as a result of their efforts in the Third World:

> Angola has leaned toward the USSR, but U.S. oil companies continue to operate there. And Mozambique has now concluded an agreement with South Africa. Egypt moved toward us and then toward the U.S. But so what? Somalia moved first to the Soviet Union and then to the U.S. So what? There were dramatic changes in the Third World; but if we talk about the final results of regional conflicts in the past fifteen years, geopolitically it is not a big deal. The geopolitical situation of the U.S. is now about the same as it was in 1972.

The significant new stress on the danger of escalation reflects the growing political influence of a school of Soviet specialists who had been emphasizing this risk in regional crises since the early 1970s.

The 1972 study edited by Zhurkin and Primakov argued that international crises had become "the main path by which the slip to global nuclear conflict could occur."[86] In a 1984 study of international crisis, Kremeniuk and Zhurkin similarly emphasized that "the dominant contradictions of our epoch are focused in the international political crises, and, in the postwar period, the danger of the outbreak of global nuclear war is manifest in them in a more naked form."[87] The risk of uncontrollable escalation of a regional crisis to the nuclear level has become a standard precept in Soviet political-military (declaratory) doctrine[88]—though Western analysts argue that Soviet military planning since the mid-1970s has anticipated a purely conventional war in Europe.[89] The Soviets appear to be seriously concerned about escalation in Europe and the Middle East, but statements regarding South Africa and Central America are largely rhetorical and directed to public opinion.

Though strategic parity has produced greater certainty at the central level of U.S.-Soviet relations, these Soviet specialists stress that certainty at the local level has decreased. They emphasize that Third World states are largely uncontrollable actors, and there is a danger that the tail may begin to wag the dog. A small country might "take several independent actions which could sharply exacerbate the course of a crisis and push the [great] powers in certain cases onto a path of more dangerous actions than at first planned. . . ."[90] In the 1980s, one Soviet specialist emphasized that in many cases "the superpowers actually follow events, they do not control. Pinochet, Duarte, Ortega, Castro or Qaddafi decide, and the big powers are left to contrive and arrange."[91] When U.S.-South African relations worsened under Carter, Botha threatened to establish relations with the USSR—as did Marcos in his final days in power.

This stress on the danger of escalation has been tied to revision in declaratory policy about the use of armed force and revolution. Soviet officials and specialists argue that the Soviet Union has always denounced "Trotskyism," "left communism," and the theory of revolutionary wars, yet this position has clearly been strengthened since the Twenty-seventh Party Congress. Gorbachev writes that, given new conditions, they "drew a conclusion about the disappearance of the cause-and-effect relationship between war and revolution."[92] In an authoritative *Pravda* article, Ye. Plimak argues that the existence of dictatorial regimes does not allow the "exclusion" of armed struggle from the agenda (particularly in cases like South

Africa and Chile), but stresses that "any local conflict has a tendency to escalate into a regional conflict, even a global one. The nuclear era demands from revolutionary forces the utmost consideration in taking decisions regarding armed struggle, a principled renunciation of various manifestations of leftist extremism."[93] The message to Soviet clients and allies is that use of force in hot spots such as South Africa or Korea could quickly lead to an explosion with unacceptable costs.

In the mid-1980s, the Soviets acknowledge, any conventional war would certainly destroy nuclear reactors, as well as nuclear weapons storehouses. Hence even a conventional war would become nuclear as deadly radiation was released. Like many elements of Soviet "new political thinking," this position was advanced much earlier by the Western peace movement (in this case the West German Green Party).

The Gorbachev regime has carried out a public media campaign about the danger of the accidental and uncontrollable factors that could lead to nuclear war. In the Soviet film "Letters of a Dead Man" (1986), which was shown throughout the Soviet Union, computer error triggers a nuclear attack, causing the slow death of the population from radiation exposure. The incident at Chernobyl was a turning point in public awareness of the danger of accident.[94]

At the Twenty-seventh Party Congress, Gorbachev stated that crises are "fertile ground" for terrorism. Soviet representatives had previously paid little attention to the danger of "catalytic" war, or *agent provocateur* scenarios.[95] In the 1980s, Georgy Shakhnazarov discussed scenarios involving third-country provocation and nuclear terrorism by citing Western science fiction novels.[96] As for actual U.S.-Soviet agreements, the Standing Consultative Commission agreed in 1985 that the two sides would consult via the hot line in the event of a third-party nuclear incident.

CONCLUSION

The recent Soviet de-emphasis of the threat of deliberate Western attack is useful to Gorbachev as he seeks a rationale for redirecting resources from the military to the domestic *perestroika*. But the new focus on inadvertent paths to nuclear war is not merely a matter of domestic political expediency. Rather it seems to reflect a long-term Soviet reassessment of the nature of threats in the international environment, as well as the increasing influence of advisers who have a sophisticated understanding of American society. Soviet theory has begun to acknowledge that Western capitalist states may not be inherently militaristic, as previous doctrine maintained.

The change has been facilitated by learning through diffusion at U.S.-Soviet meetings and conferences, where progress has been made toward developing a common language on avoiding inadvertent war and crisis. The Soviet military must increasingly compete with civilian specialists' assessments of the threats facing the Soviet Union. Recently a new Scientific Coordination Center was established in the Soviet Foreign Ministry to coordinate academic research on arms control and integrate it into the foreign policymaking apparatus. In general, Gorbachev has taken steps to reassert civilian control over the professional military, which under Brezhnev exercised its almost exclusive prerogative over matters of nuclear strategy and technical weapons systems. Gorbachev's reference at the Twenty-seventh Party Conference to the danger of becoming "captive to technology and military-technocratic logic" was not directed toward the West alone.[97] This reassertion of civilian control may work against one risk-reduction measure proposed by the United States in 1983—the military-to-military hot line.

Soviet specialists in the Gorbachev era are re-examining past crises, particularly the Cuban missile crisis, and drawing lessons for current policy. Those lessons are being institutionalized through risk-reduction centers and other measures to make inadvertent war less likely. These developments are likely to improve prospects for further institutionalization of measures to provide for mutual policy adjustment to head off crises.

NOTES

1. In addition to American and Soviet members of the Joint Study, I am indebted to William Jarosz, Jeffrey Legro and Stephen M. Meyer, who offered valuable comments on earlier versions of this chapter.
2. V.V. Zhurkin, S. Karaganov, and A. Kortunov, "Vyzovy bezopasnosti: starye i novye" (The Challenges of Security: Old and New), *Kommunist* no. 1 (January) 1988, p. 47.
3. Mikhail Gorbachev, *Perestroika: New Thinking for Our Country and the World* (New York: Harper and Row, 1987), p. 138.

4. See Bruce Allyn, "Soviet Views of Confidence-Building Measures," in J. Borawksi, ed., *Avoiding War in the Nuclear Age: Confidence-Building Measures for Crisis Stability* (Boulder, Colo.: Westview Press, 1986), pp. 116–30. For a useful historical overview of U.S.-Soviet negotiations, see Barry M. Blechman, "Efforts to Reduce the Risk of Accidental or Inadvertent War," in Alexander L. George, Philip J. Farley, and Alexander Dallin, eds., *U.S.-Soviet Security Cooperation* (New York and Oxford: Oxford University Press, 1988), pp. 466–81.

5. At the Conference on Communist and Workers' Parties in 1969, Brezhnev stated: " . . . many comrades present here remember the speech of Mao Zedong in this hall at the 1957 Conference. With striking ease and cynicism he spoke about the possible destruction of half of humanity in the event of a nuclear war." Brezhnev then referred to a Peking newspaper article that called for "both a conventional and a large nuclear war with Soviet revisionism." See *Mezhdunarodnoe soveshchanoe kommunisticheskikh i rabochikh partii: dokumenty i materialy* (International Conference of Communist and Workers' Parties: Documents and materials) (Moscow: Politicheskaia literatura, 1969), pp. 197–98.

6. Andrei A. Gromyko, *Pamiatnoe*, vol. 2 (Moscow: Politizdat, 1988), p. 133.

7. *Pravda*, July 14, 1963.

8. M.S. Gorbachev, *Perestroika*, p. 144.

9. See the classic study by N.P. Poletika, *Vozniknovenie pervoi mirovoi voiny* (The Emergence of the First World War) (Moscow: Izd. sotsial'no-ekonomicheskoi literatury "Mysl'," 1979), p. 12. Soviet explanations have traditionally stressed that Lenin "proved" or "uncovered" the "nonaccidental" essence of World War I (V.A. Kremeniuk, *"Krizisnaia strategiia na sluzhbe imperializma* ('Crisis Strategy' in the Service of Imperialism) (Kiev: Izd. Politicheskoi literatury Ukrainy, 1979), p. 12. Soviet writings distinguish between short-term precipitating causes and long-term causes. The murder of Austrian Archduke Franz Ferdinand in June 1914 was, Soviet historians stress, merely the "pretext" used to unleash a historically determined war.

10. See the study by the Institute of General History *Prichiny vozniknoveniia vtoroi mirovoi voiny* (Causes of the Emergence of the Second World War) (Moscow: Nauka, 1982), pp. 4–5.

11. V. Matveiev, "The Danger of Accidental War," *International Affairs* no. 9 (September 1962), p. 78 (emphasis in original).

12. See, for example, the theoretical treatise by Colonel S.A. Tiushkevich, *Neobkhodimost' i sluchainost' v voine* (Necessity and Chance in War) (Moscow: Voennoe izdatel'stvo ministerstvo oborony Soiuza SSR, 1962) and the 1965 edition of the authoritative *Marksizm-Leninizm o voine i armii* (Marxism-Leninism on War and the Army), cited by Stephen Meyer,

"Soviet Perspectives on the Paths to Nuclear War," in Graham T. Allison, Albert Carnesale, and Joseph S. Nye, Jr., eds., *Hawks, Doves and Owls* (New York: W.W. Norton, 1985), pp. 187–88.

13. Soviet participants in the October 1987 Cambridge conference (see Chapter 4) argued that Khrushchev believed that Soviet actions in Berlin were "political gamesmanship" not worth risking war. The complete transcript of the conference is available at the John F. Kennedy Library, Dorchester, Mass. (David A. Welch, ed., *Proceedings of the Cambridge Conference on the Cuban Missile Crisis, October 11–13, 1987*, hereafter referred to as *CCT* for "Cambridge Conference Transcript").

14. S.A. Mikoyan, "Karibskii krizis, kakim on viditsia na rasstoianii" (The Caribbean Crisis: How It Appears from a Distance) *Latinskaia amerika* no. 1 1988, pp. 70–71. This article is based on information from his father, Anastas Mikoyan, and his personal recollections. Sergo Mikoyan reports that Khrushchev consulted with Politburo (then Presidium) members Anastas Mikoyan and Frol R. Kozlov, as well as Foreign Minister A.A. Gromyko, Defense Minister Malinovsky, and S.S. Biriuzov, commander of strategic rocket forces. A.I. Aleksev, who replaced Sergei Kudriatsev as ambassador to Cuba, was soon included in the deliberations.

15. This accords with Graham T. Allison's speculation in *Essence of Decision: Explaining the Cuban Missile Crisis* (Boston: Little, Brown and Company, 1971), pp. 106–7.

16. Castro is reported later to have expressed his dismay that Cubans had not been consulted on camouflage measures. The sites could easily have been disguised as agricultural projects, he maintained, had the Soviets only asked for help (Sergo Mikoyan, *CCT*, p. 48).

17. In Robert Kennedy's words, the U-2 shootdown marked a turning point where ExComm members expected that the United States and Soviet Union were "preparing to do battle." But recent evidence suggests that the shootdown did not affect immediate policy choices; see David A. Welch and James G. Blight, "An Introduction to the ExComm Transcripts," *International Security* 12 (3), Winter 1987/88, 19–20.

18. Seymour M. Hersh, "Was Castro Out of Control in 1962?" *Washington Post*, October 11, 1987.

19. Stephen Meyer notes the Soviets' perplexing "failure to place nuclear charges on their strategic bombers and missiles during the 1950s and much of the 1960s—a period when the United States aspired to a massive, disarming first-strike capability." He concludes that "the Soviet political leadership apparently feared the loss of political control (or an accident) more than the threat of surprise attack by the United States" (Stephen M. Meyer, "Soviet Nuclear Operations," in Ashton B. Carter, John Steinbruner, and Charles Zraket, eds., *Managing Nuclear Operations* (Washington, D.C.: Brookings, 1987), pp. 487–88).

20. Meyer, "Soviet Nuclear Operations," pp. 489, 518.

21. Ibid., p. 490.

22. Meyer, "Soviet Perspectives," pp. 182–87.

23. *Khrushchev Remembers*, tr. and ed. Strobe Talbott (Boston: Little, Brown, 1970), p. 504, and *Khrushchev Remembers: The Last Testament*, tr. and ed. Strobe Talbott (Boston: Little, Brown, 1974), pp. 513–14.

24. See A. Shevchenko, *Breaking with Moscow* (New York: Knopf, 1985), p. 118.

25. See Michael McGwire, *Military Objectives in Soviet Foreign Policy* (Washington, D.C.: Brookings, 1987), pp. 361–62.

26. McGeorge Bundy, transcriber, James G. Blight, editor, "October 27, 1962: Transcripts of the meetings of the ExComm," *International Security* 12 (3), Winter 1987/88, 37.

27. V.V. Zhurkin and V.A. Kremeniuk, "Podkhod SShA k mezhdunarodnym krizisnym situatsiiam," *Sovremennaia vneshnaia politika SShA* (Moscow: Nauka, 1984) vol. 1, p. 380.

28. The 1962 understanding served as the basis for resolving the 1969 Cienfuegos submarine base incident (Raymond L. Garthoff, *Détente and Confrontation* (Washington, D.C.: Brookings, 1985), p. 80). After U.S. deployment of intermediate-range missiles in Europe, Col. General Chervov specifically ruled out placing new missiles in Cuba in retaliation, reaffirming the 1962 understanding (*New York Times*, October 18, 1983). A leading Soviet specialist claimed that deployment of U.S. missiles in Europe violated the 1962 understanding (Vitaly V. Zhurkin, "O strategicheskikh stabil'nosti," *SShA: ekonomika, politika, ideologiia*, no. 1, 1986, p. 25.

29. Alexander George, *Managing U.S.-Soviet Rivalry: Problems of Crisis Prevention* (Boulder, Colo.: Westview Press, 1983), pp. 381–82.

30. *Mezhdunarodnoe soveshchanoe*, p. 288.

31. See A.A. Gromyko and A. Kokoshin, *Brat'ia Kennedi* (The Brothers Kennedy) (Moscow: Mysl', 1985), p. 201. See also V. Zhurkin and V. Kremeniuk, "Podkhod SShA," p. 380.

32. See, for example, V.V. Zhurkin, *Literaturnaia gazeta*, September 19, 1980.

33. H. Sonnenfeldt and W. Hyland, "Soviet Perspectives on Security," Adelphi Paper no. 150 (London: IIIS, 1979), p. 18.

34. At the 1969 Conference on Communist and Workers' Parties, which occurred during the year of the Sino-Soviet border clashes, Brezhnev made a scathing attack on Mao and the "provocative" role of China in crisis situations, asserting that Peking had assisted imperialism by "playing an instigating role in moments of acute international crisis" (*Mezhdunarodnoe soveshchanoe*, p. 288).

H.R. Haldeman asserts that the USSR made several overtures to the United States in 1969 proposing a joint attack on Chinese nuclear installations, but Soviet commentators have dismissed these statements as deliberate disinformation intended to exacerbate Sino-Soviet relations. For the official response by Tass, see *New York Times*, February 18, 1978, pp. 1, 12. If the Soviets actually made such overtures, they may have been intended as a scare tactic against the Chinese; or the idea may have been the view of a single Politburo member (e.g., Marshal Grechko, as Shevchenko asserts). There does appear to be strong evidence of Soviet interest in joint efforts against any country that launched a provocative nuclear attack. During the SALT negotiations, Ambassador Smith reportedly received a Soviet note proposing a "bilateral agreement providing for joint retaliation against any country that launched a provocative nuclear attack" (Gerard C. Smith, *Doubletalk: The Story of SALT* (Garden City, N.Y.: Doubleday, 1980), p. 141. Kissinger writes that the 1973 Agreement on the Prevention of Nuclear War had its origins in a Brezhnev proposal to renounce the use of nuclear weapons against each other and to "prevent" situations whereby actions taken by third parties might lead to nuclear war. Kissinger interprets this as "a virtual U.S.-Soviet military alliance designed to isolate or impose our will on China or any other country with nuclear aspirations" (Henry Kissinger, *Years of Upheaval: The Story of the First Strategic Arms Limitation Talks* (Boston: Little Brown, 1982), p. 275). The final agreement included a U.S.-Soviet pledge to engage in "urgent consultations" if a crisis situation arose threatening war.

35. V.V. Zhurkin and Ye. M. Primakov, eds., *Mezhdunarodnye konflikty* (Moscow: mezhdunarodnye otnoshenye, 1972), p. 23.

36. See Alexander George, *Managing U.S.-Soviet Rivalry*, chap. 5.

37. V. Kremeniuk and V. Zhurkin, "Podkhod," p. 388.

38. Ray Garthoff, *Détente and Confrontation*, p. 14.

39. V. Gantman, ed., *Mezhdunarodnye konflikty sovremennosti* (Moscow: Nauka, 1983), pp. 4, 83.

40. V. Kremeniuk, "Sootnosheniye mezhdu global'noi strategii i regional'-noi taktikoi" (The correlation between the global strategy and regional tactics) in *Sovremennaia vneshniaia politika SShA* (Moscow: Nauka, 1984) vol. 2, p. 152.

41. Interview with *Der Spiegel*, published in *Pravda*, April 25, 1983. Also in Y.V. Andropov, *Speeches and Writings*, 2nd ed. (Oxford: Pergamon Press, 1983), p. 323.

42. *New York Times*, March 30, 1988, p. A11.

43. Joint study discussions.

44. Raymond Garthoff, *Détente and Confrontation*, pp. 671-73.

45. Personal communication, April 1984. A Soviet specialist has also argued that the détente atmosphere contributed to the resolution of the 1973 crisis involving the U.S. nuclear alert (V.V. Zhurkin, *SShA i mezhduna-rodnopoliticheskie krizisy* (Moscow: Nauka, 1975), pp. 299-300).

46. Chernenko's "norms of relations among the nuclear powers" included: (1) to consider the prevention of nuclear war to be the principle goal of

foreign policy and to hold urgent consultations if situations arise fraught with the danger of nuclear conflict; (2) to renounce the propaganda of (global or limited) nuclear war; (3) to commit to a no-first-use policy; (4) not to use nuclear weapons against a nonnuclear power; (5) to prevent nuclear proliferation; and (6) to eliminate nuclear weapons step-by-step (*Pravda*, March 3, 1984).

47.   For a discussion of the propaganda use of broad declarations on disarmament, see Schevchenko, p. 101.

48.   E. Glenn, D. Whitmeyer, and K. Stevenson, "Cultural Styles of Persuasion," *International Journal of Intercultural Relations*, 1977, 52–66.

49.   Igor Andropov, Soviet delegate to the Stockholm Conference, CDE Plenary Statement, February 7, 1984.

50.   See *New York Times*, May 30, 1988, p. 6.

51.   For a review of American literature and a statement of the Soviet position by an official of the Ministry of Foreign Affairs writing under a pseudonum, see E.N. Shcherbakov, "Diskussia v SShA vokrug 'mer doveriia' v iadernoi oblasti" (The Discussion in the USA of Nuclear 'CBMs'), *SShA: ekonomika, politika, ideologiia*, no. 10, 1985, 84–89.

52.   *Pravda*, November 25, 1982.

53.   Andropov: "Given the swift action and power of contemporary arms, an atmosphere of mutual suspicion is especially dangerous. Even an absurd accident, an error, a technical fault, may have tragic consequences. It is important, therefore, to take the fingers off the launching buttons, to put arms on a reliable safeguard" (*Pravda*, December 22, 1982). Ustinov: "The quantity of nuclear warheads on both sides directed against the other's military targets has increased; the time has been sharply decreased for making a responsive decision to a nuclear attack or an unintended emergent nuclear situation; trust between states has been undermined" (*Pravda*, May 21, 1984). Kulikov: Deployment of American Euro-missiles "would make it practically impossible to prevent a conflict resulting from an error or technical fault" (*New York Times*, October 14, 1983).

54.   In the early 1980s, Soviet writings hopefully cited domestic and allied opposition to American Pershing deployment as a factor that threatened the power base of U.S. "ruling circles" (*Mezhdunarodnye konflikty sovremennosti*, p. 34).

55.   For example, at the November 1985 Geneva summit meeting, Gorbachev noted the danger of an "accidental encounter in space," which would activate computers and result in unwise political decisions (*Sovetsko-amerikanskaia vstrecha na vysshem urovne Zheneva 19–21 Noiabria 1985* (Moscow, 1986), p. 30).

56.   See M.M. Mil'shtein, "Ob ugroze 'sluchainogo' vozniknovneniia iadernoi voiny" (On the threat of 'accidental' emergence of nuclear war), *SShA:*

ekonomika, politika, ideologiia, no. 10, 1986, 10; V.C. Yemel'ianov, *O vozmozhnosti 'sluchainoi' voiny* (Moscow: Nauka, 1985); and review of William Ury, *Beyond the Hotline,* by A.A. Arazumov in *SShA: ekonomika, politika, ideologiia,* no. 10, 1986, 104–6.

57. The first Soviet study that dealt specifically with "international-political crises" was V.V. Zhurkin and Ye. M. Primakov, *Mezhdunarodnye konflikty.* The long tradition of U.S. literature on international crises was analyzed from a Soviet point of view in V.V. Zhurkin, *SShA i mezhdunarodno-politicheskie krizisy.*

58. See, for example, William Ury and Richard Smoke, *Beyond the Hotline-Controlling a Nuclear Crisis,* Report to the Arms Control and Disarmament Agency, 1984.

59. See V.V. Zhurkin and Ye. M. Primakov, *Mezhdunarodnye konflikty.*

60. V.I. Lenin, *Collected Works, Polnoe sobranie sochinenii,* 5th ed., vol. 49 (Moscow: Politicheskoi literatury, 1970), pp. 369–70.

61. See sections on typology of conflict in *Mezhdunarodnye konflikty* (1972) and *Mezhdunarodnye konflikty sovremennosti* (1983).

62. M.S. Gorbachev, *Pravda,* September 17, 1987. In his news conference after the 1988 Moscow summit, Gorbachev twice used the phrase "balance of interests" (*New York Times,* June 2, 1988, p. A18).

63. See Zhurkin and Primakov, *Mezhdunarodnye konflikty,* 1972, p. 36.

64. Alexander George, *Managing U.S.-Soviet Rivalry,* pp. 381–82.

65. F. Burlatsky, joint study discussions, Moscow, February 1985.

66. For a summary of the Western literature, see Alexander George, "The Impact of Crisis-Induced Stress on Decision-Makers," in Institute of Medicine, *The Medical Implications of Nuclear War* (Washington, D.C.: National Academy Press, 1986), pp. 529–52.

67. M.S. Gorbachev, Report to the 27th CPSU Congress, trans. in *Current Digest of the Soviet Press* 38 (8), 1986, 27. See also A.G. Arbatov and A. Saveliev, "Sistema upravleniia i sviazi kak faktor strategicheskoi stabil'nosti," *Mirovaia ekonomika i mezhdunarodnye otnosheniia* no. 12, 1987, 16.

68. V. Lukov and V.M. Sergeev, "The Patterns of Political Thinking and Perception of International Crises," The Round Table Conference, Zurich, January 1981.

69. V. Lukov and V.M. Sergeev, "Opyt modelirovaniia myshleniia istoricheskikh deiatelei: Otto Fon Bismark, 1866–1876 gg," in *Voprosy kibernetiki: logika rassuzhendii i ee modelirovanie* (Moscow, 1983).

70. V. Gantman, *Mezhdunarodnye konflikty sovremennosti,* chap. 3.

71. In an unpublished Soviet dissertation on international crisis (1978), M.F. Dorogovstev observes that the phenomenon of crisis had not received adequate attention in Soviet literature, suggesting that bourgeois studies

had given it a bad name. See M.F. Dorogovstev, "Mezhdunarodnyi krizis: istorikoteoreticheskie aspekty problemy" (Moscow: Institute of Sociological Research, Soviet Academy of Sciences, 1978).

72. See Ye. Primakov, *Istoriia odnogo sgovora (Blizhnevostochnaia politika SShA v 70-e—nachalye 80-ikh godov)* (Moscow: Politizdat, 1985).
73. *Mezhdunarodnye konflikty sovremmenosti*, p. 62.
74. V. Kremeniuk and V. Zhurkin, "Podkhod," pp. 371–77. Soviet writings fault the Schelling approach because it overlooks other dimensions of conflict, most importantly its historical, deeper sources.
75. See, for example, Stephen S. Kaplan, *Diplomacy of Power: Soviet Armed Forces as a Political Instrument* (Washington, D.C.: Brookings, 1981); Francis Fukuyama, "Nuclear Shadow-Boxing: Soviet Intervention Threats in the Middle East," *Orbis*, Fall, 1981, 579–605. For a discussion of the political and operational requirements for effective crisis management and the major threats to it, see Alexander George, "Crisis Management: The Interaction of Political and Military Considerations," *Survival* 26 (5), September/October 1984, 223–34.
76. Anatoly A. Gromyko, *President Kennedy's 1036 Days* (Moscow, 1971), p. 149. V.M. Kulish, *Military Force and International Relations* (Moscow, 1972); trans. by U.S. Joint Publications Research Service #58947, May 8, 1973, p. 103. Cited in Jeffrey Legro, "Soviet Views on Crises: Political and Military Aspects," Working Paper for *Avoiding Nuclear War Project*, Rand/UCLA Center for the Study of Soviet International Behavior (January 1987).
77. A 1987 study, for example, discusses the argument that the Soviet side could use its capacity to destroy U.S. land-based strategic forces "to force the United States to make political concessions. . . ." But it hastens to add: ". . . this kind of adventurism is incompatible with Soviet policy. . . ." (Raold Sagdeev and Andrei Kokoshin, eds., "Strategic Stability Under Conditions of Radical Nuclear Arms Reductions" (Moscow, 1987), p. 19).
78. See Shevchenko, pp. 254–55.
79. M.S. Gorbachev, *Materialy XXVII s'ezda kommunisticheskoi partii sovetskogo soiuza* (Moscow: Politicheskaia literatura, 1987), p. 65.
80. Ibid., p. 75.
81. Mikhail S. Gorbachev, *Izbrannye rechi i stati* (Selected Speeches and Articles), vol. 4 (Moscow: Politizdat, 1987), p. 240.
82. Adam B. Ulam, *Dangerous Relations: the Soviet Union in World Politics, 1970–1982* (New York: Oxford University Press, 1983), pp. 153–54, 311–12.
83. V. Zhurkin, et al., "Vyzovy," p. 49. They write, "in the majority of conflicts involving underdeveloped nations the Soviet Union supports govern-

ments of national-democratic and socialist orientation (in Afghanistan, Nicaragua, Angola, Ethiopia, Mozambique) in their battles with anti-government bandits and mercenaries. This imposes on the USSR a much greater political responsibility and economic and military burden than the U.S."

84.   See Francis Fukuyama, *Moscow's Post-Brezhnev Reassessment of the Third World* (Santa Monica, Calif.: Rand Corporation, R-3337-USOP 1986). See also "Gorbachev and the Third World," *Foreign Affairs*, 1986, 715-31.

85.   V.A. Kremeniuk, "Sistema vzaimodeistvii mezhdunarodnikh konfliktov sovremennosti" (The System of Interaction of Contemporary International Conflicts), in *Mezhdunarodnye konflikty sovremennosti*, p. 292.

86.   Zhurkin and Primakov, p. 19.

87.   V. Kremeniuk and V. Zhurkin, "Podkhod," p. 370.

88.   For example, the Warsaw Pact Declaration of October 1985 stated that "any local conflict in the current tense international situation is fraught with the danger of escalation (*pererastanie*) into a clash of major, even global scale (*Pravda*, October 24, 1985).

89.   Stephen Meyer, "Soviet Perspectives," pp. 182-87.

90.   Zhurkin and Primakov, p. 20.

91.   Personal interview, Moscow, May 1987.

92.   M.S. Gorbachev, *Perestroika*, p. 147.

93.   Ye. Plimak, "Voprosy teorii: Marksizm-Leninizm i revoliutsionnost' kontsa XX veka" (Questions of Theory: Marxism-Leninism and the Character of Revolution at the End of the Twentieth Century), *Pravda*, November 14, 1986, pp. 2-3.

94.   In September 1986, Shevardnadze noted that Chernobyl involved a human mistake, adding "Even more so there is no guarantee against nuclear mistakes in a war" (E.A. Shevardnadze, *Za novoe myshlenie v mirovoi politike* (Moscow: Politizdat, 1986), p. 7).

95.   In 1968, Henry Trofimenko elaborated a scenario in which West Germany, seeking revenge for its defeat in World War II, might disguise one of its vessels with Soviet markings and launch a nuclear missile as if it were an attack from a Soviet ship or submarine, provoking the United States to launch a major attack against the territory of the Soviet Union (H. Trofimenko, *The Strategy of Global War* (Moscow, 1968), pp. 49-50). This scenario was in line with official Soviet statements designed to raise fears about Bonn possessing nuclear weapons, and it probably was an oblique reference to China—given Soviet concerns about that nation's provocative activity.

96.   G. Shakhnazarov, "The Logic of the Nuclear Era," *20th Century and Peace* no. 4, 1984, 10.

97.   M.S. Gorbachev, Report to 27th CPSU Congress, p. 28.

SOVIET VIEW

Viktor A. Kremeniuk

Khrushchev's conclusion in 1956 that there was no "fatal inevitability" of a new world war retains fundamental importance to this day. The mere recognition of the possibility that East and West could find ways to settle their differences in a peaceful manner, that both societies were potentially capable of living together without war, was a great leap forward from the gloomy perspective that dominated thinking in the 1940s and early 1950s. This conclusion formed the basis for a possible common pardigm in crisis management and crisis avoidance, the subject of Bruce Allyn's chapter.

As Allyn correctly notes, the subject of international crisis began to be studied in depth at research centers in the USSR after publication in 1972 of the book *Mezhdunarodnye konflikty* (International Conflicts), edited by Vitaly Zhurkin and Yevgeny Primakov. The basic Soviet approach has been to analyze international crises as the result of deeply rooted contradictions in world politics, stemming from inequality between nations or classes. When these contradictions cannot be resolved through compromise or other political means, acute crises can emerge. The actual driving force of a crisis is the policy of governments or political parties that consider armed force to be a major means to resolve contradictions and conflicts. Conflicts develop at an uneven pace: periods of quiet growth, undetected by outside observers, may give way to very precipitous, even revolutionary development. The moments of rapid change are the crisis proper.

The foreign policy of a state can either exacerbate an emerging crisis or help prevent it from escalating to a more acute level. Ordinarily these effects are deliberate, but sometimes a crisis develops so spontaneously that policies have unintended effects. The beginning of World War I provides a vivid example.

After the October Revolution in 1917, Lenin wrote that Soviet Russia was encircled by an unfriendly bourgeois environment that might attempt to use force against the revolutionary state—as was used against France in the 1790s. But, Lenin stated, the primary goal of the Soviet state would be to work for peaceful co-existence, or "peaceful co-habitation" with the bourgeois states. This was an essential element of the Soviet position during the Genoa Conference in 1922.

In this respect, Khrushchev's conclusion that there need be no war between socialism and capitalism was a return to Lenin's idea. It was based upon an intuitive understanding of what was actually occurring in international relations. The strategic balance still greatly favored the United States. Yet the Soviet capacity to inflict a second strike against American territory, should a crisis on the Soviet periphery evolve into a major showdown, was already a factor of significant political importance. It provided a basis for a more equitable, more balanced relationship with the United States, suggesting an accommodation that could satisfy both sides. In the period of heightened international dynamics caused by the wars of national liberation and the process of decolonization, Soviet-American relations might, it was assumed, become a pivotal point of stability for the entire international system.

The view persists in America that it was Soviet policy to create crises through support of national-liberation wars. But the Soviet government's position at that time was in complete accord with the UN Charter and the UN Declaration of 1960 (on the right of the oppressed and colonial nations to self-determination). Moreover, this position did not directly threaten U.S. interests, since the United States was not a colonial empire and did not support, at least officially, the colonial wars of its allies. Thus the American charge that the Soviet Union created crises by supporting wars of national liberation was seen in our country as a new guise for continuing the belligerent brinkmanship of the 1950s.

The Cuban missile crisis played an especially important role in this respect. First, it proved that a nuclear war between the two nations was not merely a plot for science fiction, but very nearly a grim reality. Second, it showed that the main problem in handling crises between the two nations, at least at that time, related to miscalculation and misinterpretation of each other's intentions. Third, both sides learned that a situation can sometimes develop autonomously and become unmanageable, beyond the control of either side. All in all, the Cuban crisis was a beginning in developing a common paradigm of crisis management; establishment of the hot line was a logical extension of that lesson, though a common approach to crisis prevention was not further developed at that time.

Other types of crises, such as the American intervention in Vietnam, involved an indirect interaction; both sides were engaged through an intermediary so as to avoid a direct confrontation. Though such interventions were regarded as a political challenge, the use of nuclear weapons was not considered appropriate.

In the 1970s, Soviet theorists concentrated on two aspects of crisis avoidance. First, as the U.S. alert during the 1973 Middle East War showed, the American administration continued to regard nuclear arms as a possible means of crisis management until 1977, when President Carter's P.D.-18 acknowledged that nuclear weapons cannot be regarded as a means of crisis management in conditions of strategic parity and proposed the rapid deployment force as a substitute. Second, studies were conducted on the possibility of a more constructive interaction between the two countries, including de-escalation, parallel restraint, and diplomatic communication. Both approaches were closely connected to the correlation of forces (the achievement of strategic parity), which was regarded as a cornerstone of a new détente relationship. Allyn has analyzed the treatment of these issues in Soviet specialist writings and official statements.

The period of détente in the 1970s followed the American debacle in Vietnam and the withdrawal of U.S. forces from that country, which, together with the 1973-74 oil crisis, had an immense effect in the Third World. The subsequent activization of political forces in those areas increased the general level of conflict. This trend was perceived differently in the Soviet Union and in the United States, a discrepancy aggravated by ill-shaped attempts to find a "linkage" between what was happening in the Third World and Soviet-American relations. Hence the greater risk of an accidental or inadvertent war, which preoccupied Soviet thinking at the time.

Allyn describes the striking asymmetry of Soviet and American understandings of what created the crisis potential in our relations during the 1970s. To a great extent, this asymmetry can be explained by different methodologies of thinking: what was regarded as an objective process in Soviet literature was considered the result of Soviet "manipulations" in American writings (and sometimes vice versa). The two countries' political and historical experience also differed. Until the early 1970s, the Soviet Union was trying to catch up with the United States, to reach nuclear parity. What the Soviet side regarded as legitimate and even beneficial for the relationship (since only parity could put it on the basis of equality), the American side perceived as a growing threat.

This misreading of intentions had a confusing impact, so that the latter half of the 1970s was a period of considerable instability in Soviet-American relations. The revolutions in Iran and Nicaragua in 1979 only increased the Americans' sense of growing vulnerability. Tension increased toward the end of the decade, exacerbated by developments in Afghanistan.

In the 1980s this asymmetry of thinking diminished. During the first half of the decade, relations were strained and full of mutual suspicions. The U.S. administration sought to regain a sense of security through harsh statements, threats, and increased military spending. Its efforts were supported by a majority of the American public and by Western Europe. At the same time, opinion became polarized, and a vocal opposition was created among those who understood that this approach to regaining a sense of security was too expensive or who were simply scared by the cold war rhetoric accompanying the growth of nuclear potential.

Throughout those years, remarkably, there were no serious crises in Soviet-American relations. It was as if both sides understood that, in a period of high tension, they simply could not afford another Cuban missile crisis. They tried to avoid any possibility of a direct confrontation; at the same time, there was an impasse in arms control negotiations and a deep freeze in other spheres of relations.

A breakthrough occurred with the *perestroika* in the Soviet Union and with the new political thinking in foreign policy. These charges made possible a fuller awareness of the scope of issues both countries faced, and greatly increased the flexibility and dynamics of Soviet foreign policy. In addition they created a climate in which it might be possible to dispel the "enemy image" that had dominated American foreign policy thinking.

Bruce Allyn analyzes in detail the new directions in Soviet writings on the subject after 1985: the view of crisis prevention as a political (not military) problem, the emphasis placed on regional crises, and the problem of accidental or inadvertent war. Serious attention has also been given to the problem of escalation, crisis control mechanisms including nuclear risk reduction centers, and the possibilities of UN mechanisms to handle regional crises. Often these issues have become the topics of Soviet-American, Soviet-Western European, and other discussions.

These discussions have begun to develop a realistic common approach to crisis avoidance and crisis prevention. Events like Chernobyl have increased shared awareness of common threats and of the need to develop a framework for a common response, both at the level of thinking and on the operational level of crisis avoidance mechanisms.

This awareness is an essential element of the Soviet understanding of the "integrity and interdependence" of the world today. If both Americans and Soviets accept this understanding, we can recognize that the scope and nature of crises have changed, acquiring new and very important dimensions of common threat. No single nation, even the mightiest, and indeed not even several nations, could deal with these threats adequately. The entire world community must be involved in devising ways to avoid inadvertent war and crisis. This joint book is a step in that direction.

SOVIET VIEW

Vitaly V. Zhurkin, Sergei A. Karaganov, and Andrei V. Kortunov

During most of the Soviet Union's history, threats to its existence have been clearly defined, their sources sufficiently evident, and there was general agreement on ways to counteract them. Discussion focused on how to survive in conditions of hostile capitalist encirclement, to prevent the creation of a united anti-Soviet front by Western countries, and to guarantee the necessary material resources to repel any attack from the West.

In our day the situation has fundamentally changed. The question of socialism's continued existence has been decided finally and irrevocably (unless, of course, the flames of nuclear war should destroy the socialist part of humanity along with the rest). Thus we now have greater freedom to maneuver in both domestic and foreign policy, allowing for a complex and considered approach to the problem of national security, taking into account both short-term and long-term tendencies, both military and nonmilitary challenges, foreign threats and possible dangers in domestic development.

On the other hand, our society must confront a widening spectrum of objective challenges. Never before has the competition between the two social-economic systems affected so many areas, never before has the interaction between socialism and capitalism on the intergovernmental level been so intense. In recent decades humanity has encountered a qualitatively new set of global problems. Unprecedented tasks appear on the horizon, connected with the establishment of the scientific-technological civilization of the twenty-first century.

Human thinking characteristically lags behind quickly changing political realities. Thus in our day-to-day thinking we naturally tend to concentrate attention on traditional threats that have already been confronted, and to underestimate unfamiliar threats that are becoming a reality. Hence the urgent necessity when evaluating the world military-political situation to avoid absolutizing past experience, to take full account of changes occurring in the world.

Traditionally, for example, the main threat of concern to the Soviet people has been some form of a repetition of June 22, 1941—

that is, an invasion from the West, whether a nuclear attack or a large-scale aggression with conventional forces. The nuclear age gives a special character to this problem, for the most dangerous military threat to our country now appears to be a nuclear attack. For instance, the deployment in Western Europe of American Pershing IIs, which could reach the Soviet capital in a flight time of about ten minutes, put the nuclear threat on Moscow's doorstep. Given current military-political realities, however, such a nuclear attack would spell unavoidable catastrophe for the aggressor as well.

Given modern forces and means, is a repetition of aggression on the pattern of 1941 even possible? In current East-West relations there is not a single conflict whose resolution would warrant resort to war. Relying on common sense, it is difficult to imagine what goals could lead Western armies to invade the territory of the socialist states. Contemporary capitalism suffers from many extremely serious problems, but none that could be resolved through military aggression against socialism. This is a major reason why no politically influential forces, either in Western Europe or in the United States, would set themselves such a task today. Even the most unbridled hawks recognize that any attempts to "abolish" or even "discard" socialism by military means would be suicidal for their own societies.

The example of Europe is telling. Even a conventional war on the European continent, saturated as it is with nuclear power stations, chemical factories, and huge stores of flammable material, would signify for all practical purposes the end of civilization there. This is particularly true of Western Europe, where the population density and the level or urbanization are higher than in Eastern Europe, and the territory is smaller. The very nature of highly industrialized society becomes a factor in the deterrence of war. Moreover it is impossible to imagine how a war in Europe could be contained to the nonnuclear level. However "limited" a nuclear war might be in the planning, its probable outcome is a radioactive desert.

Clearly the overwhelming majority of the U.S. and Western European population does not want to fight a war, especially an aggressive one. The decision to place American intermediate-range nuclear missiles in Europe significantly complicated the political situation in many nations of the region.

Soviet foreign and domestic policy of recent years objectively facilitates the unmasking of the myth of a "Soviet threat" and erosion of the "image of the enemy." Already a new image of the USSR has begun to form. Some in the West seek to take advantage of a paradox of the problem of security. In the past, an appropriate level of closedness and secrecy in foreign and military policy was considered important for the strengthening of national security. Particularly since advanced technical means of observing the other side had not yet been developed, this closedness deprived a potential adversary of confidence in the accuracy of any information it obtained. It compelled a degree of caution and restraint. But the very same closedness led the opposing sides to prepare for actions on the basis of a worst-case scenario, thereby fueling the arms race. Today the counterproductive nature of such closedness is becoming more and more obvious. It allows our adversaries to present a distorted interpretation of Soviet actions. Only openness allows us to convey effectively the aims of our policy to the peoples of other nations, to convince them of the peace-loving intentions and plans of the USSR. That is why measures to increase openness in our foreign policy and military activity have tremendous significance for the strengthening of Soviet security. They do not intensify threats but, just the opposite, weaken them.

The possibility of military aggression will continue, since bourgeois democracy cannot completely contain the aggressiveness of militarism. Witness the U.S. invasions of Grenada and Libya, its intervention in Lebanon, its undeclared wars against Nicaragua and Afghanistan, the shows of military force in the Persian Gulf, and the application of military force by Western European governments (to speak only of the current decade). Nevertheless, Western (bourgeois) democracy throws up definite obstacles to the unleashing of a large-scale aggression, a major war between the two systems. The history of the American intervention in Indochina underscores this point. The Pentagon has been forced to recognize the limitations placed on its actions by democratic institutions, by the unwillingness of people to sacrifice their lives and well-being in aggressive wars.

In Europe, because the two sides' military capabilities are approximately in balance, NATO armed forces cannot count on a successful attack. The conduct of large-scale offensive operations requires substantial superiority in basic types of armaments. And given current technical means of verification and the system of confidence-building measures, a secret mobilization of any armed forces would be extremely difficult.

Does this mean that there is practically no threat of war in Europe? It is not possible to answer this question categorically. The tremendous military potentials amassed there, oversaturated with nuclear weaponry, could under certain circumstances lead to a rapid escalation of an accidental crisis. If, as planned in NATO headquarters, there is a massive deployment of the latest conventional weapons, which are especially powerful and destructive, and have a clearly offensive character, then military-strategic stability on the continent would be undermined. (The more militaristic forces in NATO are demanding precisely such "compensation" for the liquidation of intermediate- and short-range nuclear missiles in Europe.) Mistrust, tension, and the threat of war could grow—as would the probability that events might go out of control.

Thus the threat of war in Europe has not yet been permanently removed from the agenda of world politics. But today's threat is qualitatively different from that which confronted nations in the interwar period or immediately after World War II. Our reactions must differ as well. Earlier the sufficient level of Soviet military power on the European continent was determined by the requirement to repel any attack. Now the task is in principle different—to deter and prevent war itself—and demands the rethinking of many traditional postulates of military strategy and operational tactics, beginning with a re-evaluation of the quantitative requirements for various types of armaments (e.g., tanks), the character of conducted maneuvers, and so on.

To ensure that war never again breaks out in Europe, levels of military confrontation must be successively reduced, and ultimately the system of confrontational military blocs, which intensifies the threat of war, must be overcome. A stable and humane system of security must be created that excludes hostility and the arms race. The Soviet-American agreement on the liquidation of intermediate- and short-range nuclear missiles in Europe may turn out to be a breakthrough in the development of the military-political situation on our continent. This agreement is a concrete step toward giving a strictly defensive character to the military doctrines and armed forces of the opposing groups in Europe. For the first time it creates the conditions needed for a reduction in armed forces and conventional weaponry in Europe, and for radical steps toward increasing stability.

Today and for the near future, a premeditated nuclear attack is just as improbable as a deliberate unleashing of a large-scale war in Europe. The tremendous efforts of our people to strengthen the defensive capability of the Soviet nation have borne fruit. Now any nation that might consider nuclear aggression knows that it could not expect to remain unpunished, no matter what means was chosen to unleash a conflict. Moreover, the use of even a small percentage of the world's strategic nuclear forces would be enough to destroy all life on earth.

Strategic nuclear parity—which means that neither side can expect to attack unpunished—has a large margin of stability. Even the most unbridled hawks in the U.S. administration, who in the early 1980s demanded the "restoration" of American superiority and pushed Washington into huge increases in military appropriations, are forced to agree. Today their voices have been stilled. Former Secretary of Defense Weinberger, who at the start of the decade called for the attainment of a U.S. "margin of safety," as was enjoyed in the 1950s, now admits that this goal is unattainable. Many highly influential American experts acknowledge that the latest round of the nuclear arms race did not improve the United States' position. Under such conditions there is a much greater opportunity for radical, 50 percent reductions in strategic offensive weapons in the near future.

Parity, as the Soviet Union is pointing out, is ceasing to be a factor in the deterrence of war. Given the numerical growth in nuclear weaponry and the increase in its flexibility and accuracy, the concept of parity (even if calculated with qualitative indices) and the concept of strategic stability (on which estimates of the likelihood of war are based) have begun to be at variance, whereas in the past they more or less coincided. We face a higher probability of an accidental, unsanctioned outbreak of nuclear war, of a rapid, uncontrollable escalation of a crisis. Thus a paradox takes shape: the threat of premeditated nuclear aggression is decreasing, but the threat of war may be increasing.

For perhaps the first time in the history of the Soviet Union, no national aggressor could conceivably encroach upon our territory. The accumulated reserve of might provides a basis for believing that such a correlation of forces will continue for a long time to come.

The advancement at the 27th Party Congress of a long-term program to create a comprehensive system of international security is an important step. It defines not only military but also political, economic, and humanitarian parameters of security. Moreover, the program recognizes nonmilitary aspects of international security as fully independent and no less important than military considerations.

Progress toward stable peace will inevitably be a long, complicated process. Even if the danger of nuclear cataclysm or any other war is completely eliminated, contradictions, rivalry, and confrontation would persist. At the same time the erosion of the military threat and the gradual transition to international peace based on a system of comprehensive security will create new conditions for ousting the elements of confrontation from international life and expanding the spheres of cooperation.

8 STRATEGIC STABILITY
Limiting Competition in Nuclear Arms

Aleksei G. Arbatov

Strategic parity between the USSR and the United States, first reached in the 1970s, is now in a critical phase of its historical development. If negotiations on deep cuts of strategic arms are successful, the maintenance of the nuclear balance at lower levels will be an indisputable condition for establishing security. As each side's nuclear potential approaches zero, regulation of stability in negotiations will demand increasing precision. On the other hand, if the dialogue on strengthening the regime of the Anti-Ballistic Missile (ABM) Treaty and reducing strategic offensive weapons fails, further increases in the level of nuclear confrontation, even if parity is maintained, will make equilibrium less effective as a factor of military-political deterrence and a source of security.

The concept of strategic equilibrium has been given different, often directly contradictory, interpretations by representatives of various governments, and even by individual specialists within one nation. Over time these ambiguities and differences have increased. The same is true of concepts such as *equilibrium, superiority, advantage, lag, stability,* and *sufficiency.* The search for points of convergence is an essential first step toward successful negotiations to reduce nuclear arms.

Although the strategic offensive forces of the USSR and the United States are relatively similar in their military tasks and means of execution (the destruction of targets at a distance of many thou-

sands of kilometers by the explosion of a nuclear device), an evaluation of the correlation of forces is complicated by three factors.
First, strategic weapons are characterized by a large number of technical parameters and peculiar characteristics.[1] Any system of strategic arms has technical and operational advantages and disadvantages
in comparison with other systems. Taking into account the different
composition, structure, and technical characteristics of the strategic
nuclear arms of the two sides and their dissimilar geostrategic situations, it is difficult to weigh net advantage or disadvantage on the
basis of well-founded measures. Still more difficult is it for the two
governments to agree on these measures in negotiations.

   Second, the correlation of strategic forces is not static, but constantly changing as new arms systems are introduced and old ones
removed. Variations in the day-by-day functioning of these complex
military-organizational-technical complexes also affect the correlation of forces.

   Third, and the most important, any analysis should take into
account each side's potential for inflicting a nuclear first strike, its
capacity to achieve its goals in war and to prevent the opponent
from achieving its goals. The essence of such an analysis lies in how
the other side might use its forces in the event of war. Military-
strategic equilibrium can provide security only when the correlation
of quantitative and qualitative characteristics of the two opposing
forces guarantees that the cost of unleashing a nuclear conflict would
greatly outweigh the desired victory. Even in the most acute crisis
situation, that is, a first strike would not be an attractive option.
Such an equilibrium would minimize the probability of a nuclear
conflict. At each stage of the reduction of nuclear arsenals, such an
equilibrium would be both a starting point and a final result of agreements to reduce the level of confrontation.

THE EVOLUTION OF THE MILITARY-STRATEGIC EQUILIBRIUM

Military-strategic equilibrium was initially understood simply as approximate equality of the sides in the quantity of strategic delivery
systems. The SALT I negotiations (1969–72) focused on land-based
intercontinental ballistic missiles (ICBMs), submarine-launched ballistic missiles (SLBMs), and heavy bombers. Verification of compliance

would be accomplished with the help of satellite photos of silos, SLBM launching tubes on submarines, and bombers at airbases. This approach, however, started to lose its meaning even before it had been agreed to at the SALT negotiations. Neither superpower has increased the quantity of strategic nuclear delivery vehicles in its force structure since the early 1970s (actually 1967 in the case of the United States). In fact the United States, while removing outdated systems, has reduced this figure from 2,360 to 1,960 units, and it seems likely that the total will be lowered further in the 1990s to 1,800 or 1,900 units. Between 1979 and 1987 the Soviet Union decreased its units from 2,504 to 2,480.

Evaluations of the military-strategic balance in nuclear delivery systems are clearly insufficient in themselves. Another criterion is the quantity of nuclear warheads, which has risen steadily in the United States since 1970, and in the USSR since 1975, as single-warhead ICBMs were replaced by new missiles with multiple warheads—that is, multiple independently retargetable re-entry vehicles (MIRVs). Agreements on strategic offensive arms should lead to a reduction in the total number of nuclear warheads and to a strengthening of the equilibrium at lower levels. This approach was reflected in the SALT II Treaty, which established limits on the maximum number of warheads for certain types of delivery vehicles, and in negotiations on START in 1986–87, which focused on 50 percent reductions of strategic offensive arms, limiting nuclear warheads to 6,000 units.

But even an approach based on warheads will not remain meaningful indefinitely. U.S. plans call for slower growth in the quantity of nuclear warheads in American strategic forces during the 1980s and 1990s than in the 1970s. The number of units rose from 5,000 to 10,000 during the 1970s, a 100 percent increase, but will grow only about 50 percent in the 1980s. In this respect the disproportion between Soviet and U.S. strategic offensive arms will be reduced.

The strategic arms race increasingly is shifting to the qualitative arena, as old arms are replaced with more modern, effective, and expensive weapons. Although they are deployed in smaller batches and at a slower rate, their destabilizing influence on military equilibrium is no less significant. The reality of the dynamic military-strategic balance in the 1980s and 1990s is quite different from the simplified formula of an "ever-increasing growth of nuclear arms." Changes in this sphere are potentially dangerous, but they take much more complex and heterogeneous forms, making it impossible to evaluate the military situation using outdated measures of the 1960s and even the 1970s. In the 1980s, the United States has persistently put forward official proposals to evaluate the correlation of strategic forces on *quantitative-qualitative criteria* (total throw-weight, total megatonnage or equivalent megatonnage). These measures are distinguished by a significant arbitrariness in the method of calculation. In practice, the U.S. measures exaggerated assessment of Soviet forces.

Throw-weight has been regarded as a "universal measure" of the strategic balance and nuclear potential. The throw-weight of a ballistic missile, as defined in SALT II, is the sum of the weights of its nuclear warheads, the mechanism for dispensing them in flight, and the means for penetrating any ballistic missile defenses. The weight of the warhead is related to its explosive power. Efforts to limit the general throw-weight of a missile involve a tradeoff: either have fewer, relatively powerful (and heavy) warheads or increase their quantity while reducing the power of certain warheads. In proposing this criterion, the United States counts on outstripping the USSR in warhead miniaturization technology, which would allow it to further lower the weight in relation to its explosive power. The United States also believes it will have an advantage in accuracy of destroying the target. In working toward an "equalization" of throw-weights, the United States proposes not to count the payload of heavy bombers— in which the United States has greater predominance over the USSR, which would fully compensate for Soviet advantages in ICBM throw-weight. If bomber payloads were counted, the two sides would be approximately equal in their capacity to raise a total nuclear payload in a single launch of strategic offensive arms.

Setting aside objective military technical differences, there is a certain logic in limiting throw-weight: to prevent an increase of the power of nuclear warheads by restricting their numbers in each side's force structure. But this logic is divorced from contemporary military-technical realities. Even if the levels of nuclear warheads were reduced to 6,000 units, the quantity possessed by each side would many times exceed the number of primary administrative-industrial and military targets of the other side. In such conditions an increase in the accuracy with which the nuclear payload can be delivered is at least as destabilizing as an increase in power. Enhanced accuracy is now generally accepted as the most "profitable" way to increase the effectiveness of destroying any target. Only if the number of nuclear warheads were reduced to less than several hundred units might the limitation of throw-weight become an effective means of strengthening the strategic stability of the nuclear balance. Moreover, reduction of throw-weight would require supplementary, highly complex methods of verification.

To some degree these considerations apply to other qualitative-quantitative parameters of strategic offensive arms: the total megatonnage (that is, the total explosive power of the nuclear weapons), the equivalent megatonnage, the capacity to destroy defended targets. In themselves none of these criteria adequately reflects the essential characteristics of the contemporary strategic correlation of forces and the tendency of its dynamic in the foreseeable future. Therefore, regardless of the feasibility of verification, these criteria cannot serve as a standard for reducing strategic potentials of the powers.

As is pointed out in the research of a committee of Soviet scholars, the notion of stability (*stabil'nost'*), or *ustoichivost'* in physics relates to how easy it is to take a given object from its existing state and how difficult it is to return it to the initial condition.[2] By analogy, when applied to the military-strategic equilibrium, the concept of stability refers to the probability and danger of the outbreak of a nuclear conflict given a certain correlation of the sides' strategic forces. Certain characteristics of the nuclear balance determine how easily one side can upset the balance and achieve superiority, and how readily the other side can neutralize these activities through responsive measures to re-establish the equilibrium; these characteristics are often understood as elements derived from this fundamental notion of stability.

THE AMERICAN CONCEPTION
OF STRATEGIC STABILITY

Since the late 1960s a version of the conception of strategic stability has been taking shape among politicians, the military, and scholars in the United States. In the 1970s this formulation became generally accepted in policy development for strategic nuclear forces and in negotiations with the USSR on limiting strategic arms. This conception also served as a justification for U.S. nuclear policy, and for a political-propagandistic campaign against the alleged "Soviet threat."

Since the late 1970s the West has persistently repeated that the USSR has "superiority," allegedly because of a supposed Soviet advantage in the number and yield of land-based ICBMs. The Soviet side repeatedly stated that its advantages in land-based missiles, which carry more than 60 percent of its warheads, were counterbalanced by U.S. advantages in sea-based missile forces and heavy bombers, which carry approximately 80 percent of U.S. warheads. The Soviet lead in number of launchers (2,494 versus 2,260) is compensated for by its disadvantage in the number of warheads (10,000 versus 14,000 to 16,000 units). On balance, Soviet publications emphasize, rough parity still exists.

In the West, however, these arguments have been questioned. American politicians and specialists, defending the official point of view, maintain that American advantages do not offset Soviet ones. To support this view, they resort not to quantitative comparisons but to the model of stability that is generally accepted in the West, based on certain scenarios of nuclear war. According to this model, the asymmetry favoring the USSR relates to first-strike capability and therefore is "destabilizing," whereas the U.S. superiority relates only to the potential for a second strike and is therefore "stabilizing." In particular, it is stated that, given the quantity, accuracy, and yield of its ICBM warheads, the Soviet Union could destroy over 90 percent of the hardened silos and control centers of U.S. land-based ICBMs; the analogous possibilities for U.S. land-based missiles are far more limited. The West admits the U.S. advantage in sea-based missiles, heavy bombers, and cruise missiles (of various basing modes), but argues that silo-based missiles in the USSR cannot be destroyed by these means. Submarine-launched missiles are said to be insufficiently accurate and to have unreliable radio communications with command centers (complicating the coordination of such a strike); heavy bombers and cruise missiles take too long to reach their targets and are presumed to be vulnerable to echeloned Soviet air defenses.[3]

In the late 1970s these arguments were used to undermine the SALT II Treaty, which supposedly did not reduce the Soviet advantage, and to justify present American strategic programs. On the same basis, in 1982–83 the United States insisted on disproportionately large reductions of land-based ICBMs, as a "destabilizing" element of the military balance. The American side has continued to link an overall 50 percent reduction of offensive strategic arms with conditions for establishing additional sublevels, with an emphasis on reducing ballistic missiles, a greater reduction of land-based ICBM warheads, especially those with multiple re-entry vehicles having more than six warheads.

A positive development in the American view of strategic stability occurred with the switch from quantitative comparisons to an analysis of how quantitative and qualitative aspects of the strategic correlation of forces affect the stability of the military balance, and the possibility and probability of a first strike. But the American conception of stability arbitrarily singles out as a criterion the correlation of the effectiveness of Soviet and American land-based ICBMs against each other, leaving other elements of strategic forces out of context. An extremely dubious scenario for unleashing a strategic nuclear strike is assumed: a limited strike at an individual component of strategic forces of the other side. No matter what the political motivation of such an attack, it is presumed that the opponent will retaliate with the same limited strikes on analogous targets, and will not use its entire surviving forces (including sea and air based) for an all-out strike on urban and industrial centers in hopes of saving its own cities from massive destruction by the aggressor's reserve forces.

A decision to inflict a first strike on the other side would entail extraordinarily high political stakes, and the probability of escalation to total destruction of cities would be extremely high. A strategy of using just one component of the strategic offensive arms (ICBMs) to strike the analogous component of forces of the other side seems highly unlikely. In all probability, even purely hypothetically, one could make a decision about a first strike only in the hope of preventing a second strike, or at least weakening it to a scale acceptable to the initiator. Further, the United States has proposed as the main criterion of stability the capability of one side to destroy with its land-based missiles the ICBMs silos of the other side. But other systems of arms—SLBMs with heightened accuracy, intermediate-range missiles, and cruise missiles—may be used to destroy silos and other hardened targets. Besides, ICBM silos are only one element of strategic forces: SLBMs, bombers, and cruise missiles are also capable of striking other strategic forces such as aircraft at airfields or submarines at base. Since both sides have significant low-vulnerability forces (submarines at sea, bombers in the air, mobile land-based ICBMs), their systems of command, control, and communications can become more important targets for a sudden strike than ICBM silos. For a strike against these targets, it would be preferable to use weapons that have high accuracy and minimal warning time. Minimal warning time can be achieved not only by a short flight time, but also by a strike from unpredictable directions and measures for counteracting radars and infrared warning systems of the other side. From this point of view, SLBMs, intermediate-range nuclear forces (MRBMs), submarine-launched cruise missiles (SLCMs), ground-launched cruise missiles (GLCMs), and in the future possibly bombers and air-launched cruise missiles (ALCMs) using the stealth technology are more destabilizing than ICBMs.

Other considerations that affect the approaches to the problem in question cannot be ignored either. For instance, the reliability of command, control, and communication systems of various types of strategic forces, on which the danger of unauthorized use of nuclear weapons mainly depends, especially in a crisis situation, may be taken as a criterion of destabilizing influence on the military strategic situation. From another angle, the question that should be asked is what nuclear weapons systems could be relatively easily and quickly involved in conventional military operations—that is, which of them erode the "nuclear threshold" and lead to an uncontrolled escalation of the conflict.

AN ALTERNATIVE APPROACH TO
THE PROBLEM OF STABILITY OF
THE STRATEGIC BALANCE

It is advisable to take two assumptions as a basis for the approach to the problem of the military strategic stability and equilibrium. First, since the stability of the balance is the main factor in preventing nuclear war, of prime importance in an analysis of this balance is not a comparison of quantitative and qualitative characteristics of strategic offensive armaments but an appraisal of hypothetical strategic objectives and possibilities for attaining them through a first nuclear strike that would start a nuclear war. The more dubious such objectives and the smaller the possibility of attaining them, the more stable the strategic balance. In this case, quantitative and other static parameters of the correlation of forces do not lose their value; they remain as a data base for strategic analysis. But they are no longer the only standard for estimating the military balance or the primary reference point for steps to reduce armaments.

Second, a dynamic analysis of the strategic balance is a complicated task, which depends on many selected assumptions, and which must account for immense uncertainties. The appraisal of the stability of the situation becomes much more meaningful if it is shared by both sides. At minimum, a certain mutual understanding is required regarding assumptions and criteria, even if differences remain in the determination of some parameters and methods of taking uncertainties into account.

Previously, to have a common basis for reaching agreements it was sufficient for the states to agree that it was impossible to win a nuclear war, that superiority was unattainable and should not be an objective of either side, and that in the reduction and limitation of armaments the rough parity of the military balance should be preserved. Now such a basis is too narrow for the progress of the talks. First, the very mechanisms of the evolution of the strategic balance have become much more complex, which makes former yardsticks increasingly less applicable. Besides, the logic of the talks has led them from the peripheral measures of limitation to rather radical steps, which, if implemented, would strongly influence the available nuclear arsenals and new weapons programs and, consequently, the strategic concepts and even operational plans of both states.

The choice of criteria for appraising the correlation of forces in this context is determined mainly by the definition of strategic aims pursued when delivering a first nuclear strike. Insofar as it concerns strategic offensive armaments, it is necessary to define the likely aims of a first strike with the only use of strategic offensive armaments on a global level, as distinct from the European or any other theater of war. According to modern strategic views, the goals pursued in such a strike may be quite diverse: demonstrating resolve, changing the nuclear balance of forces in one's favor, attempting to disorganize the combat operations of conventional armed forces, destroying the military and industrial potential as a whole or even individual industrial sectors.

It seems, however, that the primary and most probable purpose of a first strike would be to decrease the power of nuclear retaliation (that is, to prevent the enemy's retaliatory strike or to considerably reduce the damage from it, as compared with a situation in which the enemy delivers the first strike). The fundamental provision of the Soviet military doctrine that has repeatedly been formulated at a high level is taken as a point of departure for an appraisal of the strategic correlation of forces and an analysis of the balance and stability. "Superiority is unambiguously understood as the achievement of a capability to deal a strike . . . in the expectation that a retaliatory strike . . . would have a lower power than under other conditions."[4]

Logically, superiority and a first nuclear strike are inseparable from each other, since superiority can be an efficient instrument of political pressure only when it ensures a real threat of using nuclear weapons (that is, a first strike at a certain level of conflict).[5]

On the basis of this doctrinal provision, the purpose of a first strike would be maximum destruction of the other side's strategic forces, including its C^3I system. The latter provision is important. The U.S. strategic theory considers versions of "limited" strategic strikes in the context of conducting a "controlled" nuclear war. According to this theory, counterforce strikes are delivered so as to limit the damage to the population and industry as much as possible ("limitation") and not to hit the other side's command and communication systems ("controllability"). Our assumption excludes the possibility of such actions as totally unrealistic. Irrespective of any other considerations, a first strike can only have as a goal the reduction of the power of retaliation. A document on Soviet military policy stresses in this connection: "Only totally irresponsible persons can assert that a nuclear war could be conducted according to some prearranged rules that have been worked out beforehand and that say that nuclear missiles must explode 'in a gentlemanly manner,' that is, only on certain targets, without destroying the population."[6]

It should be pointed out that the damage-limitation in a nuclear conflict, being a quite plausible strategic task, can hardly be a political goal of a state in war. The most reliable way of reducing damage to any power would be to prevent the outbreak of a nuclear conflict. The matter is further complicated by the fact that even a completely successful disarming strike, which fully prevents retaliation (and such a probability is practically precluded for the attacker), would all the same inflict on the aggressor tremendous, if not irreparable, damage from radiation and other fatal consequences of thousands of nuclear explosions for the environment, including the possibility of "nuclear winter." This corroborates the correctness of Mikhail Gorbachev's conclusion that nuclear war cannot be a continuation of any sensible or rational policy.[7]

Nonetheless, a nuclear cataclysm may well be a continuation of a certain military strategy that has gone out of political control and is operating according to its own laws. Political goals of states may come into collision and evolve into a military conflict, which may involve direct use of conventional armed forces and armaments against each other. In this case, tactical and shorter-range nuclear weapons deeply integrated into conventional forces and weapons of NATO and the Warsaw Treaty Organization may promptly be used in the theater of war. It is in this situation, when the stakes involved and the losses from the conflict have already become tremendous—if the leaders of the warring nations cannot stop the escalation of combat operations and settle the conflict peacefully—that strategic logic threatens to gain the upper hand over political common sense. When a strategic nuclear strike of the other side seems inevitable or very probable and when the estimated difference in damage between striking first or second is relatively great, the decision may be taken to deliver a pre-emptive strategic strike.

Several other factors may push in the direction of taking such a step: vulnerability of the military and political leadership and the command and communication system for the nuclear strike; the "blurred" levels of conflict, when tactical and shorter-range nuclear weapons at the theater may trespass the territory of the great powers and deal strikes at their strategic weapons, along with conventional arms; the loss of control by the high command over the operations of its strategic forces; and so on.

In such conditions when a direct armed clash occurs, irrespective of the original political motives and goals of countries concerned, the strategic correlation of forces, the equilibrium or, on the contary, the superiority of one of the sides, may prove a decisive factor in deciding on a first or pre-emptive strike by strategic offensive forces. And since the talks and agreements on the limitation and reduction of armaments deal with the strategic correlation of forces, they are precisely the tool that may primarily serve the objectives of reducing the probability of nuclear catastrophe.

Obviously, the military strategic balance, being the basis for preventing nuclear war (that is, preventing a first nuclear strike) and the opposite of the "superiority" in the clear-cut above-mentioned sense of the term, presupposes as an ideal the total absence of such a capability on both sides. But in reality, in view of the colossal destructive power of stockpiled nuclear armaments, the extremely short flight time to targets, the high accuracy and global range, the strategic forces of any side cannot remain absolutely invulnerable to the other side's first strike. Both sides are capable of partially weakening the power of the enemy's retaliatory strike by their first strike.

Besides, even if neither the USSR nor the United States had an advantage and their capabilities in this respect would be equal though very considerable, such a parity could hardly be regarded as a reliable basis for preventing war. Having no superiority in peacetime, the states can expect to gain it during the war by delivering a first strike and in any case will seriously fear such a step from the opponent. In an acute crisis situation, this may be an additional stimulus for attack or pre-emption. The above considerations are precisely the reasons that make necessary such a notion of "stability" of the strategic correlation of forces, including "equilibrium" as one of its states.

Various approaches may be used in selecting criteria of stability of the nuclear balance and determining the methods of calculations. Each of these approaches has its advantages and disadvantages. One of them is being developed at the Department on Disarmament and International Security of the Institute of World Economy and International Relations at the USSR Academy of Sciences (in cooperation with the Committee of Soviet Scientists in Defense of Peace and Against Nuclear Threat and the Institute of U.S. and Canadian Studies of the USSR Academy of Sciences). It is based on the analysis of a number of parameters. This approach is aimed at the elaboration of a general criterion of the strategic stability of the nuclear balance between the USSR and the United States on a global scale, a stability that is evidently inversely proportional to the probability of a first strike.[8]

STRATEGIC STABILITY AND C³I

Having reviewed the evolution of the strategic balance and compared U.S. and Soviet views of stability, we now turn to the crucial issue of command, control, communications, and intelligence (C³I), which is of particular relevance to our joint study of avoiding inadvertent war and crisis.[9]

As strategic weapons systems have become more effective, key elements of C^3I have become more vulnerable; in some instances they are more subject to the destructive power of nuclear explosions than are the weapon systems themselves. A direct attack on the C^3I system might well be more effective in preventing retaliation than a strike against strategic forces. In any case, an aggressor attempting to weaken the power of its opponent's second strike will make its task significantly easier by taking out the system of C^3I. The development of antisatellite systems and other space-strike systems would further endanger C^3I. Given a crisis in the world military-political situation, this vulnerability will exert a serious destabilizing influence, as it might stimulate a pre-emptive strike.

Soviet and U.S. strategic C^3I systems of command and control consist of three main elements: (1) early warning systems, information gathering and processing systems (early-warning, photographic, and electronic intelligence satellites, radars, and radio interception stations); (2) command centers of political and military control (both stationary [underground and ground] and mobile [land, air, and sea based] centers); and (3) the systems of communication that link the first two elements with each other and with those who carry out orders of the leadership (the crews of submarines carrying nuclear weapons and strategic bombers, and ICBM launch control operators). This complex enables the military-political leadership to maintain control over strategic forces in peacetime and to bring these forces to full combat alert in a crisis situation ("negative control") and, if necessary, to transmit the order for their direct use ("positive control").

The specific characteristics of strategic arms allow varying degrees of centralized control. ICBMs deployed in silos are, from the perspective of negative control, the most reliable leg of the strategic triad. Because of redundancy in the system of space, atmospheric, and underground lines of communication, which are duplicated many times over, the military-political leadership is confident that military orders will be transmitted and received, and the activities of those who carry out the orders will be kept under control.

Strategic bombers are in a different situation. Reliable communication with air bases makes it possible to transmit an order for urgent takeoff. But once airborne, heavy bombers can maintain radio communication only within certain zones. This restriction makes them vulnerable and raises doubts whether communication with aircraft will be able to ensure control over the execution of all orders from the command center. Moreover, should strategic aircraft leave the defined zones, communication with them may be completely severed.[10]

It is much more difficult to exercise negative control over the sea-based elements of the strategic triad. Since reliable two-way communication systems are not available and the airborne relay retranslational systems are vulnerable and complex in function, the United States has introduced a command system in which the center exercises no technical negative control over submarines carrying nuclear weapons (SSBNs) while they are on military patrol. Thus in principle the crew of an SSBN is technically able (but not organizationally authorized) to unblock and launch SLBMs without the sanction of the central command. Such a probability, even if very small, compels the Soviet Union to view SSBNs somewhat differently than in the United States, as to their impact on the stability of the strategic balance—although official American spokesmen and experts insist that the high survivability of submarines ensures their "stabilizing" role. Soviet SSBNs, according to accessible data, are equipped with more reliable blocking mechanisms for nuclear weapons; that is, they operate under a regime of strict negative control from center. This control is facilitated by the fact that most submarines patrol close to Soviet shores (with the aim of more reliable defense from NATO antisubmarine defenses).

Thus the current C^3I system of military command and control does not allow the military-political leadership to control all nuclear weapons to an equal degree. In time of crisis or during the beginning of military activities the unreliability and vulnerability of C^3I could play a sharply destabilizing role, including the probability of loss of control over one's own strategic forces.

The improvement of combat performance of weapon systems has undermined both sides' confidence that various elements of C^3I could survive a nuclear strike. As a series of research studies has shown, fundamental elements of C^3I are threatened by types of arms already in existence. For example, cruise missiles (especially sea-based cruise missiles, which can deliver surprise strikes against long-range detection facilities because their flight is concealed). Particularly dangerous in this regard are the new sea-launched ballistic missiles with increased counterforce capabilities. Their short flight time, often counted in minutes, and the unpredictable strike azimuths create a real threat that warning systems might be suddenly destroyed, along with important centers of control, air bases, airborne command points, and channels of communications. Such a danger in periods of crisis increases the likelihood of nuclear war.

The report of the Committee of Soviet Scholars notes, "the specific characteristics of a given strategic correlation of forces that either enhances or diminishes the probability of a nuclear exchange in an acute conflict situation are of paramount importance to the maintenance of stability of military parity."[11]

Paradoxically, then, along with the enhanced survivability of certain systems of strategic arms, the C^3I systems remain the most vulnerable component of each sides's strategic potential. Airborne command posts are now considered to be the least vulnerable component of the battle management complex, while strategic aircraft are seen as an ever more vulnerable component of the strategic triad.

THE CONCEPT OF LAUNCH-ON-WARNING

Given the complexity and growing vulnerability of C^3I, specialists discuss two basic approaches to resolving the problems: either simplify the tasks of C^3I and concentrate on increasing its survivability, or decrease emphasis on survivability in order to satisfy the growing operational demands of strategic forces. In the sphere of strategic arms there seems to be a tendency to move down the second path, which is fraught with dangerous and largely unpredictable consequences. This tendency is illustrated by efforts to increase by all means possible the rapidity of action of C^3I and the introduction into operational plans of the concept of "launch-on-warning" (that is, the launching of a missile after information about the activation of the opponent's strategic systems has been received and confirmed). The debate over the use of Minutemen silos for basing the American MX-ICBM is a case in point. Opponents of fixed basing argued out that the vulnerability of the MX in silos was a destabilizing factor, which forced an orientation to launch-on-warning, thus raising the risk of war.

The evolution of the strategic correlation of forces has been spurred on primarily by new U.S. initiatives in the arms race, which have objectively undermined strategic stability. The emphasis on launch-on-warning could be dangerous in certain situations. Because less time is available for taking a decision in response to information about an attack or to an unanticipated nuclear danger, the probability of an error or a miscalculation grows, especially in moments of crisis. The short flight time of contemporary weapons systems, along with the reduction of warning time due to the deployment of cruise missiles and future systems using "stealth" technology, will make it impossible to evaluate and double-check information carefully, to weigh decisions about retaliatory actions. Moreover, certain actions that might be taken by the probable opponent in conditions of crisis might be interpreted as the beginning of attack, even if the adversary's intentions were merely (for example) to ensure higher combat readiness of its strategic forces for more reliable deterrence. This problem might arise with such planned measures of U.S. operational activities as the take-off of strategic bombers from air fields, after which they may move beyond reach of detection; the transfer of airborne C^3I components, to air patrol; the deployment of additional SSBNs and nuclear submarines with cruise missiles in the sea and their approach to the opponent's coastline; deployment of mobile land-based ballistic and cruise missiles from garrisons; the approach of bombers to the zone of ALCM launch; dispersion of tactical nuclear munitions from depots; the delegation of nuclear release authority from the center to the field; and so on.

History shows that wars practically never begin, and certainly are not fought, according to the strategic and operational plans developed during peacetime by the general staffs. In a political sense, pre-war crisis situations most frequently have developed unexpectedly, overturning the foreign-policy premises upon which military planning was based. Whether or not crises spill over into a military conflict, they are generally accompanied by high indeterminacy in governmental decision-making, contradictory information and evaluations of the actions and intentions of the opponent, and uncertainty as to the probable consequences of one's own actions. As for the military aspects, peacetime strategic and operational planning most frequently fails when states were plunged into a war with qualitatively new weapons materiel, untested in combat and massively deployed in troops. The existence of huge modern arsenals of diverse nuclear weapons, whose application would probably destroy human civilization and even life on earth, exacerbates the unpredictability, the drama, and the danger of crisis situations that may go out of control.

The prominent Soviet historian Daniel Proektor notes:

> The irrationality of political and military thinking and actions of the leaders of aggressive countries are not simply qualities of individuals, but a result of many interwoven and logically interconnected events and circumstances. . . . Can we speak about the logic of war? For aggressors who admit the rationality of a world war, it is the logic of the absurd. Initially erroneous decisions give rise to others, just as false. . . . If a leader is "programmed" for a military solution, he will resort to it—although it contradicts the situation and leads to catastrophe. Another leader, even with peaceful programming, who makes an erroneous decision in a crisis situation also turns out to be no better off.[12]

Two further circumstances exacerbate the problem. First, in recent decades the strategic conceptions and military plans of the USSR and the United States, of the Warsaw Pact and NATO, have developed in large measure independently of each other, based on different premises about how a conflict might arise and develop, different scenarios and goals of the application of military force by the two sides. Each side, of course, took into account the capabilities and intentions of its probable opponent, but evaluations were often based on its own images of the opposing side, without the necessary analysis of the adversary's genuine motives and plans.

For example, NATO's military plans have traditionally been based on the concept of stage-by-stage military escalation, according to which, after an exacerbation of the political situation and mutual threats, large-scale conventional military activities begin on land, sea, and air. At a certain point they escalate to the use of tactical nuclear weapons, then intermediate-range, and later "selective" strategic strikes by strategic forces. Still later, if the conflict continues, there is total annihilation of population and industry. This five-step "escalation ladder" has never been recognized or accepted by the Soviet Union and its allies, since the use of intermediate- and short-range nuclear arms would be tantamount to a nuclear strike deep inside their territory. Therefore in Warsaw Pact military strategy and planning, the first use of nuclear weapons is regarded as the transition to the nuclear phase of the conflict, which will not have a limited character, but will inevitably escalate to global catastrophe.[13] At the same time the principles of the use of tactical nuclear arms (for example, nuclear mines, artillery, anti-aircraft missiles, antisubmarine missiles and torpedoes) are profoundly intertwined with the operational planning of NATO conventional forces. But the military concepts of the Warsaw Pact admit the possibility of using conventional weapons against the opponent's nuclear weapons.[14] Since the two sides' strategic views, premises, and plans are so different, there is a great danger that in a conflict situation the same events would be very differently perceived by the opposing parties, leading to a catastrophic miscalculation of each other's actions and intentions.

A second major problem is the need for coordination within military machines of unprecedented scale. The need is acute, reflecting the growing power, range of action, complexity, mobility, and interdependence of types of services, arms, units, and armaments. It places an enormous burden on the system of intelligence, information assessment, control and communication. As never before, troops' execution of combat tasks depends on the strict fulfillment of plans for transfer to high combat readiness, deployment for combat operations, and thoroughly coordinated execution of missions. This condition relates primarily to strategic nuclear forces, but ever more so to conventional forces and weapons.

For all these reasons, a crisis will leave little time available for political leaders to evaluate the situation and make a decision. They may face a terrible dilemma: whether to wait for a clarification of the situation and improvise, plunging their armed forces into chaos, and surrendering enormous advantages to the other side if it decides to attack, or to act according to some previously elaborated operational plans (which may not correspond fully to the specific military-political situation). The greatest threat of unleashing nuclear war today, it seems, lies in this conjunction of political, psychological, and military-technological factors. If during the calm of peacetime, the leaders do not devote sufficient attention to strategic and operational plans, the crucial elements of political common sense will not temper the purely military logic, which naturally is always directed to the maximally effective execution of combat missions. Political leaders risk losing control over events at the most decisive moment.

The danger of an uncontrollable unleashing of nuclear war is significantly increased by certain concepts, such as the delegation of nuclear release authority to the field, certain measures of transferring forces to high combat readiness and launch-on-warning. The conception of launch-on-warning is particularly dangerous. In theory a deterrent to a potential aggressor, launch-on-warning in a real crisis situation could increase the probability of a breakdown of the military-political system of mutual deterrence. The more that strategic forces and their systems of warning, command, and control are oriented toward launch-on-warning, the fewer possibilities remain for a thorough evaluation of the situation, a weighing of responsible steps and their implementation.

On several occasions during the postwar period the United States raised the alert level of its strategic forces in reaction to international events, and also to perfect the procedure. The Soviet Union, as authoritative Western research attests, has never engaged in such activities.[15] Thus, there has not been a single instance when both main nuclear powers simultaneously undertook operations to transfer their strategic forces to a high alert level, which could have been fraught with unforeseen consequences. The same point could be made about the delegation of nuclear release authority. To delegate such authority in conditions of crisis (on the assumption that there will be no time to launch upon warning or inflict a second strike) risks calling forth unpredictable consequences. The side that takes such a step could be trying to demonstrate to the opponent that its strike will not achieve the goals of "decapitation." If the opponent perceives such delegation as clear evidence of preparation for a first strike, it will have a strong incentive for a pre-emptive attack. Therefore the vulnerability of C^3I and its reliance on quick action in such conditions would create an additional threat, that a political crisis will escalate to an armed clash, a conventional conflict to a nuclear catastrophe.

Thus miscalculations or mistakes by those having responsibility for launch-on-warning could well unleash an unintended nuclear war. The delegation of release authority may set the stage for uncontrollable escalation, since it could prove difficult to re-establish central control of nuclear forces, particularly in the naval and air legs of the strategic triad.

Efforts to modernize C^3I with the aim of strengthening its survivability seem generally well-founded and rational. But while increasing its survivability, programs in this area may also create a new danger— the establishment of systems of command that provide the capability to conduct prolonged, controlled nuclear war. In the structuring of U.S. armed forces, such an effort is being made under the pretext of strengthening deterrence.

In theory, the goal of strengthening strategic stability and holding the two sides' potentials to reasonable sufficiency would be advanced by a C^3I possessing certain characteristics. First, the system should be capable of surviving a surprise attack, but it does not have to withstand direct nuclear strikes longer than through several hours of calculated nuclear strikes. Second, the system should make it possible to check and assess information on an attack, to take a reasoned decision, transmit an order to the surviving forces for a second strike against the aggressor, and control the execution of the strike. Thereafter the system could cease functioning. Such a C^3I system would be sufficiently simple, and all its basic components should be duplicated: warning systems and means of rapid assessment of the consequences of an opponent's nuclear strike, mobile land and airborne command posts, and communication channels. The nation's leadership should exercise absolute negative control, having uninterrupted stable two-way communication with its forces even after the enemy's attack, so as to estimate the surviving forces and, if necessary, to transmit the command to retarget for a second strike.

Such a system would differ in essential ways from the kind of C^3I necessary to conduct a protracted war. It would require high survivability but does not have to be quick-acting to conduct launch-on-warning, to carry out extremely complex operations to restructure war plans, and recoordinate strikes in accordance with the rapidly changing combat conditions of a nuclear war. Insofar as the demands for survivability in case of a surprise attack must be traded off against the remaining functions in a technical and economic sense, a renunciation of all objectives but survivability would make the system more reliably able to fulfill the primary and clearly limited tasks of maintaining the capability for a second strike.

Thus the influence of C^3I on the whole spectrum of strategic interrelations of the two sides is becoming an increasingly topical problem. The USSR and other countries of the Warsaw Pact have proposed a discussion and comparison of the military doctrines of the opposing military-political groupings, in particular the principle of nuclear no-first-use and the Soviet initiatives in nuclear disarmament. These questions are especially acute as the threat to C^3I is increased by new, more effective weapons systems, both nuclear and "exotic," including space weapons developed for the SDI program.

CONCLUSION: PROSPECTS FOR NEGOTIATIONS

Prospects for arms limitations, taking into account the factor of C^3I, must be analyzed primarily in terms of strengthening strategic stability. Possible steps include a renunciation by both sides of delegation of nuclear release authority and of launch-on-warning. Along with lowering the threat to strategic forces, measures to reduce the threat to $C^3 I$ should have special, if not primary importance.

One step might be to agree to renounce the development and deployment (or agree to drastic limitation) of sea-based counterforce systems, both SLBMs and cruise missiles, because of their clearly destabilizing nature. The short flight time of SLBMs and the impossibility of detecting the deployment and flight of cruise missiles create the greatest threat to $C^3 I$—both $C^3 I$ infrastructure (radars, command posts, communication centers) and centers of the military and political leadership. Such an agreement (either separate, or in the framework of a wider understanding), fortified by confidence-building measures (for example, an agreement that SSBNs and submarines with cruise missiles should always remain outside an agreed-upon zone off the other country's coastline), could significantly strengthen strategic stability.

How could deep cuts of strategic offensive arms simplify the tasks assigned to these forces? Major surpluses of strike weapons, constituting overkill potential will inevitably encourage the elaboration of more sophisticated concepts for their use; new forms and methods of targeting; and various concepts of "prolonged and limited" nuclear war and of "victory" in such war. Stability will also be strengthened by the introduction of common sense into strategic planning, parallel reductions of weapons to a level of minimum sufficiency (e.g., to a level of inflicting unacceptable damage to major industrial centers in a second strike).

Measures to reduce the probability that a conflict will escalate, that a crisis will become a military confrontation, have special significance in strategic relations of the two sides. It would therefore be expeditious to begin advance notification not only of military maneuvers, but of certain activities of strategic forces (with explanation of their goals)—for example, the flushing of significant numbers of SSBNs from their ports or the take-off of strategic bombers from air fields. It is also essential to further modernize the hot line between the leaders of the two countries, and undertake practical activities to create centers to eliminate crises. The Soviet-American agreement signed on September 15, 1987, on the creation of risk reduction centers, including the protocol, was an important step on this path.

Also helpful would be discussions of military doctrines and concepts, a mutual renunciation of means of political pressure, and renunciation of concepts of protracted nuclear war. Political leaders' acknowledgement that there can be no victors in a nuclear war must be reinforced by practical activities, testifying to the sincerity of both sides.

An exchange of views on C^3I would be very useful. By the logic of new thinking in security, both sides should be interested in increasing the survivability and reliability of these systems, making them simpler and less vulnerable; thus the problem of reducing the threat to C^3I can become an integral part of negotiations to limit and reduce strategic offensive arms, or to ban antisatellite weapons and other forms of space strike weapons.

To evaluate strategic offensive arms from the point of view of stability, one must envisage a composition and structure that optimally satisfy the requirements of defense. As long as nuclear weapons continue to constitute the core of the leading powers' military might, both sides must do everything possible to ensure that these weapons are not used. As strategic offensive arms are limited and reduced, with a final goal of full liquidation, an intermediate objective could be the establishment of a force structure to minimize the risk of nuclear use in a crisis situation (either as a deliberate step or as a result of fear of attack or uncontrollable escalation of a conflict).

Clearly it is not enough to have the relatively invulnerable nuclear forces needed to inflict a devastating second strike. Such forces and the corresponding C^3I systems must also fully exclude the possibility of an unauthorized or accidental use of nuclear weapons; a key element will be reliable two-way communication, which would enable the leadership to abandon the idea of delegating launch authority to such forces in a crisis period (that is, to maintain strict centralized [negative] control over them). Finally, it would be expedient to have forces that would remain capable of implementing a second strike without necessitating a launch-on-warning rule. Only then can we speak about strengthening strategic stability and lowering rhe risk of thermonuclear war.

NOTES

1. Fundamental among these are the power and quantity of warheads, the accuracy of placing them at their targets, their technical reliability, their

range, their flight time, the type of basing, the capability of multiple use, the flexibility in retargeting, the level of military readiness, robustness before and after launch, reliability and character of communication with points of control, the probability of unsanctioned use, the cost of production and use, dependence on other means, and so on.

2. Committee of Soviet Scientists for Peace and Against the Nuclear Threat, *Strategic Stability Under the Conditions of Radical Nuclear Arms Reductions* (Moscow, 1987).

3. Caspar Weinberger, *Annual Report to the Congress FY 1986*, Washington, D.C., 1987, pp. 62–63.

4. Dmitry Ustinov, "To Avert the Threat of Nuclear War," *Pravda*, July 12, 1982.

5. Theoretically, superiority in strategic armaments may be connected with the strategy of a retaliatory strike, but in this case that superiority would not mean superiority in strategic capabilities that could be used for a real threat of the use of nuclear power.

6. Dmitry Ustinov, "Against the Arms Race and the Threat of War," *Pravda*, July 25, 1981.

7. Mikhail Gorbachev, *Perestroika: New Thinking for Our Country and the World* (London: Collins, 1987), pp. 140–41.

8. See Institute of World Economy and International Relations (IMEMO), *Yearbook 1988* (Moscow, 1988), chap. 13.

9. This section was written in collaboration with A. Savel'iev. The term C^3I is here equated with the Soviet term *system of battle management and communications.*

10. B. Blair, *Strategic Command and Control* (Washington, D.C.: Brookings, 1985), p. 196.

11. Committee of Soviet Scientists, op. cit., p. 7.

12. D.M. Proektor, *Mirovye voiny i sud'by chelovechestva* (Moscow, 1986), p. 15.

13. N. Ogarkov, *Istoriia uchit bditel'nost'* (Moscow, 1985), p. 68.

14. See *Voenno-tekhnicheskii progress i vooruzhennye sily SSSR* (Moscow, 1982), p. 301.

15. Ashton B. Carter, John Steinbruner, and Charles Zraket, eds., *Managing Nuclear Operations* (Washington, D.C.: Brookings, 1987), pp. 76–77.

AMERICAN VIEW

Albert Carnesale

What is "strategic stability"? As Aleksei Arbatov points out, analysts interpret this term in quite different ways. The differences are not entirely cultural: American defense specialists do not all attach the same meaning to the term, and neither do their counterparts.

The term *stability* is used in discussions of U.S.-Soviet relations to describe several related notions, including the predictability of the nuclear arms competition ("arms race stability"); the degree to which cooperation rather than competition dominates the U.S.-Soviet relationship ("political stability"); and the extent to which each side (but especially the other side) is deterred from starting a strategic nuclear war ("strategic stability"). Arbatov's primary focus (and that of this commentary) is on strategic stability.

Until about five years ago, participants in U.S.-Soviet discussions of stability pretty much talked past each other. Americans focused rather narrowly on the technical aspects of the issues, basing their views and their remarks largely on computer simulations of strategic nuclear exchanges. Soviet participants preferred to avoid technical detail and to focus the discussion on political stability. In recent years, however, the Americans have come to recognize the relevance of the political dimensions of stability, the Soviets to appreciate the importance of the technical aspects. Arbatov's analysis of strategic stability demonstrates that progress has been made.

To deter a strategic first strike one must persuade the adversary that the ultimate consequences of a nuclear war initiated by its strike would be worse for its side than the consequences of not launching an attack. (Note that the choice is *not* between striking first and striking second: the alternatives available are to launch a first strike or to wait.)

In times of relatively good relations between the potential adversaries, it seems unlikely that the other side plans soon to launch a strategic attack, and "waiting" is the functional equivalent of avoiding strategic conflict. But if relations are strained, as during a crisis, the "wait" option will seem to carry a significant risk that the other side will strike first. In a crisis, then, the leader believes he must choose between a nuclear war in which he strikes first, and a substantial likelihood of a nuclear war in which the other side strikes first. The deeper the crisis, the more likely it will seem that "waiting" will result in the worst of all outcomes: a nuclear war in which his side is the victim of a first strike. (The term *crisis stability* refers to strategic stability under crisis conditions.) Under current and reasonably foreseeable circumstances, avoiding a strategic nuclear conflict is better than having one, regardless of which side might start it. But if nuclear war were certain to occur, the side that struck first would have an advantage.

How could one make a "rational" decision on whether to strike or to wait? The decision maker surely would ask several questions: If my side strikes first, how likely is it that the other side will retaliate? What would be the effects of their retaliation, and what would be the likely ultimate consequences of the conflict? If my side waits, how likely is it that the other side will strike first? What would be the effects of their first strike, and what would be the ultimate consequences of the conflict? None of these questions could be answered definitively; only crude estimates (often guesses) would be possible.

The effects of the conflict would not be confined to the territories of the two sides, but would be felt worldwide. Some consequences would be virtually immediate (e.g., death and destruction caused by the explosive blasts of detonating nuclear weapons); others would be delayed for days, months, or years (e.g., death from starvation or from cancer induced by radioactive fallout). Specific outcomes would take incommensurate forms: deaths of innocent civilians, political leaders, and combatants; destruction of homes, workplaces, schools, transportation and communications networks, and weapons systems (both nuclear and nonnuclear). Could any of these consequences plausibly be considered a "benefit" of nuclear war? Almost everything about nuclear war is bad. Perhaps only destruction of the other side's weapons qualifies as unambiguously beneficial.

To any rational leader, the expected costs of nuclear war (though impossible to calculate with any degree of confidence) must overwhelmingly outweigh any (comparably uncertain) benefits. Given the current forces of the two sides, whether one goes first or second makes relatively little difference to the outcome of an exchange.

But there is some difference, and it can become important if one believes that the other side intends soon to strike first, for it is better to pre-empt than to be pre-empted. To date, there has been relatively little advantage to striking first and neither side has believed that the other intended soon to begin a strategic nuclear war; consequently deterrence has prevailed. The challenge is to assure that the strategic situation remains equally stable in the future.

Arbatov points out that measures such as numbers of strategic nuclear delivery vehicles, numbers of nuclear warheads, missile and bomber throw-weight, megatonnage, equivalent megatonnage, and reliably prompt hard-target kill capability have limited value as indicators of strategic stability. He is right to criticize those Western analysts whose determination of stability has been based on the calculated outcomes of hypothetical nuclear exchanges in which only the ICBMs of the two sides are involved as attackers and as targets. It is hardly surprising that the Soviet side emerges victorious from a nuclear duel involving only ICBMs, since its ICBM force carries more than 60 percent of its strategic nuclear warheads, while the U.S. ICBM force carries only about 20 percent of its warheads. Even if *all* of the ICBMs of one side could be successfully destroyed in a first strike by the other, the surviving nuclear weapons on submarines and aircraft would be far more than sufficient to deliver an unacceptable level of retaliatory damage. In the absence of revolutionary breakthroughs in real-time targeting of mobile ICBMs, in antisubmarine warfare, and in defenses against ballistic missiles and aerodynamic vehicles—none of which appears imminent but all of which are possible—both sides are likely to retain substantial survivable retaliatory forces for the foreseeable future.

But retaliation also requires a system of command, control, communications, and intelligence ($C^3 I$) capable of implementing the retaliatory blow. Arbatov maintains that the "increased vulnerability of some key elements of $C^3 I$ [raises] serious fears that a direct attack on the system of $C^3 I$ can be more effective in preventing retaliation than a strike on the strategic weapons as such." How serious should those fears be?

The weaknesses and strengths of the $C^3 I$ system vary among the elements of the strategic triad. [For a thorough discussion of $C^3 I$ vulnerabilities, see Ashton B. Carter, "Assessing Command System Vulnerability," in Ashton B. Carter et al., eds., *Managing Nuclear Operations* (Washington, D.C.: Brookings Institution, 1987), pp. 555–610.]

In this context, Arbatov claims that "ICBMs deployed in silos are the most reliable element"; that there are "doubts whether communication with aircraft will be adequate to control fulfillment of all orders from the command center"; and that submarines, lacking reliable two-way communication and capable of launching SLBMs "without the sanction of the central leadership," do not perform the stabilizing role attributed to them by American officials and experts. It's not that simple.

The vulnerability of the ICBM force places special requirements on the associated C^3I system. This system may be relied upon (a) to launch some or all of the ICBMs on warning or under attack, and/ or (b) to ride out the attack and retaliate effectively with the surviving ICBMs. Launch-on-warning and launch-under-attack are difficult and dangerous strategies, and measures taken to ease their implementation (e.g., predelegation of launch authority, automation of decision making) tend to render them all the more dangerous. Yet the strategy of riding out the opponent's first strike has grown less and less attractive as the ICBM forces have become more and more vulnerable.

As for aircraft, their survival depends on dispersal on warning of an attack. Under some circumstances, they may temporarily lose line-of-sight radio communication with their bases; however, there are several means by which they communicate over the horizon (e.g., satellite and rocket-launched transmitters). Moreover, even when the aircraft are dispersed, the nuclear weapons in the bombs and cruise missiles they carry remain under "negative" control: they cannot be armed unless and until the aircraft receives an Emergency Action Message (EAM). Thus, if communication with the aircraft is severed after dispersal but before receipt of an EAM, there is no danger of unauthorized nuclear use.

Because missile submarines at sea are the least vulnerable element of the triad, their C^3I requirements are the least demanding. There is little time pressure; no matter how intense the attack on C^3I, eventually an EAM could be transmitted and received, and the missiles could be launched.

These arguments indicate that, contrary to Arbatov's assertion, missile submarines are the *most* stabilizing strategic systems and silo-based ICBMs the *least* stabilizing. While this brief analysis is hardly conclusive, it does demonstrate the complexity of the relationships between C^3I and strategic stability.

Arbatov's recommendations for strengthening strategic stability are of particular interest. His call for structuring strategic forces so that they need not be launched on warning to fulfill their retaliatory role is well founded and constructive. Unfortunately, history indicates that both superpowers consistently have sought to maximize the survivability of their own forces and to minimize that of the other side. (This reflects both sides' acceptance of Carnesale's Theorem: "Weapons are dangerous and destabilizing if and only if they are the other side's weapons.") In fact, either side's reliance on launch-on-warning increases the danger of an inadvertent nuclear war involving both sides. It is clearly worth pursuing unilateral and bilateral actions (such as improving the survivability of C^3I and agreeing to deep reductions in counterforce weapons) that reduce the danger.

Among Arbatov's specific proposals, the renunciation of launch-on-warning and of predelegation of nuclear release authority appears totally unverifiable. Other proposals, such as exchanging ideas about military doctrine, modernizing the hot line, providing advance notice of flushing missile submarines from ports or bombers from airbases, and banning antisatellite weapons, have been, are being, and should be discussed by our two governments. At least one suggestion—renouncing the "creation and deployment of sea-based counterforce weapons, both SLBMs and cruise missiles"—may be both unverifiable and counterproductive. In any event, these and other proposals for strengthening strategic stability deserve careful analysis and consideration by Americans and Soviets alike—and, where appropriate, mutual implementation. Aleksei Arbatov is absolutely right in observing that, so long as the leading powers maintain nuclear arsenals, "it is necessary to apply maximum efforts so that these weapons are not used."

LOOKING FORWARD
Windows of Opportunity

9 WHERE SHOULD WE GO FROM HERE
An American View

Seweryn Bialer

Recent developments in the Soviet Union hold enormous promise for U.S.-Soviet relations. If these developments are matched by half as much new thinking in the United States, they could significantly improve superpower relations and reduce the risk of war.

In this chapter I will first summarize the new thinking in general, and its application to Soviet security policy and foreign policy in specific. Then I will examine the new thinking's roots in *perestroika*. Finally I will outline various steps, suggested by the new thinking that could significantly improve superpower relations.

THE "NEW THINKING"

Impact and Depth

The impact of the new thinking will not be merely domestic. Although the new Soviet leadership's efforts to improve national performance rest primarily on domestic circumstances, the domestic changes will invariably influence security policy and foreign policy.

Moreover, the new leadership understands that a successful foreign policy requires domestic strength and order. In this respect Gorbachev differs from his predecessors. Khrushchev was a gambler who used cheap bluffs as tools of foreign policy. Although Brezhnev helped his country achieve strategic parity with the United States, he also allowed Soviet domestic power to dwindle until it could no longer support a global, ascending power. Gorbachev, in contrast, recognizes the relationship between foreign policy success and domestic strength. Thus his domestic program, with its emphasis on new vitality and progress, also stands as his most basic foreign policy statement.

The foreign policy implications of *perestroika* have been recognized by the new Soviet leadership. The general secretary noted the linkage when talking to the editors of *Time* in the spring of 1987: "You know our domestic plan of *perestroika*, draw your own conclusions about what kind of a foreign policy these plans require."[1] Foreign Minister Edward Shevardnadze expressed the idea more explicitly: "if foreign policy is an extension of domestic policy . . . and the goal of diplomacy is to form an external environment that is favorable for internal development . . . then we are compelled to recognize that the backwardness of our power and its steady loss of status is partially our fault too."

Overall, Gorbachev's changes seem to be serious and deep-rooted. People who have scoffed at the new thinking as "mere words" should remember that policy changes generally begin with words, and words should be taken especially seriously when they are pronounced by an authoritative leader in a centralized and ideological state. Some of Gorbachev's words, moreover, have already been translated into actions.

In fact, the scope and radicalism of the individual changes may point to a fundamental change in Soviet foreign policy. It is generally accepted that such domestic influences as ideology, international aspirations, and capabilities determine the range of options considered by the leadership; the selection of specific policies is then strongly influenced by international conditions and interactions with other states. I believe that the new thinking indicates a fundamental shift in the parameters that determine the options to be considered. The changes, in other words, are not only tactical (relating to short-term changes of form), and not only strategic (relating to intermediate changes of direction), but also *programmatic* (relating to long-range changes of goals).

Rethinking National Security

Conclusions Prompting Change. Change has been most significant in the area of national security. Here domestic conditions are especially closely linked to Gorbachev's reforms. It seems that the changes rest on three basic conclusions reached by the Soviet leadership.

First, the Soviet Union cannot achieve strategic superiority over the United States. Superiority in this context can be defined in either of two ways: as the ability to strike first and limit the American retaliation to acceptable losses, or as the ability to achieve so great a strategic preponderance as to undermine the credibility of the extended American deterrence and to hamper the decisiveness of American leaders in international crises.

Second, the strategic parity between the superpowers has become fragile. The United States might achieve a strong lead in the arms race, particularly as it expands into space, where the West enjoys a decisive technological advantage.

Third, if the arms race continues at its present pace the Soviets will have to increase their absolute expenditures; an expanded arms race would, of course, require even greater expenditures. Increasingly, the race will focus on high-technology advances in nuclear weapons delivery systems, and high technology consumes scarce, valuable human and material resources. These are the very resources needed for Gorbachev's economic reforms: his *perestroika* requires the Soviets to broaden their priorities beyond the military-industrial sector and to accumulate reserve economic resources for the difficult transition to the new managerial system. These vulnerable economic reforms could be immensely complicated, and potentially sidetracked entirely, by the arms race.

These three conclusions have strongly shaped Gorbachev's "new thinking" in national security. Specifically, the Soviets have modified their definition of national security and re-evaluated the concept of nuclear deterrence.

The Traditional Definition. From almost its beginnings, the Soviet state's view of national security has been unusually expansive. Its principal roots are two: the lengthy Soviet experience of international isolation and clashes with other powers; and the Leninist doctrine of imperialism, which held that revolutions invariably grew out of wars. This view of national security was expressed in Stalin's forced industrialization, the creation by force of the East European Soviet empire, the concept of "capitalist encirclement," the belief in the inevitability of wars between the Soviet Union and the West, Khrushchev's international offensive in the Third World, and Brezhnev's military buildup beyond any definition of sufficiency. To be sure, every major country seeks to reduce potential threats and pursues a "damage-limiting" philosophy. Yet the Soviet leadership seems to go farther, as if only "absolute security" would suffice.

The concept of absolute security, however, contains its own contradiction. It demands measures and policies that other states will find threatening to their own interests, prompting them to adopt countermeasures that ultimately diminish Soviet security. If the USSR can feel secure only when other countries feel insecure, the Soviet concept works against global stability.

At the Twentieth Party Congress in 1956, Khrushchev declared that wars were no longer inevitable. In the 1970s the Soviets achieved strategic parity with the United States, a breakthrough they had sought from the beginning of the cold war. Yet neither the ideological innovation nor the strategic achievement seemed to dislodge the traditional concept of national security. Soviet military doctrine remained unchanged; the Soviet military buildup continued apace.

Elements of the New Definition. Given this background, Gorbachev's changes—the first authoritative revisions of the traditional concept—are particularly remarkable. He has redefined the notion of national security in the nuclear age, taking into account Soviet-American strategic parity. Three elements of this revision are central.

First, the notion of *nuclear sufficiency* recognizes that nuclear buildup beyond the level of mutual assured destruction is meaningless. A far lower level of nuclear weapons would reduce psychological tensions, diminish the danger of an accidental nuclear strike, and increase the security of the superpowers and the world.

The concept of *common security* (or *mutual security*) acknowledges that Soviet military security is threatened when the United States feels militarily insecure. Therefore, in considering a military buildup, the Soviets must take into account the probable effects on American defense policy, specifically the danger of a costly arms race cycle that will not increase either side's security. It has been said that simple truths are the most difficult to comprehend, particularly for highly ideological political leaders. Gorbachev's conceptual departure from national security to common security, obvious and undramatic though it may seem, represents a revolutionary shift in the basic principles underlying Soviet defense policy. If the conceptual change results in policy changes, the importance will be immense.

The third key element is Gorbachev's addition of nonmilitary factors such as economic power, to the concept of national security. When the general secretary refers to national security today, he speaks of domestic morale and order, the country's vitality, and the state of its alliances. Whereas traditional Soviet thinking viewed new weapons as the best guarantor of security, Gorbachev is saying that the USSR will be most secure by participating in a strict arms control regime, cutting its nuclear forces significantly, devoting more attention to the civilian economy, and considering even difficult foreign policy compromises. In a nation where national security has always been the paramount concern, this expansion of the concept may be essential for Gorbachev's domestic programs to succeed (and his own political career to survive).

The Effect on Nuclear Deterrence. Gorbachev's re-evaluation of nuclear deterrence may seem to be firmly grounded in Soviet tradition. Although deterrence represents the fundamental basis (and probably the only rational basis) for American and Soviet strategic policies, the Soviet political-military establishment has always rejected the concept. The American idea of nuclear deterrence (in Russian, *atomnoe ustrashnenie*), Soviet officials have said, is mere blackmail. Specifically, they have dismissed the idea that the United States must be prepared for a Soviet nuclear attack against itself or its European allies.

But Gorbachev's critique of deterrence is different. He accepts the psychological nature of the concept and focuses his objections on two consequences of deterrence. First, the internal logic of deterrence produces an unending nuclear arms race, because neither side can be certain it has (and is perceived to have) enough strategic weapons to render a nuclear attack prohibitive. Second, the internal logic of deterrence requires both sides to integrate nuclear forces into their armed forces and to undertake contingency planning for nuclear war. If nuclear forces are to deter, each side must believe that any attack it launched would meet a nuclear response.

On the basis of this critique (which I view as realistic), Gorbachev advocates two actions. First, the superpowers should retreat from the deterrence concept by totally eliminating strategic nuclear forces. Second, to accomplish the first goal, they should reduce force levels and prevent weapon modernization.

How seriously should we treat these prescriptions? The first seems utopian. Some wags in Moscow have said that only two people in the Soviet Union and the United States believe that nuclear arms can be eliminated: Gorbachev and Reagan. Gorbachev's second prescription, in contrast, seems to be serious and promising. It fits into the new leadership's general conclusions about security matters, and it has found its way into Soviet arms control policies and proposals.

Rethinking Foreign Policy

Gorbachev has made less significant changes in foreign policy than in security policy for several reasons. Most basically, the goals of foreign policy are less clear-cut. Security policy aims to prevent an attack on a country's territory (or that of its allies) and to secure victory in case of war. Foreign policy has far more complex purposes.

More specifically, the two superpowers' goals in foreign policy conflict to a much greater degree than do their goals in security policy. The two sides share the principal security goals of stability and peace. The long-range Soviet-American conflict, on the other hand, is based on real differences in values and interests. With an improvement in relations, the two superpowers may cease to be mortal enemies, but they will remain global rivals for the foreseeable future.

The Soviet foreign policy task is complicated by the blunders and entanglements inherited from Brezhnev. Gorbachev must speedily end some of Brezhnev's costly or foolish foreign adventures, while preventing any further decline in Soviet status and preserving credibility domestically and internationally. The dilemma is exemplified by Afghanistan: the USSR has clearly wanted to end the war for a long time, but until recently it was unwilling to pay the price—accepting the eradication of Afghan communism.

Certain factors have encouraged foreign policy change, however. Many arguments can be made against striving for Soviet aggrandizement. The Third World has proven more resistant to Soviet encroachment. The East European empire's stability has become questionable. The West's economic-technological superiority has increased. At the same time, the Soviets have perceived a substantial decline in the threat posed by traditional adversaries—the United States, NATO, China. An authoritative article in a theoretical journal of the Soviet Communist Party, published in January 1988, includes a statement unprecedented in Soviet history: "The Soviet Union is not in danger of war from the United States and NATO."[2]

Overall, then, Gorbachev's domestic changes have been mirrored by some notable changes in foreign policy. The new direction was succinctly stated by foreign minister Edward Shevardnadze, speaking in June 1987 at the Soviet Diplomatic Academy. "The main thing," he said, "is that the country not incur additional expenses in connection with the need to maintain its defense capacity and protect its legitimate foreign policy interests. This means that we must seek ways to limit and reduce military rivalry, eliminate confrontational features in relations with other states, and suppress conflict and crisis situations." The new direction rests on changes in several underlying premises.

Recognition of the Effects of Soviet Behavior on Others. Every student of international relations knows that a country's international behavior reflects the actions of other states as well as domestic and historical elements. The Soviets, however, have largely refused to recognize the first factor in analyzing the actions of other nations. They would not admit, for example, that many actions of the United States came as responses to Soviet actions. In discussing Afghanistan, they focused on why the Americans had reacted as they had, without examining the wisdom or propriety of the invasion. In explaining the demise of Soviet-American détente, they blamed the Americans and viewed Soviet actions as largely immaterial.

Some signs suggest that this Soviet astigmatism may be clearing up. Most significantly, Gorbachev's concept of common security shows that he recognizes the relationship between Soviet actions and American actions. Yet this is only a beginning. Most Soviets continue to view American foreign and security policy as unrelated to Soviet policy. Until Soviet policymakers recognize that their own decisions shape the decisions of the other side, rational analysis and lasting agreements will be impossible.

New Meaning of Peaceful Coexistence. Although the concept of peaceful coexistence originated with Lenin, its meaning has changed. Lenin and Stalin believed that Soviet revolutionary, expansionist pressure against capitalist countries could not continue without interruption. Under adverse conditions, they believed, the Soviets should retrench. Peaceful coexistence, then, was simply an enforced pause in the ongoing attack on capitalism, a breathing space (*peredyshka*) that would last only until conditions favored another round of revolutionary expansion. Peaceful coexistence and ultimate war between the Soviets and the West were not seen as inconsistent.

The concept acquired a somewhat different meaning under Khrushchev, the first Soviet leader to understand the international realities of a nuclear age. Wars between capitalist and Sovietist countries, he proclaimed, were no longer inevitable. For him and for Brezhnev, peaceful coexistence meant the continuation of Soviet expansion without war.

Under Gorbachev, both this interpretation and Lenin's concept of breathing space have been abandoned. For Gorbachev peaceful coexistence seems to mean that Soviet foreign policy must be insulated from communist ideology. In *Pravda* in July 1987, an adviser to the Soviet leadership wrote: "Interstate relations . . . cannot be the sphere in which the outcome of the confrontation between world socialism and world capitalism is settled."[3] Gorbachev said, in his book *Perestroika*, "We have taken steps necessary to rid our [foreign] policy of ideological prejudice."

For a domestic audience, of course, the Soviets must minimize such changes. Moderating the revolutionary process abroad was justified, one high-ranking party intellectual told a Western academic, by something Lenin had written: "situations may arise when the interests of humanity at large take precedence over the class interests of the proletariat."

Soviet leaders thus have suggested that their nation intends to abandon its role as the "helper of history" that prods the world toward the inevitable victory of socialism. If their international behavior fulfills their stated intentions, the new definition of peaceful coexistence will represent a fundamental change in the Soviet-American conflict.

Recognition of Interdependence. Global interdependence increased exponentially during the third industrial revolution, in science and culture as well as the economic sphere. Widely discussed in the West, this phenomenon has only begun to get attention in the Soviet Union. Marxist and Leninist concepts cannot explain it.

Historically, the Soviets have had trouble grasping the idea of a global economy in general, and its consequences for individual industrial countries in particular. Under Stalin the Soviet Union developed, except in the initial phase of industrialization, as a virtual autarky. Stalin's successors rejected economic self-isolation, but the Soviet economy played only a marginal role in the global arena. For example, the USSR resembles an underdeveloped country in the structure of its exports, including the dominance of raw materials. Similarly, imports and exports of goods, credit, and capital constitute a very small proportion gross national product, far less than in any industrial country.

Other communist leaders have emphasized the importance of global economic links and have viewed economic relations as an element of modernization. Examples include the dramatically unsuccessful program of the Polish leader Gierek in the 1970s and the current programs in Hungary and China. The Soviets, in contract, do not see economic relations as a part of modernization.

The new Soviet leaders have apparently adopted a realistic view of the broad pattern of technological progress. During the late stages of the second industrial revolution and throughout the third, technological progress in the industrial countries has been internally generated, rather than dependent on imports. The globalized economy has introduced common thresholds and standards. As one Japanese industrialist put it, "What exists is already obsolete." Even keeping pace with the common standards requires a nation to nurture home-grown technologies. The new Soviet leaders have recognized that although capital imports and joint ventures may complement domestic technological progress, they cannot substitute for it.

Technological progress, however, requires a nation to open its economy to the global circulation of theoretical and applied sciences, managerial methods and skills, and capital. Organizational, social, and cultural patterns may also require adjustment. Although Gorbachev's policies and economic reforms move in the right direction, toward greater openness, little real progress has been made so far. Adequate plans would nurture technological progress (a) by moving the Soviet Union into the global economy, science, and technology, and (b) by encouraging managerial interests in technological progress through domestic policy. The goal is not to become another Japan, but merely to modernize enough to keep the Soviet Union from falling further behind the capitalist states.

If the new thinking about interdependence ultimately produces new policies, it may have significant consequences for international relations. Economic and scientific needs would have to play a much greater role in Soviet foreign policy formation than has been possible under traditional security requirements. If scientific and cultural sectors are to take part in global interchange, Soviet secrecy would have to diminish markedly. Soviet enterprises would have to enter international competition, to expand the islands of modernity inside the Soviet economy. It remains an open question whether, in the long run, the political requirements of Soviet power will permit such transformations.

The new understanding of interdependence may foster a new view of international phenomena that goes beyond strictly economic, scientific, and cultural issues. This new view would stress shared interests, and it would abandon the notion that international relations is a zero-sum game. Such thinking, so alien to the traditional Soviet world view, would need a long gestation period before it could significantly influence Soviet international relations. Moreover, the Soviet elite would have to see signs of a similarly nonantagonistic approach in the West, which is not yet apparent.

The Policies of International Relations. In addition to such broad and fundamental concepts, Soviet new thinking also concerns itself with more concrete matters. For example, it appears that Soviet policymakers are determined to avoid new military adventures abroad. The Soviets seem to be changing, steadily if undramatically, the way they evaluate opportunities in the Third World—their assessment of the value of intervention and especially of the opportunity costs. The leaders have decided to reduce substantially the commitment of resources abroad. Some cuts are politically easy, such as those to the "front line" black states in Southern Africa. Others are politically difficult and potentially dangerous, such as those to their East European vassal states.

Policy toward the East European empire is also changing. Since Gorbachev took power, the Soviet Union has demonstrated greater flexibility concerning these countries' domestic affairs.

Still another change concerns the Soviet approach to capitalist countries. A new emphasis on radical arms controls initiatives has produced an escalating peace offensive in the capitalist countries, and the resulting public pressure has encouraged Western leaders to seek better relations with the Soviets.

Most important are the changing policies concerning general international relations. The Soviet leadership wants more stable and predictable relations, particularly with the major capitalist, industrial states. In their dealings with the capitalist countries the Soviets are demonstrating greater flexibility and trying to paper over existing political points of contention, though not as yet offering any major concessions (for example, the Soviets have yet to make concessions regarding the islands they occupied after WW II, which are still claimed by Japan). Improved relations are valued in part as a way to obtain economic help for Soviet domestic efforts.

The Policies of A Defensive Détente.   The new Soviet thinking about security and international relations is potentially of great importance for the entire world, but it cannot instantly alter Soviet policies. So far relatively few Soviet officials and specialists fully understand the new thinking and its policy implications. Still, some elements of the new thinking have already found their way into security and foreign policy.

Although Gorbachev's overall goal appears to be a détente with the entire capitalist world and China, he seems particularly interested in the United States. For the Soviets, the détente of the 1970s was an offensive move that fueled their expansion. This approach rested on several factors: American weakness, Soviet greed, traditional Soviet ways of thinking, and the Soviets' lack of experience with the limitations of even superpowers. The result was an ignominious death for 1970s détente. Circumstances in the late 1980s and the 1990s promise to be different, and the Soviet leadership is now eager for a different, *defensive* détente.

Precisely what the Soviets want from defensive détente, and what they are willing to pay, remains unclear. How much are the Russians willing to sacrifice in terms of long-term international ambitions? Are they willing to demilitarize the global conflict? To steer clear of vital Western interests? How deep and tenacious is the new thinking? How will it develop, and what practical consequences will it have? Such questions must be answered before the United States can respond to the new Soviet thinking.

PERESTROIKA: THE ROOTS
OF THE NEW THINKING

Many people, particularly the fiercest critics of the Soviet Union, have long insisted that significant changes in its foreign and security policy would require changes in the domestic system. Such domestic changes have begun to appear, and they seem to be moving in the hoped-for direction. Three aspects of the domestic reforms are particularly relevant to Soviet foreign policy: the complexity and timetable of the reforms; their liberal direction and its probable consequences; and the process of demilitarizing Soviet society.

The Timetable of Domestic Reform

The current Soviet emphasis on domestic reform is unprecedented in the post-Stalin era. Gorbachev seems to be turning the Soviet leadership away from foreign policy toward such domestic concerns as galvanizing a moribund economy and mobilizing an apathetic public. The remaining international goals are subservient to the domestic reforms—for example, insulating the domestic reform process from international challenges, obstacles, and interventions.

But how long will domestic concerns remain predominant? The Soviet system's crisis is serious and multidimensional. Over time, during a gradual education in office, Gorbachev has used increasingly ominous terms to define the situation he inherited, and increasingly radical terms to define the reforms necessary to reverse it. He has said that the results of his reforms will be clear by the year 2000. But many Western experts (and some Soviet experts), believe that Gorbachev's reforms will require more than a generation to bear fruit.

Different reforms, of course, will progress at different rates. Within a decade, the Soviet standard of living is likely to improve, as will agricultural and industrial productivity. Technological progress will probably come about more slowly. "Regardless of what we do," a top Soviet scientist told his American colleagues, "the gap in crucial areas of high technology, particularly computers, between America and Russia will dramatically *increase*, at least until the year 1995. If by the year 2000 we can prevent the gap from further opening, it will be a miraculous success."

Even partial achievement of Gorbachev's goals is likely to take a lifetime of his leadership. If he is replaced by another reformer with a different modernization program, progress will take even longer. If Gorbachev loses power to a nonreformer, the scenario changes substantially.

In short, the Soviets' attention will remain focused on domestic affairs for a long time. As Gorbachev said to an American, "Our country is very big, and our people do not take to new fashions [novshestvo] very easily. It will take us a long time to get our country moving. But when we achieve it, things will move faster." The first part of his statement is certainly true; the second remains to be proven.

The Process of Liberalization

The Soviet domestic reforms have a liberal flavor. The new freedoms, however fragmentary and limited, have passed an important point. No longer are they implemented only from above; now they enjoy a momentum of their own. Several situations have already exposed the Soviet leadership to the perils of democracy: the Yeltsin affair; the creative intelligentsia's growing fearlessness; and the nationalistic disturbances in Kazakhstan, the Baltic Republics, and Transcaucasia. At the same time elements of a "civil society" have appeared in the Soviet Union: freer flow of information, open debates, increased truthfulness in communications, greater autonomy of the professions and the creative community, and the spontaneous appearance of (by the Soviets' own account) some 30,000 voluntary clubs and associations.

If this process continues, its impact will be significant. The Soviet public will become more knowledgeable about the world outside. A new, nonmanipulated public opinion will appear, which Soviet leaders will have to consider in crafting foreign policy. Already the war in Afghanistan, formerly a taboo subject, has become widely and intensely discussed; the discussion has probably made Soviet leaders even more eager to end that calamitous adventure.

The Process of Demilitarization

Under Gorbachev's predecessors the Soviet Union was the most militarized industrial country in the world. The leadership promoted a cult of the military in Soviet society. In public discourse the military could not be criticized. In education and culture, patriotic themes were commonplace. Among professions, the military enjoyed the greatest degree of autonomy. The officer corps was largely a closed caste. The core of the high command exerted substantial political influence.

Inside the Soviet government, military concerns dominated decision making on foreign issues, reflecting both the importance of military power for achieving political goals and Soviet leaders' view of the role of force in the international arena. In addition, the Soviet high command enjoyed an important advantage in security policy-making: a monopoly of expertise. The cult of secrecy and the compartmentalization of Soviet management kept the military and civilian establishments apart from each other. Military leaders held almost total control over military evaluation, military doctrine, and the preparation of military options for the political leadership.

In the domestic sphere, the military was accorded the principal economic emphasis. In fact, the burden of military expenditures was largely responsible for the Soviet economic crisis. Western sources estimate that military expenditures accounted for between 12 and 20 percent of the gross national product, a proportion two to three times that of the United States. More important, military expenditures have drained civilian resources and limited capital formation. By lowering the technological level of the economy as a whole, the expenditures have even constrained future military capabilities.

By now, in the fourth year of Gorbachev's rule, the Soviet military's profile has been significantly reduced. The military's prestige has fallen because of its inability to win the war in Afghanistan.

Gorbachev's control over the Soviet high command, moreover, is strong and seems to be growing. In his second year he started to purge the upper echelons. During the deep embarrassment that followed a young West German's landing his plane in Red Square, Gorbachev replaced field rank officers (an estimated 200 officers of the rank of general). In choosing his minister of defense he passed over two dozen senior marshals and generals and appointed General Yazov, a close associate with little political ambition. He retired a number of military intellectuals from active service and assigned them to the central party apparatus in Moscow. He sought to create a military affairs think tank (like the RAND Corporation in California), based in a military department but staffed by civilian specialists; the military was encouraged to grant the civilians access to classified military information.

Such changes have already resulted in competing, civilian-produced formulations of Soviet defense policies, priorities, and expenditures. Gorbachev is following the advice Khrushchev offered in his memoirs: "Who in our own country is in a position to intimidate the leadership? It is the military . . . the military is prone to engage in irresponsible day-dreaming and bragging. Given a chance, some elements within the military might try to force a militarist policy on the Government. Therefore, the Government must always keep a bit between the teeth of the military."[4]

HOW FAR CAN WE GO?

The new thinking presents enormous opportunities for Soviet-American relations in the next decade. Substantial progress may be possible in arms control, crisis prevention, and cooperative ventures. The visionary targets outlined here may not be fully realizable—but they are definitely worth pursuing.

Arms Control

Strategic Reductions to Finite Deterrence. After the superpowers eliminate their medium- and short-range nuclear weapons, they should negotiate a succession of strategic arms agreements to reverse the arms race through a series of disarmament steps. By the end of the century strategic forces should have been reduced to a very low, "nuclear sufficiency" level of finite deterrence. This level would be adequate for deterrence, yet low enough that neither side could launch a first strike or readily "break out."

Point Defense. The finite deterrence level might combine offensive strategic weapons (land, air, and sea based) with strategic point defense of command structure and second-strike capabilities. By mutual consent, strategic offensive and defensive weapons should be barred from space, and space testing of such systems should be limited.

Limits on Testing. If nuclear tests cannot be completely banned, the superpowers should agree to limit the frequency, number, and upper yield of tests. The agreement should be subject to on-site inspection.

Bans on Chemical and Biological Weapons. Through mutual agreements the superpowers should eliminate or at least drastically reduce such exotic weapons as chemical and biological agents. Again, strict provisions for mutual verification should be included.

Reduction of Others' Arsenals. At some point the superpowers should negotiate with other nuclear powers (Great Britain, France, China) to restrict the number and modernization of their strategic weapons. The goal should be a global finite deterrence system.

Nonproliferation. The superpowers should reach a nonproliferation agreement applicable beyond the small circle of countries that already possess nuclear weapons (including Israel). The superpowers should enforce the agreement by all available means, including military actions.

Conventional Reductions. With the dramatic cuts in strategic forces and the elimination of medium- and short-range nuclear arms, the conventional military balance will become more important. Beyond the START agreement, it is virtually inconceivable that any strategic agreement can be reached without a parallel agreement on conventional forces. In fact, it would be unwise to reduce the level of tactical nuclear weapons drastically without an agreement on conventional forces (and so, until a conventional agreement is achieved, the triple zero option for Europe is both militarily unsound and politically destabilizing).

Accordingly, the superpowers and their alliance systems should negotiate intensively about the size, structure, and deployment of conventional forces in Europe, concentrating on force size and mode of deployment. Force size must be reduced asymmetrically, reflecting the Soviet advantage; the effort must concentrate on central assault units (the heavy divisions) and must go beyond force withdrawal to require that some elite conventional units be disbanded. The central goal of the agreements should be clearly defensive deployment in Central Europe that would preclude the other side from launching a surprise attack. The agreement should, of course, be fully verifiable beyond the use of national means of verification, and it should be accompanied by an agreement to undertake regular trust-building steps.

Crisis Prevention

Regional Conflict Resolution. The superpowers did not create regional conflicts and civil wars, which are largely initiated and shaped indigenously. Yet such conflicts generally touch the interests of the superpowers, prompting one or both to intervene, directly or indirectly. During the coming decade, regional conflict is likely to continue in key Third World countries, and perhaps to intensify.

Regional conflict poses a substantial threat to the superpowers' relations. War is most likely to result, not because one superpower makes a premeditated attack on the other, but rather because a regional conflict, involving both superpowers' vital interests and substantial commitments, escalates out of control. Accordingly, it is essential that the superpowers keep regional conflicts from reversing the positive trend in national security. Such a policy should have four primary aims.

First, it should demilitarize Soviet-American relations as they relate to these conflicts. The superpowers should avoid any direct participation by their troops or proxies, and any large-scale participation by their military advisers or security advisers.

Second, the superpowers should be prevented from using military materiel supplies to fuel the regional conflicts; the flow of weapons to Third World countries from the superpowers and their allies should gradually be reduced.

Third, the policy should dampen the superpowers' crusading spirit toward Third World conflicts, and build firebreaks between their ideologies and their foreign policies.

Finally, the superpowers should steer clear of Third World situations that could produce dangerous, difficult-to-control confrontations. Third World client states tend to be unreliable, and they may try to involve their powerful patrons in settling escalating conflicts. To reduce the danger, the superpowers should create institutional mechanisms of communication, crisis prevention, and crisis management. They should also regularly exchange information about the limitations they have imposed on their client states' use of offensive weapons. And they should agree that, whenever one superpower negotiates in a regional conflict, the other superpower will also be brought in.

Delink Eastern Europe. The cold war came about largely because of the Soviets' establishment of an empire in Eastern and Central Europe. The greatest obstacle to normalizing relations may well be the continuation of this empire and the Soviets' insistence on the right, under the Brezhnev Doctrine, to intervene, militarily if necessary, in the domestic affairs of its vassal states. From time to time, one must expect, broad social strata and even parts of the communist political elite in Eastern Europe will express their unfulfilled aspirations. Turmoil is likely even if the Soviets liberalize the countries' economic policies, give their leaders greater autonomy, and grant their citizens increased personal freedoms. Reforms may even unleash major sociopolitical unrest, given these countries' growing aspirations toward independence and self-determination.

Such unrest presents a dilemma. The Soviets cannot respond by direct military intervention or by Soviet-engineered "internal invasion" without violating the spirit of normalization. Yet neither can the Soviet Union be expected to surrender its clear and legitimate national security interest in the buffer states.

Lasting normalization will require the Soviets to separate their interest in the buffer states from the countries' evolution toward independence and freedom. Change will come only gradually, but it should be apparent within a decade. If it is not, Soviet-American relations will probably fall hostage to the vagaries of Soviet imperial policies and the unpredictable behavior of Eastern European nations and political elites.

Cooperative Ventures

It has become axiomatic to observe that Soviet-American relations are no longer a zero-sum game. The accuracy of this observation depends not only on the superpowers' objective interests, but also on their perceptions of each other based on their overall relations. The steps outlined above, especially successful arms control agreements, should help the superpowers reduce tensions, begin building trust, and expand cooperative ventures in a wide range of areas: ecological concerns, basic scientific research, educational and cultural exchanges, medical research, tourism, information flows, safety norms for the peaceful exploitation of nuclear power, and regular exchanges through the media.

PERESTROIKA's PROMISE

If Gorbachev's *perestroika* continues, it will affect the Soviets' long-range foreign and security policies both directly (by altering the Soviet concepts and perceptions of the international arena) and indirectly (through the influence of domestic factors on the formation of foreign and security policy).

To be sure, Soviet long-term international aspirations will remain high. Gorbachev and his colleagues are highly ambitious, and they seem to be free of the psychological insecurities that plagued the previous generation. As adversaries in world diplomacy they are more intelligent and more adaptable than their predecessors—and thus more dangerous opponents to American leadership.

Yet for a long time Soviet international aspirations will be tempered by domestic and international constraints. As a result, we will have unprecedented opportunities to improve Soviet-American relations. Americans must explore the opportunities created by *perestroika* and the new thinking. Instead of limiting our aims to a few arms control treaties, we should attempt to establish a Soviet-American dialogue geared toward reassessing the basic strategic and political elements of the conflict. Could such a reassessment succeed? The chances seem better than ever, not only in the Soviet Union but in the United States as well.

NOTES

1. *Pravda*, September 2, 1985, p. 2.
2. V.V. Zhurkin, S. Karaganov, and A. Kortunov, "The Challenges of Security—Old and New," *Kommunist* no. 1, (January 1988).
3. Yevgeny Primakov, "Novaia filosofia vneshnei politiki," *Pravda*, July 10, 1987, p. 4.
4. Nikita Khrushchev, *Khrushchev Remembers: The Last Testament*, trans. and ed. Stroke Talbott (Boston: Little, Brown, 1974), pp. 540–41.

10 WHERE SHOULD WE GO FROM HERE
A Soviet View

Georgy A. Arbatov

Previous chapters have spelled out the lessons the USSR and the United States have learned about constraining conflict and preventing dangerous crises. These lessons are a good foundation, but in today's world they are not enough. Regional crises are too costly in an interdependent world, and no longer seem to offer the possibility of a victory for either nation. We need a new code of conduct based on new political thinking. A new set of crises, of a long-term and less evidently acute nature, challenges us. These new crises, which involve such problems as global financial instability and environmental breakdown, may prove even more threatening than the regional crises of the past. This chapter addresses the need for new thinking about both traditional and nontraditional types of crises.

Is it possible for the USSR and the United States to cooperate in preventing and coping with these crises? Or are we doomed to repeat the downfall of détente? Certain international trends are in our favor, such as the decline in the role of military power and the democratization of world politics. So too is both sides' need to focus on domestic problems. The chapter concludes by examining the lessons each nation has learned, or is learning, that point to the benefits of reducing our armaments and conflicts.

NEW THINKING ABOUT TRADITIONAL CRISES

Crisis situations and conflicts of a local and regional character have existed throughout history. In our own time such conflicts have been played out against the backdrop of a global East-West confrontation, which has been called a cold war. Regional conflicts in turn aggravate this global confrontation, exacerbating tensions in the political, economic, and ideological spheres. Local conflicts also destroy economic ties between regions of the world and, within these regions, sow the seeds of enmity and mistrust between neighboring states.

Some believe the fear that a local conflict might escalate to a general nuclear catastrophe exerts a deterrent effect in regional crises. Certainly, fear of a nuclear war restrains the leaders of the great powers, which directly or indirectly participate in these conflicts (as in the Middle East crises of 1967 and 1973). But the leaders of states and political movements directly involved in regional conflicts have by no means always experienced this fear. It is impossible to be confident that in any situation they will manage to control their behavior, protecting the world from a dangerous escalation. Moreover, the great powers have not typically given "preventive treatment" to regional threats, but rather have allowed such crises to occur, even used them in their own interests, while seeking to control them within acceptable limits.

As the catastrophic, suicidal consequences of a nuclear war became clear, the search intensified to define "acceptable" scenarios of military conflicts on lower levels. Nuclear weapons have become a powerful catalyst for the development of new variants of brinkmanship. Some nations seem to have interpreted the recognition of the impossibility of nuclear war as a license to conduct wars on a lesser scale. The entire postwar period has been studded with local, "limited," regional, and other conflicts, not to speak of political crises.

Such terms as "limited conflicts" should not delude us. For whom and in comparison with what can regional hostilities be considered "low-intensity conflicts"? For the great states and in comparison with a general nuclear war? Yes, of course. But for those countries on whose territory these conflicts are conducted, their intensity is by no means low. These are bitter wars, which lead to enormous human sacrifice and material destruction.

Thus during the Korean War 1.7 million people perished; the French and American intervention in Vietnam cost the Vietnamese people 3 million lives; the civil war in the Congo took more than half a million lives; the colonial wars of the Netherlands in Indonesia led to the destruction of a million people. Together, the local wars and armed conflicts unleashed since World War II have taken an estimated 20 to 25 million lives—twice as many as World War I.

Unlike wars of the "classical" type, contemporary regional crises and conflicts have taken the civil population as their primary victim. Typically only 5 to 10 percent of all losses in a regional conflict fall upon the military; the remaining losses are suffered by people who have no relation to the military actions.

Even leaving aside the moral issues, we must bear in mind that "small," local, regional wars and conflicts today entail a special danger. Unfolding against a background of global tension, they become a kind of "forward defensive position" of a large conflict (right up to nuclear war)! Conceivably a local conflict might unexpectedly detonate a general catastrophe. Moreover, local crises and conflicts erode the whole system of international relations. By aggravating tension and mistrust, they facilitate the international arms trade, give rise to streams of refugees, encourage international terrorism, and, in sum, shatter the bases of contemporary world order and international law.

In our days, therefore, the very concept of a "local conflict" is questionable. A conflict or crisis can be local in its scale, in the territory enveloped by military activities, but it is generally global in its effect on the system of international relations.

IS VICTORY POSSIBLE IN
A REGIONAL CRISIS?

Today it is generally agreed that no nation could achieve victory in a nuclear war, which would mean general catastrophe. Even a large "conventional" war in Europe is widely regarded as suicidal, given the concentration of nuclear power stations, chemical factories, and stores of fuel oil and toxic substances existing on the continent. But what about local conflicts in other regions of the planet? Can they be an effective instrument of foreign policy today? This question, in my view, has not yet received proper scientific analysis.

I do not want to oversimplify the answer. But in recent years the attacking side has gained simple victories only in the very smallest conflicts. I can think of only two examples, strictly speaking: the Falklands and Grenada. I am not sure one can yet conclude that in more major conflicts the application of military force does not promise results. But the history of recent decades is pushing us toward such a conclusion. Since World War II success in regional wars has been very rare, and typically linked with serious political costs. A new outburst frequently ensued, bringing the war's accomplishments to nought. Therefore I conclude that *in our days a local war has ceased to be an effective instrument of foreign policy.*

This truth, I think, is becoming more widely recognized. I have in mind the encouraging new tendency taking shape in the most acute crisis points of our planet: in Central America, in Kampuchea, and in Afghanistan. People are still perishing there, the shooting has not died down, but a striving toward national reconciliation is more clearly manifest. Common sense dictates the necessity of dialogue. And these conflicts, linked with civil wars, are of the type most difficult to settle, always distinguished by particular bitterness.

THE NEED FOR A NEW CODE OF CONDUCT

Of course, local and regional crises cannot be resolved from positions of abstract moralizing. First of all, it is necessary to see that such conflicts are various in nature. Some are instigated from outside, mainly by the great powers (by support of so-called "freedom-fighters," for example). This is one of the most typical manifestations of the cold war. Our approach to these conflicts will be dictated by our approach to the cold war in general—specifically, whether we consider it inevitable or are ready to put an end to it.

Crises of a second type grow on local soil, from causes not directly related to cold war. Indirectly, however, they influence East-West relations. They can result in general damage, insofar as general tension prevents the greatest powers from undertaking joint efforts to end them. (Indeed, the superpowers may be selling arms to one side or the other.) A typical example is the Iran-Iraq War.

A third category of conflicts arise in connection with complex, often inevitable processes of internal changes in a country. Although a normalization of relations along the East-West axis might help resolve conflicts of the first and second types, it is impossible to imagine the emergence of a new global Holy Alliance of the great powers, guaranteeing the status quo in all corners of the planet.

What is needed is *a new code of conduct.* Such a code must be based on new political thinking and could be implemented only in conditions of demilitarized international relations, developed cooperation, and a truly contemporary understanding of the complex processes of the development of human society. Without denying the utility of the hot line and the nuclear risk reduction centers, I believe the threat of conflicts cannot be eliminated without a more profound transformation of the entire system of international relations.

In this regard one must give some thought to terrorism. Recent decades have seen a significant increase in the practice of terror as a means of political struggle. This development is alarming, especially as modern society, with its complex economic infrastructure, communications network, nuclear power stations, chemical factories, fuel storehouses, and so on, offers so many highly attractive targets for terrorist actions. So far, however, we have done very little to arrange effective international cooperation in the struggle with terrorism. What steps should we take? First of all, we should not maintain double standards in questions of international terrorism. Actions considered to be terrorism in certain contexts should not be regarded in others as feats of self-sacrificing "freedom-fighters." Moreover, it seems to me, it is extremely important to recognize the indissoluble link between terrorism and military-political confrontation. Today we would hardly encounter such a range of terrorism in countries of the Third World had we managed to cut off or at least essentially limit the international arms trade. Ten years ago the USSR and the United States conducted negotiations on conventional arms transfers, and we consider it extremely important to return to them.

NEW THINKING ABOUT
NONTRADITIONAL CRISES

In addition to crises of the "traditional" type, there exists another type, which are long-term in character and develop independently from concrete political decisions taken in the USSR and the United States. We often underestimate the significance of these crises, since they do not threaten immediate catastrophe. In the long term, however, the damage they do to the international community may be even more significant than the consequences of a regional conflict of the usual type. Among the most notable of these to nontraditional crises are North-South relations and ecological problems.

North-South Crises

North-South relations are troubled by a long list of problems: currency-financial difficulties, debt, the "arms race of the poor man" (i.e., in the poorest, most backward regions of the world), the brain drain of the developing countries, and many others. If substantial progress is not made toward resolving these problems, we may find that successful efforts in other directions are frustrated and do not significantly improve the world situation.

We can no longer afford to dissociate ourselves from the growing economic problems of the Third World. Both the West and the East have made such attempts in the past. We in the Soviet Union often said that the problems of the developing countries were the legacy of colonialism, for which we were not to blame. Accepting responsibility for our former colonial ventures in the Caucasus and Central Asia, we had taken from ourselves what was necessary to stimulate their growth and equalize the levels of their development with the central regions of the country. The other great powers, we argued, should give the same help to their former colonies.

In general, this position is logical, even irreproachably correct—but correct from the point of view, let us say, of old political thinking. The new political thinking presupposes a more profound view of politics and even a grounding in moral principles. We understand that no country today has a right to withdraw from global problems, whether or not it bears responsibility for their origins. Such an approach, it seems to me, together with compassion and morality, reflects a correct understanding of one's own national interests—"enlightened egoism," so to speak.

What are the true economic interests of the developed countries of the West? Clearly, their leaders cannot ignore the alarming fact that the productive capacities of the developed countries are growing much faster than effective demand. Certain of these countries are simultaneously the main consumers and main competitors in the production of basic goods. Insofar as they produce not for charity, but for profits, the potential is accumulating in the world economy for very serious conflicts.

Efforts to develop a new international economic order (NIEO) are of general interest. This idea emerged in the 1970s as an expression of an economic requirement of both the South and the North. Insofar as the countries of the Third World were the initiators, we still understand NIEO as a means of resolving the problems of the poor countries. But all countries are in need of a new international economic order.

Interdependence among nations has been increasing rapidly, stimulated by the scientific-technical revolution. It is increasingly difficult to understand who is more dependent upon whom: the debtor upon the creditor or the creditor upon the debtor, the consumer of oil upon the supplier or the other way around. The most developed countries are turning out to be more dependent upon the outside world, with which their development is inextricably linked. In the poor countries, problems are appearing and growing that strike the rich countries like a boomerang. International relations are steadily becoming more complex, developing not simply from bipolarity toward multipolarity, but toward a world combining contradictions and conflicts with a unity, an integrity, in all its diversity.

In this world the successful economic development of each individual country will most probably depend on the general state of the world economy—the world economy in the genuine sense, not in the current sense in which all participants of the world community must constantly search for a mutually acceptable, stable balance of interests (not forces, but interests) of a great number of countries. Imperial policy, like isolationism, will be increasingly counterproductive—not only politically unacceptable, but economically obsolete. I do not see how it will be possible to continue traditional approaches to the problems of security, and political and economic relations, without dooming the international community to chaos and dangerous shocks. Rather than a utopian dream, the new world and regional political and economic order is becoming a condition of survival.

At present, the potential for crises of the nontraditional type is growing with each year. One alarming tendency is the steadily widening gap in development between the North and South (I exclude a small group of so-called new industrial states). This problem has already become one of the top issues on the global economic and political agenda. In conditions of interdependence, such a gap worsens the global economic situation, furthering the disintegration of the international trade and currency system, exacerbating regional conflicts. The task of creating a new system of international stability, and the prevention of crises of the traditional type, requires constant attention to the problem of development. It is no secret that economic backwardness most often turns into social instability, giving rise in turn to political crises.

In recent years the attempts of developing countries to fulfill their debt obligations have undermined their economic position and prospects for development. These trends are a consequence of the unfavorable tendencies that emerged in the 1970s, linked to the growth of inflation and a reduction in the effectiveness of applying capital on the international scale. Yet clearly all participants in the international economic exchange must share responsibility for this outcome. It is not the fault of the developing countries, and the consequences cannot be borne only by the debtors, especially as they are physically unable to pay their debts.

An Approach to North-South Crises

A complex approach to the problem of development clearly should include multiple complementary measures. First of all it is necessary to create a qualitatively new attitude in developed countries, in both West and East, toward the development of the Third World. Without a supporting shift in broad public opinion, we are unlikely to manage to increase our assistance to the Third World and thus to hasten its development.

Further, the international community should undertake serious efforts to perfect the international trade and currency system, with the goal of creating a better climate for the trade of developing countries. Today more than half of world trade falls under various restrictions or suffers the deforming influence of subsidies.

Economic assistance to developing states has encountered many problems. Clearly the quantity of this assistance can and should be increased, but the structure of the assistance rendered is no less important. To date a very significant part of this assistance is directly or indirectly linked to the supply of arms and other measures relating to security. Quite often this aid is rendered economically ineffective;

it slows development and heightens military tension. It is necessary also to increase aid for the creation of projects in developing countries, directed toward overcoming the most acute manifestations of poverty. Joint efforts by firms of capitalist and socialist countries could play a positive role here.

Crises of the nontraditional type have various sources. There is the problem of international debt (by the end of 1987, the debts of developing countries reached $1.2 trillion; the burden exerts a depressing influence on the economy of these countries, feeding the explosive situation in the international credit and currency mechanism, and through this the whole system of international economic and political relations). There is the world food production problem, which, although it has been somewhat ameliorated since the food crisis of 1972–74, is by no means a thing of the past, especially in Africa. There is the global energy problem, threatening new shocks in the coming decades and demanding the formulation of a strategy for the development and use of the world energy-resource base in the interests of future generations as well as ourselves. In all these areas our two countries have the capacity to play an important role, given recognition of our responsibility before the world community and the necessity of wide bilateral and multilateral cooperation.

Ecological Crises

The rapidly increasing process of ecological destabilization will necessarily affect economic development. Every decade 7 percent of the world's soil resources is lost. In the arid regions of the earth almost 80 percent of the agricultural land is in some danger of becoming desert. Primarily because of loss of land resources in forty developing countries, agriculture in the 1980s has yielded a grain harvest that is less per head than in the 1950s. Every two years forests the size of Finland disappear from the planet. Every day, on average, one species of life completely disappears from the earth, decreasing the genetic foundation of the planet. The "ecologization" of contemporary production, the prevention or neutralization of the dangerous consequences of environmental pollution, will demand ever-increasing scientific, technological, and material resources. In fact, given current tendencies, economic activity may reach a level at which further growth of gross national product will bring more costs than wealth. This new correlation poses the question of the compatibility and mutually conditioned nature of economic and ecological tasks.

These problems have long been discussed. But it seems to me that something new has appeared in recent years. The tragedies of Chernobyl and Bhopal, the poisoning of the Rhine, and acid rain have begun to bring home to people the impact of ecological problems on human survival and on world security. Today security should be examined in the context of resolving economic and ecological problems.

CAN WE COOPERATE?

The new character of the threats to survival, particularly in the spheres of economy and ecology, demands new approaches to problems, encouraging collaboration and, in particular, the cooperation of the two greatest powers in the world, the United States and the USSR. The greatest need is to limit the military rivalry and political hostility. This step in itself would make it possible to concentrate resources and attention on the real problems discussed above. Still better would be to move from such passive forms of cooperation to active joint projects in the economic and ecological spheres, keeping in mind both bilateral and global dimensions, and to arrange cooperation in public health, culture, and other areas.

Even working together, of course, our two countries cannot resolve the problem of international crises. The USSR and the United States, after all, comprise only 10 percent of the population of the planet. In the long term, our opportunities to influence the development of world events will most likely be reduced, not increased. All the same, these opportunities are very significant. The economic and military power of the Soviet Union and the United States, the breadth of their political interests, extending through virtually all regions of the planet, place upon the two nations special responsibility for the preservation of peace, the strengthening of international security, and the provision of favorable conditions for the social and economic development of all humanity.

What should be done first? It seems to me we should begin by acknowledging and surmounting old mistakes, delusions, and errors. If we look at the history of international relations in recent decades, it is difficult to resist the conclusion that the superpowers' view of the Third World as an arena of confrontation and rivalry helped to pull many of its countries into the orbits of cold war, pushing them down the path of militarization and excessive military expenditures, hastening the emergence of acute crises. To this day smouldering conflicts instigated from outside undermine the already very weak economies of a host of countries and regions.

A principled new approach is needed toward the countries where the overwhelming majority of humanity lives. It is necessary to assist the developing world not only with aid, but with a new policy. That policy should proceed from respect, from a refusal to treat the Third World as an arena of confrontation, from the understanding that it is not "ours" and not "yours." The Third World will develop not in order to please us or you, but for its own sake, for its own interests, taking its own course. The sooner everyone understands this, the fewer mistakes we will make. And the sooner we renounce our rivalry, the more effectively we will assist the world of developing countries in resolving its problems and the more we will be able to organize joint efforts in the interests of development.

Can one imagine the developing world as a sphere of cooperation rather than an arena for rivalry? With all due caution suggested by the history of recent decades, I do not consider such a prospect utopian. At any rate, I think none of the Soviet or American participants in our joint study would disagree that such a prospect now appears much more plausible than when we began the project. Before our eyes Soviet-American relations have improved substantially. In East-West relations as a whole, progress has been achieved in arms reduction; we have set deadlines for the withdrawal of Soviet troops from Afghanistan and agreement has been achieved on some of the most important questions of a political settlement; in the resolution of the Kampuchea problem, light has begun to appear at the end of the tunnel. And that is not to speak of the creation of Soviet-American nuclear risk reduction centers.

For balance, one recalls some developments that heighten our anxiety. For us in the Soviet Union, the conceptual formulation of the so-called Reagan Doctrine has been alarming. This doctrine, as we understand it, signifies the readiness of the United States to render various types of assistance, including military assistance, to political groups and movements in countries of the Third World struggling against regimes, parties, and forces in power that are recognized by the world community (often the United States even has diplomatic relations with them), just because they are not to Washington's liking. One public appearance by President Reagan left many in the USSR with the impression that he was not averse to extending this doctrine to the countries of Eastern Europe.

I see the privatization of American foreign policy as another very dangerous tendency. Before our eyes the key factors of American foreign policy, including arms deliveries to explosive regions of the Third World, have been transferred into the hands of individuals and organizations having semiofficial or even no official status. These people and organizations in essence were subordinate to no one and responsible to no one. It is impossible to conduct negotiations or reach agreements with them. Such arrangements undermine the fundamental principles of the contemporary system of international relations and international law. The leadership of the state in foreign policy turns into a fiction, sharply reducing the possibility of settling regional conflicts and increasing the likelihood of their uncontrolled escalation.

A third source of anxiety is the tendency toward unilateralism in the policy of the United States. The endeavor to rely only upon oneself in world politics, the preference for unilateral actions over multilateral efforts, the unwillingness to make concessions, even in response to concessions by the other side—all this damages the existing system of international relations with its legal mechanisms, institutions, and so on.

So today we encounter an odd interlacing of completely opposed tendencies, positive and negative. It is not surprising that this gives rise to uncertainty, which in itself can slow the forward movement in Soviet-American relations.

Time and time again, both at home and in America, I have heard much the same description of relations between our two countries: a period of improved relations, of détente, during the 1970s was succeeded by a new paroxysm of cold war and arms race. Some attribute this reversion to the fact that even in the years of détente the Soviet Union and the United States were unable to agree on a mutually acceptable code of behavior in the Third World. People wonder whether the current warming in relations will turn out to be another fleeting episode, to be replaced by the next attack of cold war—just as summer is inevitably followed by autumn, and then winter.

This is no simple question. We are not yet able to forecast political developments with the accuracy that characterizes weather predictions. In politics, of course, we are not observers, but participants in the events we are trying to predict. Keeping this in mind, I would risk saying that we have come quite a way since the 1970s. Three major trends stand out: the decline in the role of military power, the globalization of world society, and the democratization of world politics.

The Decline in the Role of Military Power

The past decade has seen a significant shift in the frame of mind in the political, social, and psychological spheres. Public opinion, political circles, and governments have begun to understand better the genuine character and scale of the nuclear threat. Today no responsible political figure would say that it is possible to conduct a nuclear war and attain victory. Politicians not only understand, but officially acknowledge that a nuclear war is suicide.

Even ten years ago many political figures, including those vested with government power, stubbornly refused to make such acknowledgements, which would have called in question the very idea of nuclear deterrence. Concepts were therefore invented to prove the "usability" of nuclear weapons and of "limited" nuclear war; plans were made for a "first (disarming) strike"; the "neutron bomb" was examined as a panacea, and so on. Such illusions were abandoned only slowly and with great difficulty.

The nuclear enlightenment of the politicians was assisted by the fact that the Soviet Union achieved nuclear parity and maintained it in the 1980s, despite the attempts of the United States to regain its strategic superiority. The active efforts of mass political movements and of scientists helped, especially in recent years.

The analysis of the consequences of nuclear war performed by the physicians' movement, honored with the Nobel Peace Prize, played a particularly large role, as did the "nuclear winter" effect discovered by scholars. It was scientifically proven that nuclear war spells the end of human civilization and of man as a biological species. If anybody still needed proof, that was provided by the tragedy in Chernobyl, which graphically brought home to all the indubitable truth: if we allow a nuclear war, no one will be able to hide from destruction.

Moreover, contemporary conditions have challenged the fundamental value of using military force. Humanity has now achieved a level of economic and scientific-technological development, and of social organization, such that none of the problems that gave rise to war in the past—the struggle for new lands, insufficient resources, the absence of markets, ideological and religious dogmas, social cataclysms or economic insolvency—can explain or justify the use of military force against other peoples. Even more important, military force in the contemporary world can no longer serve any rational political goals. Experience in the 1980s clearly demonstrates that it is becoming practically impossible to achieve victory even in a regional conflict (unless on an extraordinarily small scale, as in Grenada or the Falklands). Regional conflicts may last years or decades, and the costs of their conduct—economic, political, moral-psychological—far exceed the advantages that might give an illusion of victory.

A great paradox opens before us: humanity has never possessed such gigantic destructive power, and has never been so constrained in its application. Never has this power been so impotent politically, even as a means of deterrence. If I understand that my opponent realizes that neither of us can set in motion the means of deterrence without committing suicide, then the very idea of deterrence proves to be doomed. Having become mutual, deterrence becomes unnecessary. Thus arises the inescapable necessity for other, nonmilitary means of providing security.

The Growing Diversity and Globalization of World Society

The agenda of world politics is changing. People are beginning to understand that the world is becoming increasingly diverse and contradictory. In the past decade the conception was still widespread that the determining tendency of world development was the gradual erasing of historical traditions, national origins, cultural peculiarities, and ideological differences under the influence of a global tendency toward standardization and unification. This view has not been borne out by the course of history. Today the era of universal political recipes, of messianic dogmas and ideological crusades, has finally become a thing of the past.

The diversity and contradictory character of the contemporary world are paradoxically combined with the globalization of the most important social-economic and political processes. For the first time in its history, humanity is becoming a single community.

The globalization of social life is manifest on at least three levels. First of all, the border between foreign and domestic policy is gradually being erased. Social conflicts and political differences, which develop in individual societies, are increasingly crossing national boundaries.

Second, states are becoming more economically interdependent. Earlier, when the relations between states were limited to the general political and military spheres, foreign trade remained in the position of a handmaiden of politics. Today politics is often a handmaiden of trade: economic differences, problems of currency policy, and trade barriers are becoming the most important concerns at meetings of the leaders of the industrially developed countries of the West.

Third, and probably most important, the historical fates of all states are becoming unified in the face of a possible nuclear conflict (and, in principle, in the face of other global catastrophes). This unity makes necessary a qualitatively new approach to the problem of national security, which would be the distinguishing feature of new political thinking.

The Democratization of World Politics

Legal and moral factors are playing a larger role in international relations. In the past the renunciation of the norms of international law and common human morality in foreign policy in the name of a narrowly understood "realism" or "pragmatism" has led to great sacrifices and suffering, and often to defeat. But such an approach was difficult to resist while nations were relatively isolated one from another, and global threats were not hanging over the human race itself. Now that such threats (nuclear, ecological, and others) have made themselves felt, the demand will grow for legal and moral-political principles and norms of behavior that are common to all. Can states in such conditions consider themselves free from such norms? Obviously they will have to shape their policy increasingly around international law and common human morality.

At the same time public opinion has been playing a larger role in the development of foreign policy—traditionally the most elite sphere hidden from public view. The 1980s witnessed an unprecedented growth in the antiwar movement: the broadening of its composition; the increasingly informed nature of public opinion on questions of war and peace; and the strengthening of its influence on the foreign policy of states. If the establishment of more equal relations *between* states can be called the horizontal democratization of world politics, then the increased role of public opinion *within* states in questions of foreign policy is the vertical axis of democratization.

We are witnesses and active participants in a process of historic significance: the swift democratization of the entire system of international relations. The principal questions of war and peace, of foreign and military policy, are becoming the object of concern and discussion in the widest spheres of public life: among physicians and scholars, cultural and church figures, farmers and workers, students and housewives. Not so long ago these problems (especially in their nuclear dimension) were the preserve of a narrow circle of specialists and the military.

Not everyone, of course, likes these changes in world politics. One sometimes hears it said that the "fashion" for "public diplomacy" is harmful, that "everyone should mind his own business," that "public decisions should be made by responsible figures." Yet never have organized efforts to shape public opinion, at home and abroad, represented such an important sphere of foreign-policy and diplomatic efforts.

THE NEED TO FOCUS ON DOMESTIC POLITICS

The problem of the domestic development of state and society has become more complex in all countries, large and small, industrially developed and developing. Economic development is problematic; social conflicts are acquiring new dimensions; the unresolved problems of ecology are becoming increasingly acute; national-ethnic problems are coming to the fore in many states of the world; and so on. Moreover, the tempo of change in our increasingly complex and contradictory societies is quickening, necessarily giving rise to the most diverse difficulties, disproportions, and problems. Such complex and heterogeneous societies as those of the Soviet Union and the United States are seriously affected by these phenomena.

Today, it appears, the dominant foreign policy interest of any state is the creation of the most favorable possibilities for successful resolution of its domestic problems (economic, social, cultural, and others). Clearly, in the contemporary interdependent world the tasks of domestic development (even for such large states as the USSR and the United States) cannot be resolved simply by shutting out the external world. The question is thus not whether to participate in international affairs, but how to participate in a way that facilitates the resolution of domestic problems.

Unfortunately, international relations have long done more to aggravate the internal problems of a state than to solve them. Competition did not strengthen, but weakened states, undermining their domestic potential. The rules of the game that evolved led to the substitution of artificial problems for real ones, of symbols of international influence and status for real criteria of achievement.

In recent years, however, a key question is being asked more often: ought we to compete in all spheres? Or has the time come to approach the problem of competition more cautiously and selectively?

WHAT THE SOVIET UNION HAS LEARNED

In the Soviet Union the search for new rules and parameters of competition has resulted in new thinking in the foreign policy area. In the 1970s, I must admit, we in the Soviet Union moved slowly, very slowly, toward the recognition of new military and political realities, to a renunciation of outdated conceptions. Lacking initiative, we even allowed the other side to foist its rules of the game upon us in some areas.

For example, we reconciled ourselves to indolent, unpromising, and fruitless negotiations. In fact, such negotiations may have been positively harmful, for they helped the other side deceive public opinion, relieve the pressure of the antiwar forces, and inspire people with a false feeling of security. The most characteristic instance is the Vienna negotiations on limiting military forces in central Europe, which began in 1974 and in fourteen years have yielded absolutely nothing. And the "stale rubbish" on the other negotiation tables, about which M.S. Gorbachev spoke in Reykjavik, could not have accumulated without our—if not participation—then connivance or at least lack of skill.

The Americans' ability to foist upon us their rules of the game was reflected in many other areas. We responded to almost every American military program with an analogous one of our own, without carefully considering the differences in economic resources, the strategic and political realities, or even (sometimes) common sense. The very possibility of "asymmetrical reaction," of refusing to compete with the West in every concrete type of armament, only recently became established in our military-political views, as many realities and our experience were subjected to a profound rethinking.

But the problem was not limited to military technology. We began to perceive that we had unthinkingly reproduced a whole series of bankrupt elements of American military conceptions—in particular, those linked to nuclear deterrence and nuclear war. Of course, many explanations could be cited: we were lagging behind; we were compelled to catch up; and that chronic "inferiority complex," multiplied by the tragic experience of World War II (not always correctly projected onto contemporary conditions), dictated its own logic of behavior, sometimes urging us on to an unjustified policy of matching the United States blow for blow, measure for measure, in policy and propaganda as well as military affairs.

As we freed ourselves from this legacy, we re-examined our conceptions about the world and our interests as well as our approaches to many political problems. We elaborated a series of new political ideas about a nonnuclear, demilitarized, noncoercive world and a concept of a comprehensive system of international security.

It is particularly important that we come to a new understanding of the problems of reducing conventional weapons and armed forces in Europe. For forty years, the view instilled in Western Europe has been that the root of the problems and the primary obstacle on the path to security is Soviet superiority in these weapons. I won't say that we never provided grounds for such claims—in the context of the nuclear superiority the United States once had and its policy of encircling the Soviet Union with military bases, it was perhaps only natural to build up conventional armed forces on the European continent to compensate.

But the situation has changed fundamentally. In the past two to three years, the USSR and its allies have offered a wide array of proposals outlining radical changes in Europe. The West has tried to simply ignore them.

Under the present conditions, it is getting harder to reject such proposals. We are becoming much more discriminating in selecting grounds for competition with other countries. For example, we believe that we should compete with the United States in creating a more attractive model of social development, in providing the best conditions for the self-realization of the individual, and in resolving the problem of ecology. Such competition will stimulate both societies; unable to rest on their laurels, they will be forced to look more critically at themselves as well as their partners.

In certain areas, however, the lessons of the past have shown us that competition between the USSR and the United States is as senseless as it is dangerous. Now the Soviet Union will not be drawn into every arena of competition defined by the Americans. For example, we will not compete with America in the creation of the SDI, or in the creation of bases and "spheres of influence" in the Third World. If U.S. actions demand a response, we will endeavor to act so that the response is rational, and where necessary "asymmetrical"; it need not be bound by the traditional rules of the game and standards of confrontation thrust upon us.

WHAT THE UNITED STATES HAS LEARNED

The process of *perestroika* within our country is also an important international factor of the 1980s, in part because it further erodes the "image of the enemy" that was and remains an integral element of the cold war and the arms race. Throughout the postwar period, the West as a whole has made a great deal of the so-called Soviet threat. It served as a starting point for ideology and policy, helping to justify military expenditures, to establish discipline within the country and in alliance relations, to divert attention from the West's own difficult problems. In a way, the very possibility of referring to the Soviet threat corrupted the ruling elites of the West, making it possible to divert attention from their own mistakes and failures, to eliminate the necessity to think, to doubt and to find new approaches. A struggle with supposed "absolute evil" covers a multitude of sins: when battling an unclean force, you can and should use all possible means, including those that in other circumstances would seem immoral and unacceptable.

But for precisely that reason a policy based on an image of the "enemy" carries the seeds of its own destruction. A conscious deception of others sooner or later turns into an unconscious self-deception. Political leaders become victims of their own false conceptions. And if deception of others is immoral, then self-deception is dangerous.

Today the image of the USSR is changing significantly. One can, of course, artificially prolong the life of the enemy image with the aid of various provocations and "dirty tricks," but only for a short time.

The pioneers of the cold war will no longer succeed so easily in exploiting the trust of their public (nor, I will add, in exploiting our former secretive approach in certain security questions and clumsiness in others, whether the discussion was about our policy and our intentions, or about the other side and its policy; often our policy was depicted in a way that did not convince our own people and only gave the West propaganda advantages).

During the 1980s, I think, America has learned something. At the beginning of the decade, the United States turned away from attempts to adapt to a changing world and resumed efforts to adapt the world to its interests and to return to an old policy, not responsive to the new realities. This was its own attempt at revenge, an attempt to "replay" history. Anticommunism was again put forward as the fundamental organizing principle of foreign policy, with military force as its fundamental instrument. Psychologically, Reagan's policy was supposed to convince American society that, after the shocks and disappointments of the 1970s, America was, as it so much wanted to believe, again turning from "defense" to "offense," that everything was within its power.

The heart of the matter was that America's exceptional position (partly real, partly imaginary) had come to an end, forcing the nation to adapt to a new environment. From the very start America was much less vulnerable to outside perturbations and dangers than other countries, and much more isolated from developments in the rest of the world. After the Second World War, the nation had reached a position of unmatched power—both military, derived from the U.S. atomic monopoly, and economic—which gave it unique opportunities and freedom of action in the world economy and politics. Many Americans started believing in earnest that the "American century" and "Pax Americana" had arrived.

By the mid-1960s the situation had already begun to change. While remaining a great and strong power, the United States began turning into an essentially ordinary nation. It could no longer seek global supremacy, and became interdependent with other nations. America turned out to be as vulnerable as the rest to many threats.

For a long time Americans refused to reconcile themselves to these painful changes. Even as the realities of life forced them to start adapting to these new conditions, American policymakers (and a considerable part of the public) were still trying to figure out some way to return to the old, comfortable, and seemingly natural order of things. Those attempts reached a peak in the late 1970s and the election campaign of 1980. Against a backdrop of economic difficulties and the unusual situation of parity with the USSR, such sentiments were catalyzed by a national humiliation: the seizure of the entire staff of the U.S. embassy in Teheran as hostages for more than a year and the abortive attempts to rescue them.

Those circumstances prepared the way for the far right's calls to "make America strong again," to force the world to "reckon" with the United States again, and to regain military superiority over the USSR. At home, old values were to be restored: reducing federal social spending to a minimum, granting new benefits and concessions to corporations, deregulating private enterprise. Beginning in 1982 there was a noticeable rise in consumption and an unusually long period of economic growth. But the benefits turned out to have been mostly borrowed. Today's prosperity was obtained through credit and investments from other states at the expense of future American generations, who will have to pay the bills. Overall debt—government, corporate, and private—doubled during the years of the Reagan presidency, reaching $8 trillion, a fantastic sum even by American standards.

In foreign policy, "Iran-gate" dealt a serious blow to the prestige of the Reagan administration and to the Reagan Doctrine. America did not succeed in occupying a "position of strength" in relation to the Soviet Union, but had to return to the negotiation table, to legalize arms control anew. Despite more than $2 trillion spent on military goals, strategic parity was not shaken. The American position in the Third World was not strengthened. There is significant historical irony: the primary foreign policy success of the Reagan administration in its last two years turned out to be the summit meeting with the USSR and the agreement on the reduction of nuclear arms. The basic political asset of the Reagan administration was the INF Treaty.

What choices do the American people have in this new situation? Among those who set the tone of the emerging discussion, two tendencies are evident. First, a realistic note has been sounded, based on the understanding that economic and political realities, the internal and international position of the country, demand radical changes in many areas. They should begin at home, and with the economy. Here the choice is obvious: either consume less, invest less, or produce more. But it is not so simple. To produce more, it is necessary to invest more. Given heightened competition on the world market, investment must be directed not only to new factories, but to science, education, and infrastructure to raise the fantastic sums necessary. Will it be necessary to reduce Americans' personal standard of living? Many observers say that this cannot be avoided. But in recent years the polarization of rich and poor in the United States has intensified; the number of the poor has grown. Reagan's successors will face not a few puzzling problems in domestic policy, especially when the issue becomes one of raising taxes and reducing public spending. This necessity will force them again and again to think about all accessible economic reserves, including a reduction in military expenditures.

This pressure alone forces a definite choice in foreign policy. The advocates of the realist tendency, it seems to me, believe that the foreign policy of the United States should help solve its domestic, particularly economic problems, even at the expense of reducing appropriations to weapons and armed forces.

But the realist tendency is countered by a second strain, which I would conditionally call traditionalist. The adherents of this school come out against changes and for the preservation of the old policy, of the old order in international relations. The traditionalist camp is not restricted to the far right. A significant number of reputedly moderate (or moderate-conservative) members of the two-party traditional foreign-policy establishment are coming out against change. Many political and public figures, specialists in military and international questions, who grew up immersed in the cold war, evidently cannot understand or accept any foreign policy outside its conceptions. Many prominent leaders are found on this side, along with important political and economic interests. The influence of the military-industrial complex makes the traditionalists a political force to be reckoned with.

Ahead lies a fierce, complex struggle of uncertain outcome. Never before has the choice been so critical. It is not the machinations of Moscow that have set this problem before America, not an individual's caprice or competing political demands, but real changes in the country itself and in the world. It cannot be brushed aside or indefinitely ignored. A choice involving radical changes is always hard to make, as we know from our own experience. Sometimes I think that America will not get by without its own *perestroika* and *glasnost*. Why *glasnost*? Because, in my view, the country absolutely needs a genuine, serious discussion, which can in no way be replaced by thirty-second television campaign "spots." Why *perestroika*? Because so much has changed that old thinking and old policy threaten to lead the country (and the whole world with it) to a deadlock, to exert the most ruinous influence on the entire international system.

CONCLUSION: A FADING OPPORTUNITY

The experience of the 1970s should have shown both superpowers and the world as a whole that time is the most valuable political commodity. A chance that presents itself should not be let slip, for a missed opportunity is almost always lost forever.

Historians will probably be quarreling for a long time about who carried the primary responsibility for the lost opportunities at the end of 1974, or the beginning of 1977. When we speak of truly major errors in Soviet-American relations, responsibility inevitably falls in some measure on both sides. In any case, the experience of the 1970s shows that an improvement of relations cannot be put off to next year or to another administration. Everything that can be done today must be done today.

It seems to me that both sides are beginning to understand the significance of the time factor. The negotiation and signing of the INF Treaty testify to this awakening. We will hope that this treaty becomes the first step to a truly stable, forward development of Soviet-American relations.

The idea that relations between East and West, including their competition, should be "humanized" is not new. Ever since the establishment of the Soviet government, "peaceful cohabitation" with the capitalist countries, as expressed in Lenin's words, was its preferred model of international relations. The history of the twentieth century, however, turned out to be exceptionally cruel. The conclusions of common sense too frequently gave way to crude force. Today, common sense seems to be acquiring greater material force, reinforced by inexorable economic and political necessity, by elementary interests in self-preservation. For this reason, there is perhaps a basis for looking to the future with growing optimism.

CONCLUSION
Windows of Opportunity

Graham T. Allison

The American and Soviet scholars who convened for this study in 1983 shared a deep dissatisfaction with the state of U.S.-Soviet relations. We were concerned about unrealistic attitudes in both governments that increased risks of war. We hoped that improved understanding could somehow strengthen the forces of common sense. None of us, however, anticipated the pace and depth of change that has occurred.

At that time, the first American INF missiles were just being deployed in Europe; the Soviet Union had walked out of negotiations. Who could have imagined that by 1988 the two nations would have signed a treaty zeroing out all intermediate nuclear missiles on both sides? In the wake of the Soviet shoot-down of Korean Airlines 007, who would have thought that the United States and Soviet Union would not only have reached an agreement to safeguard air traffic in the North Pacific, but also established risk reduction centers in both capitals to address a much broader array of possible accidents? Soviet withdrawal from Afghanistan without victory was literally inconceivable to both American and Soviet experts.

In 1983, no one in either country envisaged the subsequent transformation in the views of the leadership of both governments. Western Sovietologists who criticized the Soviet economy and system half as sharply as General Secretary Gorbachev does today were

309

regarded as dogmatically anti-Soviet. No one could have forecast in 1983 that the president who was then proclaiming the Soviet Union "the focus of evil in the world" would five years later be walking arm-in-arm in Moscow with "my pal" Gorbachev and signing arms control agreements.

Two cardinal factors have fueled the recent changes in U.S.-Soviet relations: the harsh facts of the real world and political leaders' recognition of those facts. Georgy Arbatov states the central point in Chapter 10: "Common sense seems to be acquiring greater material force, reinforced by inexorable economic and political necessity, by elementary interests in self-preservation." Thus the recent changes represent not so much a heroic leap of faith as a heroic recognition of facts.

The preceding chapters document widespread agreement among American and Soviet scholars about both the causes of the evolution of the U.S.-Soviet relationship and the directions in which that relationship should be nudged. Our principal conclusions are four.

First, the past four decades without war between the United States and the USSR provide clues to the possibility of forty more years of peace. Even in the period of greatest strain, the two superpowers were able to adhere to primitive rules of prudence that kept their conflicts from escalating to war. Gradually they built up these rules, supplementing them with more explicit agreements and even codes of conduct, and with procedures and institutions to ensure behavior consistent with intent. A dawning recognition of the nuclear facts of life emerged first in practice—even when that practice was diametrically opposed to governmental declarations. Over time, experts in each country began to articulate these facts and the primitive rules they inspired. Later, leaders of each country stated such facts and rules out loud. Often these statements led to agreements between the two governments and to institutions and procedures. The chapters of this book document such an evolution in thinking and practice about nuclear weapons, nuclear accidents, arms control, European security, and the competition in the Third World. The interplay of what Marxist scholars call "objective" factors (here called "facts") and "subjective" factors, particularly perceptions of hard facts, in shaping operational policy remains a fruitful subject for further investigation.

Once the Soviet Union had acquired nuclear weapons, it was just a matter of time before the United States came to recognize a real interest in seeing that those weapons were not launched accidentally. That mutual interest in preventing accidental or unauthorized uses of nuclear weapons led to the Surprise Attack Conference in 1958, conversations in the 1960s about mechanisms for precluding unauthorized use, the Accidents Measures Agreement (1971), and in 1988 the establishment of risk reduction centers in Washington and Moscow that will work to further reduce the impacts of accidents.[1] In Europe, long before either government dared voice such a conclusion, both alliances implicitly recognized that military efforts to change the artificial boundaries left by World War II would be self-defeating. The Helsinki Accords provide a framework within which relations between Eastern and Western Europe can evolve without the use of force. Also encouraging are the development of institutions and procedures such as those that guarantee the security of Berlin, the Conference on Security and Cooperation in Europe (CSCE) review of the Helsinki Accords, and ongoing negotiations regarding confidence-building measures.

Second, the principal danger of war between the United States and the Soviet Union arises from the uncontrollable. Over the past several years, views in both governments have converged on this point. This consensus has been reflected in, and even influenced by, our group's conversations and analyses. We agree that the chief nuclear danger now lies not in a premeditated decision to initiate a nuclear war, but in uncontrollable factors that could lead from some accident or incident in Eastern Europe or the Third World through a process of unintended escalation to a war neither Washington nor Moscow would have chosen.

Third, the participants in this joint study conclude that the United States and the Soviet Union now face significant windows of opportunity. A combination of realism about nuclear risks, shared interest in defusing dangers posed by the uncontrollable, urgent domestic priorities in each country, and increasingly important new threats such as terrorism and proliferation are shifting the balance of shared and competing interests. Together with changes in the leadership of both governments, these factors give both nations a chance to move beyond the cold war over the next decades to a relationship of peaceful competition.

Fourth, a stable, sustainable relationship of peaceful competition is a realistic aspiration. It does not require the transformation of either nation. It starts from where we now stand: with the rules of prudence, codes of conduct, and procedures and institutions for avoiding war that have emerged over the past four decades. It extends and enhances these accomplishments to stabilize the arms competition, reducing numbers and risks. In time, it should involve reassessing the balance of competing and cooperative interests and greater collaboration in pursuing shared interests—for example, in combating terrorism, nuclear proliferation, and the spread of advanced technologies like ballistic missiles. It means moving beyond a cold war mentality to a conception of competition and cooperation without war or the threat of war between the U.S. and the USSR.

So much has changed so quickly that some Americans and Soviets have begun to fantasize that "peace has broken out." They declare that the time has come finally to declare an end to the competition between the two superpowers. They call for dismantling cold war structures of the past like NATO and building U.S.-Soviet relations on a new foundation of cooperation. Unfortunately these advocates overlook the remaining realities of enduring conflict. If taken as a guide to policy, their views can lead only to future disappointment.

Based on our candid discussions, my own conclusion is quite different. Much has changed, and much more can change *if* we take advantage of current windows of opportunity. We have a chance to (1) *recognize* what has been accomplished—realistically and without exaggeration; (2) *institutionalize* the emerging foundation for a relationship of peaceful competition; and (3) *test* Gorbachev's word, challenging him to translate his intriguing proposals into actions that advance Western interests while meeting Soviet requirements. Prudently pursued, such an agenda should increase prospects for a stable, peaceful competition that can be sustained.

COMPETITIVE AND COOPERATIVE INTERESTS: WHAT DIVIDES US? WHAT MIGHT UNITE US?

Many American and Soviet interests conflict, fueling fundamental competition. First among these are values and ideals. For the United States, individual freedom, human rights, democracy, and market-based economies are not just preferences, but deep values that define Americans. Americans tend to be cynical about Soviet values and ideology, given past gaps between proclaimed ideals and Soviet governmental practices. But even cynics can recognize significant differences between American values and Soviet socialist ideals of social justice, economic and social rights, and equality of results. Today the American zeal for values that would "make the world safe for democracy" appears to be a more divisive influence than Soviet ideological commitments to the triumph of socialism.

A second source of conflict is the stark fact that each nation threatens the other's existence. Consequently each tries to match the other's threat and thus to deter by stalemate the use or threat of force. Each maintains, and continuously modernizes, a strategic arsenal that threatens the existence of the other, spurring a competitive effort to keep up and wherever possible to maintain a margin of safety. And the rival's continuing development of nuclear forces and plans to execute a devastating attack sustain the suspicion that someone over there doesn't like us.

Third, each superpower threatens other vital and near-vital interests of its adversary. From the American perspective, vital interests include two other major geopolitical centers of value: Europe and Japan. The Soviet Union also poses threats to U.S. interests and resources, markets, and even prestige as each competes to be "number one." For the Soviet Union, the United States appears to threaten not only the Soviets' Eastern European empire, but also the legitimacy of its regime. Soviet fears of American or Western encirclement, and of Western domination of resources and markets, have a more substantial basis in fact than most Americans recognize. And although the priority of the Third World has declined, both superpowers still regard the success of allied and client states as an important indicator of power and prestige.

Hostile domestic elites and bureaucratic interests constitute a fourth, less important cluster of factors that divide the United States and the Soviet Union. President Eisenhower noted the significance of the "military-industrial complex." General Secretary Gorbachev points to "the rapacious appetites of weapons manufacturers and influential military-bureaucratic groupings."[2] Though often exaggerated, these factors are real, and indeed have a legitimate foundation in each society's demand to assure its national security. But like any bureaucratic monopoly, they acquire influence of their own and would persist for decades even if the threat they were created to meet had subsided.

These conflicting interests are counterbalanced by complementary interests that encourage cooperation between the United States and the Soviet Union. First among these is each superpower's stake in survival. Each poses a threat to the other's existence; neither can execute that threat without triggering an equivalent response. When the only alternative to mutual destruction is mutual survival, the two nations have an overriding common concern.

Second is an array of other threats to each nation, including the proliferation of nuclear weapons to other states and even terrorist groups; the spread of highly sophisticated conventional weapons, including ballistic missiles; Third World wars that risk escalation to conflict between the superpowers; destruction of the common environment; and terrorism. Neither nation by itself can adequately address these threats. As major stakeholders in the current international system, they have incentives to cooperate with each other and with other nations to manage these threats.

Third, each nation wants to provide for its security at the lowest feasible level of cost and danger. The United States currently spends 6.5 percent of its gross national product on defense, and the Soviet Union's defense efforts consume some 15 to 20 percent of its GNP. Resources devoted to defense are not available for domestic investment or consumption and thus constitute a handicap in the economic competition with other nations. If the political leaders of each country conclude that there is no feasible use of military power against the other, both superpowers will recognize an interest in stabilizing their rivalry in ways that permit reductions in their military expenditures.

A fourth reason for greater cooperation is the fact that parallel efforts can be more effective in dealing with issues beyond the superpowers. Parallel actions by the two nations have produced gains for each in the resolution of particular regional problems, including Soviet withdrawal from Afghanistan, conclusion of the war between Iran and Iraq, the projected Vietnamese withdrawal from Cambodia, and the settlement of conflicts in Angola and Namibia. Parallel actions have inhibited the spread of nuclear wapons and technologies that provide infrastructure for nuclear weaponry. Without concerted efforts by the superpowers, problems like terrorism and the spread of advanced conventional technologies will prove insoluble. Finally, gains from exchanges of goods and people, while modest, can benefit both. Scientific, technical, and cultural exchanges, and the visits of tourists and students all help to break down the stereotypes and misperceptions fostered by different ideologies and world views.

In assessing the current balance of competing and cooperative interests, it is worth noting explicitly the contrast with those of the late 1940s and early 1950s. Then the Soviet ideological and military threat to Europe and Japan loomed large; today those geopolitical centers of value have recovered economically, politically, and even militarily. Then the Soviet commitment to "wars of national liberation" in the Third World created a deep divide; today the era of decolonization has passed, and the Soviet government appears to have reassessed its stakes in Third World revolution and recognized that it is less influential there. In the era of Stalin, virulent communist ideology and ruthless communist practices assaulted American values; today Gorbachev's *glasnost, perestroika,* and democratization take initial, but significant steps in the direction of shared Western values. Over the past forty years, the threats to U.S. interests posed by actors other than the Soviet Union have been few; over the next four decades such threats will rival those posed by America's principal adversary.

Standing back from current events, and attempting to look objectively at the scales that weigh real interests, I find that the factors leading to competition seem rather evenly balanced by those that should promote cooperation. Were a new Hitler to emerge as a threat to the United States and the Soviet Union, both governments of the superpowers would undoubtedly set aside their differences to make common cause against him. (President Reagan reportedly surprised General Secretary Gorbachev at the first summit in Geneva by observing that if a Martian threat to earthlings were to emerge tomorrow, the American and Soviet leadership would immediately begin working together to meet that threat.[3]) Without such a clear and present danger to concentrate the mind, much greater levels of statesmanship will be required to strike an appropriate balance. "Objective" forces seem unlikely to decide the issue. Rather, under current conditions, U.S. and Soviet leaders have both the opportunity and the responsibility to choose.

In sum, if one takes a sober view on a timetable of decades, the reasons for cooperation between the United States and the Soviet Union seem at least as powerful as the factors that fuel competition. Stable, sustainable peaceful competition between the superpowers thus appears within the reach of enlightened statesmanship.

WINDOWS OF OPPORTUNITY

A combination of factors has carried the U.S.-Soviet relationship beyond cold war to the current period of opportunity. The substructure of these new opportunities is *new thinking*, beginning with Gorbachev's recognition that the current Soviet system is failing. A system that depends on command and control to direct the economy, the polity, and the society is not producing the economic product, the technology, or the vitality to compete successfully. Not only is this Soviet system falling further behind the United States, Western Europe, and Japan, it is losing ground even to the new industrial countries of Asia. As French President Mitterrand has observed, Gorbachev is the first Soviet leader to understand the failure of the socialist economic system.

That failure is evident in an economy that achieved 5 percent growth in the 1960s, 2 percent in the first half of the 1970s, and virtually zero growth by the early 1980s. The military now consumes at least 15 to 20 percent of the nation's product but cannot prevent a Cessna from an absurd landing in Red Square, and allows Afghan rebels to defeat the mighty Red Army. Alone among industrial nations, the USSR has seen reductions in average life expectancy. Its technological base still has not produced for general consumption a personal computer, when countries such as Taiwan and Korea manage to market second- and third-generation PCs around the world.

Gorbachev put it bluntly: unless the trend of the last decade is reversed, the Soviet Union will not enter the twenty-first century as a great power. The core of his response has two elements: common sense and pragmatism.

Nothing is more revolutionary in the Soviet system than common sense. Previously, ideology so distorted common sense, and required so many epicycles of rationalization, that most Soviet citizens knew more certainly what was not true (namely the things that were said officially) than what might be so. In contrast to the Orwellian character of past Soviet rhetoric, Gorbachev is clearly committed to a great deal more of "calling things by their real names," as he says.

Gorbachev's pragmatism is also heretical. It means a willingness to experiment and explore alternative ways of achieving a goal. Historically, Soviet planning has presumed a central monopoly of wisdom in analysis of problems and design of the plan, and a monopoly of power in assigning players the roles they should perform. In contrast, pragmatism requires individuals who are engaged and active enough to think for themselves and to adapt as they go.

At its core, Gorbachev's "new thinking" is essentially a radical rejection of Stalinism, which ruled the Soviet Union for more than half a century. Like Luther's denunciation of papal authority, Gorbachev's acknowledgment that the Communist Party has no "monopoly on truth" has earth-shaking implications. *Glasnost* is predicted on the obvious idea that truth emerges from discussion and debate among many people, each of whom has a piece of reality. *Perestroika* revises the notion of an economy planned by all-knowing central authorities in favor of greater local autonomy, incentives, and, over time, market forces. As the Gorbachev revolution continues, we should expect to see other repressive features of the Stalinist society scrutinized and then buried.

On the American side of the relationship, there has also been considerable new thinking. Indeed, one Soviet participant in this project asked provocatively, which government's perceptions have changed more—the Soviets' or the Americans'? Gorbachev is extraordinarily different from his predecessors, but the change from Reagan I to Reagan II is also remarkable. The first indicts an "evil empire" that "lies, steals, and cheats" and thus cannot be trusted in any arms control agreements; the second seeks agreements to constrain arms, recognizes the need to live and let live, and makes his motto "trust but verify." Some of the strongest supporters and ideological soul mates of Reagan I are the most vicious critics of Reagan II. The newspaper ads comparing Reagan's new policies to Neville Chamberlain's appeasement of Hitler stand as rude reminders of how much Reagan has changed.

Beyond new thinking in both capitols, a second major opportunity-creating factor is the priority of problems at home. Gorbachev is clearly seeking to subordinate foreign policy to domestic concerns. Restructuring the Soviet economy and revitalizing the Soviet society are tasks that will require decades or even generations. Given the priority they require, Gorbachev recognizes, domestic problems will absorb the attention of the Soviet leadership. They cannot succeed without substantial relaxation of the competition with the United States in the international arena.

Under President Reagan, American leadership was slow to recognize the extent of domestic problems: federal budget deficits of

$150 billion annually that transformed the world's largest creditor into the world's largest debtor; a trade deficit of similar proportions that threatens the entire international financial system; and deep problems of long-term productivity and international competitiveness. Analogies between American economic difficulties and the fundamental problems of the Soviet economy are fascile and misleading. Nonetheless, properly recognized, these issues will demand priority from any post-Reagan administration.

Third, as superpowers in a world approaching multipolarity, the United States and the Soviet Union are both experiencing a decline in their power *relative* to the rest of the world. For the United States this decline was sharpest in the decades following World War II, as substantial American assistance spurred the recovery of Europe and Japan. In 1945–65, the U.S. share of world GNP fell from nearly 50 percent to 22–24 percent. Contrary to popular mythology, this share has not declined since then but has been maintained. (Interestingly, prior to World War II the U.S. share of global product was also 23 percent; the best forecasts for the next two decades indicate it will be maintained. The Soviet Union's piece of the global pie grew slightly in the first fifteen years after the war but has decreased to 11 percent in the last fifteen years, a decline that seems destined to continue during the next decade.) The international political stage will become increasingly crowded as regional powers, international organizations, and multinational actors grow in number and influence.

Fourth, the external environment is posing increasingly serious threats to the interests of each superpower. The risk of nuclear war predominates. Should a confrontation between the United States and the Soviet Union in the Persian Gulf, Asia, or Europe lead ultimately to nuclear war, no one would judge the cause to have been worth the consequences. This risk of inadvertent war that neither wants is a clear and present danger that should mobilize concerted action. No development adds more risk of uncontrollability than the proliferation of nuclear weapons to other states. In 1961, President Kennedy predicted that by the 1970s there would be fifteen to twenty-five nuclear powers. In fact, there are only six in 1989, though several nations stand at an ambiguous threshold.[4] Understanding their parallel interest in nonproliferation, the United States and the Soviet Union have acted in concert through the Nonproliferation Treaty, by coordinating actions to limit the supply of nuclear technology, and by sharing information about developments in countries that seek to acquire nuclear weapons.

The spread of modern conventional weapons also threatens the Soviet Union and the United States. While each remains a major supplier of conventional arms to other nations, each is beginning to recognize this common interest and to act informally to limit the spread of some categories of modern conventional weapons, including ballistic missiles.

The postwar era has seen more than 100 wars between third parties. In 1988, twenty nations were engaged in active military conflicts. Such conflicts are not only destructive in themselves; they pose serious threats to U.S. and Soviet interests and thus risk U.S. or Soviet involvement, which could escalate to war. The two superpowers thus have parallel interests in preventing conflicts between other states, controlling them, or bringing them to a conclusion where possible—and in any case restraining their own involvement.

Finally, a growing number of global problems threaten both superpowers, including environmental changes such as the depletion of the ozone layer, which could have catastrophic climatic effects; global hunger; and terrorism. If the superpowers thought hard about their real long-term interests, they would address these parallel interests more urgently.

GUIDELINES FOR PEACEFUL COMPETITION

The contributors to this book have identified a number of central guidelines for peaceful competition, rooted in the relationship between the United States and the Soviet Union that has emerged over four decades. Principal guidelines include:

Realism in recognizing facts; common sense in analyzing implications.
   If war between the United States and the USSR would destroy both, what follows? A simple, common-sensical imperative to constrain those dimensions of competition that risk war. If "a nuclear war cannot be won and must therefore never be fought," then, as President Reagan has noted, while "we don't have to agree with the Soviet leaders, we do have to find some way to live with them." However simplistic these truths, they have long eluded leaders of both governments. No recent change has been more dra-

matic than the erosion of ideology and dogma—in both leaderships—toward realism and common sense.

Recognition of each other—as a sovereign state; as a legitimate government; as a nation that has equal rights; and as a co-equal superpower (at least in the military dimension), which therefore shoulders a special responsibility. Recognition of "equality" and "equal security" does not mean denying fundamental differences, nor does it imply "moral equivalence." Rather, as in domestic law, equality recognizes each party's independence, rights, and capacity to make unilateral choices in its own realm and to reject the terms of any agreement it judges contrary to its sovereign interests.

Respect for the real differences that divide the two nations. As former President Nixon said, "Respect is important between friends; indispensable between enemies." Or in President Reagan's words, the two governments "owe each other the tribute of candor about our differences." General Secretary Gorbachev expressed his commitment to continue a serious dialogue with the U.S. president even though "sometimes we say unpleasant things to each other and even say them in public and in rather sharp words."[5]

Regular communication and consultation. Given the pace of events and the locus of decision-making, traditional diplomatic channels of communication have been expanded by upgraded hot lines between heads of state and regular summits that help leaders and their subordinates understand each other's views, hopes, and fears. Regular meetings between heads of state, and even more frequent discussions among secretaries of state, secretaries of defense, military chiefs, and lower levels, clarify vital interests, reinforce a common understanding of constraints, and permit the identification of issues on which parallel actions or agreements can advance both parties' interests.

Negotiation of agreements, on a case-by-case basis in a businesslike manner, that advance each party's conception of its own interests. Arms control will remain at the top of the negotiating agenda because preventing nuclear war is the overriding common interest. Small steady steps to reduce risks help build a peaceful relationship in other dimensions. Agreements to limit regional conflicts, permit trade and investments, and allow greater scientific, technical, cultural, and human exchange permit each side to realize more of its own interests.

Establishment of institutions and procedures to make agreements operational. Bilateral institutions and procedures such as the standing consultative commission on SALT or the nuclear risk reduction centers provide mechanisms for interpreting and enforcing agreements. Multilateral institutions and procedures, such as the Conference on Security and Cooperation in Europe (CSCE), the International Atomic Energy Agency (IAEA) for nonproliferation, or the UN Security Council with its peace-keeping function, can often be even more effective in settings that engage independent interests of many sovereign states.

Respect for human rights at home and abroad. As the European heads of government stated in 1987, "Respect for human rights and freedom is a prerequisite for confidence, understanding, and cooperation."[6] Building on the UN Charter, the Universal Declaration of Human Rights, and the Helsinki Final Act, continued efforts to improve human rights without exaggerated publicity or propaganda contribute to a sustainable relationship. While the links between freedom for citizens at home and the prospects for a peaceful U.S.-Soviet relationship are subtle, they are real and powerful. Greater freedom at home engenders greater trust abroad not only by increasing transparency but also as a result of consistency between declaration and behavior.

In sum: regularization of the competition to constrain forces that threaten war, or the risk of war, and channel efforts toward joint gains and cooperation. Competition in some areas would be self-defeating. The use of force against the adversary or its allies would probably lead to a war that destroyed the values each society is determined to preserve. Competition in those dimensions must therefore be tightly regulated. Agreements, institutions, and procedures must be developed to minimize the possibility that competition could lead to war. In other areas, competition between values and views of the two societies can be productive—spurring each to more vigor and creativity than it would otherwise muster. Which political and economic system can better meet the needs of its own population? Which will better realize cultural and spiritual aspirations? Which model will attract the hearts and minds of other citizens of the world? Answers to these questions should be left to the competition and determined by the results.

TESTING GORBACHEV'S WORD

Ideally, perhaps, a book that results from a joint Soviet-American project would conclude with a section entitled "testing U.S. and Soviet willingness to establish a framework of peaceful competition." But as analysis reaches the point of policy recommendations, it becomes hypocritical to feign independence of national ethnocentrism. Thus this final section is written from an acknowledged American perspective and focuses on testing Gorbachev.

Do we want Gorbachev to succeed? Where his actions advance American interests and move toward a more secure, peaceful world, the answer must be yes. Consider the alternatives. Another Soviet leader might pursue similar internal reforms, just more slowly and with a less active foreign policy dimension. An equally plausible historical analogy, however, would be the Austro-Hungarian government of 1914, which sought to exploit its military advantages of the moment to avoid what otherwise promised to be decades of relative decline.

The United States cannot assume that Gorbachev will remain in power, or that the Soviet Union's long-term objectives have changed. Gorbachev's main purpose is to guarantee and enhance the Soviet Union's position as a great power. To that end, he seeks breathing space, *peredyshka.* He is trying simultaneously to secure his position in the struggle for power at home; provide a framework that will let him shift resources from defense to more productive investments; and maintain a posture plausible enough to allow him to constrain Western arms through arms control. At the same time, he is sorting out what he really thinks about a confusing, changing international environment. Rather than having formulated a long-term plan that maps the future, Gorbachev and his associates see the world as being in flux as they venture into uncharted territory.

Restructuring the Soviet economy and society will require decades or even generations. If the Soviet Union turns inward for a decade or two and concentrates on rebuilding its economic strength; if Gorbachev judges that international stability, and specifically a reduction of conflict with the United States, is an essential precondition for Soviet focus on internal affairs (and if this conclusion leads him to pull back from Afghanistan, Africa, and Central America and to moderate Soviet policies in the Middle East); if his reforms produce greater freedom for Soviet citizens, a more open society, and reduction of ideologically motivated expansionism—the United States can applaud his initiatives. Where cuts in Western forces and defense expenditures are demanded as the price of reductions in Soviet threats to us, the U.S. government should act with a clear view of its net advantage.

A strategy of testing Gorbachev is not without risks, however. As the USSR passes such tests, some in the West will proclaim prematurely that peace has broken out. Others may be lulled. We could be tricked. The web of interdependence we spin could entangle the West more deeply than the Soviet Union. Nevertheless, the United States and its allies should encourage Gorbachev's progress in advancing purposes we espouse. His reforms could produce a more competitive Soviet economy that would make the USSR a more formidable adversary some decades hence—but if so, the character of that Soviet Union is likely to be unrecognizable.

My central proposition is that Gorbachev's "new thinking" holds the promise of fundamental improvements in the U.S.-Soviet relationship. But it is evolving. To be fully developed in the Soviet Union and appreciated in the West, the new thinking must be put to the test by an American strategy that begins by taking Gorbachev at his word. We should adopt a working hypothesis that Gorbachev really means what he says, and that, as an intelligent leader, he also understands the logical implications of his statements. The challenge for American policymakers is to lead the West in formulating equally far-reaching proposals for Soviet actions that advance Western interests in the cause of peace through propositions Gorbachev cannot refuse (if he means what he says). Tests can be devised along four dimensions of the U.S.-Soviet relationship: arms control, regional conflicts, human rights, and participation in international institutions.

In arms control, start with what Gorbachev has said. Leaving aside his rhetoric about eliminating all nuclear weapons, his more realistic statements essentially reject Clausewitz's proposition that war is an extension of political struggle by other means. Instead Gorbachev says:

> The fundamental principle of the new political outlook is very simple: nuclear war cannot be a means of achieving political, economic, ideological, or any other goals. . . . Security can no longer be assured by military means. . . . Attempts to achieve military superiority are preposterous. . . . The only way to security is through political decision and disarmament.[7]

If Gorbachev believes this, what might the Soviet Union be prepared to do?

In the first instance, it should begin to restrain the growth and modernization of the Soviet military establishment. Over time, in concert with Western reductions, Moscow should be prepared to sharply reduce and restructure Soviet military forces. But note the gap between word and deed. The evidence to date—continued increases in defense spending, modernization of both nuclear and conventional forces, deliveries of new equipment to front-line forces, and the character of field exercises—suggests that Gorbachev's fine phrases have yet to be translated operationally in the military realm.

Gorbachev has already passed one important test, however: he accepted the U.S. proposal for the elimination of intermediate nuclear forces. When that proposition was first put forward by the Reagan administration in 1981, it was declared a "nonacceptable demand" by the Soviet leadership, and most American experts concurred. (In fact, it had been designed within the U.S. government as an offer the Soviets could never accept.)

To achieve this treaty, Gorbachev made significant concessions to the United States: exclusion of equivalent British and French forces, inclusion of the shorter-range Soviet SS-23s among weapons to be destroyed, and, most startling, acceptance of highly intrusive verification procedures on Soviet territory, a demand Moscow had for decades rejected. Indeed, many American arms controllers had given up on this demand, agreeing with the Soviet claim that it was "unreasonable" since it violated natural Soviet conservatism and the character of Soviet society. Note the formula for NATO's success in this case: a reasonable though radical proposal combined with persistence and hard bargaining. It should be emulated on other fronts, including strategic arms control.

What do Gorbachev's words imply for the Soviet Union's strategic arsenal? In a June 1988 *Pravda* article, Vadim Zagladin, a deputy head of the Central Committee's international relations department, admitted that the Soviet Union "proceeded for a long time, for too long, from the possibility of winning a nuclear war."[8] If Gorbachev no longer believes that a nuclear war can be won, or that threats of nuclear war are useful, then he should be prepared to eliminate strategic nuclear forces acquired for that purpose.

In short, Gorbachev should now be prepared to restructure his nuclear arsenals in ways that reduce the possibility, or threat, of surprise attack; that would mean eliminating the first-strike weapons Americans fear most, namely the Soviet heavy land-based missiles (SS-18s). U.S. proposals in START, which call for a 50 percent reduction in numbers of warheads, are a step in the right direction, though not bold enough. A serious test of Gorbachev's provocative views would propose elimination of all weapons that are best suited for use in a first strike, and thus all MIRVed heavy land-based missiles that have hard-target kill capability.[9]

The USSR poses its greatest military threat to American vital interests in Europe. There thirty forward-deployed divisions of the Red Army in Eastern Europe, along with dozens more divisions in the Soviet Union's western military districts, stand equipped, trained, and regularly exercised to conduct a surprise attack that moves rapidly west to defeat and occupy Western Europe. To meet this challenge, NATO maintains combined conventional and nuclear forces and a doctrine of "flexible response" that includes the possible use of nuclear weapons to meet even a conventional attack. Nowhere would Gorbachev's rhetoric offer more promise for the West—if thought leads to equivalent action.

Gorbachev has referred to Europe as a "common security house" in which tenants can legitimately provide for their own security, but not by filling their apartments with explosives that could destroy the building. In 1986, Gorbachev confounded Western experts by accepting the Western concept of an Atlantic-to-the-Urals arms reduction zone. In 1987, he began making these ideas more operational by calling for the elimination of the capacity for surprise attack or offensive operations. That will require, he recognizes, asymmetric reductions where there are "imbalances and asymmetries in some kinds of armaments and armed forces on both sides in Europe, caused by historical, geographical, and other factors." He continues, "We stand for eliminating the inequality existing in some areas, but not through a build up by those who lag behind but through a reduction by those who are ahead."[10] To that end, at the June 1988 U.S.-Soviet summit in Moscow, Gorbachev proposed an ambitious scheme to transform the conventional force balance in the Atlantic-to-the-Urals area. The plan involves four steps: an exchange of data on the conventional forces in the zone, to be verified by on-site inspections; the identification and then elimination of asymmetries in the forces of the two sides; 500,000-man reductions in each alliance's manpower in the zone; and the restructuring of conventional forces in Europe to give them a solely defensive orientation.

It is an indictment of U.S. leadership in NATO that such politically promising suggestions have been spelled out over the past three years by Gorbachev alone, essentially talking to himself. Listening to proposals that could significantly reduce the threat to Western Europe, allied publics naturally conclude that Gorbachev seems more interested in peace than President Reagan. NATO should immediately take up Gorbachev's offer of an exchange and verification of data about the military forces on both sides.[11] Our positive response should set the terms of reference for such an exchange, to include a detailed order of battle broken out to the level of regiments or battalions and including the location, designation, and subordination of units, as well as manning levels and equipment by type and model. This information about NATO forces is publicly available; in the Soviet Union such data has been a top military secret since 1917. NATO's acceptance of Gorbachev's proposal offers a low-cost, high-benefit trial of his readiness to do business here.

NATO should attempt to craft arms control agreements that reduce the Warsaw Pact's capabilities for surprise attack and large-scale offensive operation. We must recognize that "nothing is as much anathema to traditional Soviet military thinking as is a defense-dominant theater strategy and force posture."[12] Here Western proposals attack Soviet offensive concepts and practices that have motivated the largest buildup of military power in history. Thus in designing agreements for reductions in Warsaw Pact operational capabilities, we should be sensitive to bureaucratic interests. The Soviet military system, like the West's, probably would be more ready to sacrifice readiness, ammunition, logistics, some weapons systems, and even force modernization than force structure or command slots. Among the elements of Soviet forces most essential to a surprise attack, and thus most important to reduce, are tens of thousands of Soviet tanks and artillery pieces in Eastern Europe and the western Soviet Union.

The West should also pursue confidence-building measures to increase transparency and constrain military activities. Initially in word, but now in the deed of the INF Treaty, Gorbachev has transformed Moscow's prior secrecy about Soviet territory, military forces, and perhaps even military doctrine. If Gorbachev means what he says, he should permit previously unthinkable levels of Western access to Soviet territory, military bases, and exercises.

NATO should seize this opportunity to propose the establishment of trip wires the Soviet Union would have to trigger in preparing to go to war. Such measures should include positioning permanent international inspectors at militarily important arms depots, airfields, fuel dumps, rail heads, and perhaps even command and control centers; specific constraints on forward deployment of tanks, artillery, bridging, and mine clearing equipment; and year-in-advance schedules for mobilizations of forces.

Few in the West believed Gorbachev's early indications, at the Twenty-seventh Party Congress, that support for wars of national liberation would no longer be a Soviet priority. His rationale had a certain plausibility: the era of decolonization having ended, this issue had become less crucial. But according to many Western Sovietologists, external expansion served an essential ideological role in justifying the Soviet regime at home. Thus little credence was given Gorbachev's assertions that the use of armed force to promote social revolution had declined in value, that the superpowers should not introduce their troops into Third World conflicts, and that regional conflicts and crises must be resolved by political means.

In 1985, most Western experts would have rejected summarily any suggestion that these words signaled impending Soviet withdrawal from Afghanistan, even after Gorbachev described that land as a "bleeding wound." Withdrawal without victory would blatantly refute the predominant Western geopolitical explanation of Soviet intentions in Afghanistan—an explanation that shaped the U.S. government's view of Soviet ambitions in the 1980s. Intervention in Afghanistan, which shares a border with the Soviet Union, was seen as a calculated step in Russia's centuries-old quest for warm-water ports, with domination of the world's strategic oil reserves as the unspoken prize. Given the commitment to this cause, Afghanistan was a war the Soviet Union could not afford to lose. All this quickly became conventional wisdom after 1980.

Yet Gorbachev has accepted defeat, with only the fig leaf of calling it stalemate. This realism is the strongest evidence so far that he may genuinely believe some of the more unlikely things he says. The consequences of the Soviet withdrawal from Afghanistan are difficult to exaggerate. The effects on the Soviet army and Soviet society may prove more profound than the impact of the American defeat in Vietnam on the United States. Such a stark refutation of the West's prevailing explanation of Soviet intentions in Afghanistan should also have effects in the West.

Gorbachev's propositions about declining Soviet stakes, influence, and interest in the Third World deserve to be more vigorously tested in other areas. In Angola, movement has begun, and the United States is finally pressing its case with Moscow. But the big disappointment has been American diplomacy in Central America—or more precisely, the lack thereof.

In his book *Perestroika*, Gorbachev explicitly supports "the peace-making efforts of the Contadora Group, initiatives by the Central American heads of state, and the Guatemala City accord." He goes on, "We are not going to exploit the anti-U.S. attitudes, let alone fuel them, nor do we intend to erode the traditional links between Latin America and the United States."[13] At the 1987 Washington summit, Gorbachev proposed "to review possibilities of promoting the process of peaceful settlement in Central America. . . . First, our idea is related to the entire Central American region. Second, it provides for reciprocal Soviet and American pledges to refrain from deliveries of weapons."[14] Though Reagan inexplicably failed to pick up the offer, Gorbachev reiterated this position at the 1988 Moscow summit, stating that "there is some movement towards a political settlement, and we must base ourselves on that process and lend our support. . . ."[15]

Soviet actions, however, contravene every operational implication of Gorbachev's words. Specifically, Moscow's shipment of arms and other military equipment to the Sandinista government of Nicaragua and to guerrillas in El Salvador and Guatemala has continued and even increased in the first quarter of 1988. Soviet-bloc economic and military aid to the Sandinistas is estimated at almost $1 billion annually. In December 1987, Sandinista Defense Minister Umberto Ortega acknowledged that the Sandinistas plan to double their armed forces to 600,000 troops, with additional supplies coming from the Soviet Union—which had promised, Ortega claimed, to supply MiG-21s.

The United States government should move immediately with the Central American presidents to propose cessation of all military aid (Soviet, Soviet bloc, Cuban, and American) to the Sandinistas and the Contras, together with effective guarantees that the Nicaraguan government will cease all material support for insurgent movements. The Central American presidents should also take the Soviet Union to task for the gap between its verbal support for the Arias plan and its continued supply of arms to guerrillas in El Salvador and Guatemala and demand that such assistance stop immediately.

Gorbachev's trenchant indictment of the Stalinist totalitarian system and its incompatibility with a successful economy, society, and culture exceeds all expectations. Who could have imagined an unstructured debate among participants in a solemn Party conference, including denunciations of individuals to their faces, on multiple sides of issues—*and on television* for all to see? The Soviet government's declaration about increased freedom of conscience for religious believers and its commemoration of the Russian Orthodox millennium have also been impressive.

Progress on emigration for refuseniks, release of political prisoners, and the elimination of psychiatric prisons for enemies of the state have been slower than we should demand, but more rapid and deeper than in any equivalent phase of Soviet history. While Gorbachev bridles at Western persistence in demanding human rights for Soviet citizens, President Reagan's firm pursuit of this issue at the Moscow summit did not prevent progress in other areas. The United States should keep pushing Moscow on human rights across the board. Both publicly and privately we should explain why a society that becomes less repressive at home becomes more trustworthy abroad.

Along the economic dimension, if the Soviet Union hopes to engage in international trade and to produce products that are globally competitive, it must reorganize its internal pricing system so that it can join the General Agreement on Tariffs and Trade, as China has been working to do. It makes sense to treat the Soviet Union in the same way as China and some Eastern European countries, providing incentives for Moscow to adopt a price system that would allow it to have observer status, and eventually even become a member of the international financial institutions. Recently launched joint ventures will test Moscow's willingness to undertake the necessary economic reforms. The West has a strong interest in the success of Soviet decentralization of economic power to heads of industries, firms, farms, and collectives. The decentralization of economic power weakens the monopoly of political authority. A totalitarian political system is not compatible in the longer run with a decentralized market economic system, because people who have economic power have power per se.

A realistic U.S. strategy would look at many other issues, including terrorism, on which Gorbachev has offered various attractive ideas: rejecting terrorism in all its guises, agreeing on the 99 percent on which we can agree, establishing an international tribunal under the auspices of the UN that would be a definitive court of justice on these issues, and imposing sanctions on any nations that violate the dictates of this court.[16] Western policy has not yet seriously addressed Gorbachev's decision to pay Soviet arrears to the United Nations and make greater use of the UN system, even suggesting the possibility of activating the military committee of the Security Council to play a larger role in resolving regional issues and peacekeeping.

What is the point of a strategy of testing Gorbachev at his word? Not just to promote truth in diplomatic declarations, or to force Western policymakers and publics to notice what really is happening in the Soviet Union. Not just to incline Soviet choices among feasible options toward decisions that advance Western interests—though that will inevitably be a part in any competitive relationship.

The primary purpose of proposing bold actions that follow logically from Gorbachev's bold words *is to set in place a sustainable structure for peaceful competition.* The United States and its allies must reach beyond containment to encourage Gorbachev's reformist instincts to restructure Soviet external relations and internal institutions. We should not exaggerate Western ability to influence Soviet developments. But we should use all the leverage we have to nudge events in directions that meet our fundamental requirements.

It would be foolhardy not to recognize the extent to which Gorbachev's words are consistent with a relationship of peaceful competition. If the U.S.-Soviet competition in the new and more demanding challenges of the next four decades is no more constrained than it has been in the past, we have little basis for confidence that we can avoid a catastrophic nuclear war. Thus both prudence and hope counsel leaders to seize the present opportunities to solidify a long-term relationship that realistically promises competition without war.

NOTES

1. For a further discussion of efforts to prevent accidental or unauthorized use, see Peter Stein and Peter Feaver, *Assuring Control of Nuclear Weapons: The Evolution of Permissive Action Links*, CSIA Occasional Paper No. 2 (Lanham, Md.: University Press of America, 1987).

2. Mikhail S. Gorbachev, "Political Report to the 27th Party Congress of the CPSU," trans. in *Current Digest of the Soviet Press* 38 (8) 7.

3. Evidently Reagan spoke so convincingly of this Martian threat that Gorbachev was initially uncertain whether he was speaking literally or metaphorically. At the Twenty-seventh Party Congress Gorbachev repeated the metaphor: "The American President once said that if the planet was threatened by a landing force from another planet the USSR and the U.S. would quickly find a common language. But isn't a nuclear catastrophe a more real danger than a landing of unknown beings from another planet?" (*Current Digest of the Soviet Press* 38 (8), 10).

4. Graham Allison, Albert Carnesale, and Joseph Nye, Jr., eds., *Hawks, Doves, and Owls: An Agenda for Avoiding Nuclear War* (New York: W.W. Norton & Co., 1985), p. 239.

5. Mikhail S. Gorbachev, *Perestroika: New Thinking for Our Country and the World* (New York: Harper & Row, 1987), p. 251.

6. Cited in Secretary Shultz's February 5, 1988 address to the Henry M. Jackson School of International Studies, "Managing the U.S.-Soviet Relationship," Dept. of State Current Policy Paper No. 1043.

7. *Perestroika*, pp. 140–41.

8. Vadim Zagladin, "We Discuss the CPSU Central Committee Theses following a Course of Reason and Humanitarianism," reprinted in *Pravda*, June 18, 1988.

9. The nub of this problem is the vulnerable MIRVed ICBMs: multiple warheads that permit the attacker to destroy more of the opponent's missiles than are expended in the attack. Such weapons provide an incentive, under certain conditions, both to strike first and to launch on warning. A nation seriously interested in eliminating the crisis instability and risk of accident inherent in such a theoretical first-strike capability would move toward low-throw-weight ICBMs carrying single warheads.

10. *Perestroika*, p. 203.

11. For a further discussion of this issue, see Robert D. Blackwill, "Specific Approaches to Conventional Arms Control in Europe," *Survival*, Sept./Oct. 1988.

12. Stephen Meyer, "The Sources and Prospects of Gorbachev's New Political Thinking on Security," *International Security* 13 (2), Fall 1988, 151.

13. *Perestroika*, p. 188.

14. Soviet Foreign Ministry Spokesman Boris Pyadyshev, *Tass*, December 16, 1987, cited in *New York Times*, December 17, 1987.

15. *Washington Post*, June 2, 1988.

16. As early as the Twenty-seventh Party Congress in 1986, Gorbachev proposed a "comprehensive security system" including "the development of effective methods of preventing international terrorism, including security in the use of means of international land, air and sea transportation," stating: "Undeclared wars, the exporting of counterrevolution in all its forms, political assassinations, the taking of hostages, airplane hijacking,

CONCLUSION: WINDOWS OF OPPORTUNITY

explosions in the street, at airports and railways stations—this is the disgusting face of terrorism, which its sponsors try to cover in various sorts of cynical fabrications. The USSR rejects terrorism in principle and is willing to cooperate actively with others to eradicate it" ("Report to the 27th CPSU Congress," trans. in *Current Digest of the Soviet Press* 38 (8), 1986, 29-31).

INDEX

NOTES ON CONTRIBUTORS

Graham T. Allison is dean and Don K. Price Professor of Politics at Harvard's John F. Kennedy School of Government, and chairman of the American delegation in the Harvard/Soviet Academy of Sciences joint study on crisis prevention and settlement. He is author of *Essence of Decision: Explaining the Cuban Missile Crisis* and co-editor of *Hawks, Doves and Owls: an Agenda for Avoiding Nuclear War* and *Fateful Visions: Avoiding Nuclear Catastrophe.*

Bruce J. Allyn is director of the Harvard/Soviet Academy of Sciences joint study on crisis prevention and settlement and associate director of the Nuclear Negotiation Project at Harvard Law School.

Aleksei G. Arbatov is head of the Department of Arms Control and Disarmament, Institute of World Economy and International Relations, Moscow. He is author of several books on military-strategic stability.

Georgy A. Arbatov is director of the Institute of USA and Canada in Moscow, a member of the Soviet Central Committee, and chairman of the Soviet delegation of the Harvard/Soviet Academy of Sciences joint study on crisis prevention and settlement. He has served as adviser to several Soviet leaders and has published numerous works on U.S.-Soviet relations.

Seweryn Bialer is Robert and Renee Belfer Professor of Social Sciences and International Relations and director of the Research Institute on International Change, Columbia University. He has authored and edited numerous books, including *The Global Rivals* (with Michael Mandelbaum) and *Soviet Paradox: Decline and Expansion.*

Fyodor M. Burlatsky is a political commentator for the *Literary Gazette*, head of the Department of Philosophy at the Central Committee Institute of Social Sciences, Moscow, and chairman of the Soviet Public Commission for Humanitarian Affairs and Human Rights. He was a speechwriter and advisor to Nikita Khrushchev during the Cuban missile crisis.

Albert Carnesale is the academic dean of the John F. Kennedy School of Government, Harvard University, and a specialist on arms control and international security matters. He was a member of the U.S. SALT I delegation. He is co-editor of *Superpower Arms Control; Hawks, Doves and Owls* and *Fateful Visions: Avoiding Nuclear Catastrophe.*

Alexander George is Graham Stuart Professor of International Relations at Stanford University. In recent years he has edited *Managing U.S.-Soviet Rivalry: Problems of Crisis Prevention* and *U.S.-Soviet Security Cooperation: Achievements, Failures, Lessons.* He is currently directing a research project on crisis management as a strategy for avoiding inadvertent war.

David Hamburg is president of the Carnegie Corporation of New York, former president of the American Association for the Advancement of Science, and former president of the Institute of Medicine, National Academy of Sciences.

Sergei Karaganov is department head, Institute on Western Europe, Soviet Academy of Sciences, Moscow.

Viktor A. Kremeniuk is a section chief at the Institute of USA and Canada, Moscow and a leading specialist on regional conflicts and negotiation.

Andrei Kortunov is chief of the section on U.S. policy in international conflict and crisis, Institute of USA and Canada, Moscow.

Vladimir Lukin is a specialist in the Department on the Far East, Soviet Ministry of Foreign Affairs. He is author of *Centers of Power: Concepts and Reality.*

Robert S. McNamara is a former U.S. secretary of defense and president of the World Bank.

Sergo A. Mikoyan is editor of *Latinskaia amerika* magazine in Moscow. During the Cuban missile crisis he was assistant to his father, Anastas Mikoyan, first deputy chairman of the Council of Ministers and a member of the Presidium (now Politburo).

Mikhail Mil'shtein is a retired Soviet general in the military department of the Institute of USA and Canada, Moscow.

Joseph S. Nye, Jr., is Ford Foundation Professor of International Security, Harvard University, and director of the Center for Science and International Affairs, John F. Kennedy School of Government, Harvard University. He is author of *Nuclear Ethics* and co-editor of *Hawks, Doves and Owls* and *Fateful Visions: Avoiding Nuclear Catastrophe.*

Georgy Shakhnazarov is a personal aide to General Secretary Mikhail Gorbachev and president of the Soviet Political Science Association. He is author of *The Coming World Order* and co-editor of *International Order: Political Legal Aspects.*

Henry Trofimenko is head of the Foreign Policy Department at the Institute of USA and Canada, Moscow. He is author of *U.S. Military Doctrine* and co-author of *Lessons of Peaceful Coexistence.*

William L. Ury is associate director of the Avoiding Nuclear War Project, John F. Kennedy School of Government, Harvard University, and director of the Nuclear Negotiation Project, Harvard Law School. He is co-author of *Getting to Yes* and author of *Beyond the Hotline.*

Vitaly V. Zhurkin is director of the Institute for Western Europe, Moscow, and a corresponding member of the Soviet Academy of Sciences. He is author of many books and articles on East-West relations.